Writing Security

Writing Security

United States Foreign Policy and the Politics of Identity
Revised Edition

David Campbell

University of Minnesota Press

Minneapolis

Published by the University of Minnesota Press
111 Third Avenue South, Suite 290
Minneapolis, MN 55401-2520
http://www.upress.umn.edu

Library of Congress Cataloging-in-Publication Data

Campbell, David, 1961–
    Writing security : United States foreign policy and the politics
of identity / David Campbell. — Rev. ed.
        p.   cm.
    Includes bibliographical references (p.   ) and index.
    ISBN 0-8166-3144-1 (hc : alk. paper)
    1. United States — Foreign relations — 1989–1993 — Philosophy.
    2. National security — United States — Philosophy.   I. Title.
    E840.C348   1998
    327.73 — dc21   98-14152

Printed in the United States of America on acid-free paper

The University of Minnesota is an equal-opportunity educator and employer.

10 09 08 07 06   10 9 8 7 6 5 4 3

Practicing criticism is a matter of making facile gestures difficult.

Michel Foucault

Contents

Preface

Uncertain times demand an unconventional analysis. The irruptions in the established order and traditional practices of statecraft have given many of international politics' customary modes of analysis an air of nostalgia. Faced with transformations that border on the incomprehensible, proclamations about the threat of ambiguity and declarations of the need for new order(s) ring out from the academies and capitals prominent in the old. One theme conspicuous among these admonitions is the aspiration to rethink security, a desire usually expressed in terms of how to expand the old register of hazards to incorporate what are perceived as the newly emergent dangers that imperil settled modes of life. While the sentiment behind this call is not without merit, its unquestioning acceptance of the supposedly determinate identities it ministers to squanders the subversive impulse and political possibilities of our time. For although the intensity of recent changes in international order accords a certain novelty to this era, the speed with which the putatively fixed pillars of our political imaginary were demolished should caution us to recognize the ubiquity of contingency on our political horizons, past, present, and future. Indeed, it would not be unreasonable to suggest that a reciprocal agonism between indeterminacy and determinacy is a fundamental condition of possibility for political life.

Pushing beyond the caution of traditional analyses, this study engages the interpretive opportunities enabled by the transformations of our time to more fully problematize the issue of "security" by contesting the settled nature of the identity conventional approaches assume. Specifically, by taking "foreign policy" to be an important (though not predominant) practice of security, and by taking United States foreign policy to be an important (though not overriding) practice in international politics, this book examines the way in which the identity of "(the United States of) America" has been written and re-written through foreign policies operating in its name. In consequence, this is a very different sort of international relations book. Instead of asking how United States foreign policy serves the national interest, it examines how, through the inscription of foreignness, United States foreign policy helps produce and reproduce the political identity of the doer supposedly behind the deed. Rather than considering the diplomatic motivations of the strategy of containment, it examines how a variety of policies in the cold war—diplomatic or otherwise—worked to contain contingency and domesticate challenges to the dominant identity of the period. And in place of the usual analysis of the "external" dangers said to threaten "domestic" society, this book offers a nonessentialist account of danger that highlights how the very domains of inside/outside, self/other, and domestic/foreign (those moral spaces made possible by the ethical borders of identity as much as by the territorial boundaries of states) are constituted through the writing of a threat. In short, then, this book is concerned with an aspect of the problematic of subjectivity in international politics rather than with the international relations of pregiven subjects.

Given the creative ferment of social, political, and literary theory concerning the problematic of subjectivity, many forms of inspiration are available to the writer wishing to interrogate conventional modes of thinking and acting in international politics. However, in this text, and for this writer, the figure of Michel Foucault looms large. But the prominence accorded here to his theorizations is not to suggest that within Foucault's oeuvre lies a complete and comprehensive alternative account of the state and identity. On the contrary, the privilege accorded to Foucault's thought—and the concomitant lack of emphasis given to other theorists who deploy complementary modes of inquiry—stands as testament to a personal history of how ideas are incited rather than a sustained judgment on the relative worth of a range of contributions. Indeed, insofar as I have been able to put forward some different accounts of issues pertaining to the state, sovereignty, danger, and identity, my theorizations need to be read as prolegomenon to a more sustained and widely sourced future rendering. One further limitation needs to be noted. Any exhaustive account of identity, particularly one indebted to Foucault, would require a thorough discussion of the resistance to the scripting of identity proffered by those with greater access to social resources. Crudely put, one would have to consider the full range of popular resistances to elite practices. Although I consider some of the theoretical issues relevant to this question in chapter 8, I have restricted the argument in the bulk of the book to the representational practices of those acting in official capacities. This narrower ambit has an obvious logistical dimension, but I think it is intellectually justified by the space for alternative interpretations made available by the open-ended and overtly figurative character of the texts of foreign policy, which allow their scripting of identity to be contested from within.

No book represents the efforts of someone working alone, least of all a book trying to expand established modes of inquiry. As such, this study might be understood as engaged in an ongoing conversation with other works that can be located at the intersection of international politics and political theory, including (but not limited to) Bill Connolly's *Identity/Difference*, James Der Derian's *Antidiplomacy*, Mick Dillon's *Politics of Security*, Mike Shapiro's *The Politics of Representation*, Rob Walker's *Inside/Outside*, and the many writings of Richard Ashley. Indeed, this is more than a figurative conversation, because I am greatly indebted to all those writers for comments on and critical readings of my work at various times in the past few years. They have all been more than generous in the intellectual encouragement and support offered. Likewise, Steven David, Richard Flathman, Bradley Klein, Alex Wendt, the Johns Hopkins Women's Studies Faculty Seminar (particularly Mary Poovey), and the participants in my graduate seminars on international political theory and United States foreign policy have all aided the development and refinement of my thinking. Although this book is not a revised dissertation, it bears witness from that time long ago to the influence of Jim George, who was instrumental in helping me set off in these directions. To an anonymous reader (later identified by himself to be Howard Caygill) I owe a number of important refinements. Finally, to Kate Manzo, words of professional and personal acknowledgment are not sufficient recognition of the unstinting support she provided, of which the reading of the entire manuscript when busy with revisions to her own book is but one example.

A Note about the Revised Edition

This revised edition of *Writing Security* includes an epilogue dealing with the increasing attention paid to identity politics and the politics of identity in international relations. While the turn of many toward these themes is welcome, if overdue, the nature of that turn often diminishes the necessarily politicized nature of those categories and the way in which interpretive positions are implicated in the overall arguments. Only if an attentiveness to these and other dimensions is maintained can the focus on the politics of identity in world politics reap the analytical rewards it promises.

The rest of the text remains as it was in the first edition save for two features. First, small editorial corrections have been made, though none of them alters either the overall thrust or the specific details of the argument. Second, because of the need to accommodate the epilogue, what was previously chapter 8, dealing with the representation of the perceived economic threat from Japan, has had to be deleted. Difficult though it was to make that decision, the publication of a version of that chapter in an edited collection issued after the first edition of *Writing Security* means that it is still available.[1]

In making the revised edition possible, I would like to thank for their encouragement and work Lisa Freeman, Carrie Mullen, and all of the production staff of the University of Minnesota Press, and Nicola Viinikka of Manchester University Press. For comments and criticisms that have helped shape the revisions and the epilogue, I would like to acknowledge (in a responsibility-free manner) the input of James Der Derian, Bradley Klein, Mark Laffey, Kate Manzo, David Mutimer, Iver Neumann, Mike Shapiro, Hidemi Suganami, and Jutta Weldes.

Introduction
On Dangers and Their Interpretation

On August 2, 1990, Iraq became a danger to the United States. For many, this was obvious—nothing could be more real and less disputable than an invasion of one country by another. Even though it was not the United States that had been invaded, this deed was regarded as a fact that could be observed and a danger that could be understood. Yet, without denying the brutality of such an action, the unproblematic status with which this episode is endowed deserves analysis. After all, an event of this kind (particularly one so distant from America)[1] does not in and of itself constitute a danger, risk, or threat. It was possible for the leadership of the United States to have concluded that no matter how much it disapproved of the turn of events, the situation did not demand a full-scale response, and the initial period of what later became understood as a crisis was taken up with political debates over how and to what extent the United States should commit itself to act. Indeed, there have been any number of examples in which similar "facts" were met with a very different American reaction: only a decade earlier, the Iraqi invasion of Iran (an oil-producing state like Kuwait) brought no apocalyptic denunciations or calls to action, let alone a military response, from the United States.

Danger is not an objective condition. It [sic] is not a thing that exists independently of those to whom it may become a threat. To illustrate this, consider the manner in which the insurance industry assesses risk. In François Ewald's formulation, insurance is a technology of risk the principal function of which is not compensation or reparation, but rather the operation of a schema of rationality distinguished by the calculus of probabilities. In insurance, according to this logic, danger (or, more accurately, risk) is "neither an event nor a general

1

kind of event occurring in reality...but a specific mode of treatment of certain events capable of happening to a group of individuals." In other words, for the technology of risk in insurance, "Nothing is a risk in itself; there is no risk in reality. But on the other hand, anything *can* be a risk; it all depends on how one analyzes the danger, considers the event. As Kant might have put it, the category of risk is a category of the understanding; it cannot be given in sensibility or intuition."[2] In these terms, danger is an effect of interpretation. Danger bears no essential, necessary, or unproblematic relation to the action or event from which it is said to derive. Nothing is intrinsically more dangerous for insurance technology than anything else, except when interpreted as such.

This understanding of the necessarily interpretive basis of risk has important implications for international relations. It does not deny that there are "real" dangers in the world: infectious diseases, accidents, and political violence (among others) have consequences that can literally be understood in terms of life and death. But not all risks are equal, and not all risks are interpreted as dangers. Modern society contains a veritable cornucopia of danger; indeed, there is such an abundance of risk that it is impossible to objectively know all that threatens us.[3] Those events or factors that we identify as dangerous come to be ascribed as such only through an interpretation of their various dimensions of dangerousness. Moreover, that process of interpretation does not depend on the incidence of "objective" factors for its veracity. For example, HIV infection has been considered by many to be America's major public health issue, yet pneumonia and influenza, diabetes, suicide, and chronic liver disease have all been individually responsible for many more deaths.[4] Equally, an interpretation of danger has licensed a "war on (illegal) drugs" in the United States, despite the fact that the consumption level of (and the number of deaths that result from) licit drugs exceeds by a considerable order of magnitude that associated with illicit drugs. And "terrorism" is often cited as a major threat to national security, even though its occurrence within the United States is minimal (notwithstanding the bombings in Oklahoma City and at the World Trade Center in New York) and its contribution to international carnage minor.[5]

Furthermore, the role of interpretation in the articulation of danger is not restricted to the process by which some risks come to be considered more serious than others. An important function of interpretation is the way that certain modes of representation crystallize around referents marked as dangers. Given the often tenuous relationship between an interpretation of danger and the "objective" incidence of behaviors and factors thought to constitute it, the capacity for a particular risk to be represented in terms of characteristics reviled in the community said to be threatened can be an important impetus to an interpretation of danger. As later chapters will demonstrate, the ability to represent things as alien, subversive, dirty, or sick has been pivotal to the articulation of danger in the American experience.

In this context, it is also important to note that there need not be an action or event to provide the grounds for an interpretation of danger. The mere existence of an alternative mode of being, the presence of which exemplifies that different identities are possible and thus denaturalizes the claim of a particular identity to be *the* true identity, is sometimes enough to produce the understanding of a threat.[6] In consequence, only in these terms is it possible to understand how some acts of international power politics raise not a whit of concern, while something as seemingly unthreatening as the novels of a South American writer can be considered such a danger to national security that his exclusion from the country is warranted.[7] For both insurance and international relations, therefore, danger results from the calculation of a threat that objectifies events, disciplines relations, and sequesters an ideal of the identity of the people said to be at risk.

These qualities of danger were evident in the Persian Gulf crisis. In announcing that the United States was sending military forces to Saudi Arabia, President Bush declared: "In the life of a nation, we're called upon to define who we are and what we believe."[8] By manifestly linking American identity to danger, the president highlighted the indispensability of interpretation to the determination of a threat, and tacitly invoked the theme of this study: that the boundaries of a state's identity are secured by the representation of danger integral to foreign policy.

The invasion of Kuwait is not the subject of this book. But it does serve as a useful touchstone by which to outline some of the assumptions undergirding this study. Consider, for example, this question: How did the Iraqi invasion become the greatest danger to the United States? Two answers to this question seem obvious and were common. Those indebted to a power-politics understanding of world politics, with its emphasis on the behavior of states calculated in rational terms according to the pursuit of power, understood the invasion to be an easily observable instance of naked aggression against an independent, sovereign state. To those indebted to an economistic understanding, in which the underlying forces of capital accumulation are determinative of state behavior, the U.S.-led response, like the Iraqi invasion, was explicable in terms of the power of oil, markets, and the military-industrial complex.

Each of these characterizations is surely a caricature. The range of views in the debate over this crisis was infinitely more complex than is suggested by these two positions; there were many whose analyses differed from those with whom they might normally be associated, and indebtedness to a tradition does not determine one's argument in every instance. But the purpose of overdrawing these positions (which we might call, in equally crude terms, realist and Marxist) is to make the point that although each is usually thought to be the antinomy of the other, they both equally efface the indispensability of interpretation in the articulation of danger. As such, they share a disposition from which this analysis differs. Committed to an *epistemic realism* — whereby the world comprises objects whose existence is independent of ideas or beliefs about them — both of these understandings maintain that there are material causes to which events and actions can be reduced. And occasioned by this epistemic realism, they sanction two other analytic forms: a *narrativizing historiography* in which things have a self-evident quality that allows them to speak for themselves, and a *logic of explanation* in which the purpose of analysis is to identify those self-evident things and material causes so that actors can accommodate themselves to the realm of necessity they engender.[9] Riven with various demands, insistences, and assertions that things "must" be either this or that, this disposition is the most common metatheoretical discourse among practitioners of the discipline of international relations.[10]

But there are alternative ways to think, and this book exhibits a commitment to one of them. Contrary to the claims of epistemic realism, I argue that as understanding involves rendering the unfamiliar in the terms of the familiar, there is always an ineluctable debt to interpretation such that there is nothing outside of discourse. Contrary to a narrativizing historiography, I employ a mode of historical representation that self-consciously adopts a perspective. And contrary to the logic of explanation, I embrace a logic of interpretation that acknowledges the improbability of cataloging, calculating, and specifying the "real causes," and concerns itself instead with considering the manifest political consequences of adopting one mode of representation over another.

As such, my argument is part of an emerging dissident literature in international relations that draws sustenance from a series of modern thinkers who have focused on historically specific modes of discourse rather than the supposedly independent realms of subjects and objects.[11] Starting from the position that social and political life comprises a set of practices in which things are constituted in the process of dealing with them, this dissent does not (and does not desire to) constitute a discrete methodological school claiming to magically illuminate the previously dark recesses of global politics. Nor is it the dissent of a self-confident and singular figure claiming to know the error of all previous ways and offering salvation from all theoretical sin. Rather, this form of dissent emerges from a disparate and sometimes divergent series of encounters between the traditions of international relations and theories increasingly prominent in other realms of social and political inquiry. It is a form of dissent that celebrates difference: the proliferation of perspectives, dimensions, and approaches to the very real dilemmas of global life. It is a form of dissent that celebrates the particularity and context-bound nature of judgments and assessments, not because it favors a (so-called) relativist retreat into the incommensurability of alternatives, but because it recognizes the universalist conceits of all attempts to force difference into the straitjacket of identity.[12] It is a form of dissent skeptical—but not cynical—about the traditions of international relations and their claims of adequacy to reality. It is a form of dissent that is not concerned to seek a better fit between thought and the world, language and matter, proposition and fact. On the contrary, it is a form of dissent that questions the very way our problems have been posed in these terms and the constraints within which they have been considered, focusing instead on the way the world has been made historically possible.[13]

Consequently, in attempting to understand the ways in which United States foreign policy has interpreted danger and secured the boundaries of the identity in whose name it operates, this analysis adopts neither a purely theoretical nor a purely historical mode. It is perhaps best understood in terms of a history of the present, an interpretative attitude suggested by Michel Foucault.[14] A history of the present does not try to capture *the* meaning of the past, nor does it try to get *a* complete picture of the past as a bounded epoch, with underlying laws and teleology. Neither is a history of the present an instance of presentism—where the present is read back into the past—or an instance of finalism, that mode of analysis whereby the analyst maintains that a kernel of the present located in the past has inexorably progressed such that it now defines our condition. Rather, a history of the present exhibits an unequivocally contemporary orientation. Beginning with an incitement from the present—an acute manifestation of a ritual of power — this mode of analysis seeks to trace how such rituals of power arose, took shape, gained importance, and effected politics.[15] In short, this mode of analysis asks how certain terms and concepts have historically functioned within discourse.

To suggest as much, however, is not to argue in terms of the discursive having priority over the nondiscursive. Of course, this is the criticism most often mounted by opponents to arguments such as this, understandings apparent in formulations like "if discourse is all there is," "if everything is language," or "if there is no reality."[16] In so doing they unquestioningly accept that there are distinct realms of the discursive and the nondiscursive. Yet such a claim, especially after the decades of debates about language, interpretation, and understanding in the natural and social sciences, is no longer innocently sustainable. It can be reiterated as an article of faith to rally the true believers and banish the heretics, but it cannot be put forward as a self-evident truth. As Richard Rorty has acknowledged, projects like philosophy's traditional desire to see "how language relates to the world" result in "the impossible attempt to step outside our skins — the traditions, linguistic and other, within which we do our thinking and self-criticism — and compare ourselves with something absolute."[17] The world exists independently of language, but we can never *know* that (beyond the fact of its assertion), because the existence of the world is literally inconceivable outside of language and our traditions of interpretation.[18] In Foucault's terms, "We must not resolve discourse into a play of pre-existing significations; we must not imagine that the world turns toward us a legible face which we would only have to decipher; the world is not the accomplice of our knowledge; there is no prediscursive providence which disposes the world in our favour."[19]

Therefore, to talk in terms of an analysis that examines how concepts have historically functioned within discourse is to refuse the force of the distinction between discursive and nondiscursive. As Laclau and Mouffe have argued, "The fact that every object is constituted as an object of discourse has *nothing to do* with whether there is a world external to thought, or with the realism/idealism opposition . . . What is denied is not that . . . objects exist externally to thought, but the rather different assertion that they could constitute themselves as objects outside of any discursive condition of emergence."[20] This formulation seeks neither to banish arguments that authorize their positions through reference to "external reality," nor to suggest that any one representation is as powerful as another. On the contrary, if we think in terms of a discursive economy — whereby discourse (the representation and constitution of the "real") is a managed space in which some statements and depictions come to have greater value than others—the idea of "external reality" has a particular currency that is *internal* to discourse. For in a discursive economy, investments have been made in certain interpretations; dividends can be drawn by those parties that have made the investments; representations are taxed when they confront new and ambiguous circumstances; and participation in the discursive economy is through social relations that embody an unequal distribution of power. Most important, the effect of this understanding is to expand the domain of social and political inquiry: "The main consequence of a break with the discursive/extra-discursive dichotomy is the abandonment of the thought/reality opposition, and hence a major enlargement of the field of those categories which can account for social relations. Synonymy, metonymy, metaphor are not forms of thought that add a second sense to a primary, constitutive literality of social relations; instead, they are part of the primary terrain itself in which the social is constituted."[21] The enlargement of the interpretive imagination along these lines is necessary in order to account for many of the recent developments in world politics, and (as chapter 1 will show) to understand the texts of postwar United States foreign policy.

In the form of a history of the present, then, this analysis begins from the incitement of "the end of the cold war," a period that is thought to portend a qualitative change in world politics. For many, the dangers of the past are a thing of the past. But one does not have to deny that world politics exhibits considerable novelty at this juncture to appreciate that United States foreign policy recognizes a range of new dangers that might occupy the place of the old. The European revolutions of 1989 and their consequences; "new global issues" such as the environment; the interpretation of drug use and trafficking as a national security issue; the representation of Japan and Germany as economic threats to security; an awareness of disease, migration, and other population issues as sources of external threat; a renewed focus on the "Third World" as the primary source of danger; the vigilance that is exercised toward new forms of violence such as "terrorism" or "Islamic fundamentalism"; and a general disquiet about the pervasive nature of ambiguity and uncertainty—all these orientations to the world stand as dangers that seem to challenge the long-standing and well-established modes of interpretation associated with the cold war.

For the most part, however, these developments have been represented in ways that do not depart dramatically from those dominant

during the cold war. To be sure, they are not represented as being re-
ducible to Soviet behavior. But these challenges are represented as dangers, located in an external and anarchic environment, which threaten
the security of an internal and domestic society, often via recourse to
violence. This provokes a question: What functions have difference,
danger, and otherness played in constituting the identity of the United
States as a major actor in international politics? To pose the question
in these terms is a little misleading, for it is not intended to suggest
either that it is a strict functional requirement of American identity
that difference and danger be articulated as otherness, or that only
certain groups or phenomena can be other. As Foucault argued with
respect to the confinement of the insane and the repression of certain
sexual practices in the nineteenth century, these were not functionally
the result of or required by bourgeois domination. The bourgeoisie
was interested not in the mad or the phenomenon of infantile mas-
turbation but in the procedural system through which such exclusions and controls were effected.[22] In other words, groups or practices
other than those targeted could have been the objects of surveillance
and discipline, while those that were targeted could have been tolerated if not accepted.

In this context, for the United States, the current period in world
politics can be understood as being characterized by the representation of novel challenges in terms of traditional analytics, and the varied attempts to replace one enemy with (an)other. In consequence,
the argument to be made here suggests that we need a more radical
response to these challenges: a response directed at the modes of interpretation that make these challenges available for apprehension,
the strategies and tactics by which they are calculated as dangers, and
the means by which they come to be other.

Addressing the issue of the roles danger and difference play in
constituting the identity of the United States involves a deconstruction
of conventional political discourse and its self-presentation, especially
that effected in the practice and analysis of both international relations
and foreign policy. In reorienting analysis from the concern with the
intentional acts of pregiven subjects to the problematic of subjectivity,
this argument proposes that United States foreign policy be understood as a political practice central to the constitution, production, and
maintenance of American political identity. In order to delineate more
precisely the relationship between foreign policy and political identity, this argument is predicated on a reconceptualization of understandings to which the conventional view of international relations

and foreign policy is deeply indebted—most specifically, a reconceptualization of identity and the state.

Identity and the State

Identity is an inescapable dimension of being. No body could be without it. Inescapable as it is, identity—whether personal or collective—is not fixed by nature, given by God, or planned by intentional behavior. Rather, identity is constituted in relation to difference. But neither is difference fixed by nature, given by God, or planned by intentional behavior. Difference is constituted in relation to identity.[23] The problematic of identity/difference contains, therefore, no foundations that are prior to, or outside of, its operation. Whether we are talking of "the body" or "the state," or of particular bodies and states, the identity of each is performatively constituted. Moreover, the constitution of identity is achieved through the inscription of boundaries that serve to demarcate an "inside" from an "outside," a "self" from an "other," a "domestic" from a "foreign."

In the specific case of the body, Judith Butler has argued that its boundary, as well as the border between internal and external, is "tenuously maintained" by the transformation of elements that were originally part of identity into a "defiling otherness."[24] In this formulation, there is no originary or sovereign presence that inhabits a prediscursive domain and gives the body, its sex, or gender a naturalized and unproblematic quality. To be sure, many insist on understanding the body, sex, and gender as naturalized and unproblematic. But for their claim to be persuasive, we would have to overlook (among other issues) the multifarious normalizing codes that abound in our society for the constitution and disciplining of sexuality. In seeking to establish and police understandings of what constitutes the normal, the accepted, and the desirable, such codes effect an admission of their constructed nature and the contingent and problematic nature of the identity of the body.

Understanding the gendered identity of the body as performative means that we regard it as having "no ontological status apart from the various acts that constitute its reality." As such, the idea that gender is an interior essence definitive of the body's identity is a discursively constructed notion that is required for the purposes of disciplining sexuality. In this context, genders are neither "true" or "false," nor "normal" or "abnormal," but "are only produced as the truth effects of a discourse of primary and stable identity." Moreover, gender can be understood as "an identity tenuously constituted in time, instituted in an exterior space through *a stylized repetition of acts"*; an identity achieved, *"not* [through] *a founding act, but rather a regulated process of repetition."*[25]

Choosing the question of gender and the body as an exemplification of the theme of identity is not to suggest that as an "individual" instance of identity the performative constitution of gender and the body is prior to and determinative of instances of collective identity. In other words, I am not claiming that the state is analogous to an individual with a settled identity. To the contrary, I want to suggest that the performative constitution of gender and the body is analogous to the performative constitution of the state. Specifically, I want to suggest that we can understand the state as having "no ontological status apart from the various acts which constitute its reality"; that its status as the sovereign presence in world politics is produced by "a discourse of primary and stable identity"; and that the identity of any particular state should be understood as "tenuously constituted in time . . . through *a stylized repetition of acts,"* and achieved, *"not* [through] *a founding act, but rather a regulated process of repetition."*

Moreover, the similitude between the body and the state exceeds the status of being simply heuristically useful if we think of gender as the effect of a discourse about primary and stable identity, in terms of what Joan Cocks has called a "regime of Masculine/feminine."[26] For Cocks the regime of Masculine/feminine is a disciplinary regime of truth that is prevalent in our culture and contains contingency through the production of "male" and "female" as stable identities. Most important, this regime effects a double move: "it imposes on each of the two kinds of bodies a particular norm and characteristic deviation, [and] it imposes on all bodies the rule that masculinity is the norm of active desire and femininity is active desire's deviation."[27] Informed by the understanding of power as productive and not confined to the boundaries or institutions of the juridical state, Cocks's regime of Masculine/feminine is one of the ensemble of practices that give rise to the "society of normalization" about which Foucault wrote.[28] Characterized by discipline and domination through multiple forms of subjugation, rather than by the uniform authority of sovereignty located in a single point, a society of normalization secures the content and confines of its identity through the imposition of a norm rather than the enforcement of a rule. In so doing, it encourages and legitimizes certain dispositions and orientations while opposing and delegitimizing others, a process that is neither deterministic in its operation nor totally hegemonic in its consequences.

Cocks's argument is directed primarily at how the regime of Masculine/feminine disciplines the sexed body. But given the culturally pervasive nature of the gender norms it is concerned with, it is not implausible to suggest that a similar regime — or at least the gender norms that it effects — operates in other domains and disciplines other identities, such as the state. Indeed, if we consider how our understanding of politics is heavily indebted to a discursive economy in which reason, rationality, and masculinity are licensed as superior to unreason, irrationality, and femininity, it is not difficult to appreciate that gender norms have also helped constitute the norms of statecraft. Therefore, in terms of the axiological dimension of spatializing practices, "the body" can be understood as being a historically well-established analog for the constitution of state identity. This becomes even more apparent when we think of how "the body politic" functions as a regulating and normalizing trope for "the political" (a discussion found in chapter 4). Moreover, central to that regulation and normalization, and to be understood as a privileged instance of the stylized repetition of acts, is foreign policy and the articulation of danger.[29] Accordingly, the identity of the state that is contained and reproduced through foreign policy is likely to be inscribed with prior codes of gender that will in turn operate as norms by which future conduct is judged and threats are calculated.[30]

But if there are no primary and stable identities, and if the identities many had thought of as primary and stable, such as the body and the state, are performatively constituted, how can international relations speak of such foundational concepts as "the state," "security," "war," "danger," "sovereignty," and so on? After all, isn't security determined by the requirements of a preexisting sovereign state and war conducted in its name as a response to an objective danger? How then can we speak of these categories once we acknowledge the non-essentialistic character of danger?

Indeed, much of the conventional literature on the nation and the state implies that the essence of the former precedes the reality of the latter: that the identity of a "people" is the basis for the legitimacy of the state and its subsequent practices. However, much of the recent historical sociology on this topic has argued that the state more often than not precedes the nation: that nationalism is a construct of the state in pursuit of its legitimacy. Benedict Anderson, for example, has argued in compelling fashion that "the nation" should be understood as an "imagined political community" that exists only insofar as it is a cultural artifact that is represented textually.[31] Equally, Charles Tilly has argued that any coordinated, hierarchical, and territorial entity should be only understood as a "national state." He stresses that few of these national states have ever become or presently are "nation-states" — national states whose sovereign territorialization is perfectly aligned with a prior and primary form of identification, such as religion, language, or symbolic sense of self. Even modern-day Great Britain, France, and Germany (and, equally, the United States, Australia, and Canada) cannot be considered nation-states even though they are national states.[32] The importance of these perspectives is that they allow us to understand national states as unavoidably paradoxical entities that do not possess prediscursive, stable identities. As a consequence, all states are marked by an inherent tension between the various domains that need to be aligned for an "imagined political community" to come into being — such as territoriality and the many axes of identity — and the demand that such an alignment is a response to (rather than constitutive of) a prior and stable identity. In other words, states are never finished as entities; the tension between the demands of identity and the practices that constitute it can never be fully resolved, because the performative nature of identity can never be fully revealed. This paradox inherent to their being renders states in permanent need of reproduction: with no ontological status apart from the many and varied practices that constitute their reality, states are (and have to be) always in a process of becoming. For a state to end its practices of representation would be to expose its lack of prediscursive foundations; stasis would be death.[33] Moreover, the drive to fix the state's identity and contain challenges to the state's representation cannot finally or absolutely succeed. Aside from recognizing that there is always an excess of being over appearance that cannot be contained by disciplinary practices implicated in state formation, were it possible to reduce all being to appearance, and were it possible to bring about the absence of movement which in that reduction of being to appearance would characterize pure security, it would be at that moment that the state would wither away.[34] At that point all identities would have congealed, all challenges would have evaporated, and all need for disciplinary authorities and their fields of force would have vanished. Should the state project of security be successful in the terms in which it is articulated, the state would cease to exist. Security as the absence of movement would result in death via stasis. Ironically, then, the inability of the state project of security to succeed is the guarantor of the state's continued success as an impelling identity.

The constant articulation of danger through foreign policy is thus not a threat to a state's identity or existence: it is its condition of possibility. While the objects of concern change over time, the techniques and exclusions by which those objects are constituted as dangers persist. Such an argument, however, is occluded by the traditional representations of international politics through their debts to epistemic realism and its effacement of interpretation. Grounded in an interrogation of discursive practices within the study of international relations and the conduct of United States foreign policy, this study seeks to show how these themes and issues are immanent to these domains. Through a rethinking of the practice and theory of foreign policy in chapters 1, 2, and 3; a discussion in chapter 4 of the dominant modes of representing danger; and a consideration of the figuration of difference at various foundational moments in the American experience in chapter 5, this book posits the validity (though not incontestability) of an alternative interpretation of the cold war, which is elaborated in chapter 6. The hope is that this analysis can highlight some of the political issues at stake in the post–cold war era, as chapters 7 and 8 argue. The epilogue evaluates the efflorescence of concern with the politics of identity by those perspectives previously inattentive to these concerns, and considers the modes of interpretation that are more adequately attuned to the issues.

One

Provocations of Our Time

The Globalization of Contingency

The demise of the cold war has been much heralded. But the causes, meaning, and implications of this political rupture (assuming its veracity) are much debated. For some, these developments are evidence that global life has consisted of a linear trajectory moving inexorably toward the final realization of Freedom in the State and Reason in History. In this context, the dramatic changes in the international order currently under way are to be understood as a victory of one idea over others; the ascendance of liberal democracy and consumer electronics to the mantle of a "universal homogenous state" in which the major political conflicts and alternative understandings of history are no more.[1] The collapse of one of the protagonists is taken by some to be retrospective validation of the conflict's intersystemic nature,[2] while a prominent line of argument is that the United States was triumphant in a great power geopolitical struggle.[3] While others would not doubt the potentially radical nature of the current historical juncture, their understanding of the impetus behind the upheavals — doubtful that history has come to an end — focuses on the long-standing commitment of dissident and marginal forces to social, economic, and cultural struggle.[4]

To proclaim the end of the cold war assumes that we know what the cold war was. Moreover, the very act of proclaiming the end of the cold war serves to write history in such a way that the cold war becomes an era the understanding of which is not problematic. In considering the issue of where we go from here, there is a tendency to uncritically accept a particular story of how we got to here. By constantly invoking the advent of a new phase in world politics, analysts tend to accept one particular rendering of the period from which we are emerging, a rendering that privileges the legitimacy of "the West" (especially the United States) in its entirety. To be sure, not all of the above assessments concur on the exact nature of the period from which we are said to be emerging, but there is a general sense of favoring one of two understandings. Either the cold war was the period of intense rivalry between the post–World War II blocs of "East" and "West," or it was the rivalry of greater duration between communism and capitalism.[5] Whichever, it is argued that the danger — either in the form of a military threat or an economic and ideological contest — posed to the United States and its allies by the Soviet Union and its satellites is no more. William Hyland offers a refrain common in contemporary U.S. debates:

> For the past fifty years American foreign policy has been formed in response to the threat posed by this country's opponents and enemies . . . Now danger emanating from Moscow is no longer the driving force of the debate. This country has to decide what role it wishes to play in the world where there is no overwhelming danger to national security and no clearly identifiable enemy.[6]

In terms of the nonessentialistic character of danger discussed in the Introduction, however, the objectification and externalization of danger that are central to contemporary assessments of security and politics in the post–cold war era need to be understood as the effects of political practices rather than the conditions of their possibility. Accordingly, one appropriate response at this historical juncture is to undertake a reflexive consideration of the past as a means of highlighting the historically constituted nature of international order in the present. It will be asserted here and argued in chapter 2 that one way of historicizing our understanding of the cold war is to reconceptualize foreign policy and reinterpret United States foreign policy in the postwar period. If we problematize the conventional understanding of foreign policy as being no more than the external orientation of preestablished states with fixed identities, and problematize the understanding that United States foreign policy in the postwar period was no more than a reaction to the dictates of an independent and hostile world, the form of international order we know as the cold war might be understood in terms of the need to discipline the ambiguity of global life in ways that help to secure always fragile identities.

Aside from the impetus of this historical juncture, this argument is incited by a strain of intellectual ferment premised on fundamental ontological assumptions that can be associated with the logic of interpretation and the reconceptualization of identity and the state (outlined in the Introduction). It is difficult to overstate the implications of this ferment for the understanding of international relations, because it goes to the very heart of how "international relations" are constituted and understood, and how the discipline of international relations understands its own history and contemporary role. Hedley Bull once argued that the theory of international relations was concerned with general propositions that may be advanced about the political relations *among* states.[7] Such a proposition would seem to many to be so obvious as to verge on the banal, but it resolves the process of understanding global life in a particular way, through the demarcation of a theory/practice divide so that theory is outside of the world it purports to simply observe. The interpretive approach, in contrast, sees theory *as* practice: the theory of international relations is one instance of the pervasive cultural practices that serve to discipline ambiguity. Experience has to be arrested, fixed, or disciplined for social life to be possible. The form that emerges through this process is thus both arbitrary and nonarbitrary: arbitrary in that it is one possibility among many, and nonarbitrary in "the sense that one can inquire into the historical conditions within which one way of making the world was dominant so that we now have a world that power has convened."[8] The "world" we so often take for granted as a foundation for knowledge and politics thus came to be, through multiple political practices, related as much to the constitution of various subjectivities as to the intentional action of predetermined subjects.

There is much more at stake here than the rise of fashionable interpretations in the intellectual domain or the coming to prominence of certain events in the international realm. The nexus between the moment of these events and the power of this mode of analysis is to be found in the contention that we live in a distinctive political time marked by the absence of a corresponding political space; that is to say, the activity of politics is no longer (assuming it once was) concomitant with the enclosure of politics (the state).[9] Indeed, these changes and our ability to comprehend them are both made possible by and help constitute the political contours of the late modern period: contours that might be characterized in terms of the globalization of contingency, the erasure of the markers of certainty, and the rarefaction of political discourse.

The globalization of contingency invokes the increasing tendencies toward ambiguity, indeterminacy, and uncertainty on our horizon.[10] While these have been long identified in academic international relations literature under the sign of "anarchy," these contingencies — from which comes their understanding as globalized — can no longer be contained within established power structures and spatializations.

Danger, in short, can no longer just be written as "out there." Security is not to be found "within." This is more than just a result of interdependence, the proliferation of threats, or the overflowing of domestic issues onto the world stage (the conventional response). This is an irruption of contingencies that renders all established containers problematic. This irruption does not simply involve the movement of problems from one domain to the other, but rather the rendering asunder of those domains and their entailments. It makes little sense to speak of politics occurring in terms of a distinct "inside" or "outside" (such as a "Third World" that is spatially beyond our borders and temporally backward) when, for example, U.S. economic policies encourage "Third World export processing zones" in Los Angeles, where manufacturers stamp their auto parts "made in Brazil" and the clothing goods "made in Taiwan" to attract lower tariffs; when demographic changes have made nonwhite children majorities in the California and New York school systems, and will make whites a minority in the United States by the year 2056; and when the poverty and poor health care in Harlem make the area a "zone of excess mortality" with a death rate for black males higher than that for their peers in Bangladesh.[11]

This globalization of contingency, this irruption of contingency, not only renders problematic the traditional spatializations of power (for example, states, alliances, political parties), it renders problematic the discursive practices that have made those spatializations of power possible. This is what is meant by the "erasure of the markers of certainty."[12] The irruption of contingency opens up the possibility of observing that foundational discourses—discourses about prior, primary, and stable identities—work to constitute the identities in whose name they operate.

Finally, this erasure of certainty brought on by the irruption of contingency has produced the rarefaction of political discourse.[13] To put it simply, although they retain some power, the conventional (and foundational) categories of ordering are exhausted. Their work can only continue by abjuration rather than affirmation; they can maintain an existence and identity by specifying exceptions and exclusions, but they are no longer able to mobilize support in terms of a prior and positive ideal. Even more important, the desire to order has itself become a source of danger in our time. Political discourse that speaks only of the interest and institutional bases of action; the need for attunement, normalization, or mastery as the technologies of order; or power as an object or ethics as a command, or of sovereignty and territoriality as the container of politics; has lost its capacity — if it ever had it — to provide security.

Integral, then, to the contours of our time is undecidability. This term (appropriated, and embellished, from Derrida) signifies neither the absence of decidability nor the existence of an ambiguous domain beyond the limits of our knowledge.[14] Rather, to speak of the undecidability of our time is to make the claim that there is an irreducible, irresolvable, "floating indetermination"[15] in both the conditions of our existence and the established ways of representing them. While there have always been frictions and resistances to the forces that seek the alignment or containment of the *aporias*, the gaps or rifts, through which being has exceeded appearance, it is probable that this condition — given the features of an era some consider as late capitalism — has been recently intensified. Perhaps more than at any other juncture, the indispensable incompleteness, ceaseless displacement, and abundant contradictions of social and political life that we witness daily suggest the limits of calculability and management have been reached. If so, the fervent hope that rationalist discourse can instantiate and secure homogeneous, stable identities can only be frustrated. With regard to understanding the cold war, this suggests that within both the practices and the interpretations that have been objectified in this era, there is considerably more slack and more indeterminacy than we might at first appreciate.

Securing the Meaning of the Cold War

Within historical circles, debate over the origins and meaning of the cold war has been — to offer an understatement — a subject of much controversy.[16] Orthodox accounts maintained that because of the structural configuration of power existing in international politics after World War II, conflict between the two greatest military powers was inevitable, particularly given the expansionist tendencies ascribed to the Soviet Union, although elite divisions and misperception within the United States also had an impact.[17] In contrast, revisionist arguments held that the logic of economic development and the political culture of American society meant that it was the United States that was inherently expansionist and the source of tension.[18] More recently, there has been a postrevisionist effort to combine some of the insights of each of these literatures in a comprehensive explanation of the cold war's genesis, although the resulting studies have looked to the nature of the international system as the source of conflict, prompting one scholar to describe them as "neo-orthodox."[19] Excluded from this predominantly American academic contestation are the writings of a largely European group of activist intellectuals who see the cold war as a "joint venture" in which the superpowers, through a historical process of mutual formation, each engaged in reciprocal incitement that effectively legitimized the other. In a manner similar to that of the American revisionists, this literature accords the domestic political requirements of each state causal primacy.[20]

The relative sophistication of these various historiographical debates has had little if any impact on the understanding of the cold war predominant in the discipline of international relations, where the cold war is understood in largely orthodox terms.[21] Given the shared epistemic entailments of historiography's orthodox realism and international relations' realist orthodoxy, this affinity is not surprising. The up-front commitment of a Louis Halle to narrativizing historiography (in which the cold war is treated "as a phenomenon that, experience has taught us, has its own dynamics; as a phenomenon that, typically, goes through a certain cycle with a beginning, a middle, and an end"), or of a Daniel Yergin to "the ineluctable features [balance of power, spheres of influence, power politics, danger] of an international system composed of sovereign nations" aligns perfectly with the assumptions and presuppositions of international relations' dominant discourse.[22] In consequence, many of the insights offered by critics of the orthodox historiography have been ignored or overlooked in international relations literature, thereby naturalizing without much debate one specific interpretation of the origins of the cold war.

Moreover, the hegemony of the orthodox interpretation within international relations has been buttressed by the metatheoretical assumptions of the critics. For all their opposition to a realist rendering of the cold war's beginnings, the formulations of scholars like Chomsky (who emphatically intones that "facts," "reality," and "the truth" exceed the ideological interpretation of the orthodox)[23] and Thompson (who wishes to ward off "supposedly 'critical' theory" through the rediscovery of "some vocabulary of rationality and rehabilitated universals")[24] exhibit a commitment to an epistemic realism that brings them closer than they might care to acknowledge to the position from which they wish to be distanced. To be sure, an interpretation like Thompson's gives considerable credence to the interplay of social and historical forces, and is in many ways more nuanced than Chomsky's polemics (valuable though they are). But for all that he argues that the cold war had an independent internal thrust such that it was about itself, Thompson also wants to maintain that there were real origins (an "existential socio-economic matrix") from which the conflict became detached.[25]

The critics' indebtedness to an epistemic realism thus aligns them more closely with their orthodox protagonists than is usually acknowledged. Although scholars such as Chomsky and Thompson manifestly offer an interpretation of the origins of the cold war, they do so on the grounds that there exists a nondiscursive realm outside of the purview of their interpretation that confers authority and legitimacy on their argument. In the exercise of this logic the critics share additional commitments with the orthodox view because proponents of this position enter (as the argument in the Introduction made clear) the realm of interpretation as soon as they undertake to say anything about the world. Indeed, Halle — who maintained that the cold war represented "an historical necessity" — reflected on the craft of historiography and willingly acknowledged that there were multiple cold wars, each of which was the effect of the fusion of interpretive horizons between the scholar and his domain of inquiry.[26] As such, many of the orthodox depictions of the cold war and their critics display an indebtedness to the *verstehen* tradition whereby "facts" are recognized as culturally derived and value laden, yet independently verifiable. This Weberian resolution was designed to overcome the paradox bedeviling scientific theory since Descartes and Hume: "How is it possible to speak of reality in human society when . . . understanding of reality is dependent upon intersubjective meaning bestowed upon it by subjectivized objects?"[27] Obvious in such foundational figures for international relations as Hans Morgenthau — particularly when in very nearly the same breath he wished to maintain both that international politics was governed by "objective laws" and that it was understandable only if analysts put themselves in the shoes of statesmen[28] — Weber's attempt to fuse hermeneutic and positivist themes ultimately faltered because of the inherent limits of the *verstehen* approach and its inability to escape the regulative ideal of the empiricist metaphysic.[29] Yet it bequeathed a powerful epistemic legacy of dualized understanding (subject/object, theory/observation, relative/universal, fact/value) that continues to govern the social sciences, and in which the inherently interpretive nature of social and political understanding is recognized but severely circumscribed.

The shared commitment of the orthodoxy and its critics to epistemic realism and a Weberian *verstehen* tradition has important consequences for our understanding of the cold war. An ensemble of practices as contingent and unresolvable as those we identify as the cold war has been rendered knowable through a variety of positions that appear to have exhausted all possible interpretations. Yet the undecidability of these practices has been curtailed rather than exhausted because of the declared faith in a distinction between discursive and nondiscursive realms by most contenders in the quest for understanding. In contrast, if we accept that there is nothing possible outside of discourse (which, as the Introduction argued, is a position different from philosophical idealism), the way is open to reconsider what was at stake in the cold war.

The Texts of Foreign Policy

That the behavior of the Soviet Union provided the organizing principle for postwar United States foreign policy is an assumption common to the orthodox theory and practice of international relations in the postwar era. Even among those who argued — contrary to the orthodox view — that there was an important relationship between foreign policy and the domestic social order in the United States, few doubted that Soviet behavior constituted a realm of necessity.[30] Consider the following statement: "I do not think that old-fashioned cold war liberalism needs any apologies. It will need them only if new evidence shows that Soviet imperialism never existed, or no longer exists, or if somebody comes up with a better alternative for dealing with it than the cold war." The author goes on to argue that "whether Soviet imperialism is a threat is a paradigm of a non-'ideological,' unphilosophical, straightforwardly empirical, question" and decries the "hope that such questions can be answered by improving one's philosophical sophistication (rather than by, say, reading intelligence reports on what the Politbureau and the Soviet generals have been saying to one another lately)."[31]

This statement is a useful jumping-off point for this argument because its author, Richard Rorty, has been influential in the antifoundationalist debates of Anglo-American philosophy and social theory. Yet, despite the sophisticated philosophical understanding Rorty brings to his scholarship — understandings that have sought to question all givens and critique all axioms — he is prepared to argue that "Soviet imperialism" is a fact of almost unchallengeable proportions that legitimizes the cold war liberalism of U.S. politics. It is as if Rorty has substituted a "historical myth of the given" for the "epistemological myth of the given" he has helped undermine.[32] Rorty is, of course, far from alone in granting "Soviet imperialism" an almost ontological status. But the disjunction between Rorty's antifoundationalist philosophy and neoconservative politics poses in stark relief the issue at the heart of this study: is it possible to provide an alternative account of postwar United States foreign policy employing the metatheoretical insights of the interdisciplinary debates in the social sciences concerned with issues of interpretation?

Rorty's orthodox rendering of the cold war invites a critique informed by an orientation in which the seemingly intransigent structures of history are effects (although very powerful effects) of a variety of uncoordinated practices of differentiation that serve to constitute meaning and identity through a series of exclusions. In this context, the imposition of an interpretation on the ambiguity and contingency of social life always results in an other being marginalized. Meaning and identity are, therefore, always the consequence of a relationship between the self and the other that emerges through the imposition of an interpretation, rather than being the product of uncovering an exclusive domain with its own preestablished identity. A reconceptualization of foreign policy along these lines is not only theoretically well grounded, but provides a means of critically exploring the open-ended character of the foreign policy texts that have been important in establishing the discursive boundaries of United States foreign policy.

National Security Council document number sixty-eight of 1950 (NSC-68) is widely regarded as having established the parameters and rationale for postwar United States foreign policy.[33] For all its subsequent importance, what is most striking about this document is the way in which a certain ambivalence about the sources of danger to the United States is glossed over by the highly figurative nature of its representation of threat. NSC-68 argued that international politics had been "marked by recurring periods of violence and war, but a system of sovereign and independent states was maintained, over which no state was able to achieve hegemony." This situation was changed in the wake of the defeat of Germany and Japan by the fact that the Soviet Union, "unlike previous aspirants to hegemony, is animated by a new fanatic faith, antithetical to our own, and seeks to impose its absolute authority over the rest of the world."[34]

In this representation, the United States is placed in a position of crisis diametrically opposed to the Soviet Union, such that the momentous issues of the time involve "the fulfilment or destruction not only of this Republic but of civilization itself." The "fundamental purpose" of the United States as a nation, NSC-68 argued, is "to assure the integrity and vitality of our free society, which is founded upon the dignity and worth of the individual." "Three realities" flowed from this: "Our determination to maintain the essential elements of individual freedom ... our determination to create conditions under which our free and democratic system can live and prosper; and our determination to fight if necessary to defend our way of life." The character of the Soviet Union, however, meant conflict between the United States and the Soviet Union was unavoidable: "There is a basic conflict between the idea of freedom under a government of laws, and the idea of slavery under the grim oligarchy of the Kremlin ... The implacable purpose of the slave state to eliminate the challenge of freedom has placed the two great powers at opposite poles."[35]

But NSC-68 was not solely concerned with the Soviet threat. The document argued that "in a shrinking world, which now faces the threat of atomic warfare, it is not an adequate objective merely to seek to check Kremlin design, for the absence of order is becoming less and less tolerable." This concern to establish an ordered international environment in which the United States could survive in line with its fundamental purpose mandated two policies: "One is a policy which we would probably pursue even if there were no Soviet threat. It is a policy of attempting to develop a healthy international community. The other is the policy of 'containing' the Soviet system. These two policies are closely interrelated and interact with one another."[36] Binding these policies together was the issue of freedom: "The hopes of frustrating the Kremlin design are centered in the strategy of freedom ... This strategy calls for the creation and maintenance of strength at the center."[37] Strength was not attainable by strategic calculus alone, for "the potential within us of bearing witness to the values by which we live holds promise for a dynamic manifestation to the rest of the world of the vitality of our system."[38]

Nor was NSC-68's concern for anarchy and disorder as the greatest dangers novel in the texts of United States foreign policy. Indeed, the majority of internal and secret assessments of the early post–World War II environment emphasized that, although the threat to the United States and Western Europe was most easily represented by the activity of communist forces and the Soviet Union, the danger being faced was neither synonymous with nor caused by them. The first paper produced by the State Department's Policy Planning Staff (PPS) in 1947 declared:

> The Policy Planning Staff does not see communist activities as the root cause of the difficulties of western Europe. It believes the present crisis results in large part from the disruptive effect of the war on the economic, political, and social structure of Europe and from a profound exhaustion of physical plant and spiritual vigor. This situation has been aggravated and rendered far more difficult of rem-

edy by the division of the continent into east and west. The Planning Staff recognizes that the communists are exploiting the European crisis and that further communist successes would create serious danger to American security. It considers, however, that American efforts in aid to Europe should be directed not to the combatting of communism as such but to the restoration of the economic health and vigor of European society. It should aim, in other words, to combat not communism, but the economic maladjustment which makes European society vulnerable to exploitation by any and all totalitarian movements and which Russian communism is now exploiting.[39]

Moreover, the nature of the struggle was not simply geopolitical, but was often represented in cultural and ideological terms:

Further deterioration might be disastrous to Europe. It might well bring such hardship, such bewilderment, such desperate struggle for control over inadequate resources as to lead to widespread repudiation of the principles on which modern European civilization has been founded and for which, in the minds of many, two world wars have been fought. The principles of law, of justice, and of restraint in the exercise of political power, already widely impugned and attacked, might then be finally swept away—and with them the vital recognition that the integrity of society as a whole must rest on respect for the dignity of the individual citizen. The implications of such a loss would far surpass the common apprehensions over the possibilities of "communist control." There is involved in the continuation of the present conditions in Europe nothing less than the possibility of a renunciation by Europeans of the values of individual responsibility and political restraint which has become traditional to their continent. This would undo the work of centuries and would cause such damage as could only be overcome by the effort of further centuries . . . the United States, in common with most of the rest of the world, would suffer a cultural and spiritual loss incalculable in its long-term effects.[40]

Even when represented in geopolitical terms, the danger posed by the Soviet Union was not considered to be primarily—or even significantly—military. When George Kennan was asked in 1946 to interpret recent Soviet statements, he wrote what has come to be referred to as the "Long Telegram," a diplomatic communication that set forth the basis of the policy of containment, and which was as figurative as the later NSC-68 in its representation of the Soviet Union.[41] Ambiguous in its characterization of Soviet "pressure" and the required policy of "counterforce," Kennan's assessment provided the basis for a number of policy alternatives. Kennan was nonetheless convinced that "it is not Russian military power that is threatening us; it is Russian political power...If it is not entirely a military threat, I doubt that it can be effectively met entirely by military means."[42] Having served in diplomatic posts in the Soviet Union prior to the Second World War, Kennan discerned a broader threat. While posted in Latvia in 1931, he wrote that "the present system of Soviet Russia is unalterably opposed to our traditional system, that there can be no middle ground or compromise between the two."[43] Nevertheless, Kennan argued that the circumstances confronting the United States in the late 1940s meant that a balance of power had to be restored to replace that destroyed in the defeat of Germany and Japan. The policy of containment required, therefore, that certain areas of the world vital to the United States must maintain political regimes "at least favorable to the continued power and independence of our nation."[44]

Kennan's assessment was adopted as the basis for U.S. policy. Even when a document such as NSC-20/4 stated that "the gravest threat to the security of the United States...stems from the hostile designs and formidable power of the USSR, and from the nature of the Soviet system" and that "Soviet domination of the potential power of Eurasia, whether achieved by armed aggression or by political and subversive means, would be strategically and politically unacceptable to the United States,"[45] it was argued that the Soviet Union was not likely to resort to war with the United States to achieve its aims. Other branches of the national security bureaucracy concurred. The Joint Intelligence Staff predicted in 1945 that the Soviets would avoid conflict for five to ten years; the CIA argued in September 1947 that the Soviets would not seek to militarily conquer Western Europe, preferring instead "to gain hegemony by political and economic means";[46] and Kennan argued in 1950 that there was no indication that the Soviets intended to attack the West.[47] The U.S. embassy in Moscow continued to report, even throughout the Korean War, that the Soviets had no desire to engage in global conflict with the United States.[48]

United States defense officials, then, clearly did not think the prospect of a Soviet military attack likely. In this assessment, they accurately concluded that the postwar condition of the Soviet military was insufficient to materially threaten Western Europe. The Joint Chiefs of Staff considered that with primitive logistics (half of the Soviets' transport was horse-drawn until 1950; roads in Eastern Europe were in such bad condition that ten to fifteen miles per hour was often the maximum attainable speed; and the rail gauges of the Soviet Union and Eastern Europe differed in size, making long-distance transport difficult), the popularly feared "blitzkrieg" of the Red Army was improbable.[49] Yet national security managers remained concerned about the prospect of losing control of "Eurasia." The basis of this concern was the view—as the PPS studies cited above made clear—that the poor and deteriorating economic conditions in Europe opened the way for anarchy that could be exploited by the Soviets to spread their influence. As Kennan had argued to the State Department in 1946, "World communism is like a malignant parasite which feeds only on diseased tissue."[50] The CIA had concluded likewise in mid-1947: "The greatest danger to the security of the United States is the possibility of economic collapse in Western Europe and the consequent accession to power of Communist elements."[51] Such assessments were the impetus behind the Marshall Plan's economic reconstruction of Europe.

The fear of anarchy and the concern for order were not limited to areas beyond the borders of the United States. Kennan wrote in 1950 that communism "had to be viewed as a crisis of our own civilization, and the principal antidote lay in overcoming the weaknesses of our own institutions."[52] Moreover, the national security bureaucracy concerned itself with the level of internal vigilance it thought necessary to meet the political dangers of the period. NSC-17 posed the following question: "From what are we as a people making ourselves internally secure?" The response was: "From the very beginning of organized living, of society, there have existed negative elements which would tear down and destroy the established order by force or violence."[53] The most dangerous, contemporary "negative elements" were those associated with communism, the report argued, which through ideas spread its "poisonous germs in every phase of American life." As an "international conspiracy," communism was "directed generally against the inherent dignity, freedom, and sacredness of the individual; against all God-given rights and values; against the Judeo-Christian code of morals on which our western civilization rests; against our established norms of law and order; against all peaceful democratic institutions." In this quest, communist influence exceeded the official membership of the party because it could also rely on the "convinced communist" who hid membership, the "fellow traveller" who was not a member, the "sympathizer" who was not in total agreement but entertained "friendly feelings," and the "opportunist" who furthered his own interests through the party. Furthermore, the conspiracy could prey upon the "confused liberal" who believed cooperation was possible, and the "well-meaning, socially minded, charitable people" who were deceived by communist slogans or fronts.[54]

The blurring of the boundary between internal and external security concerns, and the overtly tropical representations of danger in the texts of postwar foreign policy neither peaked nor culminated in the late 1940s and early 1950s. If we trace the evolution of the Basic National Security Policy documents drafted and redrafted throughout the 1950s, we can witness the overt concern of foreign policy making's inner sanctum with these political formulations. In so doing, it is worth remembering that when dealing with NSC documents, we are not concerned with texts written for public consumption. Although many of these themes would later appear in the rhetoric of partisan speeches and statements, all the citations (here and above) are taken from documents repeatedly stamped "Top Secret" and originally intended only for the eyes of a select few. That such a restricted audience, one normally thought to be removed from the more colorful aspects of political life and endowed with the ability to see the world as it really "is," should be actively concerned with the figurative representation of its mission necessarily requires us to rethink the meaning of foreign policy making. We should no longer regard those who occupy the secretive domains of the national security state as being outside of the cultural parameters of the state in whose name they operate.

At the end of April 1953, the National Security Council Planning Board began consideration of a revised Basic National Security Policy document. Taking NSC 149/2 as its starting point, a number of alterations were proposed in the opening section, entitled "General Objectives," which set the basic purpose and theme of U.S. national security policy.[55] The Psychological Strategy Board proposed a complete rewrite—keeping only the first paragraph—which included some particularly strident declarations about the "life and death struggle thrust upon us by World Communism" and the need to rebuild the "spiritual" and other "sinews of victory."[56] The Office of Defense Mobilization supported the major changes contained in the Federal Civil Defense Administrator's proposal and added a couple of changes of its own, most notably the redraft of paragraph 2e to read "To build up a vigorous national morale, with appropriate attention to protection against poisoning of the springs of information, subversion, sabotage and espionage."[57] The Defense Department offered a number of suggestions, including the addition of the words "which recognize the essential dignity and worth of the individual" to the statement of American values in paragraph 1.[58] On June 10, 1953, the NSC approved the outcome of these deliberations in the form of NSC 153/1. Of the proposals quoted here, only the Defense Department's line (to which the words "in a free society" had been added) were included.[59] Only three months later, a new revision was begun (as a response to Stalin's death) in which the general objectives were once again redrafted. Finalized in NSC 162/2, they highlighted the Soviet threat to "the security, free institutions, and fundamental values of the United States."[60]

Thereafter, Basic National Security Policy was reviewed on an annual basis. NSC 5501 replaced NSC 162/2 in January 1955, though it kept most of its general objectives intact.[61] The following year the NSC Planning Board added a new preamble to the national security review. Although it did not alter the general objectives, NSC 5602/1 began with the following declaration:

> The spiritual, moral and material posture of the United States of America rests upon established principles which have been asserted and defended throughout the history of the Republic. The genius, strength and promise of America are founded in the dedication of its people and government to the dignity, equality and freedom of the human being under God. These concepts and our institutions which nourish and maintain them with justice are the bulwark of our free society, and are the basis of the respect and leadership which have been accorded our nation by the peoples of the world. When they are challenged, our response must be resolute and worthy of our heritage. From this premise must derive our national will and the policies which express it. The continuing full exercise of our individual and collective responsibilities is required to realize the basic objective of our national security policies: maintaining the security of the United States and the vitality of its fundamental values and institutions.[62]

This preamble was retained without alteration in NSC 5707/8 of 1957,[63] but was revised the following year, adding after the third sentence above a new paragraph: "Our constant aim at home is to preserve the liberties, expand the individual opportunities and enrich the lives of our people. Our goal abroad must be to strive unceasingly, in concert with other nations, for peace and security and to establish our nation firmly as the pioneer in breaking through to new levels of human achievement and well-being."[64] Maintained without revision in the 1959 policy review, expressions similar to this also found their way into the more detailed outline of basic policy that followed the preamble. NSC 5906/1 added to the list of U.S. policy objectives the following paragraph: "*h*. To preserve, for the people of the United States, the basic human concepts, values and institutions which have been nourished and defended throughout our history."[65] This objective thus stood alongside (for example) the need to avoid—or if necessary, prevail in—a general war, and to accelerate changes in "the Sino-Soviet regimes," as a "basic guide in the implementation of all other national security policies" approved by the president.

This constant and deliberate (re)writing of national purpose and the objectives of security policy by those in the often clandestine corridors of power has not been restricted to the period for which documents are available. Although most of the confidential and top secret documents in which these figurations are likely contained have yet to be declassified, many of the public declarations of purpose since the beginning of the 1960s have manifested similar themes. In a campaign speech, John F. Kennedy declared, "The enemy is the Communist system itself—implacable, unceasing in its drive for world domination. For this is not a struggle for the supremacy of arms alone—it is also a struggle for supremacy between two conflicting ideologies: Freedom under God versus ruthless, godless tyranny."[66] Secretary of State Dean Rusk maintained that:

> Our foreign policy derives from the kind of people we are and from the international environment in which we live. It is relatively simple, relatively long term, and nonpartisan...Our supreme aspiration is "to secure the Blessings of Liberty for ourselves and our Posterity." This means that the beginning of our foreign policy is the kind of society we build here at home. Our example casts its shadow around the globe. Our words about freedom and justice would ring hollow if we were not making it apparent that we are trying to make our own society a gleaming example of what free men can accomplish under the processes of consent.[67]

Reagan was equally emphatic about the meaning of America when he proclaimed in 1983 "the undeniable truth that America remains the greatest force for peace anywhere in the world today...the American dream lives—not only in the hearts and minds of our countrymen but in the hearts and minds of millions of the world's people... who look to us for leadership. As long as that dream lives, as long as we continue to defend it, America has a future, and all mankind has reason to hope."[68] But neither the passage of time nor the decline of the perceived Soviet threat has assuaged the desire to (re)produce in the texts of foreign policy declarations of the nation's meaning and purpose. For example, a 1990 public report from the State Department details at length how "America's soul is its myth" of moral righteousness and obligation, national mission, abundance, and international duty.[69]

Scripting the Self

The postwar texts of United States foreign policy certainly located the dangers they identified via references to the Soviet Union. But they always acknowledged that the absence of order, the potential for anarchy, and the fear of totalitarian forces or other negative elements that would exploit or foster such conditions — whether internal or external — was their initial concern. It was NSC-68, after all, which declared "even if there were no Soviet threat" the United States would still pursue a policy designed to cope with the "increasingly intolerable absence of order." In effect, then, a document as important as this recognized that the interpretation of the Soviet Union as the preeminent danger to the United States involved more than the absorption of sense-data by an independent and passive observer. To say as much is not to exculpate the Soviet Union from all responsibility or to argue that it was the repository of all that was sweetness and light: such a proposition would be preposterous. What this argument does suggest is that it is equally erroneous to relieve the practitioners of American statecraft from all responsibility for making the world in which they worked. Even within the mainstream literature of international relations, the interpretation of the specifics of the Soviet military threat has always been contestable.[70] And the foreign policy texts have demonstrated that even when the Soviet threat was assessed in geopolitical terms, it was often understood as a political rather than a primarily military danger. Indeed, despite considerable differences in the order of magnitude of each, over the years U.S. policy makers have cited a range of threats: world communism, the economic disintegration of Europe, Red China, North Vietnam, Cuba, Nicaragua, Libya, "terrorists," drug smugglers, and assorted "Third World" dictators. None of these sources posed a threat in terms of a traditional calculus of (military) power, and none of them could be reduced solely to the Soviet Union. All of them were (and are) understood in terms of their proclivity for anarchy and disorder.

Most important, just as the source of danger has never been fixed, neither has the identity that it was said to threaten. The contours of this identity have been the subject of constant (re)writing: not rewriting in the sense of changing the meaning, but rewriting in the sense of inscribing something so that that which is contingent and subject to flux is rendered more permanent. While one might have expected few if any references to national values or purposes in confidential documents prepared for the inner sanctum of national security policy (after all, don't they know who they are or what they represent?), the texts of foreign policy are replete with statements about the fulfillment of the republic, the fundamental purpose of the nation, God-given rights, moral codes, the principles of European civilization, the fear of cultural and spiritual loss, and the responsibilities and duties thrust upon the gleaming example of America. In this sense, the texts that guided national security policy did more than simply offer strategic analyses of the "reality" they confronted: they actively concerned themselves with the scripting of a particular American identity. Stamped "Top Secret" and read by only the select and powerful few, the texts effaced the boundary between inside and outside with their quasi-Puritan figurations.

In employing this mode of representation, the foreign policy texts of the postwar period recalled the seventeenth-century literary genre of the jeremiad, or political sermon, in which Puritan preachers combined searing critiques with appeals for spiritual renewal.[71] Later to establish the interpretive framework for national identity, these exhortations drew on a European tradition of preaching the omnipresence of sin so as to instill the desire for order, but they added a distinctively affirmative moment:

> The American Puritan jeremiad was the ritual of a culture on an errand — which is to say, a culture based on a faith in process. Substituting teleology for hierarchy, it discarded the Old World ideal of stasis for a New World vision of the future. Its function was to create a climate of anxiety that helped release the restless "progressivist" energies required for the success of the venture. The European jeremiad thrived on anxiety, of course. Like all "traditionalist" forms of ritual, it used fear and trembling to teach acceptance of fixed social norms. But the American jeremiad went much further. It made anxiety its end as well as its means. Crisis was the social norm it sought to inculcate. The very concept of errand, after all, implied a state of *un*fulfillment. The future, though divinely assured, was never quite there, and New England's Jeremiahs set out to provide the sense of insecurity that would ensure the outcome.[72]

Whereas the Puritan jeremiads were preached by religious figures in public, the national security planners entreated in private the urgency of the manifold dangers confronting the republic. But the refrains of their political sermons have occupied a prominent place in postwar political discourse. On two separate occasions (first in 1950, and then in 1976), private citizens with close ties to the foreign policy bureaucracy established a "Committee on the Present Danger" to alert a public they perceived as lacking resolve and will to the necessity of confronting the political and military threat of communism and the Soviet Union.[73] More recently, with Pentagon planners concerned about the "guerrillas, assassins, terrorists, and subversives" said to be "nibbling away" at the United States, proclamations that the fundamental values of the country are under threat have been no less insistent. As Oliver North announced to the U.S. Congress: "It is very important for the American people to know that this is a dangerous world; that we live at risk and that this nation is at risk in a dangerous world."[74] And in a State Department report, the 1990s were foreshadowed as an era in which divergent political critiques nonetheless would seek equally to overcome the "corruption" and "profligacy" induced by the "loss" of "American purpose" in Vietnam through "moral renewal."[75] To this end, the rendering of Operation Desert Shield-turned-Storm as an overwhelming exhibition of America's rediscovered mission stands as testament.[76]

The cold war, then, was both a struggle that exceeded the military threat of the Soviet Union, and a struggle into which any number of potential candidates, regardless of their strategic capacity, were slotted as a threat. In this sense, the collapse, overcoming, or surrender of one of the protagonists at this historical juncture does not mean "it" is over. The cold war's meaning will undoubtedly change, but if we recall that the phrase *cold war* was coined by a fourteenth-century Spanish writer to represent the persistent rivalry between Christians and Arabs, we come to recognize that the sort of struggle the phrase denotes is a struggle over identity: a struggle that is not context-specific and thus not rooted in the existence of a particular kind of Soviet Union.[77] Besides, the United States–led war against Iraq should caution us to the fact that the Western (and particularly American) interpretive dispositions that predominated in the post–World War II international environment—with their zero-sum analyses of international action, the sense of endangerment ascribed to all the activities of the other, the fear of internal challenge and subversion, the tendency to militarize all responses, and the willingness to draw the lines of superiority/inferiority between us and them—were not specific to one state or one ideology. As a consequence, we need to rethink the conventional understanding of foreign policy, and the historicity of the cold war in particular.

Two
Rethinking Foreign Policy

The Constitution of the Foreign

Many of the official proclamations that represent the United States focus on questions of identity. The Constitution encourages the people to form a "more perfect Union" and "insure domestic Tranquility," while the Pledge of Allegiance speaks of one nation "indivisible." At the same time, other proclamations speak of difference. The oath of allegiance—given to those being naturalized as citizens of the United States—declares the need to defend the Constitution and laws of the country against "all enemies, foreign and domestic." Who are these enemies, foreign and domestic, that citizens are to be distinguished from? Consider the following questions:

> Are you or have you at any time been an anarchist, or a member of or affiliated with a Communist or other totalitarian party?

> Have you advocated or taught, by personal utterance, by written or printed matter, or through affiliation with an organization (a) opposition to organized government; (b) the overthrow of government by force; (c) the assaulting or killing of government officials because of their official character; (d) the unlawful destruction of property; (e) sabotage; (f) the doctrines of world communism, or the establishment of a totalitarian dictatorship in the United States?

> Have you engaged in or do you intend to engage in prejudicial activities or unlawful activities of a subversive nature?

> Are you afflicted with psychopathic personality, sexual deviation, mental defect, narcotic drug addiction, chronic alcoholism, or any dangerous contagious disease?

> Are you a pauper, professional beggar, or vagrant?

> Are you a polygamist or do you advocate polygamy?

Have you committed or have you been convicted of a crime of moral turpitude?

To officially join the society of the United States, these are among the questions you will have to answer. For a citizen of a country other than the United States wishing to change status from that of "non-resident alien" to "permanent resident alien," document number I-130 of the Immigration and Naturalization Service specifies the undesirable qualities that mark those who will not be permitted to enter the indivisible union that seeks domestic tranquillity.[1]

The passage from difference to identity as marked by the rite of citizenship is concerned with the elimination of that which is alien, foreign, and perceived as a threat to a secure state. Accordingly, this passage shares a similar purpose with those undertakings we associate with conventional understandings of foreign policy. Moreover, the figurations of identity/difference that characterize this process remind us of the texts of foreign policy considered in chapter 1. But is there a connection between the daily activities of a domestic government agency that scrutinizes immigration applications for their evidence of naturalization, and those practices we traditionally associate with foreign policy? Is the foreignness of "aliens" qualitatively distinct from the character of the existing citizenry in whose name presidents, secretaries of states, and diplomats are represented to the world? Does the foreign-ness of the characteristics indicated by the Immigration and Naturalization Service's questions afflict only those from the external realm? Does the inside of a state exist in marked contrast to the outside? What is at stake in the attempt to screen the strange, the unfamiliar, and the threatening associated with the outside from the familiar and safe, which are linked to the inside?

These are not the orthodox questions posed by the discipline of international relations and those concerned with the traditional study of foreign policy. Contemporary scholarship has been for the most part content to see foreign policy explained as a state-centric phenomenon in which there is an internally mediated response to an externally induced situation of ideological, military, and economic threats. There are a number of ways in which this understanding can be subject to critical scrutiny. We can begin — as chapter 1 began — with a reflection on the recent transformations in the international order that have served to render the conventional wisdom of postwar international relations increasingly problematic, and argue that the current historical juncture provides us with an opportunity that is potentially far richer in its implications for foreign policy because it suggests the need to problematize established modes of understanding. Somewhat differently, we can begin with the etymology of the word *foreign*, noting that it was not until Bentham coined the phrase *international* in the late eighteenth century that *foreign* came to be firmly associated with the different character of other nations.[2] *Foreign* always signified something that was on the outside and therefore distinguished from the inside, but the parameters that constituted the demarcated space differed greatly from our contemporary understanding. In the first recorded use of *foreign* in the English language, the thirteenth-century term *chamber foreign* represented a private room in a house. From then until the seventeenth and eighteenth centuries, *foreign* served to indicate the distance, unfamiliarity, and alien character of those people and matters outside of one's immediate household, family, or region, but still inside the political community that would later comprise a state.

Either way, there is more to understanding the constitution and importance of what we consider to be "foreign" than is suggested by considering as "foreign" those characteristics found (and kept) outside the state. This chapter suggests that as "foreign" as these concerns to foreign policy seem, there is a connection—warranted by the texts of postwar American foreign policy—that prompts the development of an alternative theorization of foreign policy. This requires that we address a fundamental question: How was it that we (meaning those principally, though not exclusively, in the discipline of international relations) came to understand foreign policy as the external deployment of instrumental reason on behalf of an unproblematic internal identity situated in an anarchic realm of necessity?

More specifically, this question concerns the problematizations that make possible our conventional understanding of global politics as international relations and of foreign policy as the province of a state. Thus, if one were operating in terms of the "levels-of-analysis" metaphor found in traditional international relations literature, the argument here would need to be regarded at a level beyond that associated with either the state or the international system.[3] The argument here is concerned with the representation of history that allows us to talk in terms of "the state" and "the international system," and the impact that problematization has had on our understanding of foreign policy. In this context, the discussion of foreign policy is not about policy per se, although it has manifest political implications. Rather, it is about how the conventional understanding of foreign policy was made possible via a discursive economy that gave value to representational practices associated with a particular problematization. The first task is to examine the conventional understanding of foreign policy dominant within the discipline and the representation of history that makes it possible.

Foreign Policy: States, Boundaries, Practices

The subfield of international relations that serves as the main body of literature on foreign policy is that of "comparative foreign policy," a field indebted to the realist orthodoxy that underpins the discipline's view of the cold war.[4] A number of reviews have provided a clear insight into the entailments and assumptions of this dominant mode of understanding foreign policy. In the introduction to a collection that surveyed "new directions" in the study of foreign policy, James Rosenau noted with approval that the conspicuous absence of "philosophical and methodological argumentation" in the collected essays was an indication of the field's passage into a "more mature era of inquiry." In contrast to earlier periods, "the epistemological foundations and methodological premises on which the analysis rest[s] . . . are largely taken for granted."[5]

These assumptions give rise to a conventional and largely unquestioned substantive focus (for scholars rather than practitioners) in foreign policy analysis: the policies of states oriented toward the external world.[6] Rosenau has provided an illuminating metaphor to describe this focus. Foreign policy analysis, he argued, "is a bridging discipline. It takes as its focus of study the bridges that whole systems called states build to link themselves and their subsystems to the even more encompassing international systems of which they are a part."[7] In this understanding, global politics comprises states, their (domestic) subsystems, and international systems. These systems and subsystems exist independently of, and prior to, any relationship that results from their joining by the "bridge" of foreign policy. That bridge is consciously constructed by the state in an effort to make itself part of the larger system and to deal with the dangers and uncertainties that larger system holds for its own security. As a phenomenon thought to be common to all states, we speak about the foreign policy *of* state "x" or state "y," thereby indicating that the state is prior to the policy. Underpinned by a commitment to epistemic realism, this understanding depends on the "explicit and grounded . . . prior conceptualizations of variables and relationships."[8] These variables are the internal factors of the state and the external conditions of the international system. The relationships involve the structure of the internal factors (the processes of decision making within the state, in which psychological interpretations act as an additional "bridge" between individuals and institutions)[9] and the interaction of the internal factors and the external conditions.[10]

Within comparative foreign policy there is another dominant tendency. This tendency, while maintaining the need to stay with the external behavior of states as the organizing principle of analysis, recognizes the inherently political and boundless nature of the subject matter. Rosenau himself notes that "those who study foreign policy must concern themselves with politics at all levels ... It is in some profound sense a discipline with limitless boundaries: the discipline is imposed by the need to reorganize inquiry around the external behavior of nation-states ... but insofar as its independent variables are concerned, the scope of the field is boundless."[11] This recognition pays homage to the fact that the study of foreign policy is located on terrain that intersects with some of the most contentious and creative debates in international relations: the role and nature of the state, the division between politics and economics, the agent/structure conceptions of sociological theory, and the tension between domestic and international factors.[12] What this suggests is the existence of a potential but undeveloped open-endedness within the comparative foreign policy literature to formulate an alternative theorization of foreign policy in the terms of the ontological assumptions outlined above.[13] When we consider the constituted and permeable nature of the boundaries that have been central to the modern world, and the effort to impose an interpretive discipline on the ambiguity of the subject matter, we can foreground those practices that have helped constitute the conditions of possibility in which we are able to speak as we conventionally do of foreign policy in the modern era. If traditional interpretations of international political practice need to be historicized, it is equally the case that the bases of theoretical understanding need to be problematized.

Bringing the logic of interpretation outlined in the Introduction to the study of global politics involves approaching the international system as an arena of practice in which some subjects emerge with the status of actors, who are sustained by a variety of practices that establish the boundaries of legitimate meaning and naturalize a particular order. In the more familiar language of international relations, this approach asks how, in a world of ambiguity, contingency, and difference, the field of practice known as "the international system" is constructed in such a way that sovereign states are said to exist in an anarchic world, and how this particular construction is considered normal, natural, and necessary.[14] Bringing these interpretive concerns to the study of foreign policy, this approach asks how foreign policy comes to be understood as the bridge between sovereign states existing in an anarchic world, a bridge that is constructed between two prior, securely grounded, and nominally independent realms. And, finally, bringing these concerns to the study of United States foreign policy, this approach asks how United States foreign policy comes to be understood solely as the external orientation of a pregiven and settled national identity.[15]

In each of these sets of questions, the conventional formulation that is being questioned — that of sovereign states in an anarchic world, foreign policy as a bridge between them, and United States foreign policy as an externally oriented practice — is represented as sustained by a traditional historical narrative that depicts the rise of the state in western Europe in a particular way.[16] Put simply, this narrative understands the state to be constituted by a secularized eschatology in which one form of social organization and identity (the church) completely gives way to another (the state) at a readily identifiable juncture (the Peace of Westphalia). Any attempt to retheorize foreign policy thus requires that this narrative, which serves as the condition of possibility for the conventional understanding of foreign policy (and international relations in general), be challenged. Such a challenge, however, does not involve writing the "true" and "correct" historical narrative to replace that which is in error. Such a challenge, rather, seeks only to establish the space for a retheorization of foreign policy via the problematization of the traditional narrative on the rise of the state. What follows is thus not simply about (re)writing history; it is also about interpreting the effects of certain historical representations on our understanding of foreign policy.

The Rise of the State: Challenging the Traditional Narrative

The rise and fall of Christendom; the overcoming of the various and diverse articulations of political community throughout the medieval period; the formation of absolutist states; the increasing centralization and intensification of political control associated with modernity and the state: these are among the significant signposts in the traditional narrative about the rise of the state. They can also be located in discourses that challenge the traditional narrative, but what distinguishes the traditional narrative as it is deployed in international relations is the attribution of a teleology to history that suggests that the emergence of independent sovereign states was a natural outcome. As

Hinsley declares, "All evolution from primitive prestate methods has been inexorably towards the establishment and the consolidation of the state."[17] This inevitability is driven by the "desire" that is "ubiquitous among men" to extend power and control beyond "the capacity of lineage and tribal forms."[18] Equally, Herz argues that "there is hardly a historical process which has been better understood and more fully described than the rise of the modern, centralized territorial state out of the socio-economic and political conditions of the late Middle Ages."[19] Both Hinsley and Herz are too subtle to subscribe to a teleological understanding without caveats, however. Hinsley notes that the ubiquity of desire notwithstanding, "the transition to the acceptance of the state has historically been a long and reversible process,"[20] while Herz maintains that "the transition from medieval hierarchism to modern compartmentalized sovereignties was neither easy, nor straight, nor short."[21] Such qualifications fail to diminish the overall imputation of teleology in their arguments; although the historical progression they invoke is not strictly linear, its end in the accomplishment of the state is not doubted. Moreover, in their figuration of the rise of the state in terms of a transcendence of the tribe and other primitive formations, these accounts offer nothing less than an edifying tale of modernization in which we witness the overcoming of chaos and the establishment of order through the rise of sovereign states.

Above all else, it is the privileging of the Peace of Westphalia (1648) as the point at which traditional anarchy gave way to modern harmony that signifies the edifying and teleological nature of such narratives. For international relations, this rendering of the Westphalian moment constitutes the conditions of possibility for the discipline. It establishes the point of origin necessary to suggest that, in contrast to the religious and political structures of the preceding millennia, the history of modern Europe since the Peace of Westphalia has been a history of sovereign states acting in a multistate system.[22] In Herz's formulation, once the territoriality and impenetrability of the state "was achieved approximately at the time of, and partly through, the Peace of Westphalia," it meant that "the basic structure of the territorial state which was to last throughout the classical period of the modern state was established. Upon this foundation a new system of international relations could and did arise. Its characteristics are indicated by terms such as 'independence,' 'sovereignty,' 'nonintervention,' and 'international law.' "[23] And, we might add, "foreign policy."

It is this historical narrative of the rise of the state in western Europe that has been ahistorically deployed by a tradition of international relations scholarship (realism) to suggest the naturalness of its representation of international politics and to undergird a statist discourse of international relations. It is a deployment that has privileged structuralist orientations of realism at the expense of historicist interpretations, with the result that the complex forms of interaction associated with the development of the state in its multiple forms are subordinated to a point of identity that stands as the negation of difference.[24] Most important, this appropriation has been pivotal in making it possible to talk about foreign policy as the external orientation of a preestablished state.

The traditional narrative on the rise of the state in western Europe has been challenged by a number of contributions from historical sociology.[25] In contrast to the statist discourse of international relations, these alternative historical narratives offer a more nuanced account of the "state" which enables a retheorization of foreign policy. What distinguishes these alternative accounts from the traditional narrative is the proposition that there was neither a clean nor a clear break between the social formations of Christendom and subsequent sovereign communities. In contrast to the implicit or explicit invocation of a distinct moment of secularization in the traditional narratives, these alternative accounts serve both to blur the strict temporal divisions and to disrupt the sense of homogenous and settled identities in any understanding of the rise of the state.

In particular, by making a distinction between *extensive* power ("the ability to organize large numbers of people over far-flung territories in order to engage in minimally stable cooperation") and *intensive* power ("the ability to organize tightly and command a high level of mobilization or commitment from the participants, whether the area and numbers covered are great or small"),[26] Mann's alternative historical narrative makes it possible to draw a number of distinctions crucial to appreciating the dynamic nature of the "state." Specifically, this gives us a greater appreciation that the forms of state that existed at the time of the Peace of Westphalia varied across "Europe," from the despotically powerful French monarchy, through the infrastructurally more organized English constitutional monarchy (albeit consumed by civil war in this period), to the weak confederacy that was the mosaic of German petty states. Each of these forms has to be distinguished among themselves, from others existing earlier (such as the federated cities of the Hanseatic League or the maritime empire of Venice), and in contrast to the considerably more intensive form of the modern state. Moreover, the development of these diverse state forms was a multifaceted process that was neither linear nor progressive.

Modernity: God, the State, and Man

Contrary to the traditional historical narrative's supposition of a complete rupture between the social functions of the church in the Middle Ages and the political effects of the state in the modern era, the alternative historical narratives discussed above suggest that common across time and space was the role of the church and the forms of "state" in securing identity amid disorder. Moreover, it suggests that insofar as the emerging "state" forms came to predominate in mediating claims of identity, they were replicating that function performed earlier by the church. It is possible to emphasize this commonality between church and state — without ignoring the complexities of "state" forms — by bringing the problematic of identity embedded in the above narratives to the fore. In this context, if we understand modernity as a condition that stands in a relationship of relative autonomy to any specific temporal location — a position in contradistinction to the traditional narrative on the rise of the state in which modernity is an easily delineated era — it is possible to address the relationship between history, structure, and identity in a more complex way. In this context, what is important about modernity is that it is not a temporal era, but rather a series of dispositions and orientations: "Once consolidated it gives modern articulations to persistent questions of meaning, the relation of human life to nature, the relation of the present to the past and the future, the form of a well-grounded order, and the relation of life to death."[27] Accordingly, our concern is not with historical periodization, but with the logic of identity and the dispositions and orientations it encourages in diverse times and places. In other words, modernity can be considered as being bound up in a discourse of "men" as much as in a discourse of the "state."

To reiterate the major conclusion of the above discussion in these terms, the demise of Christendom in the sixteenth century produced a "deep breach" in the position of individual subjects when the "entire social order became unhinged."[28] Previously located in an established structure of responsibilities that situated them as believers in a church and vassals in an estate, the spiritual and secular developments of the period rendered both increasingly insecure as points of identity. In a situation of chaos, subjects looked to a new order (emerging "states"), just as they had looked to the church during the demise of the Roman Empire as a solution for a crisis of social identity. To be sure, this representation of Christendom's role in securing identity is overdrawn: the church was riven with disputes and was anything but a settled identity itself, the papacy lacked coercive means to enforce its governmental ambitions and existed in an uneasy relationship with the emperors it sanctioned, and its teachings incompletely penetrated into the domains of everyday life. Yet without overlooking or underplaying these tensions and limitations, it is fair to say that whatever unity there was in the Middle Ages was made possible by the church.[29] Moreover, for the argument being made here, the issue is one of highlighting the logic of identity within Christendom and its similarity with or divergence from the logic of identity in a system of states.

In this context, what Christendom had achieved in providing a resolution to the crisis of identity was the construction of a social order that put things in their "proper" places and legitimized the result. The preservation of order (such as it was) among the disparate political communities of the medieval period was made possible by Christendom's location of difference within a larger framework of order centered on God as the ultimate point of identity. The monotheism of Christianity encouraged loyalty to a universal authority that transcended particular social structures: the individual was in a relationship with the divine, a situation that encouraged a universalistic and radical element that led it into conflict with centralized empires. However, God as the spiritual point of identity transcendent over earthly matters was also in a mediated relationship with the temporal order through the church hierarchy. The extensive horizontal relations of power that distinguished Christendom—the bishoprics, monasteries, and estates—were organized in terms of vertical relations of power that hierarchically structured the church with the pope and his agents (bishops, abbots, and clerics) as further points of identity. As the only authoritative and extensive source of power in medieval "Europe," the church came to intensively structure secular life. Far from being a specialized *ecumene* that was not concerned with worldly power, the church was to have a lasting impact on the forms of social and political power that would eventually give rise to the state. Through the papacy and its subordinated officers, it was the custodian of civilization, a legitimizing force that provided sacral authority to secular rule, the arbiter of intercommunity disputes, the organizer of the defense of Christendom, and a source of pacification that made possible increasing economic relations within "Europe." Christendom's comprehensive nature was thus derived from its ability to link its normative regulation of horizontal space to its spiritual regulation of vertical space. This hierarchical intensity of social order and its spiritual underpinning were matched by the vertical structure of the authority relations that guaranteed this order and ensured continued acceptance of the legitimate boundaries of meaning and identity for "man."

When Christendom emerged as the resolution of the identity crisis in the Roman Empire, it was deeply embedded in the infrastructural relations of power of the empire; there was no discrete historical breach that gave rise to a completely original ordering of identity and difference. With the demise of Christendom, the rise of new forms of identity associated with the state equally need to be seen as embedded in the infrastructural relations of power of the order they were replacing. In the case of the church, this is not difficult to appreciate. Aside from its immediate secular involvement with emerging state forms through its extensive power relations throughout "Europe," the problematic of power associated with Christendom (horizontal extensiveness secured through vertical intensity) was the schema onto which the relations of power associated with the transformations of feudalism, absolutism, capitalism, and the state were mapped.[30] By the eighteenth century the state had come to occupy the position that the church had once held, though the content of that position was yet to fully develop.[31]

In the wake of Christendom and the advent of absolutism, the figure of identity was moving from the transcendent and universal plane of God and his agents to the territorial and temporal level of the monarch in the state. This shift can be represented by the Peace of Augsburg (1555), the Peace of Westphalia (1648), and the Peace of Utrecht (1713). This is not to suggest — as the traditional historical narrative and statist discourse of international relations does — that the signatories to these documents acted as representatives of organic, unitary, sovereign states. These resolutions to the religious and civil conflicts that were the source of upheaval in "Europe" did sublimate the religious identities of the signatories to the mutual integrity of the states they represented. But the settlements divided "Europe" into Catholic and Protestant spaces and subsequently spurred the interstate construction of the continent.[32] Although the "state" of the late seventeenth century was still a very different form of political community from that we have known by the same name throughout the twentieth century, these developments meant that "two possible competing terrains of social relationships, the local and the transnational, declined in significance; the state, religion, and the economy became more intertwined; and the social geography of the modern world emerged."[33]

The implications of this for the question of securing "state" identity can be illustrated by reference to a debate in German social theory.

In *The Legitimacy of the Modern Age,* Hans Blumenberg questioned the idea that the modern idea of progress was nothing more than the secularization of eschatology.[34] Blumenberg argued instead for appreciating the role of Christianity in bringing about the condition of modern "self-assertion" that characterized the increasing dominance of state forms in late medieval "Europe."[35] The modern age was to be seen as something that neither emerged completely from Christendom nor was historically novel. There was instead a continuity between the period of Christendom and the later period marked by the dominance of state forms. This continuity stemmed from the way problems were posed rather than from the particular solutions that were offered. The problem to which modern "self-assertion" — the rationalist tendencies of science, art, and individualism — was a response was that resolved by divine omnipotence: the securing of identity in a world of difference. While the form of the problem had not changed, the historical context in which it was offered had. After the demise of Christendom, the problem of securing identity was posed in terms of how to handle contingency and difference in a world without God.

To explain the relationship between disparate solutions to similar problems, Blumenberg employed the metaphor of a system of positions occupied and reoccupied in the service of securing the identity of "man." Under Christendom, divine providence was the teleology that determined the quality of the world for "man" and therefore the necessary mode of behavior required of "men." Faced with contingency and unable to find the solution in God, "man" reconstructs the world through "self-assertion": "Deprived of God's hiddenness of metaphysical guarantees for the world, man constructs for himself a counterworld of elementary rationality and manipulability."[36] This construction is not free of resistances, nor is it entirely volitional. The position that was occupied by the teleology of divine providence is reoccupied by the notion that the world has an endangering quality that prescribes man's basic mode of behavior. Specifically, this quality is marked by the metaphor of the "unfinished world" — a world that is ambiguous, uncertain, and dangerous — which is a condition of the possibility of human action: "The 'unfinished world' becomes the metaphor of a teleology that discovers reason as its own immanent rule that up until then had been projected onto nature."[37] The "unfinished world" provides the necessary teleology for human action because a complete world means that all the activities of "men" would be for nothing. If the world is unfinished, uncertain, and dangerous, then the vocation of "man" is to take part in its (hoped for but never realized) completion.

Blumenberg's arguments were also situated in contrast to some of Carl Schmitt's arguments about state sovereignty.[38] Schmitt maintained (in concert with the traditional historical narrative) that all the significant concepts of the modern doctrine of the state were secularized theological concepts: one simply replaced the other, untainted by any previous form. In contrast — although accepting that Christendom played a considerable role and agreeing with Schmitt that political and theological absolutism were mirror images — Blumenberg argued that the transfer of sovereignty from God to the state was not simply the result of secularization. He maintained that ending the religious and civil wars that necessitated the Peace of Westphalia was achieved "by means of the transfer of the category of the unconditional friend/enemy relation onto conflicts between the national states that were in the process of integrating themselves."[39] The *intrastate* sources of conflict between various religious factions were thus transposed into *interstate* conflicts between the emerging state forms, making the religious conflicts central to the actual process of state making then under way. This transfer of the conflict, however, was neither conscious nor direct: "The symmetry of the development of internal conflicts between absolute positions and the setting up of an absolute agent may be describable as an 'inducing process' but hardly as the transfer of specific attributes of one realm to the other."[40] In other words, the secular state did not adopt in a unilateral or uncoerced way the theological attributes of the warring factions of which it was composed. In the context of the fractionation of Christendom, there was an "inducing process" that produced a situation whereby the sovereign state in a dangerous world came to occupy the position previously held by the divine omnipotence of the church. Although the resolution was secular, the problem was spiritual.

Central also to this "inducing process" was the transition from feudal to capitalist economic relations. But the outcome of all this was only a territorially coordinating state that remained relatively weak in relation to its social base; it lacked any real organic, unitary, or intensive power structure until well into the nineteenth century. As an emerging substitute for divine providence, the state found itself only half able to occupy the position into which it had been induced. Its extensive and horizontal power relations were expanding but were not yet matched by an intensity on the vertical level that would have replicated the achievement of Christendom in securing identity against difference. Moreover, this was an achievement made all the more difficult by the culture of the Enlightenment.

Crudely summarized, the Enlightenment had been an attack on ecclesiastical authority through the instruments of reason and scientific rationality. Although the nineteenth-century Romantics contributed to the subsequent and popular characterization of this period as the victory of reason over faith, experience over intuition, science over religion, and modernity over tradition, the outcome was not quite so clear-cut. To be sure, the authority of the church had been fundamentally and successfully challenged, but this did not extinguish the role of faith, for it remained necessary to maintain the improved condition of contemporary existence.[41] The problem was that once the "death of God" had been proclaimed, the link between the world, "man," and certitude had been broken. Neither a divine teleology nor the application of reason and rationality alone could provide the grounds for the maintenance of identity in the state. An ambiguous situation arose in which there was (and is) a demand "for external guarantees inside a culture that has erased the ontological preconditions for them. Modernity is thus an epoch of secret insistence jeopardized by its own legacy of truthfulness and honesty: its bearers demand that every hidden faith be exposed, but faith is necessary to ground the superiority of modern life."[42]

In this context of incipient ambiguity brought on by an insistence that can no longer be grounded, securing identity in the form of the state requires an emphasis on the unfinished and endangered nature of the world. In other words, discourses of "danger" are central to the discourses of the "state" and the discourses of "man."[43] In place of the spiritual certitude that provided the vertical intensity to support the horizontal extensiveness of Christendom, the state requires discourses of "danger" to provide a new theology of truth about who and what "we" are by highlighting who or what "we" are not, and what "we" have to fear.

This is not to suggest that fear and danger are modern constructs that only emerged after the relative demise of Christendom. On the contrary, the church relied heavily on discourses of danger to establish its authority, discipline its followers, and ward off its enemies. Indeed, although this disposition was important to the power of the church throughout its history, for the three centuries between the Black Death of 1348 and the Peace of Westphalia in 1648, the agents of God propagated a woeful vision of life marked by a particular attitude toward death.[44]

Thinking that Western civilization was besieged by a horde of enemies (Turks, Jews, heretics, idolaters, and witches, to name but a few), the church saw the devil everywhere and encouraged introspection and guilt to such an extent that a culture of anxiety predominated. The literary tradition of *contemptus mundi* ("contempt for the world"), which was pivotal to the culture of anxiety and the acute sense of endangeredness it encouraged, bespoke hatred for the body and the world, the pervasiveness of sin, the fleeting nature of time, and the fragility of life. Moreover, it was this "evangelism of fear"[45] that produced a preoccupation with death. As the promise of an escape from earthly vices, the religious leitmotif of "salvation" obliged all those who sought this transcendence "to think continually about death in order to avoid sin, because sin plus death could land them in Hell."[46] Meditation on death was thus the principal form of a moral pedagogy that sought to ensure salvation.

In fostering an evangelism of fear, with death as its impetus and salvation as its goal, the cultural agents of the period were not simply responding to danger as an external condition. The required familiarity with death demanded of individuals an eternal vigilance against the self: "One should always keep death in mind, just as one would always mount guard against an enemy who might suddenly appear" (indeed, for essayists like Montaigne, *death* was a synonym for *enemy*).[47] But it was this vigilance against the self, encouraged by the experience of finitude and required in the name of salvation, that constituted the conditions of *contemptus mundi* from which one sought salvation. In the *Specalum peccatoris* ("Sinner's Mirror")—a manuscript attributed to Saint Augustine—the author declares, "Consideration of the brevity of life engenders contempt for the world," and continues: "Is there anything that can increase man's vigilance, his flight from injustice, and his saintly behavior in the fear of God more than the realization of his [future] alteration, the precise knowledge of his mortal condition and the consequent thought of his horrible death, when man becomes nonman?"[48] The logic of the evangelism of fear thus ferments the very conditions that it claims necessitate vigilance against the enemies of the self; put simply, it produces its own danger. The evangelism of fear and its logic of identity are not just of the past, however. In our own time, argues Delumeau, we can witness their operation:

> Does not our own epoch help us to understand the beginnings of European modernity? The mass killings of the twentieth century

from 1914 to the genocide of Cambodia—passing through various holocausts and the deluge of bombs on Vietnam—the menace of nuclear war, the ever-increasing use of torture, the multiplication of Gulags, the resurgence of insecurity, the rapid and often more and more troubling progress of technology, the dangers entailed by an overly intensive exploitation of natural resources, various genetic manipulations, and the uncontrolled explosion of information: Here are so many factors that, gathered together, create a climate of anxiety in our civilization which, in certain respects, is comparable to that of our ancestors between the time of the plague and the end of the Wars of Religion. We have reentered this "country of fear" and, following a classic process of "projection," we never weary of evoking it in both words and images...Yesterday, as today, fear of violence is objectified in images of violence and fear of death in macabre visions.[49]

To talk of the endangered nature of the modern world and the enemies and threats that abound in it is thus not to offer a simple ethnographic description of our condition; it is to invoke a discourse of danger through which the incipient ambiguity of our world can be grounded in accordance with the insistences of identity. Danger (death, in its ultimate form) might therefore be thought of as the new god for the modern world of states, not because it is peculiar to our time, but because it replicates the logic of Christendom's evangelism of fear.

Indeed, in a world in which state identity is secured through discourses of danger, some low tactics are employed to serve these high ideals. These tactics are not inherent to the logic of identity, which only requires the definition of difference. But securing an ordered self and an ordered world—particularly when the field upon which this process operates is as extensive as a state—involves defining elements that stand in the way of order as forms of "otherness."[50] Such obstructions to order "become dirt, matter out of place, irrationality, abnormality, waste, sickness, perversity, incapacity, disorder, madness, unfreedom. They become material in need of rationalization, normalization, moralization, correction, punishment, discipline, disposal, realization, etc."[51] In this way, the state project of security replicates the church project of salvation. The state grounds its legitimacy by offering the promise of security to its citizens who, it says, would otherwise face manifold dangers. The church justifies its role by guaranteeing salvation to its followers who, it says, would otherwise be destined to an unredeemed death. Both the state and the church require considerable effort to maintain order within and around themselves, and thereby engage in an evangelism of fear to ward off internal and external threats, succumbing in the process to the temptation to treat difference as otherness.

In contrast to the statist discourse of international relations, this understanding proffers an entirely different orientation to the question of foreign policy. In addition to the historical discussion above, which suggested that it was possible to argue that the state was *not* prior to the interstate system, this interpretation means that instead of regarding foreign policy as the external view and rationalist orientation of a preestablished state, the identity of which is secure before it enters into relations with others, we can consider foreign policy as an integral part of the discourses of danger that serve to discipline the state. The state, and the identity of "man" located in the state, can therefore be regarded as the effects of discourses of danger that more often than not employ strategies of otherness. Foreign policy thus needs to be understood as giving rise to a boundary rather than acting as a bridge.

But this argument is itself so "foreign" to the conventional understanding of international relations that it needs to be further substantiated. This is to be done by reference to one of the classic theorists of international relations whose work is taken to support the conventional view of international relations and foreign policy being retheorized here. In chapter 3 we consider Thomas Hobbes's *Leviathan* in terms of modernity's entailments to demonstrate, first, that Hobbes's text can be read as supporting the argument being made here, and second, that the traditional reading of Hobbes is what helps gives rise to the conventional understanding of foreign policy.

Three
Foreign Policy and Identity

Hobbesian Strategies

Within the discipline of international relations there is a widely recognized if imperfectly understood "Hobbesian tradition"; a tradition in which Hobbes is regarded as having providing the pivotal images of anarchy, conflict, the state of nature, and war that are taken to be the conditions of possibility for international relations and our conventional understandings of foreign policy.[1] Regardless of the nuanced understanding of Hobbes's contributions that some within the discipline have exhibited, the more frequent casual references to this tradition use the name of Hobbes to evoke a "commonsense" understanding the entailments of which are more extensive than indicated by the simple reference that is offered. Robert Gilpin provides a particularly clear example when he remarks in his discussion of the fundamental assumptions of realism that "as Thomas Hobbes told his patron, the Second Earl of Devonshire, 'it's a jungle out there.' Anarchy is the rule; order, justice, and morality are the exceptions."[2]

The basic features of this "Hobbesian tradition" are said to proceed from an "individualist anthropology"[3] to the construction of a political theory in which the security of individuals and their ability to engage in commodious living is threatened by their existence in a state of nature, but achieved by their mutual surrender of sovereignty to a common power. The implications for international relations are taken to evolve from the transference of Hobbes's understanding of individuals within the state to the realm of relations between states. This logic is succinctly presented by Hedley Bull. Bull is far from being the only person to argue for the significance of Hobbes's work for international relations,[4] but his reasoning is particularly clear on how this comes to undergird subsequent realist understandings of international relations and foreign policy, thereby making his position worthy of examination.

Bull argues that although international relations was a subject of peripheral concern for Hobbes (a mere cupboard in the vast mansion of his philosophy), his account of conflict within states is integrally linked to relations between them. The commonwealth formed to bring an end to the rancorous religious and civil conflicts that were Hobbes's primary concern serves also as the source of protection from foreign invasion.[5] Hobbes's understanding of international relations, argues Bull (a "rigorously systematic" understanding that makes him a figure of "towering importance" who provides "the principal impetus" for realism), comes when Hobbes "makes his celebrated appeal to the facts of international relations":[6]

> But though there had never been any time, wherein particular men were in a condition of warre against one another; yet in all times, Kings, and Persons of Soveraigne authority, because of their Independency, are in continuall jealousies, and in the state and posture of Gladiators; having their weapons pointing, and their eyes fixed on one another; that is, their Forts, Garrisons, and Guns upon the Frontiers of their Kingdomes; and continuall Spyes upon their neighbours; which is a posture of War.[7]

Bull concludes that "from this and comparable passages in *The Elements of Law* and *De Cive* we are entitled to infer that all of what Hobbes says about the life of individual men in the state of nature may be read as a description of the condition of states in relation to one another."[8] A number of logical objections can be raised against the complete transference of the state of war from the realm of individuals to the realm of states, objections that Bull sometimes notes. In the first place, this transference fails to give the significance deserved to the first sentence of the famous passage that Bull quotes from Hobbes. This declares that there never was a time in which the state of war was the general condition among all individuals. Hobbes states in chapter 13 that "the savage people in many places of America" live in such a condition, as do subjects in a civil war, but that he "believe[s] it never was so, all over the world."[9] Second, the quotation from Hobbes that is so often cited usually (as above) omits an important sentence that follows immediately from the declaration of states existing in the condition of war. Hobbes continues: "But because they uphold thereby, the Industry of their Subjects; there does not follow from it, that misery, which accompanies the Liberty of particular men."[10] The state of nature among states is, according to Hobbes, qualitatively different from that among men; because states are the guarantors of their subjects' rights and property they recognize each other as free *personae morales*. Bull and others recognize this qualification, though as Smith has noted, later realists were less aware of the distinction that Hobbes made between the two realms.[11] Moreover, unlike individuals who are autonomous and equal—and thus in a condition of perpetual insecurity because they are situated in an environment of scarcity—states exist in different structural relations whereby they are both more unequal and less vulnerable.[12]

In this context, the war of all against all in international relations did not produce the misery of civil war but was "pared down to a purely interstate relationship . . . war became a means of princely politics, guided by *raison d'etat* and reduced to the common formula of a European balance of power."[13] This interstate relationship resembles more a conception of international society and less an understanding of pervasive conflict. That the end result of Hobbes's schema should be the existence of sovereign states in a network of relationships that was considerably less destructive and violent than the original state of nature is hardly surprising given that these states were supposed to be the site in which civil and international war was mediated: "Logically it was impossible for them to be in the same position as that which they transformed."[14]

These critiques raise serious and fundamental objections to the use of Hobbes's state of war to undergird a crude realist understanding of international relations (an understanding that makes possible the conventional representation of foreign policy) as the perpetual struggle for power among states in a pervasive condition of anarchy. However, all these critiques proceed from one important starting point. These critiques all treat Hobbes's text as a transparent rendering of the social and political reality of the time. Implicitly or explicitly, they support the contention that *Leviathan* stands as a factual, historical narrative intended to educate his and subsequent generations about the perils of their ways. We can object to this understanding by maintaining that Hobbes was not a historian, that he was "not a collector or reporter of past and present facts."[15] This is not an objection based on the arbitrary disciplinary grounds that divide up intellectual activities. It is an objection based on the proposition that in seeking to overcome civil war, Hobbes self-referentially took the condition of civil war as evidence for his proposition that peace could only be restored by a return to the status quo ante. In other words, Hobbes's conclusion of a powerful state is implied in the premise of civil war; individuals are always described as "subjects," that is, as people subordinated to a higher sovereign authority.[16]

Moreover, in the famous chapter 13 discussion of the state of nature where Hobbes denies its universal applicability, he declares that where "there were no common Power to feare" —a condition *"which men that have formerly lived under a peacefull government"*[17] have known— there would be civil war. But the absence of a common power to fear is not a feature that characterizes contemporary society, for men have formerly lived under peaceful government. Clearly, then, it is the fear of slipping *back into* the state of nature should men give up their allegiance to the sovereign power in the state, rather than an argument that men should proceed *from* the state of nature *to* the state, that is the force behind Hobbes's reasoning. Hobbes needs to establish this dire prospect as the grounds from which his radical prescriptions can be judged as worthy of pursuit.[18] In this context, *Leviathan* comes to be seen as a text implicated in, and fundamental to the form of, modernity's discourses concerning the "state" and "man." An explication of this theme will demonstrate its significance for the conventional understandings of international relations and foreign policy. But it is worth noting that this reading will emphasize—indeed, probably overemphasize—the role fear and danger play in Hobbes's rendering of identity and order. This reading is not designed to foreclose the possibility of an alternative interpretation.[19] Instead, its concern with the constitutive nature of fear and danger is intended to problematize international relations' realist rendering of fear and danger as either natural conditions or instrumentalities deployed by settled identities.

Hobbes begins *Leviathan* with a statement significant for the subsequent way in which his political theory is framed. It is a statement that indicates that his political theory is directed toward the discourse of "man" through the discourse of the "state":

> Nature (the Art whereby God hath made and governs the world) is by the *Art* of man, as in many other things, so in this also imitated, that can make an Artificial Animal... *Art* goes yet further, imitating that Rationall and most excellent worke of Nature, Man. For by Art is created that great LEVIATHAN called a COMMON-WEALTH, (in latine CIVITAS) which is but an artificial man.[20]

"Man" imitates nature through art to construct an artificial "man" in the form of the state, and the state is a form of rational "man." The state is not the author of "man" and "man" is not the author of the state. Neither agency nor structure are prior or determinant. "Man" and the state are simultaneously constituted; each is constitutive of the other and cannot be without the other. "In other words, the primary question is not one of analogies or parallels but one of the simultaneous emergence of 'inner' and 'outer,' or 'us' and 'them' in the development of Hobbes's concept of the state."[21]

Hobbes's intention is to theorize an end to religious and civil conflict by arguing for a renewed commitment to the transfer of sovereignty, which first enabled the emerging state forms of seventeenth-century "Europe." This argument takes place in the period of Christendom's declining authority, but it does not presuppose a complete secularization of social and political life. On the contrary, the state at the center of Hobbes's theory is a temporal body that takes the place of God. Once subjects "conferre all their power and strength upon one Man or Assembly of men," they are united in a commonwealth. The result "is the generation of that great LEVIATHAN, or rather (to speak more reverently) of that *Mortall God, to which wee owe under the Immortall God, our peace and defence.*"[22] In occupying the place of God, the state has a need for some mechanism (or art) to occupy the place of the "Feare of things invisible" that was the product of ignorance, the seed of religion, and the genesis of the civil conflicts.[23] That mechanism or art is the sanction that exists in a new fear: the fear of anarchy, danger, and the subsequent return to the state of nature that would be possible were fear not to be permanently located in a common power of which all are in awe. The victory of reason over rhetoric and of knowledge over superstition that is marked by submission to a common power is a major achievement, but it is not something that is self-sustaining. The battle is constantly being fought and victory has to be constantly sought. A mechanism that can perpetuate this continual struggle is necessary because "even if the struggle between enlightenment and superstition were won by the forces of reason, their victory would never be so secure that their enemies could be forgotten."[24] As a consequence, the state of nature is a sanction, a threat, a discourse of danger, and not a description of an unproblematic reality:

> The state of nature is shock therapy. It helps subjects to get their priorities straight by teaching them what life would be like without sovereignty. It domesticates by eliciting the vicarious fear of violent death in those who have not had to confront it directly. And when one confronts the fear of early and violent death, one becomes willing to regulate oneself and to accept external regulations that will secure life against its dangers. The fear of death pulls the self together.

It induces subjects to accept civil society and it becomes an instrumentality of sovereign control in a civil society already installed.[25]

Ironically, then, the overcoming of fear requires the institutionalization of fear. But fear and danger are put into place by reason rather than (as previously) by superstition. Reason understands that because there is "a general inclination of mankind, a perpetuall and restelesse desire of Power after power, that ceaseth only in Death," the desire for peace, unity, and a contented life dispose "man" to obey a common power.[26] In obeying this common power "man" is doing more than subjecting himself to authority; he is forming himself to be a member of the order that ensures arts, letters, and society and saves him from the life that is "solitary, poore, nasty, brutish, and short."[27] Such is the fifth law of nature, "compleasance":

> that is to say, *That every man strive to accommodate himselfe to the rest.* For the understanding whereof, we may consider, that there is in mens aptnesse to Society; a Diversity of Nature, rising from their diversity of Affections; not unlike to what we see in stones brought together for building an Aedifice. For as that stone which by the asperity, and irregularity of Figure, takes more room from others, that it selfe fills; and for the hardnesse, cannot be easily made plain, and thereby hindereth the building, is by the builders cast away as unprofitable, and troublesome: so also, a man that by asperity of Nature, will strive to retain those things which to himselfe are superfluous, and to others necessary; and for the stubbornness of his Passions, cannot be corrected, is to be left, or cast out of Society, as combersome thereunto . . . The observers of this Law, may be called SOCIABLE . . . The contrary, Stubborn, Insociable, Froward, Intractable.[28]

In this metaphor of the stones brought together by builders to construct an edifice lies the central textual strategy of Hobbes's political theory: a strategy of otherness designed to discipline the self. Because the "unformed matter of the World, was a God, by the name of *Chaos*,"[29] order requires discipline. And because there is a propensity to diversity in "man" and society that can readily undermine order unless corrected, "man" must remove his "irregularity of Figure" and accommodate himself to the rest. If he does not undertake this self-discipline, he will be cast out of society and signified as troublesome, cumbersome, stubborn, unsociable, and intractable.

To be cast out is not to be physically removed but to be politically marginalized. Hobbes's text is replete with examples of others from whom the self of rational, disciplined "man" must be distinguished. Most obviously, the reference to "savage people" in chapter 13 is in contrast to the unnamed but ever present "civilized people," who have lived (and hopefully continue to want to live) under peaceful government in an ordered society. The implication is that unless the power of the sovereign is reinscribed, "we" run the danger of becoming like "them." Hobbes does make this move explicit in other texts. In a short essay written at the same time as *Leviathan* he distinguishes "the civility of *Europe,* from the Barbarity of the *American* sauvages."[30] In the *Elements of Law* he asked the rhetorical question: without the developments of arts and sciences, "what do we differ from the wildest of the Indians?"[31]

In a similar vein, there are numerous references to the contrasts between those who are good and evil, mad and sane, drunk and sober, and modest and arrogant.[32] In later sections of *Leviathan* metaphors of disease and illness are employed to understand disorder within the society: commonwealths are dissolved not by external violence but by "intestine disorder"; large numbers of men rebel, just as children's bodies break out into "biles and scabbs" when they are not purged of illness; the struggle between temporal and spiritual powers in society is akin to "epilepsie" in the body; a mixed government is equated with "a man, that had another man growing out of his side, with a head, armes, breast, and stomach, of his own"; the immoderate greatness of a town or corporation in the commonwealth, and those who dispute the sovereign power, are like "wormes in the entrayles of a naturall man."[33]

Hobbes argues that the "antidote of solid Reason" is all that is required to overcome these maladies.[34] Hobbes's continual invocation of reason and rationality indicates the importance of the strategy of otherness to his enterprise. The strategy of otherness is not just an occasional rhetorical device employed by Hobbes to make a point with clarity; it is at the very heart of his political theory. Reason and rationalism are not simply modes of thought that are desirable; they are dispositions that are produced through differentiation from their opposites. The narrative of *Leviathan* is, therefore, not just an instance of scientifically rigorous argument that derives its form from an admiration for Euclidean geometry. The narrative of *Leviathan* is a polemic *for* science and the rationalism of the Enlightenment. It is actively engaged in molding a consensus around one orientation to life at the expense of another. In this context, the opposition of reason and rhetoric that Hobbes employed in the *Elements of Law* is replaced in *Leviathan* by the contrast between knowledge, reason, and science on the one hand, and ignorance, superstition, and magic on the other. The forces of light and the forces of darkness are engaged in the struggle between enlightenment and superstition.[35]

The strategies of otherness are pivotal to *Leviathan* and, as a consequence, integrally related to Hobbes's understanding of international relations. Hobbes's strategies of otherness are directed at the treasonous subjects who wish to subvert the state, but they give rise to the problematic through which it is possible to impose discipline on a wider domain and to constitute the ambiguity and upheaval of seventeenth-century "European" politics as an ordered multistate system in a chaotic world. The metaphor employed by Hobbes in his discussion of the fifth law of nature indicates how this is achieved. In constructing the edifice that is the ordered polity (the state), "man" forms and disciplines himself so that he can take up his rightful place in the walls. These walls are the fundamental structures in the building, but they do more than simply constitute the form of order that arises. The walls, or boundaries, that are constructed serve to separate the inside from the outside. But the boundary both separates and joins, thus making it impossible to conceive of a space that could be traversed by a bridge between independently existing realms. The spaces of inside and outside serve to delineate the rational, ordered polity in which good, sane, sober, modest, and civilized "man" resides from the dangerous, chaotic, and anarchical realm in which the evil, mad, drunk, arrogant, and savage people are found. The division between inside and outside, and the normative distinctions between the two realms, means that these strategies constitute a world in which sovereign states exist in a condition of anarchy and war.

The work of this problematic is not the result of a thought experiment. This coeval emergence of the inside and the outside is made possible by the transference of "the right of war from *within* the group and the restriction of the right of war to relations *between* groups."[36] The consequence of this is that "man," the "state," and "international relations" are mutually constitutive. No one authors the other. Multiple strategies of otherness give rise to identities that only exist in historically specific and spatially defined locations. Moreover, these strategies of otherness made foreign policy possible: "Nothing but [Hobbes's] strict separation of exterior and interior realms could make it possible to core an area of foreign policy out of the welter of religious jurisdictions."[37] Hobbes's text can be read, therefore, as indicating that comparative foreign policy's understanding of its own domain of study is seriously impoverished. Foreign policy was not something subsequent to the state or the interstate system, but integral to their constitution. Foreign policy was not a bridge between two distinct realms, but something that both divided and joined the inside and the outside, the state and the interstate system.

Foreign Policy: War, the State, and Man

To this point, the argument has sought to demonstrate: (1) how the conventional understanding of foreign policy depended on a particular representation of history in which the rise of the state is understood as the result of one form of social organization and identity (the church) completely giving way to another (the state) at a readily identifiable juncture (the Peace of Westphalia); (2) how an alternative historical representation makes it possible to understand the state as emerging through an "inducing process" in which it comes to offer a novel solution to a traditional problem, and thereby effects a historically specific resolution to the more general problematic of the constitution of identity through the negation of difference; and (3) how the project of securing the grounds for identity in the state involved an "evangelism of fear" that emphasized the unfinished and endangered nature of the world. In this sense, the discourses of danger that were pivotal to the church—where the fear of death disciplined lives via the promise of salvation—were rearticulated by (as Hobbes put it) the mortal god of the state, such that anarchy, danger, and a fear of slipping back into the state of nature effected political order through the promise of security. As a consequence, instead of seeing the state as made possible by a secularized eschatology, we can conclude that the state "is a ministry for collective salvation through a generalized politics of resentment."[38]

Put simply, the principal purpose of this historical and theoretical exegesis has been to show that it is an impoverished understanding to regard foreign policy as a bridge between preexisting states with secure identities. Given the alternative standpoints from which one can appreciate the coeval emergence of the "state" and the "international" system, it is not possible to simply understand international relations as the existence of atomized states that are fully fledged intensive entities in which identity is securely grounded prior to foreign relations. The consequence of this argument is a fundamental reorientation of our understanding of foreign policy. Foreign policy shifts *from* a concern of relations *between* states that take place *across* ahistorical, frozen, and pregiven boundaries, *to* a concern with *the establishment of the boundaries* that constitute, at one and the same time, the "state" and "the international system." Conceptualized in this way, foreign policy comes to be seen as a political practice that makes "foreign" certain events and actors.[39] Those events and actors that come to be "foreign" through the imposition of a certain interpretation are not considered as "foreign" simply because they are situated in opposition to a pregiven social entity (the state). The construction of the "foreign" is made possible by practices that also constitute the "domestic." In other words, foreign policy is "a specific sort of *boundary-producing political performance.*"[40] This conception thus differs greatly from arguments that maintain either that domestic influences are important in the construction of foreign policy, or that international influences play a role in structuring domestic politics.[41] Both these perspectives rely on granting the domestic and the international realms existence prior to history and politics. In each case, the "domestic" and the "international" are regarded as independently existing sovereign presences that exert influence over each other.

Premised on the ontological assumptions of ambiguity, interpretation, representation, and discipline, this retheorization of foreign policy understands foreign policy to be one of a range of practices that make up the discourses of danger that serve as "an art of domesticating the meaning of man by constructing his problems, his dangers, his fears."[42] Foreign policy is one part of a multifaceted process of inscription that disciplines by framing man in the spatial and temporal organization of the inside and outside, self and other: i.e., in the "state." These practices do not operate in terms of a domestic society that is pregiven, nor do they signify an absolute and preexisting space from which the threats to domestic society emerge. Their very operation frames the domestic society in whose name they claim to be operating through their claim to know the source of threats to domestic society and "man." In this sense, we can understand "international politics" as "a practice of the inscription of the dangerous, the externalization and totalization of dangers, and the mobilization of populations to control these dangers—all in the name of a social totality that is never really present, that always contains traces of the outside within, and that is never more than an effect of the practices by which total dangers are inscribed."[43] Importantly, "man," understood as the identity of the social totality that is effected, is intrinsically gendered.[44]

The practices that impose boundaries and establish meaning through a reading of ambiguity—practices that can be said to operate in nonpurposive ways approximated by Bourdieu's understanding of the "conductorless orchestration of collective action and improvisations" and Foucault's "strategies without a knowing strategist"[45]—usually locate the dangers to "man" in terms of threats emerging from other domestic societies. The dilemmas of international politics (e.g., nuclear war, interstate conflict, environmental degradation, or the relative autonomy of global capital) are conventionally understood as being composed of threats to a pregiven, already constituted and well-bounded identity in the form of the state. Clearly, such issues are vitally important, but an understanding of them does not depend solely on their interpretation as threats or their identification in the external, anarchic realm. Given all the possible locations of threats in an unfinished and endangered world, locating them in the external realm has to be understood as serving a particular interpretative and political function.

The principal impetus behind the location of threats in the external realm comes from the fact that the sovereign domain, for all its identification as a well-ordered and rational entity, is as much a site of ambiguity and indeterminacy as the anarchic realm it is distinguished from. When we speak of "man" we refer to more than just individuals or national types; the meaning of "man" incorporates the form of the "domestic" order, the social relations of production, the various subjectivities to which they give rise, the groups (such as women) who are marginalized in the process, and the boundaries of legitimate social and political action. It is easier to recognize the constructed character of "man" in societies other than our own (consider the attention given to "socialist man")[46] than to acknowledge the centrality of this practice to the "West."[47] But there are, in principle at least, a multitude of ways in which society can be constituted: the possibilities are limited only by the practices that focus on certain dangers, in a manner like the concerns exhibited by the U.S. Immigration and Naturalization Service questionnaire. But such dangers are not objective conditions and they do not simply reside (as represented) in the external realm. Threats to identity are equally prevalent in the challenges to the dominant enframing of "man" from within. For some, feminism, homosexuality, and support for social ownership of the relations of production are as threatening as a foreign enemy. Inscribing domestic society, arriving at a representation of the state involves, therefore, a double exclusion. The interpretations of domestic society resistant to its inscription must be excluded from the internal realm: "In effect, differences, discontinuities, and conflicts that might be found *within* all places and times must be converted into an absolute difference *between* a domain of domestic society, understood as an identity, and a domain of anarchy, understood as at once ambiguous, indeterminate, and dangerous."[48] This first exclusion is matched by a second, the purpose of which is to "hide" the status of the first as an exclusion. For the inscription of domestic society to appear as unproblematic, it is not possible for it to be understood as having the status of one interpretation among many. All interpretations that seek to expose the inscription of "man" as a representation that should be historicized and problematized have to be excluded themselves.

Reconceptualizing foreign policy in these terms also affects the understanding of what is effective foreign policy. In this context, "successful" instances of foreign policy can be understood as instances where the double exclusionary practice operates continuously in the face of resistant interpretations about "man." For example, Australian society was originally enframed as Anglo-Saxon through the transposition of a perceived threat to cultural integrity and economic well-being from Chinese gold diggers in the 1850s into a fear of Chinese invasion in the 1890s. This served to ward off an emerging nationalist drive for an independent republic by maintaining that Australia's defense could not be secured outside the British empire. The differences within became the differences between in such a way that the resulting domestic order was seen as natural and alternatives were marginalized. This disposition—in which internal threats made possible external dangers and external dangers controlled internal threats—came to provide the interpretive matrix through which all subsequent instances of Australian foreign policy were understood.[49] "Unsuccessful" instances of foreign policy are those where the double exclusionary practice does not operate, thereby allowing the recognition that the boundaries of domestic society can be disputed, so that the grounds of state legitimation become the site of political contestation about interpretations of "man."[50] In such cases, the inscription of danger is not able to transfer the differences within to the differences between, leaving political struggles to focus on the appropriateness of domestic policy to the dangers emerging (it is argued) from the external realm. For example, the Carter administration sought to make understandings of the international arena more complex by making East/West relations less central and highlighting North/South perspectives and global issues as the concerns they were. But neither the administration nor any other group could locate those new threats in a single, identifiable source. Without the internal/external nexus that had been at the base of postwar American identity, the administration's international strategy succumbed to the neoconservative effort to close off the domestic challenges of the 1960s and 1970s by reinscribing a cold war domestic identity through the externalization and totalization of threats in the Soviet Union.[51]

The need to discipline and contain the ambiguity and contingency of the "domestic" realm is a vital source of the externalization and totalization of threats to that realm through discourses of danger. But the achievements of foreign policy for the state are not due to any inherent characteristic of the state existing in an endangered world. The effectiveness of foreign policy as one political practice among many that serves to discipline ambiguity and construct identity is made possible because it is one instance of a series of cultural practices central to modernity operating within its own specific domain. This can be understood by reference to Ashley's discussion of the "paradigm of sovereignty."

The paradigm of sovereignty is not a paradigm in the Kuhnian sense of a conceptual resource that man applies to make sense of the world: it is a problematization in the Foucauldian sense that serves to discipline the ambiguity and contingency of history by differentiating, hierarchizing, and normalizing the site in which it operates.[52] But it is also more than that. Ambiguity is not disciplined by reference to a pregiven foundation. That "foundation" is constituted through the same process in which its name is invoked to discipline ambiguity.

The paradigm of sovereignty operates on the basis of a simple dichotomy: sovereignty versus anarchy. Although these terms have special significance within the discourse of international relations — a significance that depends on their effectiveness elsewhere — sovereignty and anarchy are replicable concepts that are pivotal for the construction of various mutually reinforcing dichotomies, such as subject/object, inside/outside, self/other, rational/irrational, true/false, order/disorder, and so on. In each instance the former is the higher, regulative ideal to which the latter is derivative and inferior, and a source of danger to the former's existence. In each instance, "sovereignty" (or its equivalent) signifies a center of decision presiding over a self that is to be valued and demarcated from an external domain that cannot or will not be assimilated to the identity of the sovereign domain.

This practice is at work in most if not all realms of contemporary life. In the discourses of politics, its operation can be witnessed when, confronting ambiguous and indeterminate circumstances, those discourses are "disposed to recur to the ideal of a sovereign presence, whether it be an individual actor, a group, a class, or a political community. They are disposed to invoke one or other sovereign presence as an originary voice, a foundational source of truth or meaning."[53] Most important, it is only those discourses of politics that replicate this heroic practice that are taken seriously as possible sources of truth and meaning. Alternative discourses that are less certain if not totally skeptical of foundations are *themselves* made objects of this heroic practice. If alternative discourses cannot be assimilated to some sovereign presence, they often find (as in the case of poststructuralism itself) that they are designated as "anarchical" and hence are themselves problems to be solved.

Although the foundation, fixed ground, or Archimedean point that provides the point of reference for modern discourse varies from site to site, one particular foundation can be considered pivotal: that is the sovereign presence of "reasoning man." An instance of the paradigm of sovereignty, it takes its form in an identifiable historical location. Around the end of the eighteenth century, modern discourse took a novel turn and invoked the figure of "reasoning man" as the origin of language, the maker of history, and the source of meaning.[54] The novelty of this turn was not the recognition of "man" as an object of knowledge—for the attempt to study "man" with objective methods had a long history—but the notion that this dimension was complemented with another to form what Foucault has termed an "empirico-transcendental doublet called man."[55] For the first time "man" was both an object of knowledge and a subject who knows. As instances of this new problematization, we can highlight the literature that was once written as advice to a particular prince that was refigured to address the wider concern of "governmentality,"[56] and the appearance of the concepts of "population" and "society" in the late eighteenth and early nineteenth centuries. Although both are now treated as naturalized terms describing an unproblematic reality, they emerge in a specific (and recent) historical context as instances of a normalizing project that has "reasoning man" at its core.[57]

The paradigm of sovereignty and its manifestation in the notion of "reasoning man" depend on and reproduce a gendered understanding of the political imaginary. Specifically, the discursive formation to which the texts of Machiavelli, Hobbes, and Clausewitz (among many others) are indebted is infused with notions of gender. These and other texts of importance to international relations and the rise of the state employ hierarchies drawn from the paradigm of sovereignty that establish both the boundaries and conduct of (inter)national politics; such hierarchies include strong/weak, rational/irrational, public/private, sane/insane, order/disorder, reason/emotion, stability/anarchy, and so on. Gender is insinuated into each of these pairs, with the first term being "masculine" and superior to its "feminine" subordinate.[58]

Most obviously, there is Machiavelli's discussion of *virtu* and *fortuna*, where *virtu* signifies the discipline and mastery needed to confront and do battle with *fortuna*, the "feminine" alliance of powers that cannot be understood or controlled and which threaten "man" and his life. In *The Prince*, Machiavelli declares: "What makes the prince contemptible is being considered changeable, trifling, effeminate, cowardly or indecisive; he should avoid this as a pilot does a reef and make sure that his actions bespeak greatness, courage, seriousness of purpose and strength . . . he lays down decisions not to be changed."[59] Equally, both Hobbes and Clausewitz can be understood as employing discourses of "danger" to constitute the impetus for political orders in which reason and rationalism play the central role. In *Leviathan*, the danger is posed by civil war and religious disputes that require a new commitment to sovereign power. But acceptance of this reinscribed sovereign power is possible only if those who are subject to it see it as a moral necessity. The morality that makes it a necessity is for Hobbes a morality of reason. In effect, "man" reasons his way to the state to secure the conditions for commodious living. This outcome privileges later understandings of the importance of reason: reason was the ending of the civil war, but because the historical premise of civil war became for Hobbes a logically necessary premise for his conception of sovereignty, the end of the conflicts through the establishment of the state came to be reason.[60] In other words, whereas reason begins as the path to the state, it ends up that the state becomes reason; it was, after all, Hobbes who came to refer to the state as the "empire of reason."[61] Moreover, sovereignty in Hobbes's formulation is highly gendered because, unable to include contingent identities or to come to terms with ambiguity, the unity and indivisibility of Hobbesian authority renders sovereignty as masculine.[62]

Similarly for Clausewitz, reason, rather than a specific prince, is the sovereign: the pursuit of *zweckrationalitat* rather than a specific political order is the culmination of Clausewitz's discourse on war. For example, Clausewitz admired the campaigns of Frederick the Great in the Seven Years' War because they were enabled by the king's "acute intelligence," "wisdom," "boldness," "resolution," and "strength of will."[63] These are durable terms of praise: they were applied to General Schwarzkopf's command of allied forces in the United States–led war against Iraq. The implication is that gendered discourses of power are synonymous with an understanding of politics in which reason, rationalism, and enlightenment values are privileged. Indeed, the latter qualities are coded terms that instantiate a particular (gendered) understanding of the political.

In sum, whether we are speaking in terms of Foucault's notion of a problematization in which ambiguity is disciplined by practices that differentiate, hierarchize, and normalize, Blumenberg's "inducing process" in which a concern with the unfinished and endangered nature of the world means that the "state" comes to occupy the position previously established by the church, Hobbes's sovereign state as a mortal god existing under an immortal God, or Ashley's paradigm of sovereignty, we are left with an overall problematic about the constitution of political/state identity. While dependent on specific historical contexts, we can say that for the state, identity can be understood as the outcome of exclusionary practices in which resistant elements to a secure identity on the "inside" are linked through a discourse of "danger" with threats identified and located on the "outside." The outcome of this is that boundaries are constructed, spaces demarcated, standards of legitimacy incorporated, interpretations of history privileged, and alternatives marginalized.

Foreign policy (conventionally understood as the external orientation of preestablished states with secure identities) is thus to be retheorized as one of the boundary-producing practices central to the production and reproduction of the identity in whose name it operates. We have to be very careful, however, in specifying the exact nature of the relationship between state-based foreign policy and political identity. Foreign policy in the conventional sense is a modern cultural artifact implicated in the intensification of power in the state. It arises in a form that we would recognize as recently as the late eighteenth or early nineteenth centuries, when organizations bearing the appellation "foreign" or "external" first appeared in a systematic form. Originally somewhat puny in size, it was not until the late nineteenth and early twentieth centuries that they took on the form of large-scale bureaucracies with global scope.[64] This growth coincided with, and contributed to, a range of developments that led to the intensification of social power in the nation-state, produced the category of "citizen," and established nationalism as the primary form of social identity by the time of World War I. These developments included different modes of apprehending time in which literary forms such as the novel and the newspaper enabled people to think in terms of the "nation"; rearticulations of the conventional understandings of time and space in domains as diverse as science, art, and industry; and the concerted effort to invent traditions, create national holidays, and rebuild capital cities so as to provide a particular historical understanding of the emergence of the modern state.[65]

Foreign policy cannot, therefore, be seen as constituting identity de novo. To explicate this, we need to draw a distinction between two understandings of foreign policy. The first is one in which "foreign policy" can be understood as referring to all practices of differentiation or modes of exclusion (possibly figured as relationships of otherness) that constitute their objects as "foreign" in the process of dealing with them. In this sense, "foreign policy" is divorced from the state as a particular resolution of the categories of identity and difference and applies to confrontations that appear to take place between a self and an other located in different sites of ethnicity, race, class, gender, or geography. These are the forms of "foreign policy" that have operated in terms of the paradigm of sovereignty and constituted identity through time and across space. Operating at all levels of social organization, from the level of personal relationships through to global orders, "foreign policy" in this sense has established conventional dispositions in which a particular set of representational practices serves as the resource from which are drawn the modes of interpretation employed to handle new instances of ambiguity or contingency. For example, in the case of the United States, there has been an intolerance of ambiguity at all levels of social life from neighborhoods to the international order that is expressed (as chapter 4 will discuss in more detail) in terms of a hierarchical ordering of self and other through figurations of disease and pollution. In other words, the first understanding ("foreign policy") has provided the discursive economy or conventional matrix of interpretations in which the second understanding (Foreign Policy) operates. This second understanding—Foreign Policy as state-based and conventionally understood within the discipline—is thus not as equally implicated in the *constitution* of identity as the first understanding. Rather, Foreign Policy serves to *reproduce* the constitution of identity made possible by "foreign policy" and to *contain* challenges to the identity that results.

Conversely, the relationship of Foreign Policy to political identity in any given nation-state should not be underestimated. We can point to James Der Derian's genealogy of diplomacy as an analog for this retheorization of foreign policy.[66] Der Derian examined not only the forms of modern diplomacy that can be dated from 1455 when the Duke of Milan established a legation in Genoa, but those forms of "diplomacy" (particularly "mythodiplomacy") that were paradigms for the way in which the fear of estrangement between "man" and God and among peoples was mediated long before there was ever a political community that could be considered a state. The point was not to establish a determinate intellectual pedigree for later modes of diplomacy, but to suggest that conventional dispositions for confronting ambiguity and estrangement were established that shaped the interpretation of later moments. While history does not repeat itself, "there are historical confrontations of power and truth which recur and generate parallel sets of mediatory rules and practices."[67] Such is the case with the relationship between "foreign policy" and Foreign Policy. Moreover, as Der Derian concluded, diplomacy does not have *a* historical origin, but rather "it emerges as the mediation of men estranged from an infinite yet abstracted power which they themselves have constructed."[68]

The same can be said of Foreign Policy. Particularly in its late modern form of "rational security policy," Foreign Policy is a discourse of power that is global in scope yet national in its legitimation. Foreign Policy is only one of a number of discourses of danger circulating in the discursive economy of a nation-state at any given time: from weather reports to Central Intelligence Agency net threat assessments, modern life is disciplined by discourses that tell us what to fear.[69] But in the context of the modern nation-state, Foreign Policy has been granted a privileged position as the discourse to which we should turn as the source of the preeminent dangers to our society and ourselves. Operating as such, Foreign Policy creates the very dangers to which we are supposed to accommodate ourselves. Much like the creature in Franz Kafka's *The Burrow*—which digs a complex maze of underground tunnels to provide security from predators thought to exist on the outside, but cannot in the end distinguish between the noise thought to come from the predators and the noise created by its own digging on the inside[70]—Foreign Policy cannot distinguish the "perception of objects from the object effects of perceptual acts."[71]

To conclude this retheorization of Foreign Policy, a couple of amplifications need to be made. The argument above paints a particularly negative picture of the processes implicated in a state's identity. It emphasizes the exclusionary practices, the discourses of danger, the representations of fear, and the enumeration of threats, and downplays the role of affirmative discourses such as claims to shared ethnicity, nationality, political ideals, religious beliefs, or other commonalities. Two reasons help justify this formulation.

If all meaning is constituted through difference (an assumption on which this analysis is based), then there can be no declaration about the nature of the self that is totally free of suppositions about the other. Although a positive declaration of some characteristic of the self might be devoid of specific reference to an other, it proffers nonetheless an at least implicit valuation of those who might be considered other. Of course, the nature of that valuation and its effects can vary considerably: a simple contrast need not automatically result in the demonization of the other, and the differentiation or distantiation of one group from another does not require that their relationship be one of violence. But insofar as the logic of identity requires difference, the potential for the transformation of difference into otherness always exists.

Moreover, in the context of Foreign Policy, the logic of identity more readily succumbs to the politics of negation and the temptation of otherness. The claim is not that Foreign Policy constitutes state identity de novo; rather, it is that Foreign Policy is concerned with the reproduction of an unstable identity at the level of the state, and the containment of challenges to that identity. In other words, Foreign Policy does not operate in a domain free of entrenched contingencies or resistances. Whichever Foreign Policy practices are implemented, they always have to overcome or neutralize other practices that might instantiate alternative possibilities for identity; and the intensive and extensive nature of the "internal" and "external" political contestation that this presupposes means the efficacy of one particular practice will more often than not be sharpened by the representation of danger.

Finally, the above argument should not be taken to suggest that the boundary-producing performances of Foreign Policy result in borders of identity that are clearly demarcated, singular, and neat. Indeed, given the inherently contingent identity that is the result of the attempt to secure a domain as intensive and extensive as the state, the boundaries are blurred, multiple, and often violent. Gloria Anzaldúa offers a particularly compelling formulation:

> The U.S.-Mexican border *es una herida abierta* [is an open wound] where the Third World grates against the first and bleeds. And before a scab forms it hemorrhages again, the lifeblood of two worlds merging to form a third country — a border culture. Borders are set up to define places that are safe and unsafe, to distinguish *us* from *them*. A border is a dividing line, a narrow strip along a steep edge. A borderland is a vague and undetermined place created by the emotional residue of an unnatural boundary. It is a constant state of transition.[72]

Rather than being just narrow topographical lines, borders are shifting horizons marked by flux and ambiguity.[73] And rather than clearly demarcating the duality of self and other, they come into existence through a triadic relationship when the presence of those who are ambiguous and liminal confounds any simple or unified representation of identity: "The definition of identity, in nations and men ... depends for its accomplishment on the recognition of that which is other, like, and simultaneously other and like, and on the abstract, objective understanding of the self that follows from this recognition."[74] It is the objectification of the self through the representation of danger that Foreign Policy helps achieve.

This process of objectification is achieved through certain recurring representations and figurations; ones that are general to foreign policy, and ones that are specific to the United States. Chapter 4 discusses those general to foreign policy in more detail, focusing on "the body" as a political metaphor and the discourses of discipline and containment that it enables, while chapter 5 considers how these figurations have functioned in certain key moments of American history—moments that are especially important to the identity reproduced through Foreign Policy discourses.

Four
Foreign Policy and Difference

The Moral Space of Identity

The performative constitution of identity: that has been the fundamental theme in this argument. Whether at the level of the body, the
individual, the state, or some other articulation, this theme has focused
attention on the boundary-producing practices that instantiate the
identity in whose name they operate. Sometimes these practices will
affirm more than they will abjure; at other times they will contain
rather than constitute. Foreign policy, being those practices of differentiation implicated in all confrontations between a self and other,
embraces both positive and negative valences. In contrast, Foreign Policy, understood as one of the practices that contingently constructs
through stylized and regulated performances the identity of the state
in whose name it operates, is more obviously dependent on discourses
of fear and danger. The concern of this chapter is how difference is figured and danger is represented through foreign policy/Foreign Policy.

Danger constitutes more than the boundary that demarcates a
space; to have a threat requires enforcing a closure on the community that is threatened. A notion of what "we" are is intrinsic to an
understanding of what "we" fear. What this highlights is that there
is an axiological level that proffers a range of moral valuations that
are implicit in any spatialization.[1] The construction of social space that
emerges from practices associated with the paradigm of sovereignty
thus exceeds a simple geographical partitioning: it results in a conception of divergent moral spaces. In other words, the social space of
inside/outside is both made possible by and helps constitute a moral
space of superior/inferior, which can be animated in terms of any
number of figurations of higher/lower. For example, in delineating
the domain of the rational, ordered polity from the dangerous, anarchic world in which it was situated, Hobbes did more than draw a

73

boundary: he enumerated the character of each realm by arguing that the former was the residence of good, sane, sober, modest, and civilized people, while the latter was populated by evil, mad, drunk, arrogant, and savage characters.

Identity is therefore more than something that derives its meaning solely from being positioned in contradistinction to difference; identity is a condition that has depth, is multilayered, possesses texture, and comprises many dimensions. As such, identity is a condition for which there can be cataloged no single point of origin or myth of genesis; the manifold, diverse, and eclectic ingredients that comprise a settled identity cannot be reduced to any single spatial or temporal source. None of this diminishes the role of difference in the logic of identity. But it does suggest that we might consider all the characteristics, traits, or distinctions that are understood as difference to be unequal in their identity-effects. Moreover, this might also suggest that some of the dispositions we combine under the category of "difference" — especially insofar as that term is often used to refer to entries in a register of marginality, such as race, class, gender, and ethnicity — are basic to the construction of the discursive field on which the dichotomy of identity/difference is itself erected.

Whether or not these reflections possess some veracity in terms of the general problematic of identity would need further consideration. But in terms of the question of state identity, they do show how the paradigm of sovereignty has historically inscribed parameters of the moral content of identity at the same time that it has disciplined ambiguity in terms of the spatial form of inside/outside. Most important in this regard is the gendered figure of "reasoning man" highlighted by Ashley. As described in chapter 3, the figure of "reasoning man" as the origin of language, the maker of history, and the source of meaning — as transcendental, yet implicated in history — is the sovereign presence, the foundational premise, from which we derive the contours of our social and political life. To be sure, this articulation of our horizons is not determinative: the question of the more precise content and nature of identity that emerges from the operations of this modern sovereign is open. Indeed, there are in principle an almost endless range of possible interpretations of "reasoning man," and these are dependent on the articulation of the form of "reasoning man" in specific historical contexts.[2] But the figure of "reasoning man" can be said to exhibit tendencies that favor the gendered understanding of reason, rationalism, and enlightenment values as the defining orientations of our existence.

But aside from the foundational works in the tradition of international relations theory — where the demarcation of inside/outside has been either overtly or covertly coded with gender norms (such as Machiavelli's *fortuna*, Hobbes's sovereignty, or Clausewitz's resolute strength) — Western political theory has often had recourse to openly theorize the state and society in other terms that instantiate the moral space of identity. This has particularly been the case when the political has been represented in terms of the body. Indeed, when the men of the *Mayflower* declared on their landing in North America that they were to "combine... together into a Civil Body Politike, for our better ordering and preservation,"[3] they were doing no more than reciting a by then common theme. It was Thomas Hobbes, after all, who entitled one of his philosophical-political tracts "The Body Politic."[4]

The Body Politic

The trope of "the body" is central to the moral space of identity: it is obviously implicated in the gendered discourses of power discussed above, and can be easily observed in any number of representations concerned with threats to order in society. We have encountered Hobbes's declaration that large numbers of men rebel, just as children's bodies break out into "biles and scabbs"; his presentation of those who dispute sovereign power as being like "worms in the entrails of a natural man"; and we have noted Kennan's concern for dealing with the "malignant parasite" of communism (among other figurations to be found in the Foreign Policy texts of the cold war). We could also note the eighteenth-century text that said of the houses of confinement that bordered European cities: "A terrible ulcer on the body politic, an ulcer that is wide, deep and draining, one that cannot be imagined except by looking full upon it".[5] In addition, there is Goebbels's declaration that the use of terror was in actuality "social hygiene, taking those individuals out of circulation like a doctor would take out a bacillus."[6]

Such accounts are manifestations of an established and tenacious discursive economy that provides the resources for representing difference as danger to the social, where the social is understood as a (naturally healthy) body. The continued efficacy of "the body politic" as a trope for social order stems from two factors: (1) there is a well-established history of representing the social as a body that precedes the rise of the state in Europe; and (2) it is a figuration that authorizes and empowers the representation of danger to the social body

in terms associated with the representation of danger to the physiological body.[7]

Dating back to antiquity, the earliest body metaphors used structural terms to describe the linkages between the head, organs, and
limbs. This conception reached its apogee in the *Policraticus* of John
of Salisbury, dated (though probably not written in) 1159:

> The state [*res publica*] is a body [*corpas quoddam*] . . . Within that state,
> the prince . . . occupies the place of the head; he is subject to the
> unique God and to those who are his lieutenants on earth, for in
> the human body the head is also governed by the soul. The senate
> occupies the place of the heart, which gives good and bad deeds
> their impulses. The function of the eyes, the ears and the tongue is
> assured by the judges and the provincial governors . . . The "offi-
> cers" and "soldiers" . . . can be compared to the hands. The prince's
> regular assistants are the flanks. The quaestors [*quaestous* or stew-
> ards] and the registrars . . . evoke the image of the belly and in-
> testines which, if they have been stuffed through excessive greed
> and if they hold in their contents too obstinately, give rise to count-
> less and incurable illnesses and, through their vices, can bring about
> the ruin of the body as a whole. The feet that always touch the soil
> are the peasants . . . Being governed by the head is especially neces-
> sary for them, because they are faced by numerous detours as they
> walk upon the earth in the service of the body, and because they
> need the firmest support in order to keep the mass of the entire body
> erect, to support it and to move it about. Deprive the most robust
> body of the support given by its feet, and it will not advance under
> its own strength but will either crawl shamefully, painfully and un-
> successfully on its hands, or will move about like brute beasts.[8]

As Le Goff notes, the anachronistic use of the term *Senate* in a
document putatively from the Middle Ages suggests that it had an
earlier origin. Nonetheless, it demonstrates the logic behind the structural conception of the body politic, a conception that Hobbes, among
others, put to great use. Indeed, in the wake of the rediscovery of Aristotle's *Politics* in 1260, the phrase *corpus politicum* gained renewed currency and was used extensively in the conservative response to the
protest literature prevalent in England after 1350.[9]

The reference to the soul in John of Salisbury's text suggests that
the Christian use of the body metaphor, which involved the less skele-
tal idea of head/heart as the organizing principle, developed in tan-
dem with that of antiquity. In Saint Paul's First Epistle to the Corinthi-
ans, for example, he employed a body metaphor that identified Christ
and his followers in a hierarchical relationship of differentiated parts

that was established by God.[10] But it was the transformation surrounding the meaning of *corpus mysticum* in Christianity that highlights
the mutuality of the secular and theological employment of the body
metaphor.

It might be thought that the idea of the church as the mystical
body of Christ was an established theological concept dating from
Saint Paul. The Carolingian theologians, however, used the term to
refer not to the body of the church or the unity of Christian society
but to the consecrated host. During the twelfth century, in the midst
of the controversy over transubstantiation, the referent deployed by
theologians for the *corpus mysticum* switched from the consecrated host
(which came to be understood as *corpus christi* or *corpus naturale*) to
the church as the organized body of Christian society with Christ as
the head. In consequence, the expression, "which originally had a litur-
gical or sacramental meaning, took on a connotation of sociological
content."[11]

This conceptual transformation took place in the period subsequent to 1150 and came to be deeply implicated in the respatialization of identity occurring throughout "Europe" in this period; this
respatialization was discussed in chapter 3 in terms of an "inducing
process" whereby the state "occupied" the position of the church, and
can be understood in terms of the parallel development of the spiritual world as the mystical body of Christ and the secular world as
the holy empire. But as Kantorowicz argues, this parallel development
"does not imply causation, either in the one way or the other. It merely
indicates the activity of indeed interrelated impulses and ambitions
by which the spiritual *corpus mysticum* and the secular *sacrum imperium*
happened to emerge simultaneously."[12] Nonetheless, the interpenetration of the theological and the secular in this period was complete: "the hierarchical apparatus of the Roman Church tended to become the perfect prototype of an absolute and rational monarchy on
a mystical basis, while at the same time the State [*sic*] showed increasingly a tendency to become a quasi-Church or a mystical corporation
on a rational basis."[13]

The interpenetration of the theological and secular domains culminated in the transference of the theological concept of the Lord's
two bodies (the host on the altar and the mystical body of the church)
to the idea of the king's two bodies, where the first was his body natural and the second his body politic. It is important to stress the non-
causal and nonpurposive nature of this transference. Kantorowicz
readily declares that "it is evident that the doctrine of theology and
canon law, teaching that the Church, and Christian society in general,

was a *corpus mysticum* the head of which is Christ, has been trans-
ferred by the jurists from the theological sphere to that of the state
the head of which is the king." He also argues, however, that even
though the discourse (in England) of the Inns of Court and the early
church might suggest a superficial and instrumental appropriation
of concepts, "the implication of all this is not that the lawyers consciously borrowed from the acts of the early Councils, but that the
fiction of the King's Two Bodies produced interpretations and defin-
itions which perforce could resemble those produced in view of the
Two Natures of the God-man."[14]

The conditions of possibility for this transference were not fully
in existence until the last bond between the *corpus mysticum* and its
sacramental heritage—a bond suggested in the way the word *corpus*
invoked the consecrated sacrifice—was diminished. Aquinas supplied
the necessary formulation when he wrote that the head and limbs together constituted a "mystical person" rather than a body. By substituting a juridical conception of *persona mythica,* this formulation diminished the legacy of mysterious corporeality that the *corpus christi*
exercised over the *corpus mysticum.*[15]

The significance of this substitution (which was obviously not a
complete break) was that it allowed the development of the idea of
the "corporation," so that the important link between the head and
the body of such an entity was one of *representation* rather than a specific materiality. When Otto Gierke wrote subsequently that the church
was a corporation because it "represent[ed] a person which cannot
be said ever to have lived, because that person is neither corporeal
nor mortal, since it is God,"[16] he was articulating a logic that had enabled two interrelated developments that further implicated the spiritual and secular realms. The understanding of representation in the
idea of the corporation allowed the pope to secure his imperial position because he could more easily rule over the corporate body of the
church than he could over the mystical body of Christ. Even more important, in diminishing the importance of the materiality of Christ's
body, the corporate church was not only able to more effectively rule
over the secular world, it was able to allow, if not encourage, the development of state forms whose material and physical capacities had
restricted their reach and importance. In other words, by diminishing
the importance of materiality as the grounds for spiritual and secular authority, this shift from the physical body to the representative
corporation permitted the securing of new political communities, the
existence of which would otherwise have been in doubt, through the
imputation of a transcendental spirit.

This is not to suggest that the notion of "body" fell by the wayside. On the contrary, it persisted, but in terms of an understanding whereby it was invested with the more secular understandings of representation and corporation. Indeed, the notion of *corpus mysticum* came to be used synonymously with terms such as *corpus fictum, corpus imaginatum, corpus repraesentatum, persona ficta*, and *persona repraesentata*.[17] It is succinctly summarized by the medieval jurist Balbus, who argued that "the people" were a mystical body, the meaning of which exceeded the sum of its parts, and the existence of which could only be grasped intellectually, since the resulting body politic or corporation was neither material nor real. As Kantorowicz notes, by using the idea of the *corpus mysticum* in such formulations of the social, theorists "brought to the secular polity, as it were, a whiff of incense from another world."[18]

Above all, this means that representation is not a concept read into these developments by analysts working at a distance; representation was central to medieval political theory and its conceptualization of the state and society. Indeed, bringing representation to the fore as rudimentary to the social body accents the extent to which the performative constitution of identity is the condition of possibility by which we have historically been able to perceive the state and its practices.

Furthermore, the representation of the social as a body involves gendered discourses of power, and the transformations surrounding the concept of *corpus mysticum* are replete with references to the dominance of the "male" over the "female." Indeed, the body of the body politic is taken to have a "female" identity to which the head (the "male" ruler) is married. As one jurist (Cynus of Pistoia) wrote in the fourteenth century: "The comparison between the corporeal matrimony and the intellectual one is good: for just as the husband is called the defender of his wife ... so is the emperor the defender of that *respublica*."[19] In a similar vein, Lucas de Penna wrote that "the man is the head of the wife, and the wife the body of the man ... After the same fashion, the Prince is the head of the realm, and the realm the body of the Prince."[20] In medieval England, the marriage metaphor was reproduced when James I declared to Parliament (in 1609) that "what God hath conjoined then, let no man separate. I am the husband, and all the whole island is my lawful wife; I am the head, and it is my body; I am the shepherd, and it is my flock."[21] Equally, Machiavelli figured the body politic as "female."[22] And in the contemporary period, such patriarchal understandings can be observed when violence by one state against another (such as the Iraqi invasion of Kuwait in 1990) is represented as "rape."

Persistent though it has been, the representation of the social as a body has not been devoid of changes. Catherine Gallagher's discussion of the impact of Thomas Malthus's theorization of the body's place in social discourse — whereby it is healthy and fecund bodies, rather than sick and decaying bodies, that are the greatest threat to the survival of the polity — points to a development that had considerable import for Victorian social thought.[23] Equally, Donna Haraway's elaboration of the shift from the hierarchical and organic body of earlier medical discourses to the understanding of the body within biomedical discourses as "a coded text, organized as an engineered communications system, ordered by a fluid and dispersed command-control-intelligence network [the immune system],"[24] contends that we could be currently located in the midst of a transformation that might have an impact on our political theorizations. These developments have meant that what now counts as a unit or actor is highly problematic: while notions of "organism" and "individual" have not disappeared, from the vantage point of the biologist they have been fully "denaturalized" and exist only as "ontologically contingent constructs."[25] In Haraway's terms, the contingent ontology of being means that "life is a window of vulnerability," such that identity and (more particularly) individuality are "a strategic defense problem" that seeks to effect the containment of contingency.[26]

Haraway's deployment of military metaphors highlights the symbiotic relationship between biomedical discourses and strategic discourses: each uses concepts derived from the other to present its argument.[27] Most important, such figurations suggest that whatever transformations there have been in the representation of the social as a body, one of its central functions has been to permit and commission the representation of danger to the social body in terms associated with the representation of danger to the physiological body. In some circumstances, the representation of danger to the body will be in terms that function as codes for gender and sexuality, such as anarchy, insanity, passion, or wildness. At other times, "because the body is the most potent metaphor of society, it [will] not [be] surprising that disease is the most salient metaphor of structural crisis. All disease is disorder — metaphorically, literally, socially and politically."[28]

Representing Danger

Danger, argues Mary Douglas, is always present at the border. Danger might involve pressure on the external boundaries, it might involve the violation of internal boundaries, it might be located in the margins of the boundary, or it might arise with contradictions from within.[29] Were there no borders, there would be no danger, but such a condition is at odds with the logic of identity, for the condition of possibility for experience entails (at least to some extent) the disciplining of ambiguity, the containment of contingency, and the delineation of borders. In other words, given that difference is a requisite for identity, danger is inherent to that relationship: "Where there is no differentiation there is no defilement."[30] As such, danger is not an external condition that can be either tempered or transcended; danger is a part of all our relationships with the world. And as Jean Delumeau concluded with respect to fear, danger can be experienced positively as well as negatively: it can be a creative force, "a call to being," that provides access to the world.[31] The issue, then, is how do we orient ourselves to danger, particularly at a historical juncture in which many novel dangers seem to abound? Can we do more than simply extend the old register of security to cover the new domains? What modes of being and forms of life could we or should we adopt? Do we have an alternative to the continued reproduction of sovereign communities in an economy of violence?

However one might begin to fathom the many issues located within those challenges, our current situation leaves us with one certainty: because we cannot escape the logic of differentiation, we are often tempted by the logic of defilement. To say as much is not to argue that we are imprisoned within a particular and permanent system of representations. To be sure, danger is often represented as disease, dirt, or pollution. As one medical text argues: "Disease is shock and danger for existence."[32] Or as Karl Jaspers maintains: "Disease is a general concept of non-value which includes all possible negative values."[33] But such concerns have less to do with the intrinsic qualities of those conditions than the modernist requirements of order and stability: "Dirt offends against order. Eliminating it is not a negative moment, but a positive effort to organize the environment."[34] One might suggest that it is the extent to which we want to organize the environment—the extent to which we want to purify our domain—that determines how likely it is that we represent danger in terms of dirt or disease. Tightly defined order and strictly enforced stability, undergirded by notions of purity, are not a priori conditions of existence; some order and some stability might be required for existence as we know it (i.e., in some form of extensive political community), but it is the degree of tightness, the measure of strictness, and the extent of the desire for purity that constitute danger as dirt or disease.

But the temptation of the logic of defilement as a means of orienting ourselves to danger has more often than not been overpowering, largely because it is founded on a particular conceptualization of "the body"; in its use since at least the eighteenth century, this conceptualization demands purity as a condition of health and thus makes the temptation to defilement a "natural" characteristic. This has endowed us with a mode of representation in which health and cleanliness serve the logic of stability, and disorder is rendered as disease and dirt. In the eighteenth century, when state forms were becoming the most prevalent articulations of extensive political community, these modes of representation began to take a new turn that intensified the capacity of representations of disease to act as discourses of danger to the social.

In France, a number of notions that would be fundamental to the medicalization of society materialized around the time of the Revolution. Including the myth of a clergy-like national medical profession and the supposition that pacific republics would be totally free of disease, these notions altered the conception of medicine and changed the functioning of the body politic metaphor. In this context, Foucault argues, medicine shifted from simply being an ensemble of practices for curing ills to a concern with the knowledge of the healthy, non-sick, and model man.[35] In association with a more widespread intellectual shift from juridical discourses that promulgated natural rules to a concern with codes of normalization, this development meant that medicine reoriented its principal focus from that which was healthy to that which was normal. In this context, "when one spoke of the life of groups and societies, of the life of the race, or even of the 'psychological life,' one did not think first of the internal structure of the *organized being,* but of *the medical bipolarity of the normal and the pathological.*"[36] This development did not mean that representations of danger ceased to function in terms of disease, dirt, or some other form of defilement. Rather, it meant that just as "the body" functioned as a trope for the social, "disease" now functioned as a trope for the pathological in opposition to the normal.

While the bipolarity of normal/pathological appears to derive its authority as a regulative ideal for society from its medical origins, this fact should not obscure the contested and problematic nature of such an understanding within the practice of medicine. Although the common effect of this bipolarity is to assume that "normal" refers to natural or desired health marked by the complete absence of disease, there have been many debates within medicine concerning the extent to which disease itself is something of a biological norm.[37] That is, few if any people are marked by the complete absence of ailments or physical problems, and most surveys show that large numbers of people

who live in a perfectly happy and satisfactory way possess physiological characteristics that depart markedly from statistical averages
and would be a source of ill health to some.[38] As a result, a medical
conclusion would be that "if the normal does not have the rigidity of
a fact of collective constraint but rather the flexibility of a norm which
is transformed in its relations to individual conditions, it is clear that
the boundary between the normal and the pathological becomes imprecise."[39] Most important, the variability inherent in physiological
norms, and their subsequent lack of universality, means that the imputation of a clear distinction between health and disease—which is
the regulative desire of the bipolarity of normal/pathological in the
political realm—is an understanding effected by a social and cultural
logic. It is not something mandated by medical knowledge. In consequence, proclaims Canguilhem: "Pathological constants have a re-
pulsive and strictly conservative value."[40]

The operation of the normal/pathological bipolarity as a politically regulative ideal can be observed in terms of the nineteenth-
and early twentieth-century concerns for degeneration and social
hygiene.[41] Although this was a period renowned for its faith in the
idea of progress, it exhibited—in much the same way as the golden
age of the Renaissance gave rise to a plethora of anxieties[42]—a widespread feeling of uneasiness in which a preoccupation with degeneration (in many ways no more than an update on the earlier cultural
obsession with the decomposition of the body) served as "the institutionalization of fear."[43] For example, in his study of the medicalization of cultural crises in France from the mid-nineteenth century
to the end of World War I, Robert Nye argues that the general sense
of degeneration and national decline that permeated that country was
located in individual conditions understood as pathologies (e.g., alcoholism, madness, and criminality), such that domestic health and
national security were part of the same frame of analysis.[44] What
emerged was not a program for national health, but a philosophy of
"social defense" in which there was a very low tolerance for deviance. Manifested in the "political dentistry" of nineteenth-century
European comic art—where bad teeth represented political dangers,
and which is a testament to "the broad acceptance of the inevitability
of violent and/or painful 'surgical' intervention as a means of pre-
serving or restoring the health of the body politic"[45]—this philosophy was spurred on in France, Nye argues, by a high level of public
concern about the nation's ability to respond effectively to German
diplomatic and military assertiveness. One of its consequences was
to effect another episode of *grande peur* on the part of the French bour-

geoisie, who by the turn of the century came to be preoccupied with the violent street crimes of groups known as "the apaches."[46] The wider community was equally transfixed. One analyst of the almanacs that served as major sources of information for those outside of French cities noted that they were concerned with, "above all, fear, fear, fear: of brigands, thieves, rape, fire, hail, floods, rabies, epidemics, violence of all sorts."[47]

What is especially noteworthy about this period is the way in which the concern for degeneration came to be preoccupied not just with the pathologies of health/illness but also with pathologies of deviance, particularly pathologies of sexual deviance, such as homosexuality. For example, Austrian psychiatrist Richard von Krafft-Ebing— the author of the mammoth *Psychopathia Sexualis* (1886)—warned that "episodes of moral decay always coincide with the progression of effeminacy, lewdness and luxuriance of the nations."[48] A popular manifestation of this attitude was found in Germany in the first decade of the twentieth century, where there was a national scandal concerning homosexuals in the top echelons of government. Indeed, "the links between decadence, homosexuality, and effeminacy were so strong that political cartoons of the period regularly connected them, delighting especially in the irony of homosexuals dressed in military garb."[49] Equally, the fin-de-siècle controversy surrounding prostitution in Victorian England exhibited a similar concern for social purity and hygiene.[50]

What these and other examples demonstrate about the pathologies of health/illness and normality/deviance is that although problems may be formulated in medical terms, they are largely animated by moral concerns.[51] This is not to deny the reality of illness; on the contrary, it is to reaffirm the seriousness of disease for the health of patients by distinguishing the social functions of medical discourse from the physiological effects of the disease.[52] Representing perceived moral concerns and social dangers in medical terms has a number of consequences. Informed by a "received view" of medical practice, it casts the danger as an aberration that deviates from the norm of health and threatens the integrity of the body or its habitual functions; it establishes a power relationship in which the authority making the diagnosis occupies the position of a doctor vis-à-vis the patient, thereby reproducing the notion that the health (or security) of the larger population is dependent on the specialized knowledge of an elite; it renders complex problems simplistically as the symptoms of an alien infection that is external in origin; and it mandates (often violent) intervention as the appropriate course of action that will result in a cure.

One salient example that illustrates many of these dimensions was the statement, common in the 1980s, that popular opposition to nuclear weapons in countries such as Denmark, Japan, and New Zealand was symptomatic of a "nuclear allergy."[53] This metaphor suggested that a worldwide nuclear warfare infrastructure was normal and desirable, that popular discontent was the result of a viral-like irritation in the polity, most likely carried and spread by outsiders, and that the national security managers occupied positions akin to doctors, enabling them to effectively diagnose and deal with the infection.

The effects of what we might call sociomedical discourse infiltrate the realms of both clinical medicine and political practice. Haraway and others have noted the salience of military metaphors within immunology.[54] Equally, the panoply of military metaphors that permeates the medical discourse on cancer — references to attack and counterattack, invasion and defense, cells that colonize, patients that are bombarded, or bodies that are subverted — has manifest consequences for understanding and treating that disease.[55] By constituting the disease as the "barbarian within," and by producing a discourse that is taken in some contexts to impute guilt, prescribe punishments, and incite violence, the figurative nature of medical discourse has consequences for clinical practice.[56] This should not come as much of a surprise: there is no reason why medical discourse should be immune (so to speak) from the tropical nature of language. Indeed, given the encounters with the unknown in the discoveries of scientific and medical research — encounters that can only be made available for understanding through metaphor — scientific discourse may be particularly prone to tropical discourse.[57] But there is an important implication to be drawn from the symmetry of medical and military discourses.

As Canguilhem's argument made clear, the regulative ideal of normal/pathological was not derived from or grounded in the knowledge of medicine; on the contrary, the scientific caste of this regulative ideal is a consequence of its social efficacy. Equally, the symmetry of medical and military discourse is not a situation brought about by the inherent truth value of one or the other of these domains. To be sure, our culture regards few arenas as more "real" than the practice of medicine or the conduct of war, yet neither can escape the tropical character of representation. The authority of each thus stems from a mutual referentiality in which the representations of one authorize the other: the imputed realism of military discourse brings meaning to medical practice, just as the assumed facticity of medicine legitimates certain forces in the social and political field. Indeed, it is the overtly tropical nature of medical discourse that enables it to be so effectively marshaled against those who constitute a danger. Consider Ronald Reagan's declaration—in response to the 1985 hijacking of a TWA aircraft in Beirut, when he was considering the option of military retaliation—that "when terrorism strikes, civilization itself is under attack. No nation is immune...If we permit it to succeed anywhere it will spread like a cancer, eating away at civilized societies and sowing fear and chaos everywhere."[58] In such discourse, there are no gray areas, no complexities, no historicized understandings, no doubts about the self, and no qualms about the nature of the response.

The performative nature of the bipolarity of normal/pathological in sociomedical discourse means that it does not depend on either a disease to be tremendously infectious or in actual existence for it to effect exclusions and command responses. For example, leprosy— which is rarely fatal, difficult to transmit, and relatively easy to cure— has been one of the most stigmatized of diseases.[59] Because of the visibility of its degenerative impact on the body, leprosy became a metaphor for social corruption and decay. When it disappeared from Europe at the end of the Middle Ages, it left behind a legacy that remained potent: an interpretative framework suffused with the "formulas of exclusion," which established "the values and images attached to the figure of the leper as well as the meaning of his exclusion."[60] The disease passed on, but its social logic and representational apparatus remained, to be employed later in the confinement of a range of social dangers including "madness." Even without a referent for its valuations, this interpretative framework associated with leprosy waited, "soliciting with strange incantations a new incarnation of disease, another grimace of terror, renewed rites of purification."[61]

What has been and remains central to the logic of sociomedical discourse is thus not the biological nature of disease, but a sense that disease is always from somewhere else. As Sontag notes, "There is a link between imagining disease and imagining foreignness." Indeed, when syphilis reached epidemic proportions in fifteenth-century Europe, "it was the 'French pox' to the English, *morbus Germanicus* to the Parisians, the Naples sickness to the Florentines, [and] the Chinese disease to the Japanese."[62] But "foreignness" does not necessarily coincide with places distant and removed: the foreign can also reside within, something that is evident when (as in the United States) disease is more readily diagnosed in the elderly, the poor, or the working class, even when other groups exhibit many more identifiably biological pathologies.[63] In the same manner, we can note how various groups within American and European domestic society have been constituted as marginal through the figurations of sociomedical discourse. Women, blacks, and Jews have at one time or another all been understood as uniquely susceptible to certain disorders. Women were diagnosed as exhibiting a high incidence of hysteria; Jews in general were believed to be prone to psychological disorders; Jewish men were thought to menstruate like women and thus be a source of social "pollution"; blacks were overwhelmingly considered insane. And for each of these groups, sexuality was medicalized as pathology and indicted as a threat to the integrity of the body politic.[64]

In sum, two things are particularly striking about these examples of the historical operation of sociomedical discourse. First, it has often been able to function either without any empirical referent from which its valuations are theoretically derived, or it has accomplished its task in direct contradistinction to available empirical sources. The moral characteristics of leprosy lived on after its demise; neither women, nor blacks, nor Jews were any more vulnerable to psychological disorders than any other groups; and Jewish men certainly did not menstruate.[65] Second, the modes of representation through which these groups are marked as social dangers effectively blend and fuse various stigmata of difference, such that each figuration of difference functions not as an image derived from a correspondence relationship but as an indicator of the various images with which it has some perceived affinity. Or, as Hayden White suggests of metaphor generally, it "functions as a symbol, rather than as a sign: which is to say that it does not give us either a *description* or an *icon* of the thing it represents, but *tells us* what images to look for in our culturally encoded experience in order to determine how we *should feel* about the thing represented."[66]

In other words, by conflating the stigmata of difference, the tropes and metaphors of sociomedical discourse call to mind certain sensations, dispositions, impressions, and—given the negative valence of such representations—doubts, concerns, anxieties, and suspicions to be associated with those groups that are the objects of attention. We need only consider contemporary representations of AIDS—in which iconography associated with syphilis, homosexuals, Africans, drug addicts, and inner-city residents is melded into an all-encompassing discursive formation so as to inscribe a boundary between the heterosexual, non–IV-drug-using, white community (i.e., those who are "normal") and those at risk—to appreciate the continued saliency of these representations.[67] Indeed, the boundary-producing effects of the discourse surrounding AIDS took a literal turn when the U.S. Immigration and Naturalization Service overruled the Health and Human Services Department and reinstated the presence of HIV as grounds for excluding tourists and immigrants from the United States. With over one million Americans already infected with this virus, such an exclusion "conveys the message that the danger is outside the U.S., is a foreigner, a stranger."[68]

What we have been discussing here, then, is "foreign policy": all those practices of differentiation implicated in the confrontation between self and other, and their modes of figuration. Although it has been argued that the representation of difference does not functionally necessitate a negative figuration, it has historically more often than not been the case, especially given the force of sociomedical discourse, that danger has been made available for understanding in terms of defilement. And given both the innately tropical nature of language and the multifarious sensibilities suffused within representations of danger, the depiction of difference is not carried out within the register of realism: we might say it takes place within an "orrery of signification," through which characteristics are ascribed to "others" on the basis of their associated valuations rather than on the basis of their ability to describe those being portrayed.[69] In this context, foreign policy might be likened to an "ethical power of segregation," whereby moral distinctions can be made through spatial and temporal delineations, constituting a "geography of evil" that allows dangers to be understood as originating from distinct and distant places.[70] This is especially the case when we are considering the domain of Foreign Policy, where the temptation of otherness has been uncommonly compelling.

Sociomedical discourse should not, however, be considered the metanarrative of otherness: it is but one instance, one series of formulations, drawn from the discursive economy of difference through which, in Western experience, identity has been constituted. Indeed, in the "orrery of signification" through which difference is figured and danger is represented, there is often considerable overlap in the articulations employed. For example, immediately after his equation of terrorism with cancer, Reagan declared that "this barbarism is abhorrent, and all those who support it, encourage it, and profit from it, are abhorrent. They are barbarians."[71] In so doing, Reagan pointed to an important interpretative tradition in Western experience: the inscription of the other as the barbarian who stands in opposition to the "civilized" self, a characterization that (as chapter 5 will demonstrate) played a vital role in constituting the identity of America and the New World. It is well illustrated by Mercator, who rationalized his cartographic representation of the world by arguing that:

> Here [Europe] we have the right of Laures, the dignity of the Christian Religion, the forces of Armes...Moreover, Europe manageth all Arts and Sciences with such dexterity, that for the invention of manie things shee may be truly called a Mother...she hath...all manner of learning, whereas other Countries are all of them, overspread with Barbarisme.[72]

That the "barbarian" invoked connotations that can be aligned with cancer suggests that, although each representation will have its peculiar entailments, each is energized by moral concerns similar to those invoked by the bipolarity of normal/pathological; these moral concerns naturalize the self (as normal, healthy, civilized, or something equally positive) by estranging the other (as pathological, sick, barbaric, or something equally negative). In the position of the estranged, we could place the heretic, the pagan, the primitive, the racially designated, the culturally inferior, the mad, the wild, the (sometimes noble) savage, the indigent, the immoral, the law-less, the queer, or...the possibilities are almost endless.[73] Each has its own emotional valence and each has its own coloring, but each makes up a network of tropes the combined valuations of which constitute a position capable of being occupied by any one of a number of identities. At one time or another, European and American discourse has inscribed women, the working class, Eastern Europeans, Jews, blacks, criminals, coloreds, mulattos, Africans, drug addicts, Arabs, the insane, Asians, the Orient, the Third World, terrorists, and other others through tropes that have written their identity as inferior, often in terms of their being a mob or horde (sometimes passive and sometimes threatening) that is without culture, devoid of morals, infected with disease, lacking in industry, incapable of achievement, prone to be unruly, inspired by emotion, given to passion, indebted to tradition, or...whatever "we" are not. The "we," though, is rarely if ever articulated in its own terms, devoid of negative associations. As Etienne Balibar argued with respect to the function of racism in securing national identity:

> The racial-cultural identity of the "true nationals" remains invisible, but it is inferred from (and assured by) its opposite, the alleged, quasi-hallucinatory visibility of the "false nationals": Jews, "wops," immigrants, indios, natives, blacks. One might as well say

that it remains forever uncertain and in danger: that the "false" are *too* visible will never guarantee that the "true" are visible *enough*.[74]

Operating in terms of this logic, and replete with similar figurations of otherness, many of the foundational moments in the American experience have been performatively constituted. In chapter 5, some of these moments are considered; we will witness how the identity of the "true" American nationals has been indebted to a discursive economy of identity/difference.

Five

Imagining America

Representing "America"

No state possesses a prediscursive, stable identity, and no state is free from the tension between the various domains that need to be aligned for a political community to come into being, an alignment that is a response to, rather than constitutive of, a prior and stable identity. Yet for no state is this condition as central as it is for America. If all states are "imagined communities," devoid of ontological being apart from the many practices that constitute their reality, then America is the imagined community par excellence. For there never has been a country called "America," nor a people known as "Americans" from whom a national identity is drawn. There is a United States of America, and there are many who declare themselves to be "Americans" (though the U.S. census form does not list "American" as an ethnic option), but "America" only exists by virtue of people coming to live in a particular place. The histories of Americans are located in places other than the one in which they live, such that "the flag and the Pledge are, as it were, all we have."[1] Defined, therefore, more by absence than presence, America is peculiarly dependent on representational practices for its being. Arguably more than any other state, the imprecise process of imagination is what constitutes American identity.

In this context, the practices of "foreign policy" come to have a special importance. If the identity of the "true nationals" remains intrinsically elusive and "inorganic," it can only be secured by the effective and continual ideological demarcation of those who are "false" to the defining ideals. "Only in a country where it is so unclear what is American," argues Michael Kammen, "do people worry so much about the threat of things 'unAmerican.'"[2] Although the historicity of the constellation of dispositions associated with being "American" is often elided in the practices through which they are reproduced, it is possible to recover from some of the foundational moments that have constituted "America" a sense of the modes of inclusion and exclusion at work. Consequently, this chapter takes a look at some of the foreign policy practices in the pivotal moments of the discovery, colonization, and founding of the republic, moments that enriched the discursive economy of identity/difference and from which contemporary articulations are drawn.

America in the European Imagination

Long before anyone dreamed of exploring a new world, there existed in Europe a sense of what would be found. Through a series of myths and utopian writings, there existed an imaginary on the horizons of European thought that prepared the grounds for later encounters.[3] As Tzvetan Todorov has argued, the imaginary through which the conquest of America was understood is deeply implicated in the question of the "other": the "self" of the Christian conquests and the identity of the "New World" under Spanish dominion were made possible by the confrontation with Amerindians.[4] While Todorov takes this confrontation to be but one instance that allows him to address the ethical dilemma of how to deal with the other, he notes that it is in many ways an exemplary confrontation for American—even modern—identity: "Even if every date that permits us to separate any two periods is arbitrary, none is more suitable, in order to mark the beginning of the modern era, than the year 1492, the year Columbus crosses the Atlantic Ocean."[5] Of course, notwithstanding contemporary celebrations to the contrary, Columbus's voyage has little to do directly with what later became the United States of America. But there can be little doubt that, given its genocidal impact and philosophical resonances, this encounter profoundly though indirectly affected the country that now exercises hegemony over the term "America."

Columbus sets out on his voyage of discovery with a medieval mentality, an interpretive framework derived from the centrality of Christendom in "Europe" in which all encounters with difference were assigned meaning in terms unrelated to what might be considered an observational imperative. Far from being a modern empiricist, for Columbus "the decisive argument is an argument of authority, not of experience. He knows in advance what he will find; the concrete experience is there to illustrate a truth already possessed, not to be interrogated according to preestablished rules in order to seek the truth."[6]

The emergence of America into world history is a product of this period of transition between the medieval and the modern. But, contrary to the conventional wisdom of historiography, this emergence is, as Edmundo O'Gorman has outlined, an act of invention rather than discovery.[7] For Columbus to have "discovered" America, he needed to have the intention of discovering something called America, or the land that became America needed to have an intrinsic being as America that revealed itself on physical contact. Neither precondition existed. Columbus's intention was to discover the eastern shores of Asia (hence the name "Indians" for the indigenous peoples of America), while the idea of territory having an essential quality is a metaphysical fantasy. But even when confronted with evidence that suggested the land he encountered was not Asia, he engaged in a variety of strategies to make experience amenable to predetermined authority. In each of his four voyages between 1492 and 1504, Columbus believed that "he had reached Asia, he was in Asia, and it was from Asia he returned. No one, nothing, to the day of his death, ever made him relinquish that cherished conviction."[8] This conviction was not surprising, because few in his time could have or would have dared to conceive of the existence of an independent continent.

The (geographical, as opposed to imaginary) impossibility of America was a consequence of the conceptions of the earth that prevailed in the late fifteenth century.[9] The globe was understood as a mixture of land and water in which the land formed an "Island of the Earth" comprising Europe, Africa, and Asia in the northern hemisphere. According to an oft-cited prophecy in the Book of Esdras (an Old Testament text in the Bible), the ratio of land to sea was six to one, which was taken to mean that all land larger than a small island was a contiguous part of the world island. The size of the world was such that it was possible for inhabitants to be unknown to one another, but the faith people had in the idea of a world island avoided invoking the theologically disreputable notion of separate antipodal lands, which would have challenged the belief in the singular origin of humanity. Although this prophecy was not the only understanding of the world's makeup with influence in this period, its argument against the existence of southern lands was commonly shared. Moreover, it was a prophecy frequently invoked by Columbus in his voyages. During his third voyage, upon encountering a freshwater river that suggested the land in sight was a large continent, Columbus declared that "I am also supported by the statements of Esdras in his fourth book, the sixth chapter... This work was approved by Saint Ambrose in his *Hexameron* and by Saint Augustine."[10]

This authority gave Columbus a geographical picture in which his likely destination consisted of a peninsula at the southernmost extremity of Asia, with the possibility of a second peninsula to the west of that, before he would encounter India. In addition, he knew that there was an extensive archipelago just off the eastern shore of Asia that included the island later known as Japan.[11] With this geographical template firmly entrenched, Columbus did not allow it to be contradicted by experiential evidence.

On the first voyage, when told by the indigenous people that the land of Cuba was an island and not part of the landmass of Asia as he believed, Columbus discredited his Indian informers in terms of questionable relevance to the issue at hand: "And since these are bestial men who believe that the whole world is an island and who do not know what the mainland is, and have neither letters nor long-standing memories, and since they take pleasure only in eating and being with their women, they said this was an island."[12] On another occasion this faith led Columbus to misconstrue the information being imparted. When the Amerindians spoke the word *Cariba*, by which they designated the cannibal inhabitants of the islands (subsequently the Caribbean), Columbus took them to be saying *Caniba*, which referred to the subjects of the Grand Khan, to whose Asian lands Columbus was attempting to proceed. At the same time as he (mis)interpreted the word in that way, Columbus understood the Amerindians to be speaking the Spanish word for *dog*, thus suggesting to him that the people of the Khan had dogs' heads. Knowing this to be preposterous (but without divulging the means by which the Amerindians could have spoken Spanish), Columbus concluded that they must be lying and that therefore they were in the service of the Khan, once more buttressing his belief that he was in Asia.[13] On the second voyage to the same region, he forced the crew of his ship — in front of a notary, with witnesses, and under threat of physical punishment and massive fines — to sign a declaration that the coastline of Cuba, which they had unsuccessfully explored, was too long to be that of an island, thereby confirming that the eastern shore of Asia had been reached.[14]

On the third voyage, however, when Columbus encountered fresh water below the equator and invoked the authority of Esdras in support of the contention that he had come across a vast landmass, his immediate observations and geographical pretexts came into sharp conflict. The question was how to account for a mainland in the southern hemisphere.[15] If all land was contiguous, as Esdras argued, this land was part of the Island of the Earth. But if part of the world island protruded so far south, the passage to the Indian Ocean was not where he imagined it, thus making it impossible for the land of Cuba to be part of the southern peninsula of Asia. To maintain his passionately held beliefs about Cuba being a part of Asia, Columbus had the option of arguing that this southern land was separate from the world island, but this would have brought him into conflict with religious authority. Columbus sought a third way out of this dilemma. To maintain theological fidelity, he argued that the southern land was the paradise that sheltered the Garden of Eden and contained a vast spring from which all the world's rivers ran, thereby accounting for the fresh water.

This hypothesis, which kept Columbus's belief in Asia intact despite the challenge of his observations, came very close to discrediting the ancient and church-sanctioned view of the world. Notwithstanding the risks, a spate of state-sponsored explorations from 1499 to 1502 to the region Columbus had chartered confirmed beyond doubt the existence of a southern landmass. The question of whether this was part of the world island now depended more than ever on the existence or otherwise of an ocean passage, so two formally unrelated expeditions were mounted to provide an answer: the 1501–2 voyage of Amerigo Vespucci, and Columbus's fourth and final journey of 1502–4. Vespucci arrived at what is now Brazil and found no passage, despite sailing so far south that he reached the Antarctic Circle before returning to Lisbon. Columbus sailed to the Atlantic littoral of what is now Honduras, proceeded south and equally failed to find the supposed waterway to Asia.

Columbus, still believing that the landmass to the north was Asia, came to argue that he had encountered the second of the Asian peninsulas, and left open the possibility that the passage was even further south. On the other hand, having traveled so far south, Vespucci believed that this land was separate from the north and thus not part of Asia; as such, it was not part of the Island of the Earth. This was a startling conclusion, but it did not as yet undermine the classical conception of the world's geography. However, if the land to the south was connected with the land to the north that Columbus had encountered, it meant that a vast landmass was — in contradistinction to Esdras — not part of the world island. Vespucci did not immediately make the case for this radical position, but he established the conditions of possibility by which a landmass comparable to Europe, Africa, or Asia could be conceived. This was not something that Columbus's argument could allow for. It is thus Vespucci, not Columbus, who creates the space in which America can be placed. Although in 1504 Vespucci goes beyond his earlier conclusions to argue for the radical position that the north land and the south land are connected and distinct from Asia (in a letter that first uses the phrase *novus mundus,* or New World),[16] he is left in a quandary: advocating the notion of plural worlds but without an alternative conception with which to complete his case. Vespucci thus creates the space for America but cannot fill it.

The final step in the invention of America is taken by the cartographer Martin Waldseemüller, whose 1507 map, published by the Academy of Saint Dié in the *Cosmographiae Introductio,* was the first text to use the term *America* for the newly encountered lands.[17] Arguing that it should be called the Land of Amerigo (after Vespucci's Christian name), it follows the tradition of using feminine forms of nomenclature and attributes a specific being to the entity with the name *America,* such that the discoverer is written as masculine.[18] Thus, a full fifteen years after Columbus sighted what he was convinced was a part of Asia, America was conceived, inscribed, and gendered as a new and separate landmass.

The importance of appreciating that America was invented rather than discovered is twofold. First, the process of exploration and interpretation was one in which new interpretive possibilities were restrained and shaped by theological and geographical pretexts. Conceiving the New World, in contradistinction to the Old World, was more a battle between modern frames of reference and medieval understandings than it was a simple act of observation and discovery, thus supporting Todorov's contention that this was a transitional period heralding many features of the modern identity we associate with "the West." The invention of America shattered conventional understandings of time and space, helping to provide an impetus by which man could transgress the boundaries of the "cosmic jail"[19] constructed by Christendom. Along with developments in science such as Copernicus's radical reconceptualization of the heavens, the world was being remade in ways that made possible tendencies that would be central to the project of modernity: European dominion over other peoples and lands, the place of science in the construction and ordering of the social polity, and the rise of technocratic and instrumentalist rationalities. The emergence of America into world history was deeply implicated in this transitional period in which tradition was being overtaken by a modern frame of reference. Accordingly, "it was not by a chance coincidence that America appeared on the historical science of Western culture as the land of opportunities, of the future, and of freedom."[20] It was the interpretive opportunity provided by the struggle between intellectual freedom and traditional authority that made America possible in the first instance.

The second important fact about the invention of America is that it was the first (but far from the last) instance of historical erasure in understanding American (and later United States) identity. The removal of the interpretive practices that made America possible from the collective historical memory of the modern nation is an instance of what will later be a well-developed disposition to privilege spatial conceptions over temporal process. The conventional and ubiquitous understanding that Columbus "discovered" America has given rise to an interpretation of mythic proportions about the origins of the modern nation that was to follow from his actions. Unable to appreciate the complex process that made America possible, while at the same time being aware that Columbus's intention was to reach the eastern shores of Asia, the conventional understanding of American origins has been strongly influenced by the implicit notion that the land that became America possessed an essence or being that emerged with physical encounter. Examples of this can be witnessed in later historical discourses that talk about the *land* of freedom, the experience of the *frontier*, and the importance of *geopolitics* for security. In each instance, the spatial is given priority over the temporal and the historical.

The exploration and interpretation of the New World is a historical moment of significant proportions in the development of the modern identity. It is a moment of intertextuality in which traditional modes of representation struggle to make sense of contemporary observations. It is a moment in which (inter)national relations are promulgated between divergent groups. And it is a moment when the intertextual and (inter)national relations are implicated in interracial relations.[21] In the invention of America, the confrontation between the European, Spanish, and Christian "self" and the "other" of the indigenous peoples is an encounter of lasting significance for the way in which it brings to the New World the orientations toward difference and otherness of the Old World.

Encountering Amerindians

Just as the geographical pretexts of medieval Europe guided the interpretations of those engaged in the process of exploration, so too the response to the indigenous peoples was the product of traditional dispositions. Indeed, it was the purpose and effect of Old World modes of interpretation to deny to the various communities of Amerindians their own discrete historicities.[22] Columbus again provides some pertinent examples. His observations of people are recorded in accounts of the landscape that describe them as only one among many objects in the new territory: the transcribed journal of November 25, 1492, reports that "hitherto, things had gone better and better for [Columbus], in that he had discovered so many lands as well as woods, plants, fruits and flowers as well as the people." On their nature, Columbus's first recorded observation of the indigenous people is that "presently they saw naked people."[23] In a similar vein, the report to the Spanish crown of Alvar Nuñez Cabeza de Vaca (a conquistador who survived a disastrous expedition that began in Spanish Florida in 1527 with three hundred men and ended eight years later in New Mexico with four men) opens with "not merely a report of positions and distances, flora and fauna, but of the customs of the numerous, barbarous people I talked with and dealt among."[24] Cabeza de Vaca's first detailed observation of the Amerindians echoes that of Columbus: "All the Indians we had so far seen in Florida had been archers. They loomed big and naked and from a distance looked like giants. They were handsomely proportioned, lean, agile, and strong."[25] In both accounts, amplified by discussions of the lack of customs, lack of religion, and apparent similarity among the indigenous peoples, the Spaniards clearly regarded the Amerindians as "culturally virgin, a blank page awaiting the Spanish and Christian inscription."[26]

In the encounter of the "self" with the "other," it was the Christian identity of the self that was privileged. Both the journals of Columbus and the report of Cabeza de Vaca are replete with self-descriptions of the Europeans as "Christians" without more than the odd reference to themselves as "Spaniards." When the influential theologian Bartolomé de Las Casas ventures an analysis of his identity at the beginning of his text on the indigenous peoples of the New World, he writes that he is "a Christian, a religious, a bishop, a Spaniard, and a subject of the King of Spain."[27] Equally, Columbus engages in the self-ascription of the Christian identity when, confronted with Amerindians talking excitedly among themselves about the presence of the Spanish, he concludes that "they are credulous; they know that there is a God in the heavens, and remain convinced that that is where we have come from."[28]

The priority accorded Christian identity had a number of repercussions for the Amerindians. It was the aim of the Spanish authorities and colonizers to spread the word of the Scriptures to everyone they encountered. Notwithstanding their erroneous perception that the Amerindians lacked customs, religion, and standards of civility, this program, through the belief that all humanity sprang from Adam and Eve, did grant the indigenous people the status of people, rather

than that of animals or the children of the devil.[29] As *The Requirement* —
a proclamation to be read to the Amerindians at every landing by the
Spaniards—declared, it was the aim of the authorities to "notify and
make known to you, as best we can, that the Lord our God, Living
and Eternal, created the Heaven and the Earth, and one man and one
woman, of whom you and I, and all the men of the world, were and
are descendants, and all those who come after us."[30]

The Requirement, of course, threatened war, forcible conversion,
and the enslavement of the Amerindians should they decide against
the Holy Catholic Faith once they had been informed of it.[31] But it
did so with the assumption that Amerindians had the human capacity to adopt Christian beliefs given the correct direction and induce-
ment. Cabeza de Vaca refers to them as "wild, *untaught* savages,"[32]
while Columbus writes of his intention to take several Amerindians
to Spain so that "upon their return they might be the interpreters of
the Christians and might adopt our customs and faith." He declares
that "Your Highness may have great joy of them, for soon you will
have made them into Christians and will have instructed them in the
good manners of your kingdoms."[33] Moreover, the adoption of the
Christian faith was not just the correct theological path, but the hall-
mark of culture and civilization. It enabled the adoption of customs,
good manners, arts, sciences, and industry. The latter is obvious in a
remark by Cabeza de Vaca, who wrote that one of his scouts described
new territory by saying "that the ground looked as if cattle had tram-
pled it and therefore that this must be a country of Christians."[34]

Although the basic humanity (albeit in a "barbarous" form) of the
Amerindians was not doubted, and the conversion and civilizing function of the conquistadors was not questioned, there was a considerable debate among the nobility and intelligentsia of imperial Spain
concerning how the Amerindians should be treated given these ends.
While the capacity of all humans to adopt Christianity and civilization
was acknowledged, there were two different orientations as to how
successful and desirable the Amerindians would be as candidates
for this transition. Columbus indicates this tension when he remarks
on the suitability of the Amerindians for slavery, suggesting that "they
are fit to be ruled" and speculating on how the idolatrous, cannibalis-
tic, and warlike Amerindians could be transported as slaves to Europe
like herds of cattle.[35] For Columbus, then, Amerindians could be Christians or slaves: no alternative identity was possible. But for Cabeza
de Vaca, the orientation of violence and the predisposition toward
slavery were not appropriate. Toward the end of his report, he comments that "clearly, to bring all these people to Christianity and sub-

jection to Your Imperial Majesty, they must be won by kindness, the only certain way."[36] These two orientations, which Todorov has designated as *enslavement* ideology versus *colonialist* ideology,[37] marked the parameters of the discourse on the Amerindians in what was the most significant debate of these issues, the Valladolid encounter in 1550 between the scholars Bartolomé de Las Casas and Ginés de J. Sepúlveda.

When new laws were promulgated by the authority of the Spanish crown to prevent slavery and ensure that the Amerindians were treated in ways that encouraged them to accept the Christian faith,[38] those conquistadors who were incensed sought arguments such as those of the royal historian Sepúlveda to defend their practices of enslavement. Drawing inspiration from Aristotle's *Politics*, which he had translated into Latin, Sepúlveda argued that hierarchy, and not equality, was the natural state of human affairs. He maintained:

> The greatest philosophers declare that such wars may be undertaken by a very civilized nation against uncivilized people who are more barbarous than can be imagined, for they are absolutely lacking in any knowledge of letters, do not know the use of money, generally go about naked, even the women, and carry burdens on their shoulders and backs like beasts for great distances. Moreover here is the proof of their savage life, like that of wild beasts: their execrable and prodigious immolations of human victims to demons; the fact of devouring human flesh; of burying alive their chieftains' wives with their dead husband and other similar crimes.[39]

Sepúlveda's views were representative of a considerable body of opinion, even in the church. The Dominican Tomás Ortiz wrote to the Council of the Indies in Spain with this opinion on the nature of the indigenous people:

> On the mainland they eat human flesh. They are more given to sodomy than any other nation. There is no justice among them. They go naked. They have no respect either for love or for virginity. They are stupid and silly. They have no respect for truth, save when it is to their advantage. They are unstable. They have no knowledge of what foresight means. They are ungrateful and changeable...They are brutal. They delight in exaggerating their defects. There is no obedience among them, or deference on the part of the young for the old, nor of the son for the father. They are incapable of learning. Punishments have no effect on them...They eat fleas, spiders and worms raw, whenever they find them. They exercise none of the human arts or industries. When taught the mysteries of our religion, they say that these things may suit Castilians, but not them, and they

do not wish to change their customs. They are beardless, and if sometimes hairs grow, they pull them out... The older they get the worse
they become. About the age of ten or twelve years, they seem to have
some civilization, but later they become like real brute beasts. I may
therefore affirm that God has never created a race more full of vice
and composed without the least mixture of kindness or culture...
The Indians are more stupid than asses, and refuse to improve in
anything.[40]

Such views, though widespread (particularly in the colonies), were
not part of the accepted orthodoxy at the imperial seat in Spain. Las
Casas had earlier argued his case before the scholars of the university at Alcalá de Henares, after which those assembled condemned
Sepúlveda's opinion as "unsound." Later, Las Casas managed to per-
suade the crown to suppress a book by his theological rival, Francisco López de Gomara, the secretary and biographer of Hernando
Cortés, which claimed that the Amerindians' principal god was the
devil; that they engaged in public sexual intercourse; that they were
sodomites, liars, ingrates, and that they were "stupid, wild, insensate
asses," among a host of other sins.[41] And when the Council of the Indies met to hear the arguments from both Las Casas and Sepúlveda
at Valladolid, the New World "conquistas" of enslavement were judged
to be evil, unlawful, and unjust.[42]

In his defense of the Amerindians, Las Casas took not Aristotle
but Christ as the point of departure for his argument, maintaining
that the fundamental opposition is between believer and nonbeliever.
But he went further, arguing that equality should be the basis of all
human policy, although such declarations were made in the name of
a very specific religion. Moreover, his descriptions of the Amerindians endow them with desirable Christian virtues:

> The Indians are of such gentleness and decency, that they are more
> than the other nations of the entire world, supremely fitted and pre-
> pared to abandon the worship of idols and to accept, province by
> province and people by people, the word of God and the preaching
> of the truth... Their rites and customs differ, but they all have in
> common the traits of simplicity, peacefulness, gentleness, humility,
> generosity, and of all the sons of Adam, they are without exception
> the most patient. In addition, they are eminently ready to be brought
> to the knowledge of their Creator and to the Faith.[43]

The massive contradictions between the accounts of violent, can-
nibalistic Amerindians and those of decent, peaceful, and humble peoples are enough to decisively indicate the power of authority over
experience in apprehending the indigenous people of the New World.

Both Sepúlveda and Las Casas argued about the origin and nature of the Amerindians in terms that were deductive, textual, and exegetical, with little or no reliance on the process of observation or experience.[44] But what is probably most startling about the encounters with the Amerindians is the way this evidence of diversity was so easily assimilated, failing as it did to unsettle any previously established modes of understanding in Europe.[45] Indeed, the representations employed in the New World returned to Europe to function as modes of internal differentiation, such that the subaltern classes of the continent were often understood in terms that derived their force from the Indies.[46]

The ease with which the differences of the New World were accommodated is most likely a function of the role "paganism" played in Europe at the time. Because the "Europe" of this period was a multiple acephalous federation secured by the transcendental authority of Christendom, the hierarchy of Christian/pagan was the most pervasive organizing principle for difference. As the most inclusive form of otherness, the category "pagan" was originally derived from the Latin *pagus,* meaning "of the countryside" or "rustic," giving it an additional secular dimension.[47] This was reinforced by the overlap between the category "pagan" and the category "barbarian," which had come into greater prominence in this period through the recovery of knowledge from the period of antiquity. Although the concept of "barbarian" as a category of difference predated the Greeks, they invested the term with significance as a concept for those who were unacquainted with Greek culture.[48] What was particularly powerful about the category "barbarian" was that it was not in any way differentiated; the Greeks did not rank those to whom it applied into a typology or hierarchy, thus making it possible to subsume incredible differences under this one sign and avoid the implications of diversity.[49]

The debate between Las Casas and Sepúlveda at Valladolid in 1550 can thus be understood as a confrontation between the two major hierarchies of identity/difference at work in medieval Europe: that of Christian/pagan in Las Casas's argument, and civilized/barbarian in Sepúlveda's.[50] There was obviously considerable overlap between these categories of otherness; pagans were most likely to be thought of as uncivilized, while Christianity itself was often the distinguishing characteristic of civilization. But there was an important distinction between these two orientations toward otherness that has significant implications in terms of the practice of colonialism or enslavement of the Amerindians. The dichotomy of Christian/pagan was not fixed by any intrinsic characteristics of humanity; one could move from the status of pagan to that of Christian by an act of reason in which one adopted the faith (one could also presumably shift in the other direction). In this context, the dichotomy of civilized/barbarian was more fixed and thought to represent more entrenched and "natural" distinctions, exemplified in Aristotle's characterization of the slave as an intrinsically inferior being. The former dichotomy is one in which identity is formulated as the starting point. The possibility of movement between the categories of Christian and pagan presupposes that all are seen as human, having the same rights and capacities (although unfulfilled) as the higher standard against which they are judged. This in-principle postulate of identity leads to the practice of colonialism as the values and figurations of the self are projected onto the equal but as yet culturally blank other. On the other hand, the latter dichotomy — of civilized/barbarian — begins from the postulate of difference, but difference in terms of the self being the higher and regulative ideal to which the other is lower and inferior. In this instance there is no possibility of projection from the self onto the other because the divide is too great and fixed. Consequently, with no hope for a civilizing mission, the practice of enslavement is the only appropriate strategy.[51]

Notwithstanding the significance of this distinction between orientations toward otherness, which proceeds from the postulate of identity versus the postulate of difference, there is one thing they share. Whenever these distinctions are called into service to fix ambiguity and judge diversity, they do so in terms of an unrequited egocentrism which, given the history of exploration and interpretation, is concomitant with Eurocentrism and what Derrida termed the "metaphysics of presence."[52] As Todorov notes, each of the orientations toward otherness begins with "the identification of our own values with values in general, of our *I* with the universe."[53] This is evident in that, his disagreements with Sepúlveda aside, Las Casas did not at this time want to end the dominion of Spain over the Amerindians and allow for self-determination. He simply wanted to replace the violence of Sepúlveda's enslavement via the military with the conduct of colonization by the priests.[54] This orientation toward the Amerindians was codified in the Royal Ordinances on "Pacification" (a term that reappeared nearly four hundred years later during the war in Vietnam) issued by the Spanish crown in 1573. These ordinances outlined the approved means by which "the Indians [are] to be pacified and indoctrinated, but in no way are they to be harmed, for all we seek is their welfare and their conversion."[55] The Spaniards believed that the manifest advantages of their presence — the conditions of justice, peace, and security, the "good habits and the custom of wearing shoes and clothes," the freedom from "burdens and servitude," and the many commodities and crafts they had made known to the Amerindians from Spain so that "they live excellently" — would ensure that many among the indigenous population would continue to "embrace our Holy Faith and render obedience to us."[56]

Las Casas was to diverge from the established and officially sanctioned policy of pacification in the period after the Valladolid debate by arguing that "there is no longer a true God (ours), but a coexistence of possible universes: if someone considers it as true."[57] As such, Las Casas's reformulated position led him to renounce hierarchy in favor of equality to the extent that he argued for the relative nature of the category "barbarian." Accordingly he came to argue — in contrast to his earlier views, without arousing any official attention, and obviously to no avail — that the Spanish crown should renounce its colonial possessions and wage war only against the conquistadors, who were seeking to impose values where they had no right. Las Casas's progressive position is of interest not only for the way it foreshadows later intellectual debates about how to understand and relate to others, but for the fact that in having come so far from the enslavement and colonialist ideologies of his time, it is still finally unable to shrug off a persistent logocentrism. Assuming the relativity of the category "barbarian" means that because "we" locate ourselves in this dichotomy, so do "they." While not privileging one or the other side of the civilized/barbarian dualism, it presupposes the universality of the dichotomy based on European experience alone. As argued in chapter 4, there is a certain pervasiveness to distinctions drawn along the boundary of the identity/difference categorization, but there are grounds for doubting the universality of the civilized/barbarian dichotomy that makes the category of "barbarian" relative.

In other civilizations where the category has been employed as an instrument of social differentiation, it has exhibited more nuanced features. In early India, those who had come into contact with Greek voyagers regarded the latter as "barbarians," but it was not a term that was rigidly dualistic, instead being overlaid with many cultural and religious distinctions that blurred its meaning.[58] What is distinctive about civilizations like India, Greece, and Spain (among others), however, is that they conceive of time as linear and progressive, so that what comes later is of a higher stage than that which existed previously. In other words, societies with this conception of time that regard themselves as civilizations require the category of "barbarian," (or "primitive," "pagan," and the like) to distinguish themselves from the period and culture prior—and hence inferior—to themselves. In contrast, societies with a conception of cyclical, repetitive time neither require nor generate an idea of "civilization" by which to define their identity and locate themselves in an evolutionary schema.[59] To be sure, Amerindian peoples had a propensity to formulate their problematic of identity in ethnocentric terms, but that logic did not compel them to adopt the terms of Eurocentrism (which needs to be understood as a historically specific form of ethnocentrism). Indeed, in the case of Europeans and Amerindians, there was little reciprocity between the two in their figurations of otherness: the Amerindians were remarkably unpreoccupied with their foreigners.[60] Even in the hostile environment of the conquest, when their very survival was at stake, no Amerindian tribe proved willing or eager to "civilize" itself in the terms laid out by the Europeans.[61]

The Irish Pretext

The Spanish encounter with the New World was a world-historical and paradigmatic moment in the relations between Europe and its others that constituted America. In terms of (the United States of) America, however, the English experience of colonization in Ireland in the late sixteenth century provides something of an interpretive bridge between the Spanish encounters with the Amerindians and the colonial experience in America. Those who undertook actions of conquest in Ireland—actions that were privately financed rather than state sponsored—were familiar with the Spanish debates on the nature of the Amerindians and later personally involved in the colonization of America.[62] The Gaelic Irish (as opposed to the Old English who were descended from participants in the Norman conquests of the twelfth and thirteenth centuries) were understood by the English colonizers in terms akin to those applied to the Amerindians by the Spaniards. Indeed, the figurations used to represent the Irish were an instance of the "Indianization of Europe," whereby the experience of the New World served as a resource for differentiation in the Old.[63] When Elizabeth I commended the Earl of Essex for his service in Ulster, which included the massacre of the Gaelic chief and two hundred of his followers during the Christmas of 1574, she spoke of his alacrity in bringing "that rude and barbarous nation to civility and acknowledging their duty to God and to us."[64] Where the boundary of civility lay, however, was not always clear. When the English military governor of Munster encountered resistance to his colonization efforts, he had the heads of slain Irish line the path that surrendering Irish had to walk before swearing an oath of allegiance.[65]

While the English conquest of Ireland has close parallels to the Spanish encounter with the Amerindians, it differs in one important respect that indicates something important about the English self. Unlike the "paganism" and "heathenism" immediately ascribed to the Amerindians because of their alleged lack of religion, the Irish seemed to be in a more favorable position due to their basic religious affinity with the imperial power. No one engaged in the conquest of Ireland ever doubted that even the Gaels were Christians, something that could potentially have been the basis for better treatment for the Irish. What should have been a saving grace for the indigenous inhabitants, however, was soon subverted in the colonizers' efforts to achieve their goals. As extreme Protestants, the English found even the Catholicism of the loyal area around Dublin known as "the Pale" worthy of harsh criticism. In this context, the Christianity of the "barbarous" areas beyond the Pale was thought to have deviated even from the despised Roman practices to incorporate (as was the case in much of medieval Europe) pre-Christian practices.

Accordingly, their Christianity notwithstanding, the Gaels were branded as "pagan." This seeming inconsistency derived from the English understanding of the relationship between civilization and Christianity. They acknowledged that one could be civilized without being Christian (as in the case of the Romans), but insisted that it was not possible to be Christian without being civilized. Christianity was thus the higher value, and to have considered the Gaels as fellow Christians — aside from the obvious difficulty of that making them equals — would have been to regard them as civilized. On the other hand, to understand them as "pagan" (then the most inclusive form of otherness available) enabled them to be treated as "barbarians."[66]

Observational or doctrinal precision was therefore no obstacle for power politics. Edmund Spenser wrote of the Irish that "they are all Papists by their profession, but in the same so blindly and brutishly informed for the most part as that you would think them atheists or infidels."[67] Tremayne went further and "found" religion totally lacking in Munster: "They regard no oath, they blaspheme, they murder, commit whoredom, hold no wedlock, ravish, steal and commit all abomination without scruple or conscience."[68] Barnaby Rich took the next logical step and declared (with just a touch of hyperbole) that because the Irish preferred to "live like beasts, void of law and all good order," and because they were "more uncivil, more uncleanly, more barbarous and more brutish in their customs and demeanours, than in any other part of the world that is known," ever more severe repression by the colonizers was not only justified but required.[69] As a consequence, the English did not fulfill their vow to "convert" the Irish to Christianity on the grounds that they were too barbarous to warrant the effort.

The English experience in Ireland indicated a disposition among the Protestants to take any margin of difference and transform it into a condition of complete otherness, regardless (or perhaps because of) the lack of distance between the self and the qualities of the other. Certainly, when the other is rigidly demarcated, it more often than not signals the existence of a fragile, endangered, and insecure self. That the English in Ireland subverted the Christianity of the Gaels and transformed it into evidence of paganism and barbarism said much about their inability to affirm their own identity without violence. This confrontation stands as an ominous precursor to colonial America, given that the extreme Protestantism of the English in Ireland was unmistakable in the Puritanism of the Pilgrims in America.

The Puritan Legacy

The Puritans were not the first Europeans to settle in North America, but they were the first to undertake the logistical work and ideological justifications required for long-term colonization. On board the *Mayflower*, shortly before their landing in 1620, the Puritans declared their intent to "combine ourselves together into a Civil Body Politike, for our better ordering and preservation."[70] Between 1630 and 1660, some twenty thousand Puritans came to America with the intention of establishing a new and permanent society. Officially driven from England because of their efforts to "purify" the Church of England by removing the remaining vestiges of "popery," the Puritans were seeking a place in which they could complete the work of the Reformation. Having previously argued that England would be the "Elect Nation"—John Milton spoke of England "holding up, as from a Hill, the new Lampe of *saving light* to all Christendome"[71]—Puritans came to regard New England and the other American colonies as the secular home of spiritual virtue. For some, this transformation of "geography into eschatology" was a blasphemous declaration of the ability to attain religious perfection on earth.[72] But for most, the exhortations to faith in the political sermons known as jeremiads—exhortations that exhibited an "evangelism of fear" designed to incite the "new chosen people" to their "destined progress" in the "city on a hill," "New Eden," or "American Jerusalem"—were no more than the means by which they would discharge their mission. In this context, the Puritans provided a powerful "myth of America," in which colonization was the fulfillment of scriptural prophecy and the subsequent American self was the product of divine intent; this mythical discourse was written into the foreign policy texts of the postwar period, as chapter 1 made clear. As a consequence, the Puritans regarded the land they came to as belonging solely to themselves, and the people and objects encountered as obstacles to their destiny.[73]

All identities in this period were endangered, but for the Puritans — possessing the fragility of identity and the rigidity of distinctions exhibited by the Protestants in Ireland, combined with the more extreme foreign-ness of the American environment — the sense of endangerment was particularly acute. The character of Puritan society in colonial America was that of a closed Christian community relatively homogenous as a result of shared religious convictions. Though transformed in later years into a merchant-dominated civic polity, it never lost the ideal of a well-ordered and confined self and society. But a well-ordered and confined self as the grounds for a secure identity and stable society is not something achieved without cost. As a consequence, the early colonials "defined themselves less by the vitality of their affirmations than by the violence of the abjurations."[74]

The sense of endangeredness that underpinned the fragility of the Puritan identity can be seen in the treatment of those within their homogenous community who were considered to pose a threat. To this end, the well-documented cases of Thomas Morton and Anne Hutchinson provide excellent examples that echo Hobbes's desire to smooth the stones of irregular figure. Morton was persecuted by the authorities of the Massachusetts Bay Colony in ways that flagrantly breached English law.[75] His "crime" was to have fraternized with the indigenous people, participating in activities that offended the sensibilities of the authorities. Morton had established a trading post on his property at Merry Mount and had lived peacefully among the indigenous people, behaving in ways that brought charges of paganism, barbarism, and sexual licentiousness. Morton's "crime" was not that he broke English statutes, but that he posed the most subversive question to the Puritans in America. In his book, *The New Canaan* (1637), Morton asked who the real wild people in the new colony were. His answer: "I have found the Massachusetts Indian[s] more full of humanity than the Christians, and have had much better quarter with them; yet I observed not their humours but they mine."[76] By finding the preconception of barbarous, uncivilized, and pagan natives to be unwarranted, he threatened the very being of the Puritan communities, for which he was twice deported and once imprisoned and fined. Anne Hutchinson, believing that the men of colonial society preached a "covenant of works" — whereby a person's salvation is made possible through earthly labors — to enhance their position in society, preached a "covenant of grace" to large gatherings of women, arguing that salvation was provided only by God and was not dependent on temporal achievement. Such action struck at the foundations of Puritan conceptions of an ordered polity, fermenting what became known as the Antinomian controversy. John Winthrop, the governor of the colony, employed sociomedical discourse to argue that the Antinomians were a "sore" on the colony for their teaching of "poison" and "venom." Bringing accusations of promiscuity, witchcraft, and papism, the authorities tried Hutchinson and her followers in 1638 and banished them from the colony — a relatively lenient punishment given that religious dissenters were often subject to bodily disfigurement or capital punishment.[77]

Colonial Identity: The Indian Other

If the fragility of identity among the settlers was great enough to construct dangers from within, the context of their settlement only exacerbated this anxiety and manifested itself in fears about what lay without. Distant from the familiar environs of Europe, the early colonists found themselves subject to an estrangement from traditional identities that magnified their condition of endangerment. In this context, the early descriptions of the people they encountered closely parallel the structure and content of Columbus's accounts of the Amerindians, with attention paid to physical attributes and behavior, suggesting that the Amerindians were seen as culturally virgin awaiting a European inscription. As such, the frames of reference through which the indigenous people could be understood were drawn from the civilized/barbarian argument of Sepúlveda and the Christian/pagan distinction of Las Casas. But the distinctions between these two modes of apprehension were not much argued by the English, who often combined both in a thorough condemnation of the Amerindians. For example, a Puritan settler troubled by the need to fulfill scriptural prophecy by conquering others' possessions combined the pagan and barbaric qualities of the indigenous peoples. In answer to the rhetorical question "What right have I to go live in the heathen's country?" he said:

> This then is a sufficient reason to prove our going thither to live lawful: their land is spacious and void. and there are few and do but run over the grass ... They are not industrious, neither have art, science, skill or faculty to use either the land or the commodities of it ... As the ancient patriarchs therefore removed from straiter places

into more roomy, where the land lay idle and waste, and none used it . . . so it is lawful now to take a land which none useth, and make use of it.[78]

Unlike the Spanish, however, who saw little evidence of religion among the Amerindians, observers such as Captain John Smith in Virginia acknowledged that the "savages" were not so savage as to have no religion.[79] But the religion they had was one in which they worshiped the devil and any frightening material thing beyond their control. The Amerindians who encountered the English were thus in a worse position than those who encountered the Spanish. To the Spanish, the Amerindians' lack of religion meant that they needed to be civilized by their imperial masters. From the English perspective, on the other hand, one had not only to teach the Amerindians about civilization and then Christianity; one first had to make them forget their own religion. In this context, it is revealing that accounts of the missionary enterprise undertaken by the English referred to the need to "reduce" the Amerindians from savagery to civilization. As the opposite of the usual "raising" of souls to a higher plane of development, it indicated that traditional customs and ingrained habits had to be removed before there could be any hope of progress. To this end, the missionaries prescribed a "veritable pharmacopoeia of remedies for their savage condition."[80] But the English efforts at proselytizing among the Amerindians were — given their starting assumptions — halfhearted at best. While the French accepted Indian culture and sought to convert as many to Catholicism as they could, regardless of their mode of living, the English insistence that civilization was a prerequisite for Christianity doomed their limited missionary work to failure.[81]

What distinguished early English encounters from those of the Spanish was, therefore, that the English ascribed to the Amerindians a more limited sense of cultural virginity. While the Spanish saw the potential for civilization among the Amerindians by coming to understand them in terms of the Christian/pagan dichotomy, the English developed a more rigid interpretation. The greater fragility of English identity when contrasted to that of the continental Europeans (a difference perhaps attributable to the Spanish and Portuguese experience of domestic cultural heterogeneity through the Jews, Berbers, and Moors, in contrast to the relative homogeneity of England),[82] meant that the nuances and differences between the two dualized understandings of the Spanish were obscured by the English. While Sepúlveda and Las Casas could engage in an extended debate over the relative merits of their distinctions and the differing outcomes for Spanish colonial policy, the English demonstrated in their conquest of Ireland a readiness to conflate the two dichotomies in a manner that enhanced the conquest of a people whose differences with the English were far less than those of the Amerindians. And the greater the margin of difference, the greater the temptation to ascribe otherness. Therefore, while accounts such as Smith's initially operated in terms of the civilized/barbarian distinction, they were reinforced by employing both the civilized/barbarian and the Christian/ pagan dichotomies in order to locate the Amerindians as so completely other that they could not aspire to the qualities of the self.

Of course, not all colonial opinion and action with respect to the Indian conformed to this pattern. Some settlers wrote descriptions of the Amerindians more akin to the image of the noble savage than to the evil creatures Smith and others claimed to have observed.[83] Reminiscent of Las Casas's and Cabeza de Vaca's declarations for a more humane policy toward the indigenous peoples, such arguments encompassed the orientation toward otherness that begins with the postulate of identity, which assumes complete cultural virginity, and ends with the policy of colonization. But the very limited nature of the settlers' missionary attempts stands as testament to the limited success of this argument in persuading colonial authorities of its merits.

The rigid English attitude toward the other reflected in their initial confrontation with the Amerindians was but one instance of a recurring propensity to attempt a clear distinction between themselves and those they encountered. With this disposition, the English differed somewhat from other European peoples in their attitudes toward the indigenous peoples of the Americas. The Spanish, Portuguese, and French—notwithstanding the extreme violence and social subservience exacted upon the people they colonized—sought to incorporate those people into their societies. In contrast, the English wanted to have little if anything to do with the indigenous people. The relationship between self and other that their position initially embodied thus went beyond the dichotomy of enslavement and colonization that Todorov outlined. The English regarded the Amerindians of this region as so totally other that their pejorative attitude exceeded the condition of otherness that proceeds from the postulate of difference. No event more vividly demonstrates this than the war against the Pequots, in which an entire tribe of Amerindians was massacred in an act of revenge.[84]

Accordingly, the interpretation of the difference between self and other that the English constructed was so complete that even the hierarchical power relations of enslavement did not sufficiently mark a clear boundary between the English and the Amerindians. Extermination, rather than colonization or enslavement, was the early English response to otherness. When this could not be achieved, physical separation was employed. Architectural constructions, such as the palisades strung from the James River to the York River in Virginia, which created a colonial "pale" that Amerindians could enter only with special permission, were the most obvious indicators of this attitude of complete otherness.[85] The laws concerning contact between people were another.

In the colonies of continental Europe, miscegenation was a common and open part of life. For example, an account of Spanish landholders in Hispaniola found that of the married men, ninety-two had Spanish wives and fifty-four had Amerindian wives.[86] But the English colonies in the West Indies and America attempted to outlaw such contact between the different peoples. Sexual relations between English settlers and Amerindians in colonial America were rare and always considered worthy of severe reproach, the opprobrium that Thomas Morton attracted in Massachusetts being a prime example. Legislation on the question sought to prevent "abominable mixture and spurious issue" and declared that mixed couples would be "banished forever."[87] Where sexual contact did occur, the laws pertaining to the children who resulted refused to recognize their liminal status. In colonial America, English attitudes and edicts concerning mulattos did not allow for any other possibility than people being "white" or "non-white," thereby designating all children who did not have two "white" parents as "black." As Winthrop Jordan observed, this meant that if the English colonist could not restrain his sexual nature and maintain the boundary between the groups, he could at least reinstate the distinction by rejecting the fruits of his exploits.[88]

Another form of intermixture between the English and the Amerindians that was legislated against was the propensity of some settlers to leave European society and live with the indigenous people. These "white Indians" were often captives taken by the Indians in conflict with the English who refused to return to colonial society even when given the opportunity. While English accounts portrayed the barbarism and heathenism of the Amerindian way of life, many of the captives found a form of social organization in which they perceived a strong sense of community, social equality, mobility, and freedom. The disjunction between the accounts of those in colonial society who encouraged legislatures (like that of Connecticut in 1642) to establish severe punishment for those who left for the Amerindians' "profane" way of life, and the stories of returning captives about the quality of their treatment, is further testament to the fragility of the English identity in colonial America. As Kammen has concluded, "More so than the Spanish and the French... English colonists were inclined to gauge their personae in terms of not becoming barbaric like the Amerindians. No theme runs more persistently or anxiously through the sermons, essays, and histories of colonial America than this one: Are we degenerating to the crudeness and paganism of the primeval inhabitants?"[89]

In one sense, this was a legitimate question: in colonial America, the distinction between inside and outside, between English and Indian, was often effectively blurred. And the boundaries between inside and outside are only constantly reinscribed when the distinction between inside and outside is ambiguous and in need of differentiation. The intensity of the concern and the tenacity of the efforts to draw distinct boundaries between the English and the Indian serve as evidence, not of the natural separateness of each, but of the actual fluidity and porousness of the boundary between their identities. The Amerindians were both inside and outside; they were deeply implicated in the creation of every mainland colony by the English. Every "discoverer" had Amerindian guides, every colonizer had Amerindian instruction on sites and crops, and every settlement traded with the Amerindians for much-needed supplies.[90] At the same time, the conditions of the early colonies were such that any attempt to maintain the fiction of civility required the externalization of barbarism. In Virginia, the first settlers endured what was known as the "starving time" — the first ten years after 1609 — for the harshness of conditions and the paucity of supplies. They lived in cavelike holes and were fortunate if they had one ladle of barley to eat per day. Colonists roamed the woods looking for nuts and berries, and when even they ran out, they dug up graves (theirs as well as Indian burial sites) to eat the flesh from the corpses. Cannibalism among the Europeans was not confined to the period after landing. Even as late as 1741, a sloop that took sixteen weeks for the trip from Belfast to Boston arrived with forty-six of its original one hundred and six passengers dead from starvation; six of them had been eaten by the survivors.[91]

To aid in overcoming these dilemmas and fears, the settlers made conscious efforts to recreate the old amid the new. As Zuckerman argues, "Three thousand miles from all they took to be civilized, beset by a bewildering plenitude of possibility, they clung the more compulsively to accustomed English habits that set themselves the more resolutely against intrusions that whispered of other ways."[92] Most obviously, this condition manifested itself in the material forms of architecture and town planning. Even when they lived among forests rich in timber, the settlers began by importing prefabricated wooden houses from England. And like their imperial counterparts in Ireland, the colonists in America erected an array of barriers—hedges, gardens, walls, forts, fences, and palisades—to demarcate their territory on the inside from the forests and lands on the outside, which existed as "enemies, strange and evil, existing only to be cleared."[93]

The strategy of the early settlers was thus to contain the barbarism within by the constant declaration of civility among themselves in contradistinction to the perceived primitivism without. To this end, the settlers affirmed a fictitious identity based on an idealized and abstracted understanding of what it was to be English and civilized.[94] Given the gap between this understanding and their experience, they had to not only reproduce the past, but also suppress resistances in the present, so that there could be a distinct boundary between the self and the other. As such, the Indian other served, like Hobbes's argument about the state of nature, as a sanction or reproach warning of the fate awaiting colonists who were not sufficiently disciplined. Against their constructed and idealized notion of civility and decency, the alleged paganism and barbarity of the indigenous people was a constant reminder of what colonists would become if differences inside and out were not confined, contained, and controlled. In this context, the maintenance and rigorous enforcement of religious tradition in the Antinomian controversy, the unjust treatment handed to those like Thomas Morton who transgressed moral limits, and the violence perpetrated against the Pequot Indians, are only some of the examples pertinent to the multifaceted effort to inscribe colonial American identity.

For all the rigidity of the colonial American attitude toward the Indian, it was not fixed in stone forever. The complete otherness of the Indian disposition was lessened when the threats to English identity were thought to have diminished. As the English situation became less precarious with the end of the extensive Indian wars toward the end of the seventeenth century, the image of the Indian became less hostile and more the subject of anthropological curiosity.[95] This change did not presage a major transformation of the colonial identity, however. The boundary between inside and outside, self and other, is never static or singular. There are a multitude of boundaries implicated in the constitution and maintenance of identity, boundaries that are as much shifting gray areas as they are distinct lines. In the case of colonial America, there were a variety of other "others" to be found that served as points of differentiation.

One important, perhaps notorious, example is that of witchcraft. The latter part of the seventeenth century was a time of political turmoil and social tension throughout Europe and within the American colonies. The English revolution and the wars of continental Europe were matched by the colonies' protracted conflicts with the Amerindians. For Massachusetts, the conflict included the period between 1684 and 1692, which saw the abrogation of the colony's charter and a bloodless coup against the government imposed by London. It was at the end of this period that the witchcraft delusion rose to prominence in Salem.[96]

Witchcraft had a long if inglorious history throughout Europe. In the period between the fifteenth and eighteenth centuries, some tens and possibly hundreds of thousands of people (over 85 percent of whom were women) were executed for crimes for which there was no evidence. Some no doubt engaged in practices of sorcery, witchcraft, and black magic, but there is no recorded case in which any material evidence — or any evidence beyond the statement of accusation or confession secured under duress — was offered to substantiate the charges.[97] Such niceties of the law did not stand in the way of witchcraft's utility as a point of differentiation, especially in societies racked by turmoil. Interestingly, witchcraft in Europe peaked during the Thirty Years' War and ended as a mass phenomenon at the same time that the Peace of Westphalia divided the Catholics and Protestants of Europe and contributed to the rise of state sovereignty.[98] This suggests that witchcraft may have been an important instance of "foreign policy" in shifting the locus of identity between Christendom and the state. Certainly its transcultural qualities of extruding or expelling individuals or groups considered outside of the society in question (the details of which were obviously context-specific), suggest it operated as a pervasive strategy of otherness.[99]

This was certainly the case in Salem, where by the time the panic had passed, hundreds of people had been accused, one hundred and fifty charged and imprisoned, and nineteen executed. For in Salem, as in other locations, the "crime" of witchcraft was different from other contraventions of the law: it involved not a material action or event, but an alleged private and ideational experience. Specifically, the statements of accusation (which, as in Europe, were used with forced confessions as the only form of evidence against the accused) professed that the guilty were part of a conspiracy to subvert order and stability by destroying the church of God and establishing the devil's kingdom. To test for the presence of the devil, authorities had those suspected of sorcery recite psalms and repeat the Lord's Prayer.[100]

Whatever the explanation(s) for the witchcraft delusion — they include fallout from the Indian wars, anxiety expressed by former captives, and social disputes — colonial authorities started to piece together a conspiracy of heresy, the Amerindians, and the devil.[101]
Combined with the growth of "heretical" sects (such as the Quakers)
on the frontier — who were seen as fulfilling the role of "fifth colum-
nists" to aid Satan's forces in the apocalyptic showdown between
the forces of good (the Puritan settlers) and the forces of evil (all others)[102] — this interpretation, linking internal and external threats, offered a taste of things to come in America.

Colonial Identity: The African Other

Concerned about those who transgressed the boundaries and threatened the frontiers of identity, settlers substituted one marginal group
for another throughout the eighteenth century in colonial America.
Probably the most significant opportunity for substitution was that
provided by the increasing importance of African slavery in the political economy of the new societies. Early European encounters with
Africans produced descriptions that were remarkably similar to the
contemporaneous accounts of the Amerindians in America. Leo
Africanus, a Spanish Moroccan Moor who converted to Christianity,
wrote the first influential description of Africans in 1526. Declaring
that the Libyans led a "brutish kind of life" marked by the absence
of "any Religion, any Lawes, or any good form of living," he maintained that:

> the Negroes likewise leade a beastly kind of life, being utterly des-
> titute of the use of reason, of dexterity of wit, and of all the arts . . .
> they so behave themselves, as if they had continually lived in a forest
> among wild beasts. They have great swarms of harlots amongst them;
> whereupon a man may easily conjecture their manner of living.[103]

Notwithstanding the many similarities, because they were introduced into colonial American society as slaves, Africans faced class
distinctions as a complementary point of differentiation to their already
subservient position in the hierarchies of culture and race. Whereas
the Indian was encountered in the wilderness as an obstacle to civilization and security, the African was brought into colonial society as
integral to the political economy from which civilization would emerge.
While Amerindians blurred the boundaries of inside and outside
through the way they were implicated in early colonial settlements,
Africans constantly straddled the same boundary by being integral
to the emerging society, yet excluded from membership in it.[104]

Given the rigid English orientation of complete otherness exacted upon the Amerindians, the Africans' status of being more inside colonial society meant that a greater effort had to be made to inscribe the boundary that kept them outside. To this end, detailed slave codes were enacted. While such codes are conventionally seen as restricting slaves, it takes only a small shift in perspective to see how they operated as codes to discipline the nonslaves. After all, these laws told the colonists, not the Africans, what they must and must not do.[105] Equally, the naming of the Africans was indicative. The Amerindians were referred to by their "proper" name or by the designation of "savage" or "pagan" — terms that allowed for the possibility of social mobility — against which the colonists called themselves "Christian" or "English." In contrast, the African slaves were simply "negroes," "blacks," or "Africans," but almost never "heathens," "pagans," or "savages," as though such terms were redundant. In contradistinction, the settlers began signifying their identity as "Christian," but then shifted to "English" and "free," and by 1680, to "white."[106] The prevailing view of the Africans was well summarized by the philosopher David Hume who enunciated an argument that repeated a refrain common to accounts of the Amerindians: "I am apt to suspect the Negroes and in general all the other species of men . . . to be naturally inferior to the whites. There never was a civilized nation of any other complexion than white, nor even any individual eminent either in action or speculation. No indigenous manufactures among them, no arts, no sciences."[107]

Colonial Americans were not likely to disagree en masse with this statement. In fact, Thomas Jefferson expounded some prejudiced views toward Africans that served to justify slavery or segregation.[108] What is noteworthy about these prejudices from a contemporary point of view is that race or color does not serve as the primary point of differentiation. Cultural characteristics such as the presence or absence of religion, reason, the arts and sciences — social factors that can be acquired and which therefore acknowledge the potential for mobility among even the most "primitive" people — remained the predominant distinguishing features of "barbaric" societies for the Europeans. In the case of the Africans, however, race and color — imputed biological characteristics that are fixed, thereby denying the possibility for "improvement" — were factors increasingly mentioned toward the end of the eighteenth century. This shift, codified in the development of the ideology of scientific racism during the nineteenth century, was concomitant with the move from "monogenism" to "polygenism" in explaining the origins of human life.[109] So long as Christianity main-

tained some force in the articulation of European identity, the belief
in the common origin of humanity remained the basic assumption
for all interpretations of human diversity. Before the nineteenth century few doubted—notwithstanding the consensus on the beastly,
barbaric, and pagan attitudes and behavior of the indigenous people—that the Amerindians and Africans were descended from the
same source as the Europeans. But with color increasingly prominent,
and early science such as that of Linneaus suggesting the negro might
be situated on the borderline that marked off the men from the apes,[110]
the dehumanization of the African was more readily accomplished.

If colonial identity was fragile and endangered by the presence
of others on its frontiers, the existence of others in its midst served
only to (again) further exacerbate the concerns. Most of the slave trade
in the first half of the eighteenth century was between Africa, the West
Indies, South America, and Europe; of the nearly four million Africans
who were enslaved before 1750, only one hundred and twenty thousand were sold to colonial America. After that date, the number of
slaves sent to America totaled between fifty and sixty thousand per
year for the remainder of the century.[111] This meant that Africans composed roughly one-third of the colonial population in this period,
while regional variations created even higher proportions in some
areas; in South Carolina, for example, Africans greatly outnumbered
the Europeans.[112] In these circumstances, the boundary between inside and outside, a boundary that was numerically threatened and
culturally imperilled, was often inscribed by an evangelism of fear
that linked internal and external threats.

In 1741, for example, New York suffered a bitterly cold winter, endured inflated commodity prices, and worried that the Spanish ar-
mada (then at war with England) was never far from the coast. Across
the river in Hackensack, two Africans were convicted and executed
of burning some barns. A short time later, fires broke out in the town,
consuming a fort, barracks, chapel, and the governor's mansion. No
evidence of who might have committed the arson was ever produced,
but on the doubtful assertions of an informer, a dance master named
John Ury was arrested, his protestations of innocence ignored. Convinced he was a disguised Spanish priest, the authorities accused
him of "popery" in fermenting a plot against the colony and had him
executed. Similarly without evidence, Africans and other suspects
were rounded up and jailed throughout the summer. After some dubious trials, four Europeans and eighteen Africans were hanged, thirteen Africans were burned, and seventy shipped out of the colony.[113]

In combining without evidence the pope, the Spanish, and the Africans in a subversive network, the New York authorities were doing no more than exhibiting an oft-repeated tendency to interpret all threats to order and stability as coming from an alliance of internal and external enemies. In Massachusetts Bay, when Thomas Morton was being persecuted, the governor speculated that he might be the agent of a foreign power sent to undermine the Puritan colony: "It is most likely that Jesuits or some that way disposed have sent him over to do us mischief, to raise up our enemies round about us both English and Indian."[114] Equally, it was perhaps more than a coincidence, though not inevitably a necessity, that the war against the Pequots coincided with the Antinomian controversy in the Bay colony. In fact, one minister in the colony made the connection explicit when he offered the observation that the Amerindians and the Familists, who respectively personified bestiality and beckoned men to licentiousness, "arose and fell together."[115] And Cotton Mather exemplified this logic when he theorized about the devilish alliance between the Quakers on the inside and the Amerindians on the outside.

Colonial Identity: The Revolutionary Moment

In 1751 Benjamin Franklin speculated about the plurality of the world:

> The Number of purely white people in the World is proportionately very small. All Africa is black or tawny. Asia chiefly tawny. America (exclusive of the new Comers) wholly so. And in Europe, the Spaniards, Italians, French, Russians and Swedes, are generally of what we call a swarthy Complexion; as are the Germans also, the Saxons only excepted, who with the English make the principal Body of White People on the Face of the Earth. I could wish their Numbers were increased.[116]

Notable for its location of English identity at the top of a color hierarchy, its claim that the Swedes and the Germans were "swarthy," and its identification of America with the Amerindians, Franklin's statement was indicative of widespread beliefs. Despite Pennsylvania's reputation for tolerance, there was considerable resentment about the "clannishness" of the Germans, who were referred to as the "Palantine Boer" in discussions on the "German problem," a shorthand way of representing the dilemma of how to disperse, educate, and assimilate such people. Franklin himself asked, "Why should Pennsylvania, founded by the English, become a colony of *Aliens*, who will shortly be so numerous as to Germanize us instead of our Anglifying them?"[117] Nor were other colonies free from this ethnic and religious xenophobia. Complaining of the increasing diversity in New Netherland (later New York), the Reverend John Megapolensis listed a variety of outsiders worthy of vituperation: "Those godless rascals . . . Papists, Mennonites and Lutherans among the Dutch; also many Puritans or Independents, and many Atheists and various other servants of Baal among the English under this Government, who conceal themselves under the name of Christians; it would create a still greater confusion, if the obstinate and immovable Jews came to settle here."[118] To ensure the religious and racial integrity of Virginia, the 1705 slave code of that colony maintained that "no negroes, mulattos, or Indians, although Christians, or Jews, Moors, Mahometans, or other infidels, shall, at any time, purchase any Christian servant, nor any other, except of their own complexion, or such as are declared slaves by this act."[119] And while there were forty Sephardic Jews in early Georgia, they needed special permission from the authorities to reside there.[120]

It seemed that at every opportunity the brittleness and sense of endangerment of the English identity in colonial America was expressed through the differentiation of the other, no matter how much they might share in common. Nonetheless, the orientation to otherness exhibited in these pejorative ethnic and religious distinctions was one that began from the postulate of identity. Unlike the policies of enslavement and extermination, founded on the postulate of difference or total otherness and directed at the Amerindians and Africans, the worst the various European groups were likely to be subject to was a form of cultural colonization designed to assimilate or "anglify" them into the dominant ways of colonial America. Certainly, transgressing the established social and political norms of accepted discourse attracted the severe legal repression accorded to those professing "traitorous," "malicious," "treasonable," and "seditious" beliefs, but such sanctions were not limited to particular ethnic, racial, or religious groups.[121]

The rapid expansion of colonial America, manifested in the doubling of the population between 1750 and 1775, added to and underscored the many existing sources of social conflict. The increasing disparities of wealth and poverty, the contradictory tensions of liberty and authority, and the search for spiritual salvation in the Great Awakening highlighted the comparative nature of the colonies' identity.[122] Prior to the middle of the eighteenth century, the settlers' sense of self had been predominantly inscribed through the exclusion and differentiation of others. To be sure, this had involved the simultaneous affirmation of an artificial and abstracted notion of European (particularly English) civility. But in the climate of increasing uneasiness about the colonies' moral state that America witnessed between 1745 and 1765 — a period in which there was a reinvigorated concern about the pervasiveness of pride, avarice, wickedness, vice, sensuality, wantonness, idleness, and intemperance — the reproduction of the boundaries of identity through comparison was matched by the normative affirmation of an idealized colonial image. The piety, purity, and brilliance of the Puritan past was invoked and combined with a reasserted sense of English civility and culture to construct an image to which all were supposed to aspire.[123] But even if it was achieved more by affirmation than by abjuration, the fragility and endangeredness of identity had not been put to rest by the discovery of any secure sense of self.

The primary symbol of importance in the attempt to imagine a community in this period was the designation "American." The use of the term certainly predated the revolutionary period, being first used to distinguish English soldiers from the American colonists they fought alongside beginning with the War of Jenkins' Ear in 1739. The English used it to label the colonists, whom they thought to be "poor soldiers, Irish papists, and fit only for cutting fascines with the negroes."[124] Prior to the 1760s, "American" was used in parlance equally with "His Majesty's Subjects" and "British colonists" to describe the settlers.[125] After the beginnings of the revolutionary protest against English imperial policy toward the colonies, "American" came to have a special political significance with two connotations. The first was one of inclusion among the Virginians, New Yorkers, and New Englanders who had (and would for some time yet) regarded themselves as distinct, while the second was one of exclusion that marked off the colonies from their imperial master.[126]

Constituting the American colonies as the United States was a process that exceeded the historical markers by which it is usually known.[127] From the early days of the English imperial reorganization, through the overtly revolutionary period between 1776 and 1783, to the completion of the documents that codified the union in 1790, the construction of the American nation was always in process.[128] In large part, this was due to the fact that the break between the colonies and their imperial center was a dispute concerning administrative and political issues rather than social or cultural differences. Opposed to taxation without representation, resentful of the new Colonial Office's political appointments and exercise of power, and fearing that worse examples of "oppression" were in the making, the colonists' dispute with London was little more than an attempt to ensure English rights for Englishmen. In actuality, those who spoke so eloquently of the conflict between tyranny and freedom desired no more than a return to the status quo ante bellum, the established and accepted way of governing that existed prior to 1757. In this sense, "both in intention and in fact the American Revolution conserved the past rather than repudiated it."[129]

This meant that the social consequences of the Revolution were extremely limited. No new social class assumed power; the men (women being excluded) who orchestrated the uprising were nearly all members of the colonial ruling class, three-quarters of whom had held some form of colonial office under the English; and the extensive tracts of crown land that were seized by the new government were not dispersed to the landless.[130] In consequence, this was a spatial not a temporal revolution. It was about the location of imperial power (London versus Philadelphia) rather than about qualitative dimensions of power. Those advocating independence thus emphasized order, restraint, and moderation in their protests, seeking as they were disengagement from an imperial center rather than reconstitution of the economic, social, and political order.[131]

These developments reinforced already pervasive tendencies in American culture to privilege the individual as the locus of agency and see America as the example for the rest of the world. Without the kind of old order being criticized and attacked in Europe — there was no equivalent of the European estates or the established church — American society was made up of "merely individuals, with or without property, and government."[132] Thereby endowed with the status of the prototypically modern society, Americans shouldered both special responsibilities and special burdens. Maintaining their leading position among nations was the goal, but it existed in a state of tension with the modes of apprehension provided by classical republican thought. Eighteenth-century Americans were predisposed to see history as the downward course of decay and degeneration (most obviously manifested in the pervasive self-doubt of 1745–65) rather than the upward swing of progress. And it was in the themes of classical republicanism that the paradox of American identity — where everything done to relieve the brittle, fragile, and endangered sense of self only contributed to the problem it was meant to solve — was most poignantly expressed.[133] For classical republicanism, "human nature was flawed; faith was fragile; freedom was always threatened. Under these conditions, virtue and constant vigilance were essential. But because peace and prosperity brought ease and indulgence, they promised certain decline."[134] In turn, this spurred the development in America of a very special sense of time which, in providing added support for the spatial character of the Revolution, had profound political ramifications. Whereas for Europeans, hope lay in the future and the prospect of a new order, for Americans, having established their social and political order through a revolution that secured what had already begun in a historical vacuum, "the past had been consolidated in a future whose integrity lay in remaining as much like the present as possible."[135]

Although the social effects of the American Revolution were minimal — indeed, perhaps because of this result — it required an ideological basis upon which to distinguish the Americans from the English. This was a requirement made all the more difficult by the colonists' attachment to an idealized and fictitious understanding of English civility. Nonetheless, from the 1760s on, the English and their culture began to be depicted by many in the colonies in terms of classical republicanism: English society was held to be morally inferior and even decadent compared to America. In the southern colonies, English ministers were disparaged as a "group of drunkards, hypocrites, scoundrels, thieves, rogues, Turks, lunatics, and asses who were ignorant, cunning, treacherous, wicked, villainous, and tyrannical."[136]

Counterposing the degeneracy, licentiousness, and immorality of the Old World with the innocence, decency, and ethics of the New manifested a particular tension for the colonists: "The very gratification they found in differentiating themselves from the Europeans by opposing innocence and corruption simultaneously jeopardized the identity they claimed as Europeans in opposition to primitive Indians."[137] By maintaining that they were not like the Europeans (particularly the English), the colonists were contradicting the fundamental tenet of their identity to that point: that they possessed the qualities of European civilization in contrast to the barbarity of the Indian way of life. Moreover, declaring that they were the paragons of innocence (aside from requiring extensive reconciliation with their frontier exploits) meant that they could not have resisted all the temptations with which they had been tantalized by the Amerindians and the wilderness for over a century. Either way, the Americans' revolutionary need to differentiate themselves from the English struck at the heart of their previously established identity, only aggravating the recurring condition of fragility and endangerment that had beset their identity from the beginning.

The best evidence of this condition was the adoption by various propagandists of the Indian as the symbol of America during the struggle with England. When the insurrectionists at the Boston Tea

Party dressed as Indians, and the cartoonists drew the Indian to signify the colonies, they were appropriating an identity that had both
thwarted and continued to elude them.[138] Furthermore, the symbolism of the Indian in the American Revolution signified the continuing
pervasiveness of the nexus between internal and external threats. At
the same time that the freedom and skills of the indigenous Americans were being celebrated by the nationalist elite, the Indians themselves were being pursued as the "rebels and traitors" the Penobscot
had been declared by a Massachusetts legislature.[139] Having fought
with the French against the colonists in the American invocation of
Europe's Seven Years' War, the Amerindians were loyal to the British
throughout the revolutionary period. It was a tenet (not entirely without justification) of colonial thought that all Indian raids during and
after the Revolution were of English inspiration. Settlers linked the
continuing imperial possession of frontier posts with the maintenance of hostile Amerindians, and republican newspapers continued
to claim that the British paid "savages" for the scalps of colonists.[140]
But the crowning evidence of this concern was the charge in the Declaration of Independence (what Jefferson called George III's "black
catalogue of unprovoked injuries") that the King "has excited domestic insurrections amongst us, and has endeavored to bring on
the inhabitants of the frontiers, the merciless Indian savages, whose
known rule of warfare, is an undistinguished destruction of all ages,
sexes and conditions."[141] The correlation of domestic insurrection and
foreign war was thus so ubiquitous that "it was writ large on the birth
certificate of the United States of America."[142]

The Amerindians were far from being the only targets of vigilance in the revolutionary period. Given the limited differences between the imperial and the nationalist elite, the Tory sensibilities of
the former were subject to repression by the latter. The proscription
of loyalist opinion in the colonies, the use of bills of attainder to outlaw suspects who could not be brought to trial, and the suppression
of "traitorous" speech, marked the revolutionary decades as a time
of conflict. Notorious among these measures was the coercive loyalty
oath. Though it predated the Revolution—and was to be revived frequently in the subsequent history of the United States[143]—it served
in this period to delineate those citizens siding with the Revolution
from the "secret enemies" who were, though not suspected of any
act approaching treason, to be considered (in Jefferson's words) "traitor[s] in thought, but not in deed."[144] By 1778 all thirteen states had
loyalty oaths or tests and punished those who would not take them
with a fine of double or triple taxation. In a precursor to internment

camps during later conflicts, those considered disloyal to the revolutionary cause were sometimes physically removed from their places of residence. In April 1776, the Virginia Committee of Safety ordered all persons in Norfolk and Princess Anne counties who supported the royal governor Dunmore to be shifted at least thirty miles into the interior, away from contact with the British. The following year, the governor of Virginia ordered militia commanders to ensure that all residents who refused to take loyalty oaths were moved out of military zones.[145]

The Treaty of Paris, which ended the War of Independence with the British in 1783, did not diminish the concern colonists had about the likelihood of internal subversion and external conflict. The British had withdrawn to the western frontier, where they were thought to be in alliance with the Amerindians, whose unceded lands (occupied by what the colonists considered "resident foreign nations") made up nearly one half of the territory of the new state.[146] Those who had manned the Continental army returned to the farms and towns to await some economic dues from the Revolution. When these were not forthcoming, revolt was fermented against the new elite in incidents such as Shays's Rebellion. Samuel Adams, who had been considered a radical during the Revolution, now implored people to act within the law and charged that "British emissaries" were stirring up the discontent.[147]

In the context of considerable uncertainty as to how national politics would be conducted and what the fate of the new nation would be, Americans searched for a way to interpret the novel ambiguity amid which they were situated. After America had emerged from a period of protracted if ill-defined conflict in which the boundaries of identity were often associated with a great power alliance (the Revolution having been a conflict in which America could be considered as having been situated in the vortex between Britain and France, with Spain in the background), it was hardly surprising that foreign affairs dominated the politics of the early national period and were the prism through which domestic differences were refracted. Above all else, it was the advent of the French Revolution and its subsequent course of events that shaped how the question of identity was handled in the 1790s.

With Americans apprehensive about the future, the French Revolution was welcomed as evidence of the universal aspiration for liberty in the face of monarchical tyranny, but feared as a threat to the moderation and constitutionalism of their political experiment. With political discourse divided by the ties of citizens to either the monarchy of England or the republic of France, the divisions that emerged in the American polity once the task of governing was begun were interpreted according to these cleavages. Although political parties were not yet official fixtures in the American political system, a fissure soon appeared between those who had supported the increased governmental powers of the revised Constitution (the Federalists) and those who opposed any move they regarded as akin to the centralization of a monarchy (the Republicans). Without a coherent program or affirmative identity, each of these groups was distinguished only by juxtaposition with the other, a process in which the alleged foreign ties of each were taken to be the determinant of domestic character.[148]

What is hard to appreciate from a contemporary vantage point is how foreign the idea of legitimate dissent and opposition was to American politics of the period.[149] The correctness of the revolutionary cause was considered beyond reproach by those who fashioned politics in the postrevolutionary period. Although some differences of opinion were expected, these were thought to concern only the divergent means that could be employed to reach shared goals. Politics was taken to be no more than the administration and management of a course that had been worked out and agreed upon through the Revolution. Any serious dissent, it was argued, could be nothing other than the machinations of an enemy determined to subvert the new approach.[150]

As a consequence, when domestic divisions became more apparent and the onset of formal factions and parties seemed unstoppable, each group traded charges that the other was in a foreign alliance that approached treason.[151] For the Federalists, the Republicans were the French party, whose despotism was akin to that found in the French Terror. For the Republicans, the Federalists were guilty of monarchical cabals that sought a return to pre-Revolution British tyranny. For both, the war between Britain and France beginning in 1793 was a resource from which to engage in a protracted domestic conflict around the issues of loyalty, patriotism, and identity.

With the presidencies of Washington and Adams, the Federalists were in the ascendancy of politics during the first years of the United States. Unaccustomed to the idea of dissent (Washington had written to Adams in 1794 declaring that "meetings in opposition to the constituted authorities . . . [are] at all times, improper and dangerous"),[152] they sought to put an end to the Republicans' opposition. When the Adams administration declared American neutrality in the conflict between Britain and France and signed the Jay Treaty with the British to restore relations after the Revolution, the Republicans charged that the United States was moving back toward the tyranny of monarchy as well as contravening the 1778 alliance with France.[153] Jefferson denounced the Jay Treaty as an alliance between "England and the Anglomen of this country against the legislature and people of the United States."[154] At this juncture, the Federalists eyed an opportunity to use foreign affairs to defeat a domestic opponent.

Anti-French feelings had been building in America ever since the Jacobin Clubs of France had been transformed into vehicles of the aggressive, xenophobic, and conspiratorial policies of the second revolutionary government in France. Originally made up of middle-class reformers and patriots favoring a constitutional monarchy with liberal politics, they became working-class organizations known as "Sociétés Populaires" after the overthrow of the monarchy in August 1792, and were involved in denouncing disloyal citizens at the behest of the Committee on Public Safety.[155] This transformation of class identity and revolutionary tactics was the antithesis of the American Revolution, making the Jacobins exemplars of subversive and seditious intent for those in power. When Democratic-Republican societies began to form in America in the early 1790s (the first being established by the Philadelphia Germans in 1793 to oppose any return to aristocracy), the Federalists argued that they were Jacobin-inspired. Ironically, they drew their inspiration from secret organizations such as the Sons of Liberty and the Committees of Correspondence employed by the Americans to overcome the British during the Revolution.[156] Nonetheless, these societies were soon condemned by foreign association. Tirades against them in the Federalist press charged they were addicted to "lying, cheating, whoredom, adultery, gaming, peculation, bribery, bankruptcy, fraud, atheism, etc." and associated with "incendiarism, the devil, or the bloody French Jacobins."[157] One Virginia woman wrote to the paper with a litany of abuse against the Kentucky Democratic Society, claiming it was "that horrible sink hole of treason — that hateful synagogue of anarchy — that frightful cathedral of discord — that poisonous garden of conspiracy — that hellish school of rebellion and opposition to all regular and well-balanced authority."[158] Combining images of anti-Semitism and anti-Catholicism into one web of anarchy, disorder, and insurrection, this writer clearly demonstrated how any opposition to the Federalist program invoked an angry discourse of danger linking what President Adams referred to as "the designs of foreign hostility and the views of domestic treachery."[159]

The domestic climate of guilt by accusation or association was replete with charges of foreign intrigue, but the rhetoric was not matched by evidence. The less than prudent activities of the French minister in America, M. Genet, helped give rise to wild allegations of Jacobins, Irish aliens, and Republicans being involved in a plot to subvert the government. It was later asserted that "the Frenchman's gold flowed freely in all channels where it could breed corruption . . . Jacobin clubs flourished; [and] democratic societies spread like a leprosy on the body politic,"[160] but no details of any attempted coup were ever uncovered. When settlers in the western reaches of Pennsylvania, Maryland, and Virginia rose in armed insurrection in 1794 against the imposition of a liquor excise, requiring the deployment of thirteen thousand federal troops to maintain order, George Washington, among others, attempted to use the situation to strike against what were termed "self-created societies" like the democratic clubs. Arguing that popular organizations were not required in a free society with representative government, authorities tried to minimize the impact of such class-based conflicts (the uprising united laborers and small farmers) by associating any protest with the intrusion of foreign influences.[161] As Abigail Adams, wife of the second president, confided to her diary, "The grand cause of all our present difficulties may be traced . . . to so many hordes of Foreigners imigrating [sic] to America."[162] While these incidents (among others) certainly established the boundaries of legitimate politics, none of them were extensive enough to discredit and silence domestic opposition, as the government was seeking. But the best chance for the Federalists' plans came with the XYZ affair.

Adams had sent a mission to France in 1797 to negotiate an end to the maritime conflict between America and France that had begun after the Jay Treaty was signed. His emissaries were met with less than diplomatic treatment, and the French demanded bribes and inflated loans for the directory then governing the country. For the Federalists, the French actions symbolized the contrast between the corruption of tyranny and the virtue of democracy. After the envoys had refused and returned to America, Congress published the records and correspondence of the mission (deleting the French agents' names and replacing them with the last letters of the alphabet), setting off a period of domestic hysteria.[163] As one Federalist newspaper propounded, "To be lukewarm after reading the horrid scenes [described by the XYZ papers] is to be criminal — and the man who does not warmly reprobate the conduct of the French must have a soul black enough to be fit for treasonous stratagems and spoils."[164]

The Federalist administration of John Adams proposed a war plan to ready America for conflict with France should an attack come and made support for it a test of loyalty and identity. The secretary of state informed a South Carolina senator that France was fermenting sedition among the Africans and would probably launch an invasion from the West Indies.[165] Washington was recalled from retirement at Mount Vernon and made commander-in-chief, and an already existing naval program was speeded up. There was no declaration of war, however, and the prospects of an invasion from France were most vivid only in the minds of the Federalists. But the boundaries of political discourse were now firmly marked by the linkage of internal and external threats. The Manichaean mood of the period was aptly summarized by *The Columbian Centinel* in 1798: "Whatever American is a friend of the present administration of the American government is undoubtedly a true republican, a true Patriot... Whatever American opposes the Administration is an Anarchist, a Jacobin and a Traitor... It is patriotism to write in favor of our government—it is sedition to write against it."[166] At the same time, the president of Yale added another liminal group to the litany of subversives when he spoke against the evils of the Illuminati, a sect he held responsible for the French Revolution, and which he believed threatened Americans to the extent that "we may see our wives the victims of legal prostitution; soberly dishonest; speciously polluted."[167]

The war with France did not come, but it was actively fought on the domestic front. Jefferson called the period the "reign of witches."[168] Vigilance committees were established to trace the movements of prominent Republicans (including Vice President Thomas Jefferson), the political loyalties of journalists and newspaper editors were closely studied, and all things French were boycotted or banished.[169] The most outstanding measures of domestic repression in the period of this nativist frenzy were the Alien and Sedition Laws. Although statutes against sedition and treason were already on the books (and used to bring cases against supposedly pro-French writers such as Benjamin Franklin Bache),[170] Federalists in Congress proposed a series of new laws to combat what they saw as the increasing threat of "aliens and other disaffected and seditious persons."[171] The Alien Friends Law made every noncitizen liable to arbitrary arrest and deportation at the president's pleasure in time of peace or war. Although the laws were never actually carried out, Adams did sign a series of blank warrants should any of those suspected be arrested. Moreover, the xenophobic climate meant that large numbers of French citizens (who for the most part had come to America to flee the very revolution the Federalists despised) returned to France as a precautionary measure. The Alien Enemies Law, which required a declaration of war to be enforced, would have stifled any group discussion or opposition. And the Sedition Law expanded the category of offenses to include the punishment of opinion in the absence of an overt act.[172] Under this statute, fourteen indictments were brought against Republican newspapers and then delayed so that they could come to trial in the election year of 1800.[173]

Aside from the containment of identity through the association of domestic dissent and foreign threats, the period of the quasi-war with France demonstrated how previously established discursive strategies of otherness could be invoked in novel circumstances to provide powerful modes of understanding. One strategy was to link a threat to the self with an internal other. For example, the French and the Illuminati were accused of having influence with the Africans, an association of evil that was supposed to confirm guilt. One writer argued that "as the plague flies on the wings of the wind, so do... [Illuminati] legions infect America. Their apostles have infused their principles into the submissive and laborious negroes."[174] A Republican newspaper attempted to reverse the tide of abuse over the alien laws by noting that "if Federalists found themselves deported, the Hottentots were a hospitable people."[175] George Washington reacted to all the venom Republicans were directing his way by protesting that he had been charged with "such exaggerated and indecent terms as could be scarcely applied to a negro."[176] And John Adams believed that the propensity for the subversion of order afoot in America meant that there would be "a return to the savage state of barbarous life."[177]

Space, Time, and Identity in America

As an imagined community, the identity of a state is the effect of ritualized performances and formalized practices that operate in its name or in the service of its ideals. Discourses of danger and the multifarious ethical powers of segregation: these are the modalities of foreign policy which, as chapter 4 argued, are animated by the regulative ideal of normal/pathological, and which (particularly in the guise of Foreign Policy) establish a geography of evil that inscribes the boundaries of inside/outside.

One would expect, in this context, that the boundaries of (the United States of) America would be written and reproduced within the parameters of this logic. By examining some of the pivotal moments in the construction of America—the moments of discovery, colonization, and revolution that continue to be represented in the contemporary era as embodying the defining characteristics of America—this chapter has sought to demonstrate how the practices of foreign policy have been integral to the (re)production of American identity at various junctures, and how the work of those practices is elided in subsequent moments. Although abjuration has been central to this process, affirmation has also been important. But what has been affirmed is a fictional representation of the past. In each of these foundational moments, at the same time that the logic of identity has succumbed to the temptation of otherness and danger has been externalized, a fictive paragon has been presented as a regulative ideal by which to make judgments. The Puritans invoked biblical scripture and its covenants; the American revolutionaries summoned their Pilgrim forebears and made them into demigods; and an endless array of modern political leaders have conjured up the Puritans and the "Founding Fathers" to be protagonists of particular positions in contemporary controversies. In each case, the exclusions effected by foreign policy are occluded, for all interpretations that seek to expose identity as a representation that should be historicized and problematized have themselves to be excluded in order for a contingent identity to be rendered secure.

America is more than a good example of the logic of identity at work in the realm of the state. In many ways, America is an exemplification of this logic, for America is the imagined community par excellence. As with all republics, America has constantly confronted the dilemma of securing legitimacy and establishing authority in a culture that renders ontological guarantees suspect. Caught in a "Machiavellian moment" whereby the republic encounters its own finitude in the effort to reconcile universal values in particular form, the (re)production of American identity has relied on a recurrent logic of foundation and augmentation such that performative statements are presented as constative utterances.[178] Each and every republic faces a similar structural requirement, for no matter how powerful or plausible are the claims of nations upon states, in no state are temporality and spatiality perfectly aligned. Each state thus confronts an *aporia* in its identity which — just as Derrida argued with regard to language and all acts of founding — cannot be overcome.[179] But in America there is a radical separation between history and geography: with neither a country nor a people to serve as a foundational referent, the *aporia* in America's identity is magnified.

An important consequence of this enlarged *aporia* is that a seemingly paradoxical relationship between time and space arises. Europeans who encountered the New World went out of their way to deny its historicity. Accordingly, the space that is America has taken on such significance that it becomes history.[180] With all its qualities present at its genesis, America is understood as the land of freedom that derives its meaning from the frontier. Born modern, " 'American' identity obviates the usual distinctions of national history—divisions of class, complexities of time and place—because the very meaning of American involves a *cultural*, not a national myth of consensus."[181] In consequence, the history of America is effectively de-historicized, for this privileging of the spatial over the temporal in American experience has given history the quality of an eternal present.

Yet, while space is a defining moment of American identity, it is an insufficient condition: the *aporia* of identity cannot be filled by the claims of geography alone. Indeed, the legitimations for this geopolitical identity are nonterritorial in character. As an entity that was literally the product of European imagination (which then struggled with that legacy as a means of asserting itself) and whose "true nationals" and ideals were always "inorganic" in nature, America has a peculiar iconic quality in that the major conflicts of its identity are ideational. From the religious conflicts of the Puritans, through the witchcraft hysteria of Salem, through the loyalty oaths and xenophobic legislation of the early republic, to the prominent place accorded the Pledge of Allegiance and the flag in modern elections, American politics has privileged the symbolic. As Jean Baudrillard observed, America begins and ends with "space and the spirit of fiction."[182]

To be sure, the political conflicts of seventeenth- and eighteenth-century America are a long way from the cold war of the mid-twentieth century. Yet there is something oddly similar about the structural logic and modes of representation in the dissension of these disparate periods. They are not identical, of course, but from the perspective of the present, we read the terms of their discourse and recognize some familiar figurations. Others have recognized the similitude: Leonard Levy has written that the revolutionary period was a "time of internal cold war in which the passionate exponents of the experiment in liberty felt besieged by its enemies."[183] In this context, we might be able to think differently about the cold war: as another episode in the ongoing production and reproduction of American identity through the practices of foreign policy, rather than as simply an externally induced crisis. Indeed, if the nexus of internal and external threats was so ubiquitous that "it was writ large on the birth certificate of the United States of America,"[184] it should not be surprising to find this logic operating each time the birth records are updated.

Six
Writing Security

The Global Inscription of Foreign Policy

The iconic quality of (the United States of) America has been sustained in the modern era because sequestered within it are intertwined filaments of secularism and spirituality. America is not exceptional in combining nationalism, eschatology, and chauvinism[1] — all republics have been endowed with a transcendental air by the inexorable role representation plays in the attempt to overcome the *aporia* of their identity — but America is an intensification of this structural quality. With the roots of its identity in Puritan experience, and with that experience being appropriated into an unyielding myth of the nation's existence in sacred time, the spiritual dimension has never been exorcised from American practices. While an evangelism of fear has been cardinal for the constitution of many states' identities, the apocalyptic mode — in which a discourse of danger functions as providence and foretells a threat that prompts renewal — has been conspicuous in the catalog of American statecraft.[2] Accordingly, an array of individuals, groups, beliefs, and behaviors have occupied the position of the Antichrist, and have been inscribed with one or more terms from the panoply of tropes of otherness found in American experience.

In this context, any number of historical events or periods might be considered as precursors to the cold war, not in the sense that they stand in a relationship of cause and effect, but rather because they exhibit similar orientations toward danger, the self, and others. Chapter 5 examined how some of the foundational periods of American experience were implicated in and indebted to the practices of foreign policy. And in the century and a half between the early national period and the onset of the cold war, any number of instances exist for which an archaeological examination of the political practices then at work would uncover similar dispositions. The nineteenth century, after all, was the time of continental expansion for the United States, in which its settlers and armed forces engaged in violent and almost constant battle with the Indians, the British, and the Mexicans (among others).[3] Understood in terms of "manifest destiny," these struggles reproduced the logic of the Puritan covenant such that the United States became for many the chosen nation, charged with the responsibility of redemption in the continuing struggle between good and evil, holding in its custody the coming millennium.[4] Moreover, the brittle, fragile, and endangered sense of self that had emerged as a consequence of the settlers' ongoing displacement from "civilization" (first from Europe, and then from the eastern states) was further aggravated in this process. As Hietala has argued, national security in the 1840s:

> was not "free," nor was it attained without constant effort. The expansionists utilized propaganda, personal vendetta, legislative legerdemain, confidential agents, covert military pressure, and offensive war to achieve their goals. The Jacksonians, in fact, felt as insecure in their world as their heirs felt in the 1940s, when the Soviet threat called forth a policy of ambitious containment. The insecurity of the 1840s prompted attempts to enlarge the United States; the insecurity of the Cold War prompted policies to hem in the Soviet Union. In both cases, anxiety was a major factor behind American actions.[5]

By the end of the nineteenth century, there is an important qualitative change in American statecraft which has direct repercussions for the cold war. Although the meaning of America had long relied on a nonterritorial conception of its purpose, it is not until this period that foreign policy regularly exceeds the geography of the identity in whose name it operates. In short, the end of the nineteenth century witnesses the global inscription of foreign policy in the practices of Foreign Policy. The identity of the United States becomes part and parcel of the state's global reach. With the domestic frontier of the United States effectively closed from the latter half of the nineteenth century (at least insofar as most Indian nations had been repressed, and the British, French, and Mexican territories of Oregon, Louisiana, and California had been acquired), the imperial expansion that was considered essential to the maintenance of liberty at home was extended to Asia and the Caribbean. The Spanish-American War of 1898 saw the gaining of Cuba; Hawaii was annexed while American forces were sent to occupy Puerto Rico, Guam, and the Philippines; and a series of notes demanding open-door status to China culminated in U.S. participation in the force to suppress the Boxer Rebellion.[6]

All these overseas adventures were justified in the same terms that had rationalized the oppression of the Indians and others at home: the need (if not duty) to civilize, educate, and look after "primitive" peoples, and the anarchy, barbarism, and danger that would flourish if the United States did not act. Indeed, President McKinley's war message justifying the invasion of Cuba in 1898 bore more than a passing resemblance to John Quincy Adams's white paper of eighty years earlier rationalizing the annexation of Florida: each maintained that the rise of barbarism in these provinces, manifested most clearly by wanton attacks on property, had induced such a decline that acts of self-defense on the part of the United States were warranted.[7] Equally, the annexation of the Philippines—the proclamation of which declared that the undertaking was done to ensure the well-being of the people "and their elevation and advancement to a position amongst the most civilized peoples of the world"[8]—was but one episode in the exercise of this logic. In later times, these formulations would undergird the war in Vietnam, justify foreign aid policies, support declarations about America's democratic purpose in the world, and warrant military quests against contemporary empires of evil.[9]

This is not to suggest that the globalization of foreign policy in this period was solely an ideological development: the changing nature of the social order brought on by the nature and scale of economic development was without doubt crucial.[10] But for all the transformations wrought by the transition from a largely agrarian, rural community to an industrialized, urban society, the fears and dangers evident in these distinct periods remained remarkably similar.[11] To be sure, different groups came to occupy the position of the other, but the figurations with which they were inscribed were drawn from the well-established narratives of otherness in American experience.

As an illustration of the ubiquitous nature of various liminal groups in this period, consider the declarations of John Hay, secretary of state (1898–1905) at the height of American colonial expansion. Hay was in a position to conduct national policy in a manner that accorded with his orientations to a variety of others, orientations that had been stridently articulated in the previous decades. Hay had responded to Custer's defeat at Little Bighorn—believing that only a poisonous conspiracy could have crushed the cavalry—with an odious poem about Comanche, the sole survivor of the "scorpion ring." Published anonymously, the poem described the dishonor "That shrouds our army's name / When all foul beasts are free to rend / And tear its honest fame," and subsequently confided to a friend that it was "a well-intentioned poem, calculated to make people kill Indians." Furthermore, he added, "I think H.H. ought to be made a Ute prisoner for a week." H.H. was Helen Hunt Jackson, the white Indian reformer of the period; the reference to the Ute was to a tribe alleged to be in the habit of raping white women.[12] Hay's comment was an instance of the interpretation in which reformers, even when not women, were understood as effeminate liberals standing in the way of "men" of action, thereby inviting (sometimes sexual) violence. It was a view propounded by Theodore Roosevelt, who warned Americans in the 1890s that they had to "boldly face the life of strife" through "hard and dangerous endeavor. Oversentimentality, oversoftness . . . and mushiness are the great danger of this age and people."[13] Indians and women were not the only targets of Hay's vitriol, however. In the wake of the 1877 railroad strikes, he wrote that "the very devil seems to have entered into the lower classes of working men, and there are plenty of scoundrels to encourage them to all lengths."[14] Hay's antilabor prejudice was most obvious in his novel *The Bread-Winners*, also published anonymously, which was an acrid attack on unions and their foreign members.[15] Some years later, he authored a political pamphlet for McKinley (*The Platform of Anarchy*) in which he charged that the devil had infected the Democrats with the spirit of revolution.[16]

Hay's register of liminal groups (women, Indians, workers, and foreigners, among others) and his objects of derision (reformers and political opponents) show the complex and multifaceted way in which the boundaries of identity can be inscribed. Although in their particular context Hay's views were neither free of resistances nor without their own contradictions, they illustrate how the practices of foreign policy discussed in chapter 4 came to operate in a particular time and place. Animated by a moral concern to distinguish between the normal and the pathological, and largely impervious to the characteristics and qualities of the other, these figurations instantiate a fictive self that has meaning principally as the negation of difference, and which then performs as a regulative ideal by which contingency can be domesticated and identity enframed. This is a process that is never completed, but in times of crisis or in periods in which there is a critical rupture that destabilizes the boundaries of identity established earlier, it is a process that assumes added significance.

The Cold War and Identity

The period we understand as the cold war was one such crisis. The 1930s and 1940s — from the depression to the early cold war — were a critical rupture in the identity of the United States that licensed widespread contestation. In this context, if an earlier identity was to be reproduced and challenges to it contained, a considerable effort of reinscription would be demanded: an effort in which the logic of identity might easily succumb to the temptation of otherness. And if that was to be the case, as will be argued here, then it is not possible to explain the cold war by reference to the objective threat said to reside in the Soviet Union. Within these parameters, though, some cautionary remarks about this proposition are in order.

The intention of this argument is not to provide an exhaustive historical narrative on the four decades subsequent to World War II with the aim of definitively explaining the sources of state conduct. Rather, in terms of the logic of interpretation discussed in the Introduction, the objective of this analysis is to consider the modes of representation through which danger was interpreted and understood, and the manifest political consequences of these modes of representation. We should also remind ourselves that the past forty-five years or so have not been a consistent era of total enmity between the United States and the Soviet Union: there have been a number of moments of diminished tension if not détente in the course of this period. Accordingly, the principal focus here is on the early and intense stages of the cold war — although this chapter will conclude with some reflections on the period in the late 1970s that some came to call the second cold war — because it is in this instance that the inscription of boundaries is most obvious.

Equally, this argument neither maintains that the foreign policy of the Soviet Union (and other communist states) was benign nor that the United States willfully fabricated a danger where none could be perceived. The events signified by reference to Berlin, Korea, Quemoy-Matsu, Vietnam, Hungary, Cuba, and Czechoslovakia are all real. But to repeat a formulation cited in the introduction, "What is denied is not that . . . objects exist externally to thought, but the rather different assertion that they could constitute themselves as objects outside of any discursive condition of emergence."[17] In other words, these events and not others have to be interpreted as threats, and the process of interpretation through which they are figured as threats employs some modes of representation and not others. There are thus two realms of selection to be traversed before something is constituted as real, and it is the latter that is being considered here. Specifically, the point this analysis wishes to sustain is that because the modes of representation through which the danger of communism and the Soviet Union have been interpreted replicate both the logic and the figurations of past articulations of danger, the cold war is an important moment in the (re)production of American identity that was not dependent on (though clearly influenced by) the Soviet Union for its character.

If we refer back to the Foreign Policy texts reviewed in chapter 1, we can start to appreciate that there was more at stake for the United States in the cold war than a simple response to a realm of necessity. A striking feature of these texts is that assessments of threat regularly begin with considerations that more traditional analyses might regard as epiphenomenal: culture, ideology, and general reflections on U.S. society. Yet, as Stephanson has noted, "Ideology, symbolism, mythology, and words are not inherently abstract: they constitute a material practice encapsulated in the foreign policy of every great power."[18] NSC-68, the document Christopher Thorne aptly called a "secular hymn to American values," is the most striking example of this, but it is far from being the only one.[19] It declares that the United States' fundamental purpose ("to assure the integrity and vitality of our free society, which is founded upon the dignity and worth of the individual") automatically places it in conflict with the Soviet Union (being the embodiment of the "idea of slavery"). In so doing, it isolated a formulation of American identity recurrent in later moments. For example, the debate concerning defense appropriations in the Eisenhower administration was conducted on the basis that the defense budget should not create a burden so great that it would destroy the very system it was supposed to defend — a system of freedom of choice for individuals, democratic procedures for government, and a private enterprise economy. For the Kennedy administration, the preservation of "Freedom under God" and the spreading through modernization of the principles of individual liberty were guiding tenets. Equally, the Carter and Reagan administrations' pursuit of "human rights" is a further instance of the U.S. concept of the self, given that this particular concept of "human rights" embodies the achievement of freedom through an "institutionalizing [of] a purified notion of individual selfhood."[20] These are arguments that claim universality for particular American values. They are arguments like those of Richard Rorty — whose comments on "Soviet imperialism" were cited in chapter 1 — when he maintains that there are major differences between the First and Second Worlds: "We have hope, and they (unless Gorbachev astonishes us all) do not. We have freedom of the press, an independent judiciary, and [free] universities . . . Such fragile, flawed institutions, the creation of the last 300 years, are humanity's most precious achievements."[21]

The constant (re)writing of the character of U.S. society in the Foreign Policy texts suggests, as the argument maintains, that the practices of Foreign Policy serve to enframe, limit, and domesticate a particular identity. The identity that is enframed refers to more than just the characteristics of individuals or national types; it incorporates, for example, the form of domestic order, the social relations of production, and the various subjectivities to which they give rise. In the context of the United States, then, identity has often been disciplined by rhetoric associated with freedom of choice for individuals, democratic institutions, and a private enterprise economy. This serves to reproduce those practices in the face of contradictory and threatening interpretations, most obviously that of a communal identity, the interests of which are served by social planning and the public ownership of property.

This dichotomy does not exhaust the variety of social orders and identities that can exist, but it does point to an important distinction that helps elucidate the character of the cold war.[22] That is, communism and the Soviet Union are not synonymous. The former predates and exceeds the latter. It is an obvious historical point, but if we disaggregate the two and recognize that communism dates from the 1840s while the Soviet Union emerges some seventy or more years later, the nature of the threat ascribed to the latter is in actuality related more to the character of the former. The Foreign Policy texts acknowledge this point insofar as they identify the Soviet challenge as being political rather than military in nature. But the implication I want to draw from this point is more extensive. It is that: (1) the well-developed antipathy toward communism in the United States stems from the way in which the danger to the private ownership of property it embodies is a code for distinguishing the "civilized" from the "barbaric" (or the normal from the pathological); and (2) this is the basis for the interpretive framework that constitutes the Soviet Union as a danger independent of any military capacity. This is not to suggest that the USSR's military was either insignificant or benevolent, but to argue, as will be illustrated below, that because the figurations of the Soviet threat in the post–World War II era were similar if not identical to those that existed prior to both 1939 and 1917, the danger was not solely derived from the existence of military hardware or the Soviet Union's international position.

To talk in terms of the cold war being a coded struggle between the civilized and the barbaric, however, is different from a view commonly expressed at the time. Many people considered the cold war to be a conflict of epic proportions in which the future of "civilization" was at stake. H. L. Mencken, for example, proposed that the United States initiate war on "the Russian barbarians," so that "in the end, if we are lucky, there will be something resembling a civilized peace in Christendom."[23] Outbursts of this nature, however, occluded the major point being made here: that the status of one of the parties as "civilized" was neither settled nor established independently of the figuration of the other party as "barbaric." Moreover, the process of settling and establishing the identity of the "civilized" depended on the ability of exclusionary practices to persuasively link resistant elements to a secure identity on the "inside" through a discourse of danger with threats identified and located on the "outside." In these terms, consider how issues such as full employment, wage justice, and child care were characterized as foreign and evil to the United States by their association with communism and the Soviet Union.

With the advent of World War II, many businessmen who had opposed the New Deal saw an opportunity to return to the economic policies of the predepression era.[24] When Roosevelt proclaimed that "Dr. New Deal" was making way for "Dr. Win the War," the agencies that had been the vanguard of liberal change in the New Deal, and had attracted the attention of congressional investigations into "un-American" practices, were being dismantled. Most important was the National Resources Planning Board, which symbolized the use of long-range planning for the reconstruction of society. When it published two pamphlets on full employment and security during the war, it was denounced by the *Wall Street Journal* as a tool of socialism advocating a "totalitarian plan" to reshape U.S. society.[25] The end of the war also witnessed an effort on the part of unions to pursue an increased standard of living for their members. Throughout the war, unions had been forbidden to strike, and although real income had increased 53 percent during that period, it was largely a consequence of overtime rather than improved remuneration. Immediately after the war, corporate profits reached record highs while real wages declined by 12 percent. At the same time, prices rose dramatically, with the consumer price index increasing 28 percent in the first sixteen days of July after the removal of price controls. In this environment, labor militancy was on the increase. A wave of strikes began toward the end of 1945. General Motors, for example, had well over one million workers go on strike. Within a year after V-J Day, some five million workers had walked off the job in the largest industries, causing a loss of 120 million work days. With the possible exception of 1919, such militancy was unheard of in the United States.[26] In response to events such as these, the magazine *Nation's Business* stated that "whoever stirs up needless strife in American trade unions advances the cause of Communism." Similarly, when women in New York fought for the retention of day-care programs that had been established during the war to allow them to work for the war effort, the *New York World Telegram* alleged that "the entire program of child care was conceived by leftists operating out of communist work cells." The campaign for day-care centers, the newspaper declared, had "all the trappings of a Red drive, including leaflets, letters, telegrams, petitions, protest demonstrations, mass meetings, and hat passing."[27]

Accordingly, while the end of World War II left the United States as the world's most powerful state, it was a state whose identity was being strongly contested by issues and protagonists like those considered above. The Soviet Union was neither the source nor the ally of these domestic challenges, yet it came to be interpreted as a danger to the nation on both counts, thereby generating a major "red scare" in which prominent citizens took to combining external threats with internal disorder. Billy Graham talked about "barbarians beating at our gates from without and moral termites from within"; J. Edgar Hoover declared there was a "force of traitorous communists, constantly gnawing away like termites at the very foundation of American society"; and General MacArthur noted that while the Soviet Union had a bomb, "New Dealism is eating away the vitals of the nation."[28] But the early cold war's red scare was not dependent for its efficacy on any military challenge launched by the Soviet Union. In the first instance, the national security managers of the period initially and correctly discounted the capacity of the Soviet Union to pose such a threat. Moreover, the high point of hysteria was directed at a Democratic administration that (as Stephen Ambrose has written) "forced the Russians out of Iran in 1946, came to the aid of the Greek government in 1947, met the Red Army's challenge at Berlin and inaugurated the Marshall Plan in 1948, joined the North Atlantic Treaty Organization in 1949, and hurled back the Communist invaders of South Korea in 1950."[29] Most importantly, the red scare that followed the end of World War II was not a novel occurrence without historical precedent. Indeed, there had been a number of instances in earlier times — not the least of which was the contestation of the 1790s discussed in chapter 5 — in which uncertain periods betokened the scapegoating of various groups.

Prelude to the Cold War

One had only to look back to the end of World War I to witness a similar logic at work. When the United States entered the war in 1917, the government turned to a range of private groups to mobilize opinion, ensure loyalty, and isolate dangers. Organizations such as the American Protective League, the Council of National Defense, the American Defense Society, and the National Security League preached the virtues of "one hundred per cent Americanism" and sought to punish those who diverged from their ideals. Some members of these groups—which embodied concerns akin to the social defense and hygiene movements discussed in chapter 4—engaged in vigilante activities, rounding up people they suspected of disloyalty and forcing them to kiss the flag. But official opinion and policy was not very different. While Wilson managed to withstand some senators' calls for martial law to be decreed, he endorsed legislation such as the Espionage Act of 1917, the Sedition Act of 1918 (it prohibited "language disloyal to the American form of government and the Constitution," outlawed words of support for the enemy, and set punishment for disrespect to the flag at twenty years in jail), and the Immigration Act of 1918 (which barred anarchists and those who sought the overthrow of government by force).[30]

Ironically, the end of the war brought greater concern and heightened calls for vigilance. Three days after the armistice, Secretary of State Robert Lansing declared that he was concerned with neither indemnities from nor reprisals against Germany; rather, he said, "I am anxious over the question of how we can check Bolshevism and the dangers which threaten the very structure of society."[31] Indeed, the Russian Revolution of 1917 troubled American and European leaders to such an extent that the peace negotiated at Versailles was as concerned with the containment of Bolshevism as with the restriction of Germany.[32] Equally, within the United States, official attention soon changed targets. Senator Lee Overman of North Carolina, who had after the armistice begun a judiciary committee investigation into the wartime propaganda efforts of German-American brewers, shifted the investigation's attention—with the Senate's approval—to "pacifists, socialists, radicals, Bolsheviks, free-love college professors, and their ilk."[33] Moreover, when unions in Seattle organized a general strike in 1919, a period of national hysteria was born. The mayor of Seattle declared that the strike was the work of those who "want to take possession of our American government and try to duplicate the anarchy of Russia." Even Wilson's moderate secretary of labor remarked that the aim was "to establish a Soviet form of government in the United States."[34] To curb the perceived danger, states enacted laws designed to prosecute radicals and outlaw the display of the red flag, while the federal government, which lacked the power to act beyond the immigration laws, rounded up thousands of aliens and deported some six hundred for political reasons. Attorney General

Palmer, whose department organized the raids that detained aliens, argued that it was possible to identify revolutionaries by their "lopsided faces, sloping brows, and misshapen features."[35]

In this climate, sociomedical discourse was the representational practice of choice. A 1920 National Security League pamphlet entitled "The Leper in the House" maintained that "Bolshevism is not indigenous to American soil. It is a disease that, like influenza and cholera, comes from overseas, and with which no native-born American would be likely to be afflicted unless there were something about him congenitally abnormal."[36] In the same year, the *Literary Digest* proposed a range of policies to meet the crisis, one of which was "Expel from the country all alien Bolsheviks, socialists, and anarchists. (Arrest and deportation of these Bolsheviki are as necessary as cauterizing a wound to prevent gangrene.)"[37] And sometimes the focus was broadened to condemn the traditional catalog of others — women, the mad, and foreigners:

> Of the arrested and suspected anarchists and communists in America, nine out of every ten are foreigners. They come from different parts of Europe — a large proportion coming from Russia, however; and some of them have spent many years in the United States. Of the American element, it is said that as a class they are less bloodthirsty and less given to violence than the foreigners. Many of them border on the verge of insanity; many others are women with minds gone slightly awry, morbid, senseless and seeking the sensational, craving for something, they know not what.[38]

Whatever the figuration, the inscription of otherness was linked to the enframing of American identity. Ole Hanson, the mayor of Seattle in 1919, published a book the following year that contained this articulation of Americanism:

> Americanism stands for liberty;
> Bolshevism is premeditated slavery.
>
> Americanism is a synonym for self-government;
> Bolshevism believes in a dictatorship of tyrants.
>
> Americanism means equality;
> Bolshevism stands for class division and class rule.
>
> Americanism stands for orderly, continuous, never-ending progress;
> Bolshevism stands for retrograding to barbaric government.
>
> Americanism stands for law;
> Bolshevism disdains law.

Americanism stands for hope;
Bolshevism stands for despair.

Americanism is founded on family love and family life;
Bolshevism is against family life.

Americanism stands for one wife and one country;
Bolshevism stands for free love and no country.

Americanism means increased production and increased prosperity for all;
Bolshevism stands for destruction, restriction of output, and compulsory poverty.

Americanism believes in strength;
Bolshevism teaches premeditated weakness and inefficiency.

Americanism has taught, and Americans have practiced morality;
Bolshevism teaches and its votaries practice immorality, indecency, cruelty, rape, murder, theft, arson.

Americanism stands for God and good;
Bolshevism is against both God and good.[39]

Hanson's catalog of identity/difference covers all the conceivable filaments of the desired American nation: religion, family, sexuality, gender, law and order, civilization, morality, and economic relations. Its concern is not with the prospects for a breaching of the state's territorial borders, but the feared transgressions of the nation's boundaries of identity. It might be dismissed as an example of political puffery were it not for the fact that it succinctly codified the contours of the xenophobic patriotism that abounded in America in the 1920s, and subsequently found its way into the confidential documents of post-1945 Foreign Policy.

Identity and the Myth of the Frontier

But the red scare of 1919 was not the point of origin for all subsequent red scares. It was itself no more than another incarnation of the logic present in events such as those surrounding the Haymarket bombing in 1886, which in turn was able to energize social forces because of the sense of danger that was associated with the events of the 1871 Paris Commune.[40] Nor were red scares dependent on the capacity of Bolshevism, let alone the Soviet Union, to act as an empirical referent. Indeed, the appellation *red* invoked the Indian wars of the frontier as much as it did the symbol of the international working class.

Newspapers in the period 1874–77 (a time of labor unrest) openly associated the rhetoric of class and Indian wars, thereby aligning the "reds" on the frontier with the "reds" in the cities. Accounts of the army's battle with the truculent natives were juxtaposed on front pages with stories of urban and social unrest, while the tropes applied to the Indians ("anarchical," "barbarous") were recycled and ascribed to the strikers. As Charles Loring Brace, a noted philanthropist noted, "There seemed to be a very considerable class of lads in New York who bore to the busy, wealthy world about them something of the same relation which Indians bear to civilized Western settlers." By figuring the workers as alien and savage, such representations enabled them to be the targets of force. One paper probably had this in mind when it maintained that the railroad strike was "Communistic and law-defying, against all law, order, and civilization."[41] These figurations, then, derived not from what Bolshevism (or anarchism, or nihilism) might or might not have been, but from a desire to demonstrate that any group orientation against the emerging capitalist order was a kind of tribalism, a throwback to a savage past, and a symptom of degeneracy.

Indeed, there is no specifiable point of origin for these modes of representation, because what they represent is the episodic eruption of an ethical power of segregation that is animated by moral concerns rather than derived from spatial or temporal causes. To be sure, each episode has elements specific to its location and participants, but in these various historical moments we witness the repetition of certain techniques of differentiation rather than the creation de novo of concerns, prejudices, and figurations. Moreover, the persistence of these techniques indicates the existence of a well-established discursive economy of identity/difference likely to be drawn upon to enable the disciplining of contingency and the representation of danger in moments of flux. And in the myth of the frontier, the United States possesses such a resource.

The frontier is a powerful and recurring image in American political discourse. When Henry Kissinger calls himself the "Lone Ranger" of diplomacy; when Vietnam is described by combat troops as "Indian country" (as was Iraq);[42] and when space exploration or plans for the Strategic Defense Initiative are tagged as the "high frontier"; the mythology of the frontier is invoked without explanation as a means of describing the situation.[43] The dominant themes of this mythology are those concerned with American history as a full-scale Indian war in which race fights race as part of the rites of modern-

ization and the development of the national state. It has also been repeated in the discourse of economic threats said to emanate from
Japan.[44]

The frontier is central to identity because it is not only an open
space beckoning those who seek success, but also the (ever-shifting)
boundary between "barbarism" and "civilization," chaos and order,
and "feminine" and "masculine."[45] Moreover, the frontier is part of
the national mission because it mobilized national energies in accord
with Puritan-like renewal. The mythology of the frontier achieves, in
this sense, more than mere description. It also provides the prescrip-
tion for action. It mandates that to ensure the survival of "civilization" the forces of "barbarism" have to be constantly repelled if not
overcome. As Slotkin writes, "At the core of the Myth is the belief
that economic, moral, and spiritual progress are achieved by the heroic
foray of civilized society into the virgin wilderness, and by the conquest and subjugation of wild nature and savage mankind."[46] This
disposition has been exhibited each time it has been argued that a
(particular) "barbarian" group only understands force and cannot be
reasoned with.[47]

It is, of course, central to the mythology of the frontier that from
the time of settlement in North America to the end of the nineteenth
century, the constitution and regeneration of the identity of the Eu-
ropean-American self has been made possible by the enactment of
violence upon the Indian other.[48] The Indians were scorned and sub-
jugated by the European settlers on a number of grounds, but most
prominent was the Hobbes-like claim that "they are not industrious,
neither have art, science, skill or faculty to use either the land or the
commodities of it."[49] Central to this interpretation was the Europeans' derision at the communal nature of the Indians' property — a
disdainful attitude that long preceded communism or Bolshevism. In
lacking private ownership the Indian was thought to lack the capacity for an individuated self and was thus without the basis for civilized society.[50] As a commissioner for Indian affairs declared in 1838,
"common property and civilization cannot coexist."[51] In 1875, another
Indian commissioner declared that "a fundamental difference between Barbarians and a civilized people is the difference between a
herd and an individual."[52] Even reformers such as Helen Hunt Jackson who were critical of American Indian policy did not doubt that
the Indians "must be set free from the swaddling bands of tribal col-
lectivism."[53] But it was not just Indians who were subject to prejudice
on the grounds that communal property and collective action were
"foreign." The emergence of trade unions in the nineteenth century

was legally opposed when various judges argued that they were irredeemably alien. When a tailors' union in New York was declared illegal in the 1830s because it was an impediment to trade, the judge in the case declared: "In this favored land of law and liberty, the road to advancement is open to all . . . Every American knows that or ought to know that he has no better friend than the laws and that he needs no artificial combination for his protection. They are of foreign origin and I am led to believe mainly upheld by foreigners." Similarly, in June 1872, when 150,000 workers marched to celebrate the winning of the eight-hour day, the *New York Times* was moved to wonder how many of the participants were "thoroughly American."[54] Such sentiments were to be expressed in one form or another in the early cold war. In a reaffirmation of the importance of property, housing developer William Levitt remarked: "No man who owns his own house and lot can be a communist. He has too much to do."[55]

A Society of Security

For all that is at stake in an invocation of the myth of the frontier, it is not possible to specify the social conditions that will necessarily give rise to a red scare. The techniques of these episodes persist without always being aroused into a full-scale eruption. For example, the Haymarket bombing prompted one such episode, whereas the assassination of President McKinley by an anarchist in 1901 did not. Equally, the first half of the 1930s — in the midst of the depression, and with a number of congressional investigations into alleged subversion providing potential institutional support — did not evince a nationwide red scare, whereas the relative prosperity of the early 1950s was the setting for McCarthyism.[56] In consequence, although labor militancy such as that in 1919 and 1945–46 opens up the possibility for a red scare, no simple economistic explanation of the contestation over identity is possible.

By the late 1930s, there was an increasing momentum within the United States to do something about things perceived to be un-American. In January 1937, Congressman Samuel Dickstein introduced a resolution calling for an investigation of all groups "found operating in the United States for the purposes of diffusing . . . slanderous or libelous un-American propaganda of religious, racial or subversive political prejudices." Three months later Congressman Martin Dies introduced a similar resolution calling for an investigation of "subversive and un-American propaganda." The two proposals were combined, and a resolution passed in May 1938 establishing the House Un-American Activities Committee (HUAC). Although Germany was the greatest international threat, Communists rather than Nazis were the targets of concern, and the committee signaled its proclivities by excluding Dickstein from its ranks because of his Jewish faith.[57] But HUAC's early importance was less its investigative endeavors than its function as the source for most of the legislative provisions that would later fuel the conduct of the cold war: the Hatch Act of 1939 (barring federal employees from engaging in political activities), the reintroduction of the Espionage Act of 1917, and the Alien Registration [Smith] Act of 1940 (establishing the registration, fingerprinting, and grounds for deportation of aliens), which was the first peacetime sedition act since the "reign of the witches" in 1798.

The invasion of the Soviet Union by Hitler's forces in 1941 stalemated many of the congressional programs designed to root out communists and their fellow travelers from the federal bureaucracy, because the wartime alliance with Stalin spawned a massive reversal in public perceptions of the Soviet Union. A *Life* special issue in March 1943 described Lenin as "perhaps the greatest man of modern times," the Russians were said to be "one hell of a people... [who] to a remarkable degree... look like Americans, dress like Americans, and think like Americans," and the NKVD was described as "a national police similar to the FBI."[58] But the propensity of official opinion to swing one way and then the other on the potential threat of communism and the Soviet Union meant that HUAC's legislative legacy lay in wait for another episode of anticommunist fervor. Indeed, what was different about this moment from previous potential red scares was that for the first time the federal government had expanded its peacetime authority to handle political dissent beyond the immigration laws. As Heale notes—in a development that aided the nexus between extensive and intensive power—it was the nationalization of American state authority that established the possibility for the overt and extensive politicization of anticommunism.[59]

What was similar about this moment to the earlier red scares was that loyalty was the issue around which the articulation of danger coalesced. In 1920 the National Civic Federation's *Review* offered the following conclusion on the danger to America:

> Therefore, please note that our present national problems are not primarily political and not primarily economic. These are important phases, but they are secondary. *Our problems are primarily spiritual, since they concern the spirit of the American people.* Loyalty to America is essentially loyalty to its ideals. Defensive loyalty is the defense of these ideals when they are in danger; constructive loyalty is the application of these ideals to new problems of national life.[60]

This assessment was something of an update on the Puritan theme of a chosen nation in which people had to believe, and the classical republican conviction that democratic polities were peculiarly susceptible to subversion by foreign influences. Together, these concerns pointed to the importance of ideological purity as the defining moment in the imagined community of America. The early cold war conformed to this schema, particularly in its overtly spiritual moments. Theologians and preachers like Reinhold Neibuhr and Billy Graham highlighted the sin and avarice of American society and were prominent in shaping public discourse: Neibuhr in his position as the establishment's official theologian, and Graham in his public crusades (during which he once preached that the paradise of Eden contained "no union dues, no labor leaders, no snakes, no disease").[61] A particularly striking example of such thinking was the way in which the words *one nation under God* were added to the Pledge of Allegiance in 1954. In a sermon attended by President Eisenhower and his wife, a Presbyterian minister argued that without this phrase, the Pledge could be applicable to any republic, even the Soviet Union, for it was lacking "the characteristic and definitive factor in the American way of life." Congress reacted immediately to Eisenhower's call for action; seventeen bills to this effect were introduced, one of which the president signed into law on Flag Day (June 14) 1954. Two years later, but in the same vein, Congress ordained as the nation's official motto the words that had been on the coins of the republic since the Civil War: "In God We Trust."[62] Given these reaffirmations of America's iconic quality, it is not surprising that the loyalty oath has had (as chapter 5 demonstrated) a venerable history in the disciplining of social and political conflict in America. In this context, Arthur Miller's play *The Crucible*, which was as much about the political climate of 1952 as it was the religious climate of 1692, was a powerful statement of the persistence of the techniques of witchcraft hysteria — charges without evidence against crimes of belief — across the centuries.

In statements made at the time, many things other than traditional national security concerns were at stake in the threat ascribed to communism. Rupert Hughes, founder of the Motion Picture Alliance for the Preservation of American Ideals, argued before HUAC's Hollywood hearings that although there was never any open communist propaganda on the screen, "where you see a little drop of cyanide in the picture, a small grain of arsenic, something that makes every Senator, every businessman, every employer a crook and which destroys our beliefs in American free enterprise, that is communistic." Albert Canwell, chair of the Washington State Legislative Fact-Finding Committee on Un-American Activities argued that "if someone insists that there is discrimination against Negroes in this country, or that there is inequality of wealth, there is every reason to believe that person is a Communist." When Truman proposed a national health insurance scheme in 1948, the American Medical Association attacked it as a "monstrosity of Bolshevik bureaucracy," and faked a quote from Lenin to the effect that "socialized medicine is the keystone to the arch of the Socialist State." And in the Rosenberg trial, the judge argued that the defendants' crime was worse than murder because they were accused of the "denial of the sanctity of the individual and [of] aggression against free men everywhere instead of serving the cause of liberty."[63]

In this context, the loyalty oath took on a renewed importance as the test that could weed out those who professed un-American beliefs. Many private employers came to use it to screen their workforce, but it was state authorities who made it a condition of many aspects of daily life. By the early 1950s, "the swearing of loyalty oaths was ... required to obtain permits to fish in New York city reservoirs, to become a public accountant in New York state, to sell insurance or pianos in Washington, D.C., to obtain unemployment compensation in Ohio, to box, wrestle, barber or sell junk in Indiana, to be licensed as a pharmacist in Texas or to become a veterinarian in the state of Washington."[64] In Texas, where the writers of school textbooks were bound by these declarations, the legislature resolved that "the American history courses in the public schools [must] emphasize in the textbooks our glowing and throbbing history of hearts and souls inspired by wonderful American principles and traditions."[65] It was the federal government that provided the impetus for this wave of ideological screening, however.

The Truman administration, in a move designed to head off congressional pressure, established a Temporary Commission on Loyalty in 1946. Its report the following year became the basis for Executive Order 9835, which set forth the procedures and standards for the examination of federal employees. The Truman order justified its concern on the grounds that "each employee of the Government of the United States is endowed with a measure of trusteeship over the democratic processes which are the heart and sinew of the United States." It then set the following standards:

1. The standard for the refusal of employment or the removal from employment in an executive department or agency on grounds

relating to loyalty shall be that, on all the evidence, reasonable grounds exist for belief that the person involved is disloyal to the Government of the United States.

2. Activities and associations of an applicant or employee which may be considered in connection with the determination of disloyalty may include one or more of the following:

   a. Sabotage, espionage, or attempts or preparations therefor, or knowingly associating with spies or saboteurs;

   b. Treason or sedition or advocacy therefor;

   c. Advocacy of revolution or force or violence to alter the constitutional form of government of the United States;

   d. Intentional, unauthorized disclosure to any person under circumstances which may indicate disloyalty to the United States, of documents or information of a confidential or non-public character obtained by the person making the disclosure as a result of his employment by the Government of the United States;

   e. Performing or attempting to perform his duties, or otherwise acting, so as to serve the interests of another government in preference to the interests of the United States;

   f. Membership in, or affiliation with or sympathetic association with any foreign or domestic organization, association, movement, group or combination of persons, designated by the Attorney General as totalitarian, fascist, communist, or subversive, or as having adopted a policy of advocating or approving the commission of acts of force or violence to deny other persons their rights under the Constitution of the United States, or as seeking to alter the form of government of the United States by unconstitutional means.[66]

In 1953, the Eisenhower administration made some important changes with far-reaching consequences to the Truman loyalty program. Shifting the emphasis from "loyalty" to "security," Eisenhower's administration defined its concern in a novel way and expanded the categories of exclusion. Executive Order 10450, which rescinded Truman's, began by stating that "the interests of the national security require that all persons privileged to be employed in the departments and agencies of the Government, shall be reliable, trustworthy, of good character, and of complete and unswerving loyalty to the United States."[67] To be sure, loyalty remained an important issue, and many people considered loyalty and security to be synonymous. But the Eisenhower executive order marks a clear and identifiable moment in the development of what Foucault has termed a "society of security." In this understanding, the state is neither a monolith that exercises power over an independent social domain, nor a settled identity that simply responds to external stimuli. Instead, the state and the social are made possible by "multiple regimes of governmentality," which employ a rationality of security that calculates the possible and the probable, and simultaneously individualizes and totalizes, asking for both the citizen and the state what it means to be governed.[68] In this context, by replacing a concern for "the democratic processes which are the heart and sinew of the United States" (the rationale of the Truman program) with "the interests of the national security," the Eisenhower program constituted in a different way the object it purported to defend. By diminishing (though not eradicating) the classical republican notion of the role of a citizen in a democratic polity, and substituting for it an abstracted and reified notion of "the interests of the national security," Eisenhower both extended the domain of the state's interest and increased the intensiveness of its concern. As a pivotal textual moment in the passage from the defense of the nation to the constitution of the national security state, Eisenhower's executive order multiplied the dimensions of being along which threats to security could be observed, thereby amplifying in the name of security the sense of endangeredness the nation would feel. This is evident in the expansion of categories of exclusion. In addition to the Truman order's classification of danger, the following was added:

> The investigations conducted pursuant to this order shall be designed to develop information as to whether the employment or retention in employment in the Federal service of the person being investigated is clearly consistent with the interests of the national security. Such information shall relate, but shall not be limited, to the following:
>
> (1) Depending on the relation of the Government employment to the national security:
>   (i) Any behavior, activities, or associations which tend to show that the individual is not reliable or trustworthy.
>   (ii) Any deliberate misrepresentations, falsifications, or omissions of material facts.
>   (iii) Any criminal, infamous, dishonest, immoral, or notoriously disgraceful conduct, habitual use of intoxicants to excess, drug addiction, sexual perversion, or financial irresponsibility.
>   (iv) Any adjudication of insanity, or treatment for serious mental or neurological disorder without satisfactory evidence of cure.
>   (v) Any facts which furnish reason to believe that the individual may be subjected to coercion, influence, or pressure which may cause him to act contrary to the best interests of the national security.[69]

The loyalty-security program in the decade 1947–57 covered some 13.5 million people, or some 20 percent of the workforce. Just under 5 million were scrutinized for government employment, with the remainder being private sector employees whose work with defense contractors brought them into the program. The scheme cost some $350 million, required over 26,000 field investigations by the FBI to pursue information of a detrimental nature, resulted in over 11,000 people losing their jobs, and uncovered no espionage or sabotage.[70] It was nonetheless a very effective program, though not for the advertised reasons.

No rationalist assessment of the program's impact can fully appreciate the social and political effects it had in inscribing the boundaries of identity. In such an assessment, social control would be the organizing principle, and the conduct of the program would be appraised on its ability to faithfully carry out its aims and scrupulously avoid any digression from established procedure. But in these terms, the loyalty-security program was conducted in a dubious manner. Many innocent people were wrongly charged and either removed from or denied employment, while many who were cleared by the loyalty and security review boards were nonetheless made by their employer to pay the same price an adverse finding would have incurred. The effects of suspicion thus exceeded the procedures and standards prescribed in the executive orders.

This had an important implication. The global inscription of danger was something that long preceded the cold war, but it was in the cold war, when numerous overseas obligations were constructed, that the identity of the United States became even more deeply implicated in the external reach of the state. What the Eisenhower security program reveals is that concomitant with this external expansion was an internal magnification of the modes of existence that were to be interpreted as risks. Danger was being totalized in the external realm in conjunction with its increased individualization in the internal field, with the result being the performative reconstitution of the borders of the state's identity. In this sense, the cold war needs to be understood as a disciplinary strategy that was global in scope but national in design. It was like earlier instances in which the practices of foreign policy enabled the conduct of Foreign Policy, but also different from them insofar as the articulation of "security" involved a new writing of the boundaries of American identity.

In this context, discipline, rather than control, was the program's modus operandi. This is not surprising given that the nature of the "crime" with which people were accused was overtly political and

ideological, and bore little if any relationship to a (traditionally conceived) threat to national security. Indeed, what these "crimes" did
achieve was not the rooting out of an objective threat, but the reproduction of a standard, an optimal mean, around which those modes
of being considered "normal" could be organized.[71] In this context,
consider a range of the charges that brought people under surveillance:

> A reliable source has disclosed that at a meeting held at the [——]
> School in [the housing development] during National Brotherhood
> Week in 1943–1944, a motion was made by one Mr. [——] that "the
> Bible should be burned and start building from there," and that
> you verbally seconded the motion and discussed it.
>
> Specifically, it is charged that you continued sympathetic associ-
> ation with a known Communist, read Communist literature and
> made pro-Communist statements.
>
> That about 1937–38 in or around [city #1, state], you actively par-
> ticipated in collecting funds for purchase of an ambulance for the
> use of the Loyalist Army in the Spanish Civil War.
>
> In connection with your study at the University of [X] in the pur-
> suit of a Ph.D. degree in 1950–51, you wrote a thesis which was based
> mainly on material from the Institute of Pacific Relations which
> was cited as a Communist Front organization by the House Com-
> mittee on Un-American Activities . . . furthermore, it is believed that
> your thesis is definitely sympathetic with the aims and ambitions
> of Soviet Russia.
>
> During 1941 and thereafter, at [city, state], and [city, state] and
> elsewhere, you demonstrated a sympathetic interest in programs,
> policies and causes of the Communist Party. During this period
> you regularly read the "Daily Worker" and openly advocated and
> supported the political viewpoint of that publication in discussions
> with fellow employees and others. In this connection you are re-
> ported to have made statements to the effect that "the downtrod-
> den masses and underprivileged people are not being treated fairly
> in the United States." It is also reported that you expressed approval
> of the political viewpoints of Paul Robeson, a long time member of
> the Communist Party.
>
> You have maintained a close and continuing association with
> your brother [name], who: a. Is a close associate of reported Com-
> munist Party members and sympathizers, including [ten named in-
> dividuals].
>
> In a sworn statement made before an authorized representative
> of the Civil Service Commission on September, . . . 1954, you stated
> that within six months after your appointment with the [agency] in
> 1942, you were aware that [C], a former employee of the [agency]
> was a homosexual. You stated that during the period of your employ-

ment, [C] had propositioned you on several occasions. Also, that approximately two years ago, you and [Employee] met [C] and [D] in the [——] Restaurant, and after a few drinks the four of you went to [D's] hotel room where you and [C] and Employee [B] and [D] participated in homosexual acts.

You have consistently been a trouble maker, antagonizer, and braggart while employed in the [Agency].

He had cohabited for some time with a woman who was not his wife.

Your statements over an extended period of time show your dissatisfaction with the U.S. form of government and your preference for the Russian or other form of totalitarian government.

You were a member of the Consumers Union which is cited as a Communist front by the House Committee on Un-American Activities.

That you: (a) Exhibited a hypercritical attitude toward society that appeared to reflect home indoctrination; (b) Were a member of a family considered as extremely radical and sympathetic to the Communist Party; (c) Had a father who: 1. Was a Communist sympathizer.[72]

When called to appear before the Security Hearing Board, those accused would be asked a range of questions by board members to elicit more information pertaining to the charges. Consider the following sample of the kind of questions that some people were asked:

What do you think of female chastity?

What was your reaction upon receiving these charges? Didn't you feel remorseful from some of the things you did in your life?

What were your feelings at the time concerning race equality?

The file indicates . . . that you were critical . . . of the . . . large property owners?

The file indicates that you were quite hepped up over the One World idea?

At one time or two, you were a strong advocate of the United Nations. Are you still?

Do you or your wife regularly attend any organized church services?

Have you ever indicated that you favored a redistribution of wealth?

Have you ever expressed yourself as being in favor of the abolition of trademarks?

Do you think that the workers in the Capitalistic system get a relatively fair deal?[73]

Like Ole Hanson's 1920 paean to Americanism quoted above, the charges and questions pursued by the Security Hearing Board were concerned with the ethical boundaries of identity rather than the territorial borders of the state. Furthermore, aside from the scant relationship between the concerns of these charges and questions and a threat to national security as traditionally understood, what is most striking about the topics ranged across is the way they parallel the issues (even today) tracked by immigration authorities when considering potential residents and citizens. Indeed, there is a Janus-faced quality to the border inscribed by these and the INS questions discussed in chapter 2: the former look inward to contain difference while the latter gaze outward to screen perceived risks. In this conjunction, we find a different appreciation of what is meant by *containment* as the pivotal strategy of the cold war. As Andrew Ross has argued with respect to George Kennan's writings, there are two meanings of containment integral to this period: "one which speaks to a threat *outside* of the social body, a threat which therefore has to be isolated, in quarantine, and kept at bay from the domestic; and a second meaning of containment, which speaks to the domestic *contents* of the social body, a threat internal to the host which must then be neutralized by being contained, or 'domesticated.'"[74] And at this conjunction of the two conceptions of containment, in an echo of Hobbes's strategies of otherness designed to discipline the asperity and irregularity of the figure of "man," we find the liminal groups that mark off the border of the state.

This refiguration of containment—away from a practice of foreign and defense policy, toward a strategy central to the constitution of a society of security—can be illustrated by three examples that exhibit the boundary-inscribing qualities suggested above. The first is the salience of sociomedical discourse in representing external as well as internal threats. We have noted before Kennan's references to disease, but (like containment) this was not an exclusively American characteristic. Perhaps the boldest postwar declaration of this kind was offered by Churchill, to the effect that Bolshevism "is not a policy; it's a disease. It is not a creed; it is a pestilence...It breaks out with great suddenness; it is violently contagious; it throws people into a frenzy of excitement; it spreads with extraordinary rapidity; the mortality is terrible; so that after a while, like other pestilences, the disease tends to wear itself out." As Stephanson notes, these formulations give the often used notion of a cordon sanitaire as the operationalization of containment added poignancy.[75] Moreover, these figurations enable a power relationship between those who make the diagnosis and those said to be afflicted. For example, when Kennan's long telegram was leaked to journalists in 1946, it was the source for an article in *Time* accompanied by a map with the heading "Communist Contagion," which showed Iran, Turkey, and Manchuria as "infected," with Saudi Arabia, Egypt, Afghanistan, and India as "exposed."[76] The implication was that the United States occupied the position of the doctor with the right if not the duty to intervene. Such a logic was also clearly manifested in the Kennedy administration's counterinsurgency plans. National Security Memorandum 182 of 1962 (with the interesting title of "U.S. Overseas Internal Defense Policy") stated that America's role is "(1) To assist in the immunization of vulnerable societies not yet seriously threatened by communist subversion or insurgency. (2) To assist countries where subversive insurgency is latent or incipient to defeat the threat by removing its causes before the stage of insurgency is reached." The diagnostician's logic was laid out in the section on intelligence: "An intelligence effort must: (a) Identify those free world countries where the threat of subversion is potential, latent, or incipient. (b) Appraise the nature and scope of the threat, the underlying causes, and the significant factors related thereto."[77]

A second example of how a strategy of containment inscribed the boundaries of identity can be found in the preoccupation of the era with the relationship between sexuality, deviance, and national strength. National strength in the early cold war era, it was argued, depended on the ability of strong men to stand up to the threats of communism. In this context, "deviant" sexual behavior became a national obsession in the United States after World War II, being one of the categories of risk in the Eisenhower executive order. The Senate issued a report in 1950 entitled "Employment of Homosexuals and Other Sex Perverts in Government," which proclaimed that "one homosexual can pollute a Government office." Within the logic of security, this concern was premised on the notion that sexual indulgence and perversion weakens the moral fiber of the individual, making them susceptible to temptation by outside forces.[78] But homosexuality as a symbol for the pathology of deviance has an established history (as mentioned in chapter 4), particularly when it is alluded to by the gendering of people or policies as feminine. During World War I, for example, an elitist patriotic group called the Military Order of the World War was agitated by the fact that Bertrand Russell— "the effeminate, pacifist representative of the 'Pink Intelligentsia' of England" —was speaking to women's peace groups in the United States.[79] The appellation "pink" (and sometimes "lavender") to represent liberal, socialist, or communist thought has an obviously gendered connotation, made clear by Richard Nixon when he argued that his opponent in the 1950 California Senate campaign, Helen G. Douglas, was "pink right down to her underwear."[80] And when the liberal intellectual Arthur Schlesinger wrote favorably of "the new virility" of postwar leaders in contrast to the "political sterility" of their opponents, he argued that communism was "something secret, sweaty and furtive like nothing so much, in the phrase of one wise observer of modern Russia, as homosexuals in a boys' school."[81]

But "deviance" was not the only object of sexual concern in this context. Just as the Eisenhower executive order listed "immoral or notoriously disgraceful conduct" alongside "sexual perversion" as inconsistent with the interests of the national security, so too the culture of the period fretted about the power of female sexuality to entice "normal" men from the moral path. The association of women and aggressive power was evidenced by the usual iconography of sensual women that adorned fighter planes and bombers; the calling of saucy women outside the home "bombshells," "knockouts," or "dynamite"; and the placing of a photograph of Rita Hayworth on the hydrogen bomb dropped on the Bikini Islands. The islands then provided the name for the revealing swimsuit that female "bombshells" could wear.[82] Of course, this fear of female sexuality—which resonated with a cultural disposition to understand conflict in terms of the clash between *virtu* and *fortuna*—was not divorced from the changes in gender relationships that the war had wrought, when increasing numbers of women entered the workforce. This transformation was accompanied, however, by an increasing emphasis on notions of domesticity, and when the war ended but danger was not overcome, domesticity became a prominent feature of the cold war's cultural terrain.[83] In this context, the nuclear family might be considered part of a strategy of domestic containment: sexuality would be contained through sexual restraint outside marriage and traditional gender roles within.[84]

Finally, the liberal response to the onset of McCarthyism provides an example of how containment was an ensemble of strategies, the effect of which was to domesticate identity, and helps illustrate the various official mechanisms that produce a society of security. In the hysteria of the red scare after 1948, liberal senators were seeking means to codify security concerns in a way that avoided a repeat of the exclusionary logic behind the internment of Japanese-Americans during World War II. In that instance, nearly 120,000 Japanese—two-thirds of whom were American citizens—were interned in ten camps designed to civilize (or "Americanize," as the director of the War Relocation Authority preferred) the inmates because of doubts about their loyalty.[85] To avoid a repetition of this, the Emergency Detention Act of 1950 (EDA) was introduced. Its purpose was to establish the committing of, or conspiracy to commit, espionage or sabotage as the legal grounds for the detention of dangerous individuals, thereby siding with the Truman executive order's understanding of a security threat. Eventually passed as Title II of the Internal Security [McCarran] Act of 1950, the EDA mandated the building of internment camps. Congress set aside money in 1952 to establish six camps for the internment of people designated under the act during an emergency—one of them was Tule Lake in California, which had held Japanese during World War II—but they were never used and no money for them was appropriated after 1957.[86] The liberal impetus of the EDA notwithstanding, two unacknowledged corollaries to its logic actually exacerbated the problem it was trying to solve. First, the fact that detention began only after an emergency was declared gave considerable power to those who could specify that exception. Second, the speedy detention of dangerous people required that information on potentially dangerous people be gathered as an ongoing project.[87] Indeed, one of the liberals' overt policies was to give the FBI greater authority over the collection of information on subversives as a way of stymieing the adhoc arrangements of political mavericks like McCarthy.

But the conduct of the FBI thwarted that intention. In 1943, Attorney General Francis Biddle ordered the FBI to terminate and destroy the Custodial Detention List, which had been begun in 1939. Biddle's reasoning was that "the notion that it is possible to make a valid determination as to how dangerous a person is . . . without reference to time, environment, and other relevant circumstances, is impractical, unwise, and dangerous [sic]." J. Edgar Hoover—who had begun his career at the FBI in 1919 with responsibility for the list of 100,000 "radically inclined individuals," a list that within a year of his employment quadrupled in size and enabled the Palmer raids—saw no such problem. In a 1943 letter to special agents that disregarded Biddle's order, Hoover wrote that "the Bureau will continue to investigate dangerous and potentially dangerous individuals."[88] The fruits of these labors were to be found in the FBI's Security, Communist, and Reserve Indexes, which were concealed from successive political authorities and expanded to such an extent that the Bureau had over 500,000 files in its central office by the early 1970s.[89]

Above all else, what was most revealing about the liberals' attempts to regularize the procedures that interpreted people as dangerous was the way they replicated earlier instances in which similar techniques of exclusion had been directed against different targets. In

World War I, for example, it was prostitutes, or women who were suspected of being prostitutes, who were interned. The Commission on Training Camp Activities (CTCA), with its Social Hygiene Instruction Division, was established after the United States entered the war in 1917 to deal with the sexual and moral aspect of the call-up. Under the guise of its "American Plan," the CTCA arrested, detained, and interned women picked up within a certain radius of all military installations. By the end of the war, some 30,000 women had been dealt with in this way. About half of those were infected with venereal disease and were ostensibly sent to hospitals or farm colonies for treatment, but most ended up in jails or workhouses for between two and twelve months. The other half, however, were only suspected of having venereal disease, and were in effect treated as subversives because their lifestyle (single and mobile) transgressed the normal boundaries of morality.[90]

This replication of earlier techniques of exclusion, particularly by liberals who sought to ameliorate what they saw as the fanaticism of McCarthy and his ilk, suggests that the application of internal security measures in the early cold war period was not an aberration brought on by the climate of the period.[91] Neither was the application of these techniques derived from the existence of an objective danger. In addition to the fact that many of the legislative instruments liberals introduced or supported in this period (such as the Communist Control Act of 1954) delegitimized internal practices by associating them with an external enemy, many others (like the Immigration and Nationality [McCarran-Walter] Act of 1952) survived both the Warren court's opinions of the late 1950s and the easing of relations with the Soviet Union. Along with the FBI's counterintelligence program (COINTELPRO, begun in the same year that the Supreme Court curtailed both the McCarran and Smith Acts), these mechanisms of security lay in wait—like their predecessors in the late 1930s—for a new episode in which they could be exercised against different groups, movements, and ideologies interpreted as dangers. And in the late 1960s, they were to rear their heads once again.

A Crisis of Culture

No period subsequent to the late 1940s and early 1950s has yet to witness an evangelism of fear similar to the extensiveness and intensiveness of that which characterized the early cold war. But there have been moments in which a new episode looked like it might be emerging. For example, after a period of massive civil, racial, and urban unrest in the late 1960s, the Nixon administration proposed to reactivate the Subversive Activities Control Board and give it renewed authority. By adding the proviso that "a policy of unlawfully advocating the commission of acts of force or violence" would be grounds for regarding a group as equivalent to those already designated as totalitarian, fascist, communist, or subversive, the administration sought a further expansion of Eisenhower's categories of exclusion. However, this amendment was ultimately rescinded.[92] In a similar vein, there were rumors that the Emergency Detention Act would be activated for the problems of the period. The House Un-American Activities Committee (which survived the 1960s, but which was renamed the Internal Security Committee before being abolished in the early 1970s) noted in a 1968 report that Title II of the McCarran Act "might well be utilized for the temporary imprisonment of warring guerrillas." The effect of this was to spur negative interest in the act, which eventually led to its repeal in 1971.[93]

Although the sense of fear spawned by anticommunism proved to be less successful as a disciplinary code by the late 1960s, there are good grounds on which to argue that the moral concerns that originally animated it, and the techniques through which it was deployed, insinuated themselves into a different form. In this and the previous chapter, we have seen how the Puritan legacy of the covenant and the jeremiad both induced and remained important to, albeit in a different context, classical republicanism with its fear of corruption and subversion. Moreover, as organizing thematics, each of these modes exacerbated the logic of identity and licensed the temptation of otherness in the performative constitution of the imagined community of America. But in the post–World War II environment, the society of security, with its catalog of exclusions that imperilled the national security, was the dominant problematization in the constitution of American identity. It did not replace or totally subsume that from which it was derived, however. Just as the shift from the church to the state (as argued in chapter 3) was a case of one occupying the position of the other and thereby providing novel answers to traditional questions, so too the transition from covenant to republic to society of security does not involve a complete breach that frees the new from the shackles of the old. Besides, for all the distinctions between these modes of identity, some common themes run through them all. Most importantly, each combines nationalism, eschatology, and chauvinism in a particular way, such that the spiritual and the secular are intertwined. As noted at the beginning of this chapter, all states share this principle, but in America it is intensified. The political discourse of the 1960s, in which the concerns of the society of security were addressed in the figurations of republicanism and with the spirit of a jeremiad, are testament to this.

Beginning in the mid-1960s, a series of developments challenged each of the fundamental principles behind cold war liberalism and propagated a sense of decline. A number of international referents were available. Changes in the global political economy produced economic conditions that limited the growth of the welfare state, demonstrated the power of Western Europe and Japan, and hampered cooperation between the industrialized nations. The United States' superiority in strategic nuclear indices was giving way to essential equivalence with the Soviet Union. And the Vietnam War vividly demonstrated the limits of American power and contributed to the world's economic dilemmas.[94] Moreover, dissent within the power blocs surrounding the superpowers — the Sino-Soviet split, France's withdrawal from NATO, and West Germany's *Ostpolitik* — combined with the assertion of sovereignty and rights by the so-called Third World, suggested to many that the easily understood bipolar configuration of global politics in the postwar era was coming to an end.[95]

But as with previous periods of uncertainty in which evangelisms of fear were generated, the sense of danger associated with this period was as much cultural as it was objective and external. The election of Richard Nixon in 1968 coincided with the open rupture of the policy elite in the wake of the Tet offensive in Vietnam earlier that year. Alongside international upheavals (the Soviet invasion of Czechoslovakia and the domestic French struggles being just two), the assassinations of Martin Luther King Jr. and Robert F. Kennedy, the violence surrounding the Democratic convention in Chicago, and the continuing protests of the civil rights, antiwar and women's movements, there seemed to be a major crisis facing the American polity.[96] A new consensus about the dissensus emerged: it was a situation that one observer characterized as "disorder within, disorder without."[97] And a new source of critique — neoconservatism — sought order out of chaos by appeals to past virtues and earlier dangers.

As former liberals who retained a commitment to capitalism with some moral vision but who were cognizant of its contemporary problems, the neoconservatives were an amorphous group who noted the failures of the Great Society, criticized the affirmative action programs designed to remedy inequality, bemoaned the lack of order at home, and became impatient with the inability to use American force abroad.[98] Traumatized by the 1960s, the neoconservatives regarded the "counterculture" of that era as an onslaught against tradition and authority, a veritable "consecration of disorder."[99] Ignoring the changing political economy and the performance of political elites as factors in the polity's problems, the neoconservatives focused on cultural explanations for the various crises. It was, they maintained, the lack of bourgeois constraints for liberal capitalism that had precipitated the problems of public policy. The English neoconservative Paul Johnson maintained that "civilized societies require institutions which restrain our passions and supplement our shortcomings. The three principle ones are the family, organized religion and the state."[100]

For the neoconservatives, sexual and racial conflict, poverty, and economic disorder were functions of what one exponent called "the twilight of authority."[101] Nisbet argued that "the giant political apparatus of the modern state, part war machine, part welfare machine, complete bureaucracy," presides over a wasteland with "the littered remains of authority, political community, family, religion, moral values and cultural excellence."[102] This litany of revolution was a consequence of the radical opposition of the 1960s, an outgrowth of what Samuel Huntington termed the "democratic distemper."[103]

Huntington regarded the democratic activity of the 1960s as a general challenge to systems of authority, public and private. The result of expanding education, among other factors, this democratic surge made demands on government that could no longer be fulfilled. The Great Society programs designed to achieve a measure of social justice after a period of sustained economic growth were a result of these demands, which could not be met by a fiscally constrained state trying to pay for the Vietnam War without raising taxes. There was thus a gap between expectations of the government and its performance at the same time that there was a disjunction between the extent of governmental activity and its authority. This "excess of democracy" was the greatest threat to democracy, according to Huntington, who, in terms akin to those of John Adams two centuries earlier, wrote:

> The vulnerability of democratic government in the United States thus comes not primarily from external threats, though such threats are real, nor from internal subversion from the left or the right, although both possibilities could exist, but rather from the internal dynamics of democracy itself in a highly educated, mobilized, and participant society.[104]

The neoconservative critique was a declaration about the state of political identity in the United States. Concerned with the demise of Enlightenment thinking about progress and problem solving, it was alarmed at the "spreading mediocrity" of American society and attitudes. With its cultural focus and concern for "faith," "nerve," and "will," the critique—in a jeremiad-like narrative that invoked classical republican themes for the society of security—did not distinguish between domestic and international domains, but linked the crises at home with the inability to act abroad. As Daniel Bell lamented, "Today, the belief in American exceptionalism had vanished with the end of empire, the weakening of power, the loss of faith in the nation's future."[105] In his terms the prospects for the future were not bright: "Despite a common culture, there is no common purpose, or common faith, only bewilderment."[106]

For some, like Norman Podhoretz, the diagnosis was equally bleak but salvation was possible with a redirection of Foreign Policy. Podhoretz argued that, like Britain in the wake of World War I, the United States in the wake of Vietnam was cultivating a "culture of appeasement."[107] In the same spirit as his colleagues' denunciations of the anti-authoritarianism of the 1960s, Podhoretz saw the cultural crisis at home as precipitating a security crisis abroad: "This malevolent legacy of the war in Vietnam, this combination of pacifism, anti-Americanism, and isolationism . . . [is] all working against American resolve to resist the forward surge of Soviet imperialism."[108] The "strategic retreat" of the Nixon Doctrine, he argued, had allowed "Soviet proxies" in the form of Cuban troops to occupy Angola and led the United States to look on while various nations had fallen to factions supported by or loyal to the Soviet Union.[109]

Podhoretz argued that there was a historical precedent for turning America around, overthrowing the "culture of appeasement," and advancing domestic and international prosperity. Taking the cold war to be a period of struggle against an unambiguous Soviet threat, and writing with the verve of a Puritan preacher, he maintained that in pulling together to combat this threat the American people "experienced a surge of self-confident energy" that had provided the prosperity and harmony characteristic of the dominant understanding of postwar American society.[110]

With order precarious at home and abroad, the neoconservative strategy was the pursuit of a stable, unified society at home through an emphasis on foreign threats as a means "to generate the requisite national allegiance and discipline."[111] As Steinfels argues, "their determination to find an overseas opponent, whether Idi Amin, Fabian socialism, Eurocommunism or Soviet power, seemed constant despite the vast difference in geopolitical and military factors."[112] In this context, international developments became less important for their impact on U.S. security "than as markers of how far America has fallen from the necessary strength of will."[113]

Yet for all their foreign preoccupations, neoconservatives argued that no factor in the crisis of authority was more important than challenges to the family. Throughout the 1960s, pressure from social forces on the inside and the outside had loosened the nexus between cold war practices and the nuclear family. Now the neoconservatives argued that it had to be reinstated and reinvigorated to arrest the social decline and moral decay of the United States.[114] Specifically, the neoconservatives maintained that the crisis of liberalism was brought on by the changed nature of the relationship between the family and the state. Because of economic pressures arising from the increasing demands (associated with the "excess of democracy") on the welfare state, taxes had been raised, inflation had increased, and the sole male breadwinner was no longer able to sustain his family. As a consequence, the married woman had been pulled into the labor force to make up the shortfall, thereby destroying the patriarchal family and, in their terms, the moral order of society. Irving Kristol argued that the welfare state was responsible for having made "the child fatherless, the mother husbandless, the husband useless."[115] The "problem of the family" for the neoconservatives was that the husband had lost patriarchal authority to the working wife.[116] The significance of this is that it promulgated a new range of groups and issues considered threatening. These included drugs, busing, crime, welfare, taxes, abortion, affirmative action, gay rights, capital punishment, child abuse, women's rights, gun control, divorce, and a general permissiveness.[117]

Valid or otherwise, the neoconservative lament of declining moral standards, the destruction of the traditional family, and a loss of will at home and nerve abroad—signified most obviously by the "Vietnam syndrome," which one writer called "le cancer Americain"—came to dominate American public discourse in the late 1970s.[118] It was a political discourse to which the Nixon, Carter, and Reagan administrations variously accommodated their Foreign Policies. The Nixon administration sought to stabilize the cold war identity of the United States by accommodating global developments in a strategy that pursued different means to similar ends. Security was to be reformulated but not fundamentally altered. The Carter administration recognized that American identity had been undermined by the struggles of the 1960s, but regarded the rigid cold war practices that had resulted in Vietnam and Watergate as responsible. For the Carter administration, to return to cold war practices would thus have been to perpetuate the excesses of applying dogma in an inherently complex and differentiated world, thereby retracing the path to the present crisis. Equally, to follow the Nixonian path of accommodation would not have provided a clear enough break with past practices and would have thus failed to differentiate the administration's own identity without addressing the problems of America's malaise. Security was to be fundamentally rewritten. The neoconservatives regarded the cold war identity of the 1940s and 1950s as having been undermined by the counterculture of the 1960s. They sought its reimposition by a return to cold war foreign policy practices. Security was to be reimposed by a return to past practices.

The election of the Reagan administration saw the implementation of the neoconservatives' evangelism of fear and, consequentially, the beginning of the second cold war.[119] But the disciplining of identity was not left to the techniques of anticommunism alone. In part because the hysteria of the early cold war could not be easily copied — though many of its strategies were reproduced — new targets of exclusion were found. Most notably, those who had once been pursued on the grounds that they or their activities and beliefs were revolutionary, subversive, or militant, were (from the mid-1970s on) subsumed under the label "terrorist."[120] As "a commodity in enormous demand . . . [but] in pitifully short supply" within the United States, terrorism replicates a number of key facets previously associated with communism, most notably the combination of the tropes of savagery, revolution, and foreign agents.[121] Once the designation of terrorist was made, anyone thought to be associated in any way with a group so defined could be placed under scrutiny. Moreover, the definition of "terrorism" is very loose and extremely wide-ranging: California state law criminalizes gang membership as "street terrorism," while local authorities in Rhode Island established in 1985 a "Terrorist Extremist Suppression Team," which served to monitor left-wing political groups and peace activists.[122]

Infamous in this regard was the FBI's COINTELPRO tracking of various groups within the United States opposed to the Reagan administration policies in Central America, particularly the Committee in Support of the People of El Salvador (CISPES). Because of allegations that CISPES was linked to the Farabundo Martí National Liberation Front (FMLN) in El Salvador, a four-year clandestine operation was mounted in 1981 to detect illegal activity among similar groups in fifty-eight cities. None was found, and the director of the FBI was forced to acknowledge in 1988 that groups like CISPES were "involved in political activities involving First Amendment rights and not international terrorism."[123] That such an extensive operation failed to find activity of the kind it was allegedly pursuing was not uncommon for the FBI. A 1976 General Accounting Office review of 19,000 open FBI case files concluded that in only seventeen were any actions being proposed by those under surveillance, while only six of those had the potential for violence. When asked, the Bureau was unable to provide any evidence to Congress that it had prevented a single act of violence through these programs.[124]

The Reagan administration's preoccupation with counterterrorism also reproduced some of the logic behind the cold war's Emergency Detention Act. Under the aegis of Vice President Bush's Task Force on Terrorism, a bureaucratic body called the Alien Border Control Committee was so convinced of the danger emanating from "communist terrorists in Central America," that it drafted secret plans, to be implemented in the event of a national emergency, to close the U.S.-Mexican border and intern all aliens in that region.[125] Equally, some in Congress during this period sought to implement similar measures. In a move that recalled the early twentieth-century effort to use the deportation of aliens under the provisions of the immigration laws as a means of disciplining political dissent, Senator Strom Thurmond, a Republican from South Carolina, introduced a proposal to establish secret hearings with concealed evidence to facilitate the deportation of "terrorists" from the United States. Eventually defeated, this initiative resurfaced in the Bush administration's 1991 crime bill, with the added proviso that associating in any manner with a group defined by the government as "terrorist" (raising money for the African National Congress, for example) qualified as "terrorism." However, this proposal met a fate similar to that of its predecessor after some Democrats and most civil liberties groups vehemently opposed it.[126]

The texts of postwar Foreign Policy reviewed in chapter 1 demonstrated two interesting things about their interpretation of the Soviet Union and its attendant dangers. First, it was the capacity of the Soviet Union to manifest political chaos — and in the absence of the Soviet Union, another country, another group, or the threat of anarchy per se — which was the motivating concern of the time. Second, the concern for the forces of disorder was represented in terms of the narratives of otherness that have been central to the American experience. The conclusion was that the cold war was a struggle that exceeded any military threat of the Soviet Union, and into which any number of potential candidates, regardless of their strategic capacity to be a threat, were slotted as a danger.

In this chapter, that proposition has been supported by a consideration of the "domestic" and cultural terrain of the cold war. Because the modes of representation through which the danger of communism and the Soviet Union have been interpreted replicate both the logic and the figurations of past articulations of danger, it has been argued that the cold war was not dependent on (though clearly influenced by) the Soviet Union for its character. Instead, I have maintained that the cold war was an important moment in the (re)production of American identity animated by a concern for the ethical boundaries of identity rather than by the territorial borders of the state. In chapter 7, a contemporary expression of the cold war in the society of security is considered.

Seven
Rewriting Security

The Crisis of Representation

If we understand the cold war to be a struggle related to the production and reproduction of identity, the popularly heralded belief that we are witnessing the end of the cold war embodies a misunderstanding: while the objects of established post-1945 strategies of otherness may no longer be plausible candidates for enmity, their transformation has not by itself altered the entailments of identity that they satisfied. In the West, the cold war was an ensemble of practices in which an interpretation of danger crystallized around objectifications of communism and the Soviet Union. In replicating both the structural and narrative qualities of earlier articulations of danger (vis-à-vis other "others"), enmity toward communism and the Soviet Union functioned as a code for the inscription of the multiple boundaries between the "civilized" and the "barbaric," the "normal" and the "pathological." In consequence, through a series of ritualized performances, each of which constituted a foundation that was subject to recurrent augmentation, the figuration of difference as otherness in the cold war rendered a contingent identity ("the West," "America") secure. Containment was thus more than a historically specific Foreign Policy strategy authored by George Kennan: containment is a strategy associated with the logic of identity whereby the ethical powers of segregation that make up foreign policy constitute the identity of the agent in whose name they operate, and give rise to a geography of evil. Any transformation in the objects of enmity might, therefore, belie the persistence of the logic they served.

In a larger sense, given the global nature of the cold war, this means that the crisis of international politics is now very much a crisis of representation.[1] The vast majority of contemporary states are multiple acephalous federations that exist as states only by virtue of their ability to constitute themselves as imagined communities. Central to the process of imagination has been the operation of discourses of danger which, by virtue of telling us what to fear, have been able to fix who "we" are. The effective discourses of danger that have led to "successful" instances of foreign policy are those that have been able to combine both extensive and intensive forms of power, so that the social identity of the community has been aligned with the political space of the state.

The crisis of representation the United States faces is unique only in the particularities of its content. The form of the dilemma is something common to all states. The state has never been a stable ground on which a fixed identity has been secured against danger: the variety of state forms throughout modernity have always been a historically contingent panoply of practices that have served to constitute identity through the negation of difference and the temptation of otherness. With the intensification of state power in the late nineteenth century, Foreign Policy helped contain and discipline the identities to which foreign policy had given rise. In our late modern era, where we find proliferating challenges that cannot be readily contained within the state, the discourse of danger associated with the discursive economy of foreign policy/Foreign Policy will have to work overtime to overcome the ever present threats to the once stable representation of an always unstable sovereign domain. The discursive economy of foreign policy will thus be taxed in its efforts to reproduce and contain challenges to the political identity of nations such as the United States.

However, for (the United States of) America — which I have argued is the imagined community par excellence, the state that requires a discourse of danger probably more than any other — the crisis of representation is particularly acute. The operation of anticommunism as a prominent discourse of danger in the United States throughout the nineteenth and twentieth centuries — with its ability to encompass the entire population, intensively structure the practices of everyday life, and offer a link between internal and external threats in ways that circumscribe the boundaries of legitimacy — is probably the best example of an effective discourse of danger. But with (as discussed in the Introduction) the globalization of contingency, the erasure of the markers of certainty, and the rarefaction of political discourse, reproducing the identity of "the United States" and containing challenges to it are likely to require new discourses of danger. Of course, talk of a shift from old to new discourses of danger drastically oversimplifies the complexity of this cultural terrain. Transformations of this kind do not occur in discrete or sequential stages, for there has always been more than one referent around which danger has crystallized. What appears as new is often the emergence of something previously obscured by that which has faded away or become less salient. In this context, there is no shortage on the horizons of world politics of potential candidates for new discourses of danger (such as AIDS, "terrorism," and the general sign of anarchy and uncertainty). Consider just one example. The environment has occasionally emerged as an international discourse of danger. For example, a focus on the environmental catastrophes of Eastern Europe has been prominent.[2] One of the effects of this interpretation has been to reinscribe East-West understandings of global politics in a period of international transformation by suggesting that "they" in the East are technologically less sophisticated and ecologically more dangerous than "we" in the West. This produces a new boundary that demarcates the "East" from the "West" in a period when the old frontiers of identity are no longer sustainable. But environmental danger can also be figured in a manner that challenges traditional forms of identity inscribed in the capitalist economy of the "West." As a discourse of danger that results in disciplinary strategies that are de-territorialized, involve communal cooperation, and refigure economic relationships, the environment can serve to enframe a different rendering of "reasoning man" than that associated with the subjectivities of liberal capitalism, thereby making it more unstable and undecidable than anticommunism.[3]

The major issues regarding the possible emergence of a new discourse of danger(s) in this period can be indicated by some questions. In terms of the reproduction of American identity along the lines established in the cold war, will any of the likely candidates be as extensive or intensive as that which they are needed to replace? In other words, are we going to witness the persistence of cold war practices even after their most recent objects of contention have passed on? Will these practices be represented in the mode of the society of security? Or, alternatively, do any of the new dangers being focused on in this juncture contain the possibility for a different figuration of American identity that would diverge from the enmity of the cold war? These questions, dealing with the rewriting of security, inform the argument in the remaining chapters. To make the analysis more specific, the first task is to consider an issue that has been officially identified a danger or threat necessitating vigilance and defense in the (so-called) post–cold war world: the incidence of drug consumption in America.

Before proceeding, an observation about the strategy of argumentation employed in this chapter is in order. It begins with a consideration of the claims of "fact" made by the policy discourses to support their articulation of danger. In discussing counterevidence, my intent is not to juxtapose one realm of fact with another. To the contrary, my desire is to demonstrate that within each realm of policy discourse it is possible to construct, in its own terms, a competing narrative that denaturalizes and unsettles the dominant way of constructing the world, thus prying open the space for an alternative interpretation concerned with the entailments of identity. Indeed, although I begin this chapter by operating largely within the terms of these policy discourses, I have attempted to politicize the terms of the debate. For example, instead of "the drug problem" or "drug abuse" I speak of "drug consumption"; instead of "drug users" or "addicts" I speak of "drug consumers" or "people addicted"; and instead of "drug traffickers" and "cartels" I speak of the "drug industry." Of course, no representation is neutral, and the terms of my discourse are certainly contestable, but their estranging quality is designed to help make obvious the way in which formulations of identity are sequestered within even the technical arguments of public policy with which we are most familiar.[4] As such, this consideration of contemporary discourses illustrates the relevance to the current period of the idea that foreign policy/Foreign Policy is constitutive of political identity.

Drugs as Danger

The Bush administration launched a much vaunted "war on drugs." In a 1989 address to the nation, the president unveiled his program by declaring that "all of us agree that the gravest domestic threat facing our nation today is drugs... drugs are sapping our strength as a nation."[5] The promulgation of a national drug control strategy was required, the administration maintained, by "unprecedented concern over epidemic levels of drug use and frightening amounts of drug-related crime."[6] Directed at the "visible effects of widespread drug use: rising rates of violent crime, serious damage to the Nation's health and economy, and strains on vital relationships between international allies," the Bush administration's drug policies were characterized as a major break with previous approaches to curb a widely perceived evil.[7] But it was the Reagan administration, of which George Bush was a member, that popularized the idea of drugs as a national security threat. In April 1986, Reagan signed a secret directive that authorized the development of policies to attack the drug supply at its source (meaning the use of the military in Central and South America), and equated the problem with terrorism.[8] Not that the previous decade was without its antidrug crusades: President Ford declared drugs a national security threat in 1974, while his disgraced predecessor put considerable emphasis on fighting a self-styled war on drugs.[9]

One can look back to even earlier precedents for the externalization of "the drug threat." Indeed, it was the international dimension of drugs that first led to antinarcotics legislation within the United States. Active in, in fact, the initiator of, international conferences to control narcotics trafficking in the early 1900s, the United States enacted domestic laws so as to have a domestic example with which to press for restrictions in other countries. Although World War I interrupted efforts to get widespread compliance to the Hague Opium Convention, section 295 of the peace treaty signed at Versailles — inserted at the insistence of Britain and the United States — meant that ratification of those accords was equivalent to the automatic ratification of the Hague convention. While international efforts continued throughout the 1920s and 1930s, it was this early convention that paved the way for the Harrison Act of 1914, the first federal law to criminalize the consumption of narcotics.[10]

The current preoccupation with drug consumption and trafficking thus has a long history. But few moments have matched the late 1980s for the level of concern — or frenzy — surrounding drugs. Public opinion polls taken after Bush's 1989 speech showed that 54 percent of respondents thought drugs to be the most important problem facing the nation; a mere 1 percent mentioned nuclear war. Previously the reverse had been the case: in January 1985, 23 percent had stated nuclear war while answering the same question, with only 1 percent citing drugs. To be sure, much of the anxiety had been fueled by media attention. The three American TV networks offered seventy-four evening news stories about drugs in July 1986 alone; in the seven months prior to the November 1986 congressional elections, one of those networks (NBC) aired four hundred stories on drugs, taking up a massive fifteen hours of air time. In addition, the weekly magazines *Time* and *Newsweek* each had five cover stories on drugs throughout that year.[11] The flavor of these accounts can be garnered from a *Time* cover story on "The Enemy Within." Relying on sociomedical discourse for its representation of the issue, it began with a 1911 epithet from William James: "The deadliest enemies of nations are not their foreign foes; they always dwell within their own borders." It then introduced the problem with an essay that spoke of a "shadow world" of "grey skulking figures," asking whether the concern was with the plague, curse, disease, tragedy, or normality of drugs. Stating that the "country [is] awash with drugs," it approvingly reported

Reagan's call for a "national crusade," and identified the "battle strategies" and "five fronts" on which the war could be waged.[12] These evocative and strident representations left little room for doubt that this was an issue that warranted the 700 percent increase in federal funding it received throughout the 1980s.[13] But when the "crack epidemic" was first being promoted, the Drug Enforcement Agency (DEA) released a report stating that the media attention had resulted in "a distortion of the public perception of the extent of crack use compared to the use of other drugs...*crack presently appears to be a secondary rather than a primary problem in most areas.*"[14] On what grounds, then, has this interpretation of danger been based? How are the declarations that the country is awash with drugs, that the nation is being weakened by drugs, and that there are frightening amounts of drug-related crime taking place, supported? An examination of the levels of drug consumption, deaths from drug consumption, and crime statistics will demonstrate that there are good reasons to doubt that the evangelism of fear surrounding drugs is actually about the narrowly defined issue of drugs.

Dimensions of Danger: Drug Consumption, Death, and Crime

The National Institute on Drug Abuse's (NIDA) household survey is the administration's authoritative source on levels of drug consumption. It has a number of methodological problems, not the least of which is that a government-backed survey dependent on self-reporting might underestimate usage in the current climate of fear. Nonetheless, what its figures showed was a decline in drug consumption. Although the Bush administration quoted these statistics as evidence of the impact of its prevention programs, the decline began well before the implementation of their strategy. For example, in 1985 NIDA reported 23 million consumers; by 1988 that had declined to 14.5 million (a reduction of 37 percent), and by 1990 the figure was down to 12.9 million (a further 11 percent decrease). With regard to cocaine—the primary concern of the current war on drugs—NIDA reported that occasional consumption had declined 29 percent between 1988 and 1990, and frequent consumption was also down from 862,000 to 662,000 in the same period.[15] Furthermore, the survey showed that cocaine consumption in the eighteen to twenty-five age group peaked in 1982 (the sharpest rise had been in the late 1970s), and that all other drug consumption in this cohort had been relatively stable between 1980 and 1985. Among those of all age groups, other sources reported that the drug of choice for daily use was heroin, whose adherents outnumbered cocaine consumers by more than two to one.[16] Such statistics point to the validity of a conclusion reached, but not acted upon, in Nixon's earlier war on drugs. A report by the White House's Domestic Council in December 1970 stated: "If the misuse of all drugs... was discussed in only medical and public health terms, the problem of drug abuse would not take on inflated importance requiring an undeserved federal response for political purposes."[17]

If overall use is declining, and that decline preceded the Bush administration, then an alternative ground for justifying the war on drugs is that high levels of consumption are concentrated among certain groups in certain areas, thereby creating a particular danger. It is in these terms that crack — a cheap cocaine derivative that is inhaled and contains between 5 and 40 percent of the pure drug — is singled out as the scourge. First reported in 1985, crack has become the symbol that has generated the representations of the inner city, minorities, and drug violence in terms of an epidemic or plague.[18] The conventional wisdom has been succinctly stated by columnist George Will: "Drugs and attendant pathologies are increasingly confined to inner-city enclaves — Beiruts without heavy artillery."[19] But Will's marginalization of the drug issue to the inner city (and, by implication, largely to blacks) is contradicted by a number of considerations. NIDA reported in 1990 that the vast majority (85 percent) of drug users were employed, students, or homemakers.[20] While the household basis of the survey might underreport inner-city drug usage, the fact that so many users held down jobs, while the inner cities are racked with high levels of unemployment, strongly suggests that drug consumption extends well beyond the inner city. Another survey of high school students who finish school has shown that almost twice as many white males (nearly 12 percent) as black males reported taking cocaine at least once in the previous year. In addition nearly half the white males, but only a quarter of the black males, reported taking five drinks in a row in the previous two weeks.[21] Even more striking are reports from New York drug treatment officials that there are more people dependent on crack among the white middle class than any other segment of the population. As a newspaper investigation concluded: "Cocaine use in all forms, snorted, injected, or smoked, is greatest amongst single white men in metropolitan areas of the Northeast and West [of New York City]."[22]

The situation revealed by the above statistics on the consumption of drugs suggests that other justifications — such as the incidence of death resulting from consumption — might be providing the impetus for the current interpretation of drugs as a massive social danger. A Drug Alert Warning Network (DAWN) run jointly by NIDA and the Drug Enforcement Agency (DEA) provides data on the number of drug-related emergencies at hospitals and the number of deaths coded as drug-related. In 1986, it reported that coroners nationwide listed 1,092 deaths as "cocaine-related." This figure probably overstates the situation, because cocaine alone was mentioned in just under 19 percent of those cases, giving cocaine an ambiguous role in mortality.[23] Other estimates, which have not disclosed their source or means of calculation, have varied: one analyst stated that 1988 saw 600 cocaine-related deaths, while the surgeon general declared that the same year saw 2,000 such deaths.[24] The government's main statistical compilation of accident mortality recorded 3,907 deaths in 1987 from all "drugs, medicaments, and biologicals." The category that includes cocaine (along with eleven other drugs) reported 852 deaths.[25] Whichever figure is used, one thing is beyond doubt: the number of deaths resulting from the legal drugs of alcohol and tobacco far and away exceeds those arising from illegal drugs. For every cocaine-related death recorded by DAWN in 1986, there were 300 tobacco-related and 100 alcohol-related deaths, while the surgeon general declared that tobacco was responsible for 390,000 deaths in 1988.[26]

As with those for consumption, the statistics on mortality from illicit drugs fall far short of providing secure grounds for a war on drugs and its attendant evangelism of fear. That leaves the connection between drugs and crime, and the incidence of such crime, as the final justification. Most government reports, although replete with hyperbolic assertions of this problem, are devoid of supporting argumentation.[27] That the United States is the most violent and crime-prone nation in the world is beyond question: its murder rate is nine times that of England, Egypt, and Greece, and eleven times that of Japan. American women are more than eight times as likely to be raped as European women, and the robbery rate is six times as high as England's, 100 times greater than in Greece, and 150 times that of Japan.[28] Some have argued that one-half of all thefts and burglaries, and 40 percent of all murders in large cities are drug-related.[29] But the relationship between America's propensity for violence and drugs is not as clear as these assertions would suggest.

In the first instance, the nexus between drugs and crime can be conceptualized in a number of different ways: it can be the result of the chemical properties of the drug (the psychopharmacological causes), the need for money associated with a drug habit (economic-compulsive reasons), or it can be associated with the industry of selling and distributing drugs (the systemic connection).[30] Focusing on homicides as the most extreme crime, very few are thought to be the result of the chemical properties of illicit drugs. One analysis of nearly 1,900 convicted murderers found that only 7 percent were under the influence of drugs alone at the time of the murder. In contrast, one-half of those considered were under the influence of alcohol.[31] Most of the violence in the drugs/crime nexus is systemic: one study of homicides in New York City found that nearly 80 percent of drug-related homicides conformed to this category.[32] Circumstances other than drugs, however, account for more than nine out of ten murders in the United States. The FBI's Uniform Crime Reports suggest that just over 7 percent of the murders committed nationwide in 1989 were in situations related to narcotics.[33] Some areas obviously have a higher incidence of drug-related homicides than others. In New York City—which has the largest number of murders of any American city—drugs are thought to be related to approximately one out of every four homicides, still well below many authoritatively announced assertions.[34] Moreover, although nationwide there has been an increase in the number of drug-related homicides, that increase has not led to an increase in the overall murder rate, which has remained relatively stable in the time since crack appeared in the mid-1980s.[35]

Even when the above figures demonstrate that the distribution of drugs is implicated in a fraction of the total number of murders, a focus on homicide statistics alone provides a distorted picture. In the first instance, contrary to claims of an epidemic, a nationwide survey of households affected by crime suggests that there has been a steady decline in the incidence of crime since 1975.[36] Moreover, if we consider the relationship between drugs and *all* categories of crime, a picture emerges that suggests they are a very minor cause of crime. In New York City, the most extreme case, some 1,400 arrests for crack possession were made each month in 1987, a rate achieved by trebling the number of police assigned to the crack units of the police department's narcotics division. Yet for all those drug arrests, in most cases the charge of drug possession and distribution was itself the most serious charge. In other words, in most drug arrests, the arrest is not made because of the arrestee's involvement in either violent or property crime. Indeed, in less than 4 percent of all drug arrests in New York City is felony violence charged, in less than 7 percent of cases is the drug charge accompanied by a charge for felony property crimes, and in less than 10 percent of the cases is there an associated weapons charge. These findings led the authors of the study that revealed them to conclude: "Violence does not appear to be strongly associated with drug dealing for either [crack or cocaine] substance."[37] This means that the crime problem associated with drugs is one largely produced by the war on drugs itself. Leaving aside the full range of public policy issues involved in such a move, if the possession and distribution of drugs was decriminalized, more than 90 percent of the "drug crimes" in New York City would vanish.[38] The image of drugs as the cause of all crime thus needs considerable revision.

At times, administration officials responsible for prosecuting the war on drugs have exhibited some knowledge of the complex and contested relationship between drugs and crime. Even William Bennett, Bush's first "drug czar," had occasion to note that most addicts did not finance their habits through crime, and that overall the nexus was one in which criminal activity preceded drug use rather than the reverse.[39] But such admissions were not factored into the national strategy, and appeared only at testing moments when more radical solutions to the issue of drug consumption were being considered.[40] On the strength of the above analysis, however, the foundations on which the current "war on drugs" is constructed are at best contestable and at worst spurious. Without denying either the pain of addiction for certain consumers or the social costs of the drug industry in certain parts of the country, it seems more than reasonable to suggest that there is a logic at work in the interpretation of drugs as a social danger that exceeds the factors most often cited as rationales.

Drugs and the Society of Security

"Social problems," one analyst has remarked, "have careers that ebb and flow independent of the 'objective' incidence of behaviors thought to constitute them."[41] What animates the careers of social problems like drug consumption or drunk driving are (as argued in chapter 4) moral concerns about what constitutes "normal" behavior in contradistinction to "pathological" behavior. In other words, the interpretation of some problems as social dangers subject to intense concern and punitive sanctions is integral to the inscription of the ethical boundaries of identity. As Joseph Gusfield has argued with regard to the issue of drunk driving:

> The laws against driving under the influence of alcohol constitute a moral drama which states the public definition of moral conduct in American life. In differentiating the drinking driver from the traffic offender these laws create an identity for the moral person and a counteridentity of deviance and guilt. The law in this area symbolizes a public commitment to the centrality of work, safety, and individual responsibility in American society. It supports and en-

hances a view of a "generalized other," of a "society" committed to the legitimacy of a style of living in which alcohol is a symbol of risk and danger and its control a mark of morality and social responsibility.[42]

The rhetoric of "the war on drugs" exhibits this moral concern quite openly. In addition to the ubiquitous intoning of the problem in terms of the threat to the strength of the nation, "drug czar" Bennett told a Washington audience in May 1989 that "the drug crisis is a crisis of authority... Drugs obliterate morals, values, character, our relations with each other and our relation with God."[43] Equally, Houston (and later New York City) police chief Lee Brown told the national conference of mayors that "drugs pose a serious threat to the very fabric of our society and are a *clear and present danger* to our way of life in a democratic society... drugs have a very special meaning. It means the destruction of our *children*. It means the destruction of our *institutions*. It means being afraid, in our *homes*, on our *streets* and in our *schools*."[44]

What is striking about Brown's characterization is that his reference to a "clear and present danger" calls up the historical analogy of the threat supposedly posed by communism to the United States. The phrase was the standard that Supreme Court Justice Oliver Wendell Holmes constructed to affirm and uphold the conviction for sedition of Socialist Party general secretary Charles T. Schenk during World War I. Socialist leader Eugene V. Debs was similarly charged under the 1918 Espionage Act after he made a speech declaring that his party would assume power and destroy "capitalist institutions." In a subsequent Supreme Court case, Holmes held that these words comprised a "clear and present danger" of impairing the war effort, and thus came under the standard he had laid down in the *Schenk* case.[45] Brown makes the connection between the two dangers unambiguous by declaring that "the major threat to our national security is *not communism, not the Russians,* but *Americans* using illegal drugs."[46] That the two threats should be linked in this way is not surprising: as chapter 6 made clear, the concern over communism was animated more by a sense of the endangered nature of the ethical boundaries of identity than by the perception of a threat to the territorial borders of the state. Moreover, the similitude between the targets and the techniques of exclusion in each case suggests that it is a challenge to the (often fictive) parameters of order and morality signified by the idea of national security that is the issue.

Women, blacks, foreigners, radicals, the "insane," and the "sexually deviant" were often the targets of anticommunism's discursive practices, and antinarcotic practices have identified the same groups. In the nineteenth century, writes Musto, "addicts were identified with foreign groups and internal minorities who were already actively feared and the objects of elaborate and massive social and legal restraints." Throughout the early twentieth century, Chinese were thought to be subverting American society with their opium smoking, blacks were said to be made violent and sexually uncontrollable by cocaine, Hindus were accused of encouraging addiction to cannabis, Mexicans were charged with introducing marijuana and fomenting crime, urban immigrants were associated with alcohol, and turbulent inner-city youth were identified with heroin. In the same era, the American Pharmaceutical Association's Committee on the Acquirement of the Drug Habit concluded that "unfortunate women" (along with blacks) were "made madly wild by cocaine." An American Medical Association report argued that if an addict was not normal and went untreated, he might become "organized and vocal, and society may awaken to the fact that he is an IWW, a Bolshevik, or what not." The American Psychiatric Association weighed in with the assessment that marijuana was "a primary stimulus to the impulsive life . . . [which] releases inhibitions and restraints imposed by society and allows individuals to act out their drives openly [and] acts as a sexual stimulant [particularly to] overt homosexuals."[47] "Deviant" behaviors have also been linked by Carlton Turner, a former White House adviser on drug consumption, who asserted publicly that marijuana use may lead to homosexuality, with the implication that it was also spreading AIDS.[48] Another Reagan-appointed official went so far as to link AIDS tests to nationalism. Dr. Cory Servas, a member of the Presidential AIDS Commission, declared that "it is patriotic to have the AIDS test and be negative."[49]

Despite the dubious basis for most of these claims—high levels of poverty, for example, made the alleged addiction of blacks to cocaine a figment of the fragile white imagination—law enforcement officials acted on such representations. Many police departments in the late nineteenth century changed the caliber of their revolvers from .32 to .38 when it was believed that cocaine-addicted blacks were physically invulnerable to the former weapons, and the mayor of New York established—at the height of the red scare in May 1919—a Committee on Public Safety to enquire into the (purportedly related) issues of heroin addiction among the young and the bombings of revolutionaries.[50]

Today the situation is little different. Contrary to the competing narrative discussed above—which argues that levels of cocaine and crack consumption among suburban whites greatly exceeds those among urban blacks and Hispanics—it is the minorities in America who have become the target of "the war on drugs." Although they make up only 11 percent of the population, the black community's percentage of drug arrests has risen from 30 percent to nearly 40 percent since the emergence of crack. One in four black men aged twenty to twenty-nine (compared to one in sixteen white men) is in prison, making it four times more likely for an American black to be imprisoned than for his peers in pre-democratic South Africa. As a result, there are more black men under the control of the criminal justice system in the United States than there are in college.[51] Likewise, the profiles that law enforcement agencies employ to identify people in the drug industry use typologies that make blacks, Hispanics, and occasionally women their major targets. For example, the Florida Highway Patrol's profiles encourage officers to look out for drivers of rental cars, drivers who disobey traffic laws, wear "lots of gold," do not "fit the vehicle," and are members of "ethnic groups associated with the drug trade."[52] In Mississippi, of fifty-seven police stops on Interstate 10 using profiles, fifty-five were for Hispanic or black drivers with out-of-state license plates on their cars. In New Jersey, on a stretch of the New Jersey Turnpike, less than 5 percent of the traffic consists of late model cars with out-of-state license plates driven by black males, but 80 percent of the arrests (though few of the convictions) on the highway fit that description. Similar profiles have also been utilized at airports since the Supreme Court ruled in April 1989 that factors such as style of dress, the amount of cash being carried, and the destination and length of stay of a prospective traveler can amount to "reasonable suspicion" for a "brief investigatory stop."[53]

Equally, the techniques of exclusion that functioned to discipline liminal groups in the early cold war—domestic intelligence collection, loyalty and security testing, and the creation of internment camps—exist today in "the war on drugs." The DEA's Narcotics and Dangerous Drug Information System (NADDIS) has computer files on more than 1.5 million people, even though less than 5 percent of that number are actually under investigation for suspected narcotics law violations. Available to other law enforcement agencies on request, this database also receives information from a variety of sources throughout the country, including the CIA's Counternarcotics Center, the FBI, and the Defense Department.[54] Even more than the extensiveness of these practices, it is the intensiveness of drug testing that is acting as a technology of order and discipline in this new climate.

The 1953 Eisenhower executive order on security testing listed "drug addiction" as one of the indicators of a risk to the national security. Still in force today, its meaning was extended by the Reagan administration's Executive Order 12564 of 1986, which made drug testing mandatory in federal agencies for employees in "sensitive positions," those for whom a "reasonable suspicion" of drug consumption exists, and for any applicant for employment in those agencies (the first category alone covers some 346,000 workers in forty-two agencies).[55] With the Drug-Free Workplace Act of 1988, this regime was extended to cover all federal contractors and grantees in the private sector. Required to certify that they operate a drug-free workplace before they can receive federal funds, individuals are now required to sign declarations as to their intentions. For example, asked to appear in a one-hour United States Information Agency television program on jazz, columnist Nat Hentoff was required to sign a "drug-free statement form," which read "I certify that . . . I will not engage in the unlawful manufacture, distribution, dispensing, possession or use of a controlled substance in the performance of the contract." On refusing to do so, Hentoff was barred from appearing in the program.[56] In response to the same law, the Department of Transportation issued comprehensive drug testing rules that apply to the four million transportation workers in the private sector.[57] Likewise, the private sector has responded enthusiastically to calls for the implementation of drug-testing and employee-assistance programs: nearly seventeen million employees work in establishments with the former, and twenty-six million with the latter, making drug tests more widespread in the early 1990s than security tests were in the early 1950s.[58] One of the reasons for this is that the private sector views these measures as a means of containing costs: "Testing is viewed as an important tool in risk classification, which allows insurance carriers to assess their potential exposure for future liability."[59]

Whatever the impetus, the potential for drug testing to be a disciplinary technique has already been demonstrated. At an industry in Maine that instituted random drug testing and tested seven out of ten people, all seven turned out to have been handpicked for the tests by management because they were on a union collective bargaining committee.[60] Moreover, the assumption that drug-testing procedures are unquestionably accurate is open to contestation. One problem with testing is that after consuming the same amount of a drug, some individuals retain higher concentrations in their urine than others, thereby making punishment dependent on the result of a drug test, a potentially arbitrary practice. But an even more serious realm of potential abuse exists prior to the implementation of a drug test. Individuals are being increasingly encouraged to monitor the attitudes and behavior of their colleagues and peers so that they can detect and report any suspicious symptoms. For example, the Johns Hopkins University, in response to the Drug-Free Schools and Communities Act Amendments of 1989, publicized its commitment to an environment free of drugs in a booklet that outlined indicators of substance abuse. Among the sixty-two factors—albeit after noting that some of the identifiable symptoms may be indicative of normal and understandable stress—the guide lists the following:

Arriving late and leaving early
Taking long lunches
Friday and Monday absences
"Putting things off"
Irresponsibility in completing tasks
Faulty decision making
Overreactions to criticism
Making inappropriate statements
Poor personal hygiene
Financial [problems]
Fatigue
Excessive feeling of boredom
Much older friends
Too much money, no money, missing money.[61]

As with the grounds for questioning loyalty and security in the early 1950s, nebulous manifestations of potentially drug-induced behavior such as these have the effect of constituting an increasingly narrow optimal mean in the tolerable bandwidth of normal behaviors. The effect of such techniques is thus not social control, but social discipline: the establishment of certain standards against which attitudes and behavior can be proscribed as legitimate or illegitimate. And in that goal, they have their predecessors. For example, the Ford Motor Company's policy of paying workers five dollars a day in the early 1900s was accompanied by the establishment of a "Sociology Department" from which thirty investigators screened applicants and monitored employees. Gambling, drinking, radicalism, and unionism were discouraged, and "proper" middle-class habits of diet, recreation, living arrangements, budgets, and morality were taught. For immigrants, English classes were mandatory, and the text used began with the statement "I am a good American." In the same vein, the Coors Brewing Company administered polygraph and psychological tests in the mid-1970s to screen out potential unionists and radicals. Together with widespread corporate policies to deal with stress, a range of addictions, and subjects suitable to "wellness" promotions, these programs are instituting disciplinary strategies designed to constitute the "normal" in contrast to the "pathological" under the sign of the "healthy" versus the "unhealthy."[62]

A logical corollary of testing and discipline is the sanction of quarantine or internment. In the early cold war, loyalty and security tests were accompanied by the Emergency Detention Act and its six internment camps for communists and other subversives should an emergency be declared—but the camps were never put into use. In the first drug war, Governor Rockefeller of New York had his staff draw up plans under which he could declare a "drug emergency" and call on other authorities to establish emergency camps in which those rounded up would be interned and quarantined—but these plans were never implemented.[63] In the current evangelism of fear begun with the Reagan-Bush declaration of war on drugs, however, internment camps have become a reality. Mississippi, for example, began a Regimented Inmate Discipline Program in 1985, in which young first-time drug felons are obliged to undergo "a 90- to 120-day regimen of grueling paramilitary training and 'psycho-correctional therapy,' consisting of lectures and discussions aimed at modifying criminal behavior." William Bennett approvingly described the purpose of such programs: "You take the first offender, particularly a young person, and he goes to boot camp—that's a lot less expensive than jail; he gets up at 4:30 in the morning, he does push-ups, he runs a good bit ... It's inexpensive, it teaches good lessons."[64] It's not clear whether these camps have become part of federal (as opposed to state) programs, but the 1991 issue of the *National Drug Control Strategy* speaks of "shock incarceration," or the so-called boot camps, as one of a number of "promising initiatives."[65]

The "war on drugs" bears all the hallmarks of a morality play designed to instantiate the ethical boundaries of identity.[66] With a relationship of dubious veracity to the "objective" behaviors thought to make it a public policy priority, the current evangelism of fear surrounding drugs has more in common with earlier targets and techniques of exclusion in the American experience. Most significantly, it is not just an internal problem with an external dimension (or vice versa). The discourse of danger that has crystallized around drugs is indebted to the discursive economy of identity/difference that has characterized earlier moments in which foreign policy practices can be observed. Accordingly, an important effect of this articulation of danger is to inscribe the very boundaries that constitute the "domestic" and the "foreign."

Drugs and the Sustenance of Sovereignty

Concern over, and legislation restricting, the consumption of narcotics in the United States has had an international dimension since the early twentieth century. Recently, presidents Ford, Nixon, Reagan, Bush, and Clinton have all characterized the drug industry as a threat to national security. In the words of Bush's secretary of defense, Richard Cheney, drugs are a "direct threat to the sovereignty and security of our country."[67] An important dimension of "the war on drugs" is thus the portrayal — in a manner that replicates almost exactly the formulations of the Soviet threat in the early 1950s — of drugs' danger to the ethical boundaries of identity in terms of a threat to the territorial borders and sovereignty of the state. In this transference of the differences within the state to the differences between states, the discursive practices of "the war on drugs" serve to inscribe the frontiers of America.

As chairman of the House Select Committee on Narcotics Abuse and Control, Charles Rangel — an African-American Democrat representing a New York City district — eagerly participated in the hyping of the drug war. In one short newspaper article commenting on cartel-related violence in Colombia, he spoke of the issue in the following terms: "violent offensive unleashed . . . urgency of the war on drugs . . . empires of doom . . . systemic breakdown . . . narco-kings . . . under siege . . . reign of terror . . . drug carnage . . . savagely attacked . . . industry of death . . . rule the world." And in the best Puritan tradition, he described how vigilance to this threat should "awaken" the American people. But in one particularly compelling paragraph, Rangel represented the issue in terms familiar to the national security managers of the early 1950s:

> Our national security and future as a stable government are at stake as well. Our survival and strength as the democratic stronghold in this part of the world is delicately intertwined with that of our neighbors to the south . . . If Colombia falls, the other, smaller, less stable nations in the region could become targets. It is conceivable that we could one day find ourselves an island of democracy in a sea of narco-politico rule, a prospect as bad as being surrounded by communist regimes.[68]

With its invocation of the domino theory once applied to communism in Southeast Asia, and its substitution of "narco-political rule" for the "totalitarianism" of the cold war, Rangel's harangue is an echo of the argument in NSC-68, and a direct reference to the Kennedy ad-

ministration's concern that America not become "a beleaguered island in a totalitarian sea."[69] Equally, Senator John Kerry, a liberal Democrat from Massachusetts who chaired the Senate subcommittee that
investigated (and confirmed) allegations of the involvement of Oliver
North's contra supply network in drug trafficking, has had no objection to portraying the issue in terms akin to Rangel's. The 1988 Kerry
report begins with an epithet from General Paul Gorman, formerly
commander of the United States Southern Command in Panama: "The
American people must understand much better than they ever have
in the past how (our) safety and that of our children is threatened by
Latin drug conspiracies (which are) dramatically more successful at
subversion in the United States than any that are centered in Moscow."
The executive summary then continues:

> There should not be any doubt in anyone's mind that the United
> States is engaged in a war directed at our citizens — the old, the
> young, the rich, the poor. Each day, with what has become numb-
> ing regularity, the American people are besieged with the news of
> the latest casualties in the drug war. . . .
> The Colombian drug cartels which control the cocaine industry
> constitute an unprecedented threat, in a non-traditional sense, to
> the national security of the United States. Well-armed and operat-
> ing from secure foreign havens, the cartels are responsible for thou-
> sands of murders and drug-related deaths in the United States each
> year. They exact enormous costs in terms of violence, lower economic
> productivity, and misery across the nation.[70]

The structure of the Kerry report's argument makes it clear that
the source of the drug problem is foreign and remote, that both agency
and responsibility lie only with those operating from abroad, and that
their less-than-human considerations result in an orgy of carnage and
costs. Its effect is to inscribe a geography of evil, absolving America
of responsibility for much of the problem (even though it notes the
country's appetite for drugs) by invoking a threat to the republic from
traditional adversaries such as "terrorists . . . saboteurs . . . spies . . . insurgents, and . . . subversives."[71] Such orientalist, Conrad-like representations, can be found in both the administration's documents (where
the organizations of "drug kingpins" are said to be located in "the
jungles of Latin America or Asia") and in media reports.[72] But they
are nowhere more obvious than in the image of "narcoterrorism."

The conflation of narcotics production and trafficking with in-
surgent and revolutionary movements in Central and South America has been an attempt, largely without foundation, to both inflate
the dimensions of the danger associated with drugs, and render it

more intelligible on a traditional national security register. United States Foreign Policy has a long history of aversion to insurrectionist groups in countries it determines important to the national interest: the Kennedy administration's National Security Action Memorandum 182 of 1962 discussed in chapter 6 is illustrative of how that threat has been perceived.[73] The power of "narcoterrorism" as a concept is that it subsumes under one banner a number of ideas, including the assertion that guerrilla movements finance their operations largely through drug trafficking, and the more believable argument that the principals in the drug industry employ extreme violence.[74] Aside from occasional and tactical alliances usually said to emerge as a response to U.S. intervention in the region, the idea that there is a natural affinity between overtly Marxist revolutionary groups such as Peru's Shining Path and the laissez-faire capitalist enterprises of the drug industry seems rather odd.[75] But this has not prevented U.S. allies such as the military leadership in countries like Argentina and Bolivia from incorporating all possible enemies into one object. After the Fourteenth Bilateral Intelligence Conference of the Argentine and Bolivian armies in 1988, a communiqué declared that "the MCI [International Communist Movement] uses narcoterrorism as a socioideological procedure for provoking social imbalances, eroding community morale, and corrupting and disintegrating Western society, as part of the strategic objective of promoting a new Marxist order."[76] Such understandings have laid the groundwork for both renewed and substantial military aid by the United States to the region's military and police forces (not known for their respect of human rights), and the commitment of U.S. military advisers, special forces, and occasional combat assistance.[77] Moreover, the foreign combat experience of the drug war is being folded back onto the domestic environment: Bush spoke of drugs breeding "the most insidious form of domestic terrorism," and equated the police with infantrymen and the DEA with Green Berets in the internal fight against the threat.[78]

The "war on drugs" is thus very much more than a metaphor, both at home and abroad.[79] In the utilization of the Defense Department and related agencies to carry out the congressional desire to "seal the borders" of America, the territorial boundaries of the state have become sites of intense power. A 1981 amendment to the 1887 Posse Comitatus Act has allowed the military to undertake civilian law enforcement, extra border patrol agents have been hired, $100 million has been spent on seven radar balloons for the southwest area, an over-the-horizon radar originally built to track Soviet bombers now works to track the aircraft of drug smugglers, the Pentagon was designated as the lead agency in early 1989 to coordinate antitrafficking efforts on the Atlantic and Pacific coasts, and the National Guard has proposed that on some nights near the Mexican border, its servicemen be camouflaged in cactus suits.[80]

But given the lack of success in reducing the level of drug trafficking, and the instances in which United States Foreign Policy has itself condoned drug trafficking in the service of other security goals, the attention focused on the threat from the outside can be seen as part of a practice that externalizes the danger of drugs as a means of sustaining the notion of sovereignty.[81] And just as foreign policy practices have subjected a number of domestic liminal groups to techniques of exclusion, Foreign Policy over the years has rendered a number of external adversaries as enemies because of (along with other indicators of malfeasance) their purported but usually unsubstantiated involvement in the narcotics trade. Japanese militarists in World War II were said to export opium so as to "soften" countries they wished to attack, and China was similarly accused. The *New York Times* declared in a 1950 editorial that "communists...are eager to get as many addicts as possible in the territory of those to whom they are opposed."[82] Iranians in 1951 (after they nationalized the oil industry), Cuba after Castro, the Soviet Union and its satellites, North Vietnam after 1962, and Nicaragua after the fall of Somoza were all likewise indicted.[83] As secretary of state, George Schultz argued in 1984 that a number of communist governments were complicit in drug trafficking, and that "smuggling massive amounts of drugs into Western nations may serve their broader goal of attempting to weaken the fabric of Western democratic society."[84]

The "war on drugs," then, replicates earlier narratives of foreign policy/Foreign Policy in the American experience. More specifically, the articulation of danger associated with "the war on drugs" operates largely in terms of the idea of the society of security that came to prominence in the early cold war. As chapter 6 argued, in abstracting and reifing "the interests of the national security" as the malleable standard by which the "normal" was constituted, the disciplinary strategies of the cold war performatively reconstituted the ethical borders of the state's identity through the containment and exclusion of the "pathological." By multiplying the dimensions of being along which threats to security could be observed—so that they included unreliable behavior, "criminal, infamous, immoral, or notoriously disgraceful conduct" (which, even in 1953, specifically included drug addiction)—these strategies both individualized and intensified their attendant sense of endangeredness. The search for security thus proliferated the grounds of insecurity.

Furthermore, the foreign policy strategies associated with the society of security in the cold war enabled the practice of Foreign Policy in that era. Communism was perceived as a danger (both during and long before the cold war) because it was thought to imperil "American" values, thereby making contention around that issue a coded struggle between the "civilized" and the "barbaric," the "normal" and the "pathological." But the ethical powers of segregation that constituted the lines of demarcation among and between groups within society also effected the transference of those differences such that they inscribed the boundaries between societies and, hence, the borders of America.

Equally, in "the war on drugs," the intensity of the location of danger within the site of the morally responsible individual is made possible by narratives of otherness important to the American experience. Accordingly, even though the actual consumption of drugs can be easily interpreted as exceeding those liminal groups to whom it is usually ascribed, the figurations and representations of this social problem reproduce previously established contours of American identity. Moreover, these practices of individualization are accompanied in their reconstitution of identity by an externalization of danger that reinscribes an (inter)national geography of evil. Just as the Soviet Union and its allies became the locus for all the world's evil during the cold war, the representation of the Andean nations as responsible for all the world's drug evil resuscitates sovereignty in the context of radical interdependence. The "war on drugs" therefore constructs sites of both "domestic" and "foreign" marginality, constituting American identity through the negation of "un-American" behavior at home and abroad.

Eight
The Politics of Theorizing Identity

A critique is not a matter of saying that things are not right as they
are. It is a matter of pointing out on what kinds of assumptions, what
kinds of familiar, unchallenged, unconsidered modes of thought the
practices that we accept rest. We must free ourselves from the sacral-
ization of the social as the only reality and stop regarding as super-
fluous something so essential in human life and in human relations
as thought...It is something that is often hidden, but which always animates everyday behavior. There is always a little thought
even in the most stupid institutions; there is always thought even
in silent habits. Criticism is a matter of flushing out that thought
and trying to change it: to show that things are not as self-evident
as one believed, to see what is accepted as self-evident will no longer
be accepted as such. Practicing criticism is a matter of making facile
gestures difficult.

Michel Foucault, "Practicing Criticism"[1]

Practicing Criticism

In posing as a question the role difference, danger, and otherness play
in constituting the identity of the United States as a major actor in
world politics, this book has sought to tackle some of the self-evident
categories and practices in our political imaginary. By questioning what
is implicated in notions such as identity, the body, the state, danger,
foreign policy, containment, security, and sovereignty, this analysis
has attempted to flush out a few of the assumptions and modes of
thought that establish the political contours of our time. By offering
a "history of the present" incited by the rituals of power evident in
the juncture many have termed the "end of the cold war," this study
has tried to investigate the codes governing and the logic behind
contemporary declarations about the new dangers and possibilities

facing (the United States of) America. And, most specifically, the critique embodied in this argument hopes in its own way to make difficult the statements sometimes offered by those involved in the study or the practice of international relations (such as those statements concerning the nature of the state and foreign policy examined in chapter 2, and those concerning the meaning and purpose of American Foreign Policy explored in chapters 5 through 7). By way of conclusion, therefore, I want to draw out some of the implications of theorizing identity in this manner for the discipline of international relations, the practice of United States Foreign Policy, and future thinking about the constitution of "the political."

Theorizing Identity and the Study of International Relations

Declarations about the state of flux in the discipline of international relations are commonplace. From studies that chronicle a renewed effort for the search for theory, to proclamations about the desirability of abandoning concepts as integral as "the state," a number of scholars in the field have surveyed with dismay the absence of an intellectual consensus.[2] High on the list of concerns of some of these analysts has been what they perceive as the insidious, unwarranted, and unhelpful advent of "foreign" attitudes associated with continental philosophy.[3] Often reciting the alleged inability of such approaches to say anything useful about the "real world," these academics have taken it upon themselves, in a moment of academic xenophobia, to sound the tocsin and awaken the discipline to the dangers of "postmodernism" and/or "poststructuralism." Deriding any work that speaks in terms of discourse or texts, reviled by what they perceive as abstruse language, and insistent that all contributions to knowledge should conform to their unargued epistemological and ontological standards, these jeremiad-like declarations seek to patrol the intellectual borders that frame the study of world politics.[4]

Others have responded in detail to similar criticisms in ways that I find compelling.[5] But because this book will likely be labeled by critics (friendly or otherwise) as "postmodern," I want to say something about such an interpretation. I have refrained—despite an open and unabashed indebtedness to the thought of Michel Foucault, among others—from self-consciously describing the critical attitude of this argument as being "postmodern" or "poststructural." This aversion is based on the way these terms have become overdetermined in scholarly and cultural circles, such that anything described as "postmodern" is immediately associated with a number of "well-known" features, even if neither the argument being analyzed nor the works from which it draws sustenance bear any resemblance to its representation.[6] For example, it is assumed that a long list of (predominantly) French thinkers are all contributors to a homogenous theoretical paradigm, when in fact there are many differences between those so associated.[7] It is assumed that the use of terms like *discourse*, *text*, and *writing* has to be referring to an exclusively discursive domain that is divorced from the "real world" of the nondiscursive, when in their disparate ways both Derrida and Foucault have made it abundantly clear that they reject the basis of that distinction and thus consider those terms to have a much wider meaning.[8] And it is assumed that there is an unassailable political quietism inherent to a "postmodern" attitude despite both arguments and actions to the contrary.[9]

Of course, my hope is that the force of this analysis will mollify if not assuage some of these concerns. But it has to be recognized that such a desire is limited — but not precluded — by the nature of the agonism that exists between the logic of interpretation (which, outlined in the Introduction, underpins this analysis) and the entailments of epistemic realism. It is not a limit that is enabled by the incommensurability of paradigms, or some such formulation, for this agonism is not something that can be resolved on methodological or epistemological grounds. It is a limit commissioned by the fact that each approach instantiates a different ethic. Epistemic realism can be considered a commitment designed to contain what Richard Bernstein has called the "Cartesian anxiety," the proposition that asserts that either we have some sort of ultimate foundation for our knowledge or we are plunged into the void of the relative, the irrational, the arbitrary, the nihilistic. As Bernstein notes, the search for a foundation and the anxiety it inculcates is more than an effort to solve the problem of the basis for knowledge and truth: "It is the quest for some fixed point, some stable rock upon which we can secure our lives against the vicissitudes that constantly threaten us."[10] However, this ethical impulse cannot be satisfied, particularly when we remind ourselves (as chapter 2 noted) that the culture of modernity necessitates external guarantees but has erased the ontological preconditions for them. It was this situation, after all, that granted to fear and danger the capacity of securing that which could no longer be reasoned into existence. As a result, epistemic realism is sustainable only through the faith of its adherents believing that they are warding off a threat. In consequence, it seems that the processes that were implicated in the rise of the state are now replicated in the traditional discourses of the relations between states. The evangelism of fear centered on death grounded the church's project of salvation; the evangelism of feai articulated in the anxiety about an unfinished and dangerous world secured the state such that security occupied the position of salvation; now the evangelism of fear enunciated by those hoping to ward off "foreign" intellectual influences works to contain the instability of their representations of the world.

Overcome with this Cartesian anxiety, traditional scholarship in international relations will probably continue to forget the silences, omissions, and limitations of the traditional approaches and maintain that epistemic realism rests on more than faith. But the ritual forgetting (which might be characterized as post-Cartesian amnesia) of the insights of diverse scholars—such as Wittgenstein, Winch, Kuhn, Habermas, Foucault, and Derrida, all of whom have in some way contributed to the logic of interpretation—can only increase the anxiety.[11] Besides, only by exorcising ourselves from the unfounded but seductive appeal that social and political life has to be organized by recourse to either one option or another, and that we can locate a secure foundation outside of politics and history, can we move toward a situation where we are equipped to deal with the issues of life and death that we confront in global life.

This is not to argue that the logic of interpretation either desires or is able to transcend the ethical dilemma of how to think and act politically given the provocations of our time. On the contrary, by refusing the search for an Archimedean point from which to orient all action and judgment, the logic of interpretation seeks to replace the command ethic of epistemic realism (with its insistence on specifying the standards for why that ground and not others) with what Connolly has termed an "ethic of cultivation," in which the ambiguity and indeterminacy of life come to be respected, and a sensitivity to the costs of containing those conditions fostered. Indeed, by refusing transcendence as an option, the logic of interpretation prepares the ground for a democratic and politicized practice: "A practice that affirms the indispensability of identity to life, disturbs the dogmatization of identity, and folds care for the protean diversity of human life into the strife and interdependence of identity/difference."[12]

I want to pursue, in the context of international relations, what this might entail, first by considering some of the implications of this argument for the conduct of United States Foreign Policy, and then more generally for how we might think of "the political." But before doing so, I want to note an important feature of this study, which—despite my caution about the overdetermined reception of "postmodernism" or "poststructuralism"—might strengthen the position of those who employ the insights associated with those terms. Through its close analysis of the texts of Foreign Policy, the cultural terrain of the early cold war, and the articulation of new dangers to the security of the United States, this book has demonstrated that those issues to which the logic of interpretation is attentive — most particularly, the ethical boundaries of identity — are part and parcel of the "real world." After all, it was in the confidential documents of postwar Foreign Policy, and the security policies of the Truman and Eisenhower administrations, that the preoccupation with those cultural and ideological issues overlooked or ignored by traditional analyses was most apparent. Equally, both the analysis in chapter 2 of the representation of history that sustains the traditional narrative of foreign policy and international relations, and the textual exegesis of Hobbes's *Leviathan* in chapter 3 demonstrated that the themes concerning identity/difference, the "normal" and the "pathological," and the "civilized" and the "barbaric" are immanent to the canons and traditions of international relations. Prolix prose or not (and only those who can claim to write with the desired force and clarity can be the first to cast a stone), these realities cannot be dismissed by recourse to a disdain for the intellectual currents that nurtured their interpretation.

Theorizing Identity and the Practice of United States Foreign Policy

We are now at a historical juncture where the demise of the Soviet Union means that policy makers in Washington are looking forward to a new era in international relations, the outlines of which they can barely discern. What is clear, however, is that the optimistic view that held that the so-called post–cold war period would be a fundamentally different era in world politics placed too much credence on the essential qualities of a supposedly independent other as the basis for an assessment of threats. Such a view was possible only because it ignored the debt that subjectivity owes to otherness and the role the requirements of identity play in giving rise to discourses of danger. What the United States–led war in the Persian Gulf demonstrated is that above all else, the cold war was not based exclusively on an orientation toward the Soviet Union. Indeed, what that event demonstrated — particularly when considered in terms of the above analysis, with its consideration of the themes apparent in the "discovery" of the New World, the colonization of Ireland, the Puritan settlement in America, and the subsequent moments of identity conflict from colonial times to the red scares of the nineteenth and twentieth centuries — was the way in which certain targets and techniques of exclusion were common to disparate historical moments. In each of those instances, for all that was specific to the time and place, there was more often than not a sense of endangerment ascribed to the activities of the other, a fear of internal challenge and subversion, a tendency to criminalize or militarize responses, a willingness to tightly draw the lines of superiority/inferiority between "us" and "them" (thereby constituting "domestic" and "foreign" sites of marginality), and an application of these figurations and representations to dangers that could be located in the external realm such that notions of sovereignty were sustained. Accordingly, the cold war was not specific to one state or one ideology. The cold war was a powerful and pervasive historical configuration of the discursive economy of identity/difference operating in multiple sites, the logic of which is outliving the demise of its most recent objects of enmity.

The "war on drugs" is but one of many manifestations of this discursive economy. But it is not a "new" threat, recently created. It is one of the many dangers constantly in circulation throughout the discursive economy that rise to prominence and are exacerbated when changes in the political conditions allow it. It remains to be seen whether it or some other articulation of danger like it can be as extensive and intensive as the anticommunist discourses of the cold war. But the major political challenge suggested by this analysis is not simply to address the specifics of the threat (though that is in itself desirable); it is to address the process whereby the subjectivity of the United States is continually in hock to strategies of otherness.

Practices of differentiation and modes of exclusion are not unique to the United States, however. For example, much of the debate about the future political and strategic horizon of the new Europe embodies this logic.[13] With the demise of the continent's neat division into competing blocs, each of which was the negation of the other, leaders in "the West" have demonstrated a pronounced aversion to the spectacle of what they see as anarchy and instability.[14] For political actors who are most comfortable with discourses of certitude and who decry the strategic danger of ambiguity, the flux of a political space without a concomitant political order is too much to handle. Indeed, this very condition has become the new domain of danger. As a lecturer at the U.S. Naval War College succinctly stated, "The threat is no longer the Russians. The threat is uncertainty."[15] And as the new domain of danger, contingency is being appropriated as a means of breathing new life into the exhausted security categories of postwar Europe. To those who have argued that the loss of the Soviet other puts NATO's existence into question, Secretary General Manfred Worner—

in a manner that explicitly linked the technology of insurance discussed in the Introduction to international relations — responded: "NATO doesn't need a counterpart, or a foe, or an enemy. There are risks, there are instabilities, so you need insurance."[16]

The debate over European security is thus preoccupied with which institutions or arrangements might be resuscitated or put in place to contain challenges, control ambiguity, and (ostensibly) provide security. The question is, though, can any inclusive security order be structured in such a way that its associated technologies of discipline do not specify exceptions and mandate exclusions? If Europe is any guide, then so long as the traditional conception of security is the terrain of the debate, the answer seems to be no. As one European community official notes: "The principle of free movement within the region is built around having solid external borders. So the internal frontiers cannot come down until measures are taken to secure the external borders."[17] Such measures, of course, involve the specification of exceptions and exclusions such as "third world" immigrants, "terrorists," drug traffickers, and others named as undesirable.[18] As such, the air of progressive internationalism that surrounds the prospects for Europe's political integration might belie — in the words of Paul Virilio — the fact that "the suppression of national boundaries and the hyper-communicability of the world do not enlarge the space of freedom. They are, rather, a sign of its disappearance, its collapse, before the expansion of an all-too-tangible totalitarian power, a technological control over civilized societies that is growing ever more rapid and refined."[19] As a consequence, and unless there is a rethinking of "the political," the prospects of a liberal reformism on matters of European security or any "post–cold war" international structure producing a benign and nonexclusive order seem dim.

These reflections demonstrate how many of the themes developed here are relevant to more than the United States. After all, America, like all states, is an inherently paradoxical entity; devoid of a prediscursive, stable identity, and unable to reveal the performative nature of its identity, it thereby relies on the regulated and stylized repetition of practices like Foreign Policy to contain contingency and secure the self. But the prior example of Europe notwithstanding, America — wanting a land that always bore its name or a people who always identified themselves as "Americans" — is the imagined community par excellence. Confronted with this *aporia* of identity, the articulation of danger, the specification of difference, and the figuration of otherness, have been especially acute for America. Moreover (as outlined in chapters 5 and 6), the intertwining of the Puritan covenant's spiritual legacy with the republic's heritage of nationalism and eschatology has produced and reproduced an identity whose chauvinism has a distinctly iconic quality, and whose security depends on the global inscription of nonterritorial legitimations. But although this has given ideational conflict (often centered around the issue of loyalty, interests, and values) a prominent place in America's heritage, the logic and practice of identity for America has been sustained by the investment of social resources. Indeed, there have been few countries that have either desired or been able to fashion a form of life in which both the discursive and political economies — even in a period of (relative) decline — have been so deeply implicated in each other and so global in their ramifications.

In these terms, the future of United States Foreign Policy rests upon considering whether the United States can develop an orientation to the inherently plural world that is not predicated on the desire to contain, master, and normalize threatening contingencies through violence. Of course, not all Foreign Policy practices can be characterized in this manner, though the fluctuations in the relationship between the United States and Japan, a country that is officially an ally, suggest that the distance between peaceful interaction and a strained association in which the dividing lines are tightly drawn can be easily and speedily traversed. Therefore, thinking about future United States Foreign Policy involves considering what it would be like to address the incidence of drug use at home without marginalizing consumers or militarizing the threat as foreign. It involves thinking about how to handle the AIDS pandemic without scapegoating certain behaviors as immoral and closing the frontiers to those who test HIV positive. It involves conceiving of a means to address international trade problems without transmitting the fiscal pressures of the world economy to liminal groups within society, or constituting the practices of one's competitors as responsible. Finally, it involves (among many other issues) reducing the tensions that give rise to political violence abroad while refraining from stigmatizing domestic political dissent as "terrorism." Most particularly, thinking about future United States Foreign Policy involves acknowledging that we are always already situated in dangerous relationships; it involves recognizing that we are indebted to those figurations of otherness that crystallize around problems interpreted as dangers; and it involves appreciating that our orientation to danger, and those representations we employ to apprehend it, are capable of reinterpretation and rearticulation. And if the force of these injunctions is accepted, thinking about the future of Foreign Policy shifts onto the terrain of how the articulation of danger effects the articulation of "the political."

Theorizing Identity and Imagining "The Political"

Our political imagination has been impoverished by the practices associated with the paradigm of sovereignty. As discussed in chapter 3, the force of the sovereignty/anarchy distinction works to contain contingency through the instantiation of a sovereign presence which then acts as a regulative ideal. In terms of the political field, this has meant that the idea of "the political" has been subsumed by and made synonymous with "the state." In effect, the state has colonized our understanding of "the political" by obscuring those practices through which it has been "fashioned in the likeness of legislated fear," and foregrounding in their place its claim to be the source of authorized articulations of danger.[20] Integral to this has been the assumption that political modalities—such as strength, resolution, boldness, will, and vigilance—associated with the regime of Masculine/feminine (discussed in the Introduction) are the natural dispositions of politics. But such a colonization and such an assumption are rendered problematic by the retheorization of identity central to this study. More specifically, such a colonization is rendered problematic by a different understanding of security that emerges from the retheorization of identity.

Security and subjectivity are intrinsically linked, even in conventional understandings. Traditional discourses of international relations maintain that alliance is one where security is a goal to be achieved by a number of instrumentalities deployed by the state (defense and foreign policy, for example). But the linkage between the two can be understood in a different light, for just as Foreign Policy works to constitute the identity in whose name it operates, security functions to instantiate the subjectivity it purports to serve. Indeed, security (of which foreign policy/Foreign Policy is a part) is first and foremost a performative discourse constitutive of political order: after all, "securing something requires its differentiation, classification and definition. It has, in short, to be identified."[21]

An invitation to this line of thought can be found in the later work of Michel Foucault, in which he explicitly addresses the issue of security and the state through the rubric of "governmental rationality."[22] The incitement to Foucault's thinking was his observation that from the middle of the sixteenth century to the end of the eighteenth century, political treatises that previously had been written as advice to the prince were now being presented as works on the "art of government." The concern of these treatises was not confined to the requirements of a specific sovereign, but with the more general problematic of government: a problematic that included the government of souls and lives, of children, of oneself, and finally, of the state by the sovereign. This problematic of governance emerges at the intersection of central and centralizing power relationships (those located in principles of universality, law, citizenship, sovereignty), and individual and individualizing power relationships (such as the pastoral relationships of the Christian church and the welfare state).[23] Accordingly, the state for Foucault is an ensemble of practices that are at one and the same time individualizing and totalizing:

> I don't think that we should consider the "modern state" as an entity which was developed above individuals, ignoring what they are and even their very existence, but on the contrary as a very sophisticated structure, in which individuals can be integrated, under one condition: that this individuality would be shaped in a new form, and submitted to a set of very specific patterns. In a way we can see the state as a modern matrix of individualization.[24]

Foucault posited some direct and important connections between the individualizing and totalizing power relationships in the conclusion to *The History of Sexuality, Volume I*. There he argues that starting in the seventeenth century, power over life evolved in two complementary ways: through disciplines that produced docile bodies, and through regulations and interventions directed at the social body. The former centered on the body as a machine and sought to maximize its potential in economic processes, while the latter was concerned with the social body's capacity to give life and propagate. Together, these relations of power meant that "there was an explosion of numerous and diverse techniques for achieving the subjugation of bodies and the control of populations, marking the beginning of an era of 'bio-power.'"[25] This era of bio-power saw the art of government develop an overtly constitutive orientation through the deployment of technologies concerned with the ethical boundaries of identity as much (if not more than) the territorial borders of the state. Foucault supported this argument by reference to the "theory of police."

Developed in the seventeenth century, the "theory of police" signified not an institution or mechanism internal to the state, but a governmental technology that helped specify the domain of the state.[26] In particular, Foucault noted that Delamare's *Compendium* — an eighteenth-century French administrative work detailing the kingdom's police regulations — outlined twelve domains of concern for the police: religion, morals, health, supplies, roads, town buildings, public safety, the liberal arts, trade, factories, the supply of labor, and the poor. The logic behind this ambit claim of concern, which was repeated in all treatises on the police, was that the police should be concerned with "everything pertaining to men's happiness," all social relations carried on between men, and all "living."[27] As another treatise of the period declared: "The police's true object is man."[28]

The theory of police, as an instance of the rationality behind the art of government, had therefore the constitution, production, and maintenance of identity as its major effect. Likewise, the conduct of war is linked to identity. As Foucault argues, "Wars are no longer waged in the name of a sovereign who must be defended; they are waged on behalf of the existence of everyone; entire populations are mobilized for the purpose of slaughter in the name of life necessity." In other words, countries go to war, not for the purpose of defending their rulers, but for the purpose of defending "the nation," ensuring the state's security, or upholding the interests and values of the people. Moreover, in an era that has seen the development of a global system for the fighting of a nuclear war (the infrastructure of which remains intact despite the "end of the cold war"), the paradox of risking individual death for the sake of collective life has been pushed to its logical extreme. Indeed, "the atomic situation is now at the end of this process: the power to expose a whole population to death is the underside of the power to guarantee an individual's continued existence."[29]

The common effect of the theory of police and the waging of war in constituting the identity in whose name they operate highlights the way in which foreign policy/Foreign Policy establishes the general preconditions for a "coherent policy of order," particularly as it gives rise to a geography of evil.[30] Indeed, the preoccupation of the texts of Foreign Policy with the prospects for order, and the concern of a range of cultural spokespersons in America with the dangers to order, manifest how this problematic is articulated in a variety of sites distinctive of the United States. Most important, though, it is at the intersection of the "microphysics" and "macrophysics" of power in the problematic of order that we can locate the concept of security. Security in this formulation is neither just an essential precondition of power nor its goal; security is a specific principle of political method and practice directed explicitly to "the ensemble of the population."[31] This is not to suggest that "the population" exists in a prediscursive domain; on the contrary, "one of the great innovations in the techniques of power in the eighteenth century was the emergence of 'population' as an economic and political problem."[32]

Furthermore, Foucault argues that from the eighteenth century onward, security becomes the central dynamic in governmental rationality, so that (as discussed in chapter 6) we live today, not in a narrowly defined and overtly repressive disciplinary society, but in a "society of security," in which practices of *national security* and practices of *social security* structure intensive and extensive power relations, and constitute the ethical boundaries and territorial borders of inside/ outside, normal/pathological, civilized/barbaric, and so on.[33] The theory of police and the shift from a sovereign's war to a population's war thus not only changed the nature of "man" and war, it constituted the identity of "man" in the idea of the population, and articulated the dangers that might pose a threat to security. The major implication of this argument is that the state is understood as having no essence, no ontological status that exists prior to and is served by either police or war. Instead, "the state" is "the mobile effect of a multiple regime of governmentality," of which the practices of police, war, and foreign policy/Foreign Policy are all a part.[34]

Rethinking security and government in these terms is one of the preconditions necessary to suggest some of the political implications of this study. Specifically, it has been the purpose of this book to argue that we can interpret the cold war as an important moment in the production and reproduction of American identity in ways consonant with the logic of a "society of security." To this end, the analysis of the texts of Foreign Policy in chapter 1, the consideration of Eisenhower's security policies in chapter 6, and the examination of the interpretation of danger surrounding "the war on drugs" in chapter 7, demonstrated that even when these issues are represented in terms of national security and territorial boundaries, and even when these issues are written in the depoliticizing mode of policy discourse, they all constitute "the ensemble of the population" in terms of social security and ethical borders. Likewise, Foucault's argument underpins the fact that these developments are not peculiar to the post–World War II period.

Given that the articulation of danger effects the articulation of "the political," the articulation of danger associated with foreign policy/ Foreign Policy instantiates "the political" as a sovereign community in an economy of violence (the state in an anarchical world), a community whose boundaries are tightly drawn, whose identity tends toward rigidity, and whose disposition toward difference can succumb to the temptation of otherness. However, as discussed in chapter 4, danger is not an external condition that can be either tempered or transcended; we cannot avoid danger and seek to move into a condition free of risk. On the contrary, danger is a part of all our relationships with the world and can be experienced positively as well as negatively: it can be a creative force, "a call to being," that can articulate "the political" in ways rich in new possibilities. The issue, then (even when thinking in the narrow terms of Foreign Policy), is how do we orient ourselves to danger, particularly at a historical juncture in which many novel dangers seem to abound? Do we have an alternative to the continued reproduction of sovereign communities in an economy of violence? Can we act in terms other than those associated with the predominant (and gendered) discourses of power?

The answer to that question is an unequivocal yes. I suggested above in a tentative way how we might think differently about some of the issues pertinent to United States Foreign Policy. Were those possibilities explored, the boundaries of American identity and the realm of "the political" would be very different from that which currently predominates, for the distinction between what counts as "normal" and what is thus "pathological" would have been refigured. Besides, the evident differences in emergent discourses of danger demonstrate how even those articulations with the most affinity do not mechanically reproduce a monolithic identity. Of course, the pursuit of new possibilities through different interpretations is often strongly contested. Even recommendations to redirect political practices so as to confront new challenges sometimes do not escape old logics. For example, the effort to address environmental issues within the parameters of international relations and national security often involves simply extending the old register of security to cover this new domain. Usually signified by the appropriation of the metaphor of "war" to a new problem, this is evident in some of the literature that advocates the importance of global cooperation and management to counter environmental degradation, where ecological danger often replaces fading military threats as the basis of an interpretation designed to sustain sovereignty.[35] Yet, as I noted in chapter 7, environmental danger can also be figured in a manner that challenges traditional forms of American and Western identity. As a danger that can be articulated in terms of security strategies that are de-territorialized, involve communal cooperation, and refigure economic relationships, the environment can serve to enframe a different rendering of "the political."

Recognizing the possibility of rearticulating danger leads us to a final question: what modes of being and forms of life could we or should we adopt? To be sure, a comprehensive attempt to answer such a question is beyond the ambit of this book. But it is important to note that asking the question in this way mistakenly implies that such possibilities exist only in the future. Indeed, the extensive and intensive nature of the relations of power associated with the society of security means that there has been and remains a not inconsiderable freedom to explore alternative possibilities. While traditional analyses of power are often economistic and negative, Foucault's understanding of power emphasizes its productive and enabling nature.[36] Even more important, his understanding of power emphasizes the ontology of freedom presupposed by the existence of disciplinary and normalizing practices. Put simply, there cannot be relations of power unless subjects are in the first instance free: the need to institute negative and constraining power practices comes about only because without them freedom would abound. Were there no possibility of freedom, subjects would not act in ways that required containment so as to effect order.[37] Freedom, though, is not the absence of power. On the contrary, because it is only through power that subjects exercise their agency, freedom and power cannot be separated. As Foucault maintains:

> At the very heart of the power relationship, and constantly provoking it, are the recalcitrance of the will and the intransigence of freedom. Rather than speaking of an essential freedom, it would be better to speak of an "agonism" — of a relationship which is at the same time reciprocal incitation and struggle; less of a face-to-face confrontation which paralyzes both sides than a permanent provocation.[38]

The political possibilities enabled by this permanent provocation of power and freedom can be specified in more detail by thinking in terms of the predominance of the "bio-power" discussed above. In this sense, because the governmental practices of biopolitics in Western nations have been increasingly directed toward modes of being and forms of life — such that sexual conduct has become an object of concern, individual health has been figured as a domain of discipline, and the family has been transformed into an instrument of government — the ongoing agonism between those practices and the freedom they seek to contain means that individuals have articulated a series of counterdemands drawn from those new fields of concern. For example, as the state continues to prosecute people according to sexual orientation, human rights activists have proclaimed the right of gays to enter into formal marriages, adopt children, and receive the same health and insurance benefits granted to their straight counterparts. These claims are a consequence of the permanent provocation of power and freedom in biopolitics, and stand as testament to the "strategic reversibility" of power relations: if the terms of governmental practices can be made into focal points for resistances, then the "history of government as the 'conduct of conduct' is interwoven with the history of dissenting 'counterconducts.' "[39] Indeed, the emergence of the state as the major articulation of "the political" has involved an unceasing agonism between those in office and those they rule. State intervention in everyday life has long incited popular collective action, the result of which has been both resistance to the state and new claims upon the state. In particular, "the core of what we now call 'citizenship' . . . consists of multiple bargains hammered out by rulers and ruled in the course of their struggles over the means of state action, especially the making of war."[40] In more recent times, constituencies associated with women's, youth, ecological, and peace movements (among others) have also issued claims on society.[41]

These resistances are evidence that the break with the discursive/nondiscursive dichotomy central to the logic of interpretation undergirding this analysis is (to put it in conventional terms) not only theoretically licensed; it is empirically warranted. Indeed, expanding the interpretive imagination so as to enlarge the categories through which we understand the constitution of "the political" has been a necessary precondition for making sense of Foreign Policy's concern for the ethical borders of identity in America. Accordingly, there are manifest political implications that flow from theorizing identity. As Judith Butler concluded: "The deconstruction of identity is not the deconstruction of politics; rather, it establishes as political the very terms through which identity is articulated."[42]

Epilogue
The Disciplinary Politics of Theorizing Identity

Border Politics

In October 1996 a sixteen-year-old boy by the name of Learco Chindamo was convicted of the murder of a London schoolmaster. Philip Lawrence's murder had become a cause célèbre in the British capital. Fatally stabbed a year earlier while trying to separate fighting pupils outside his West London school, Lawrence's murder was seen as emblematic of an education system in crisis, a population subject to violent crime, and a society in moral decay. In the weeks after Chindamo's conviction, Lawrence's widow, Frances, won substantial media attention and public support with her call for a moral crusade.

In representing the conviction of Chindamo, the *Daily Mail*—widely regarded as the voice of "middle England"—employed an impressive array of foreign policy strategies that tapped into a series of contemporary discourses of danger. Chindamo's father was "a mafia thug" serving fifteen years in an Italian jail; his mother was a "Filipino [who] lives on benefit in [a] three bedroom council flat"; and his stepfather was "a heavy drinking Moroccan on the dole for years." Chindamo's mother was said by one of her relatives to have come to London because she "heard that Britain had a good welfare state and the children could be well-off . . . even if she wasn't in work." Her situation was said to have been quickly aided by the "Left-wing Camden Council in North London [which] was running a special scheme to house immigrants." Although "said to be in poverty and living on the British taxpayer," Chindamo's family were reputed to always have enough money "for those little extras such as computer games, an occasional visit to the Philippines, new clothes and a mobile telephone." Despite such providence, the paper detailed how Chindamo led a life of crime, frequently being caught with weapons at school, that led him to join a series of gangs including the "Triad-style street gang called Woo Sang Wu."[1]

In its interweaving of tales about welfare abuse, dysfunctional families, foreign immigrants with malevolent intentions, continental Europeans and non-Europeans as racialized others, and violent crime, the *Daily Mail* drew upon a series of discursive practices prominent in late-nineties Britain.[2] The dying months of Conservative rule were marked by a manifest public anxiety about threats to the United Kingdom's sovereignty said to flow from the expansion of the European project.[3] Despite the political changes brought on by Labour's sweeping electoral victory in May 1997—the Foreign Policy element of which another paper trumpeted under the banner "Goodbye, xenophobia"— British policy remains attentive to concerns about national identity in a globalizing world.[4]

It might seem odd to begin the epilogue to this book with an example from beyond the United States, no matter how much the themes echo some of the American instances discussed previously. Although it bears witness to my migration as much as anything else, this story helps make an important point about *Writing Security*. Similar specific readings could be offered from a range of cultural, national, and political sites, and while *Writing Security* does not offer a universal theory of Foreign Policy (at least in the narrow social-scientific sense), these reflections suggest that the argument does offer a means for interpreting cultural contestations and political issues implicated in foreign policy/Foreign Policy in domains other than the United States.[5] While such concerns in the United States and elsewhere are normally confined by the sovereignty problematic to being either "domestic" or "foreign," the central theme of *Writing Security* concerns the needs to rethink those practices and their representations so as to appreciate the role they play in bringing into being the very domains of inside/outside and domestic/foreign, with their associated figurations. These interpretive concerns were also directed at the discipline of international relations, and as developments in that field to be discussed below demonstrate, appreciating the way practices of "foreign policy" operate in domains other than the state remains crucial.

In the time since the first edition was published, many of the themes evident in United States foreign policy/Foreign Policy have replicated the themes highlighted by *Writing Security*, albeit in different contexts with varying articulations. The continued salience of the drug problem, the various irruptions of sexual politics, the militarization of elements of the American Right exemplified by the Oklahoma bombing, the proliferation of anti-alien and anti-immigrant policies, and the specter of trade wars have all functioned as sites in which political identities are performed through the operation of foreign policy, sometimes with links to "external" threats.[6] Likewise, the fervent casting around for new dangers in the form of countries such as Iran, Iraq, Cuba, North Korea, and other so-called "rogue states"; conditions such as environmental degradation, population growth, migration flows, and refugee movements; divergent belief systems such as "fundamentalist Islam"; the culture clash of incommensurable civilizations; and even previously unimaginable possibilities such as "killer asteroids," has been conducted in ways not unfamiliar to the identity politics of the Cold War.[7] Similarly, the struggle to articulate "the national interest" given what some regard as the "balkanizing" dangers of multiculturalism, the conduct of the Gulf War, and the contentious response (or lack thereof) to conflicts such as Bosnia, Rwanda, and Somalia, have all employed practices common to the nexus of foreign policy/Foreign Policy.[8]

To establish whether, beyond the initial proposition being offered here, such developments fully replicate the arguments of *Writing Security* would take another complete volume.[9] This epilogue, in contrast, while maintaining that the themes of the book are of continuing relevance, will focus on a range of issues begged by the political and theoretical stance embodied in the argument. The contingency and flux of the post–cold war period has provided a moment that furthered the cause of already existing critical theories, and triggered a pluralization of critical approaches in international relations. The resulting ferment has helped to breathe interdisciplinary life into an all-too-often self-referential field, thereby opening up the space for creative interpretations of world politics. These developments have not always been welcomed with open minds by those in positions of intellectual authority. In this epilogue, I want to explore the disciplinary politics evident in the reaction to these changes. Specifically, I want to consider the growth in international relations' scholarship dealing with questions of political identity since *Writing Security* was first published, and the way the disciplinary reaction is a form of discipline that renders the new as "foreign" and "dangerous." This is not to suggest that this book and the proliferation of such scholarship are causally connected. To the contrary, this book is part and parcel of that growth. But five years after its original publication is a good time to reflect on how scholarship of this kind has proliferated in both approach and substance and how facets of the discipline have reacted to it, while considering elements of my own arguments.

Border Patrols

The declarations of intellectual danger directed at so-called postmodernists (a term with which I still have many, many problems) by the self-declared guardians of international relations, which were first discussed in chapter 8, have not abated in the period since that was written. If anything, their intensity and frequency have increased and appear to be directly correlated with a stubborn avoidance of intellectual engagement. It appears that the consequences of ceasing attempts to delegitimize perspectives they find abhorrent are feared.

And abhorrent they do find them. What is most interesting about the conventional critics of "postmodernism" is the unvarnished vehemence that adorns their attacks. Accused of "self-righteousness," lambasted as "evil," castigated for being "bad IR" and "meta-babble," and considered congenitally irrational, "postmodernists" are regarded as little better than unwelcome asylum seekers from a distant war zone.[10] Of course, had the critics reached their conclusions via a considered reading of what is now a considerable literature in international relations, one would repay the thought with a careful engagement of their own arguments. Sadly, there is not much thought to repay. What will be engaged, however, are their strategies of containment and gestures of rejection designed to confer pariah status on those they oppose.

An example that justifies this conclusion comes from Justin Rosenberg in an otherwise interesting piece. Rosenberg proposes that a critical tradition in international relations could be founded on the principles of inquiry enunciated by C. Wright Mills in *The Sociological Imagination*. As one way of dismissing a particular set of alternatives to his argument, Rosenberg declared that "the intentions of postmodernism towards Enlightenment conceptions of reason hardly bear thinking about."[11] Such a move was neither accidental nor ancillary to Rosenberg's argument, and indicates something important about the politics of these gestures. For Rosenberg to be able to present his proposal as novel and progressive required the (inaccurate) assertion that no other perspective(s) had even the intention of addressing the matters that rightly concern him. In consequence, this remark serves to highlight probably the greatest limit to Rosenberg's (and others') imagination: the policing of legitimate and illegitimate courses of inquiry in an argument that seeks to break down intellectual and political barriers.

This dismissive gesture starkly contradicts Rosenberg's own observation that the difficult task of pursuing freedom and responsibility "is not, and arguably cannot ever become, the exclusive preserve of any one intellectual method or political position."[12] Ironically for one who might regard himself as indebted to Marxist traditions of critique, Rosenberg's gesture places him in the company of a number of supposedly liberal analysts of international relations who are seemingly frightened by the prospect of thinking through unsettling alternatives. The most (in)famous example of this is Robert Keohane's argument, framed in terms of "rationalists" versus "reflectivists," where the latter group of critical theorists have to meet certain (supposedly neutral) empiricist standards concerning research agendas, hypothesis construction, and testing before they could be taken seriously in the field.[13] Another is John Ruggie's attempt to problematize modernity in international relations through an analysis of the status of territoriality, where Ruggie disavows the possibility that "postmodern" approaches may have something to say about what he explicitly identified as the cultural category of postmodernity.[14] In an all-too-common move — exhibiting the "strategy of condemnation by refraction" — Ruggie argued via a few secondhand sources that there was no need to consider the potential contribution of so-called postmodernism to ethics and politics in our time.[15]

It's always odd to find those who proclaim their faith in Enlightenment principles publicly stating that they refuse to think about some alternatives — alternatives that many Enlightenment thinkers themselves presaged. It's equally disturbing to find that those who are so insistent about evidence and rigor fail to heed their own advice when it comes to dealing with attitudes they regard as dangerous. Not that an engaged reading by the critics would necessarily produce an enlightened critique. John Mearsheimer attempted an interpretation, but his bizarre conclusions suggested that the frames of reference he brought to the account were profoundly limited. Mearsheimer lumped together an odd bunch under the banner of "critical theory" (e.g., John Ruggie was included) and then read them superficially as arguing for the priority of language in the name of peace, a form of philosophical idealism bolstered by a dash of old-fashioned liberalism.[16] And even those interventions offered in a wholly more generous spirit can nonetheless rely on some dubious claims about "postmodernism."[17]

All of which suggests some remarks about representing "postmodernism" are in order. Although these remarks invoke a number of themes already addressed partly in chapter 8, the above criticisms necessitate their continued discussion. While it would have been preferable to be in a position to enter debate with a variety of critics about the substance of various arguments, that debate cannot commence until the legitimacy of critical work in international relations is granted, and at least some appreciation of the concerns that animate it is registered.

The trouble with "postmodernism" is that it is a homogenizing label used more often by critics than alleged adherents. More than that, "postmodernism" has become a metaphor that evinces a tenuous relationship to the argument so described. That is because, as Hayden White has argued:

> The metaphor does not *image* the thing it seeks to characterize, *it gives directions* for finding the set of images that are intended to be associated with that thing. It functions as a symbol, rather than as a sign: which is to say that it does not give us either a *description* or an *icon* of the thing it represents, but *tells us* what images to look for in our culturally encoded experience in order to determine how we *should feel* about the thing represented.[18]

In this sense, "postmodernism" has become a metaphor for a range of cultural and intellectual anxieties about life in an age of uncertainty. "Postmodernism" thus does not describe the work of a particular group of thinkers. Instead, as an important site of foreign policy, the term "postmodernism" functions as a way of directing our attention and establishing a negative disposition toward a set of characteristics with which we would all be concerned were they to be unproblematically advocated by anyone. As was noted in the Introduction to *Writing Security*, incantations about "postmodernism" thus speak derisively of "the notion that discourse is all there is . . . the subject is dead, I can never say 'I' again; there is no reality, only representations."[19] They warn against the dangers that flow from the notions supposedly central to "postmodernism," such as the idea that "all is permitted," "every interpretation is equally valid," or "we have no capacity to make judgments." And they herald the fear of the resultant dissolution of ethics, truth, and the possibility of politics, along with a host of other virtues thought to be derived from and ensured by an understanding of the Enlightenment as a definable historical event. Yet when it comes to offering up argumentation and evidence for these ringing declarations being conclusions justifiably drawn from the works mentioned—standards of reason they are supposedly defending—many of the critics are found wanting. Few if any have noticed, for example, that both Derrida and Foucault, though for different reasons, neither used nor endorsed the term *postmodern*.[20]

Much of the problem comes from the implicit and misleading historical periodization associated with the prefix *post-* in *postmodernism,* something that a good number of the critics insist on reading literally and superficially as advocating a complete break with modernity. Fredric Jameson, despite his own doubts about post-Marxist perspectives, provides the basis for a crucial distinction that enables a more sophisticated appreciation. Jameson has argued that "it is safest to grasp the concept of the postmodern as an attempt to think the present historically in an age that has forgotten how to think historically in the first place."[21] In this sense, "postmodernism" can refer to an *interpretive analytic,* a critical attitude that attempts, contrary to contemporary forces, to "think the present historically."

Jameson also argues that, although "postmodernism is not the cultural dominant of a wholly new social order," it can be thought of as "the reflex and the concomitant of yet another systemic modification of capitalism itself."[22] In this sense, "postmodernism" is a *cultural, social, and political problematic* marked by the rearticulation through compression of time and space in the modern world. Much of the confusion surrounding the concept of "postmodernism," and much of the hostility directed toward those thought to be operating under its influences stems, I would argue, from the conflation of these two senses. Those deploying the interpretive analytic are mistakenly thought to be celebrating if not fomenting the dangers that flow from the apparent depthlessness and heightened speed of the cultural problematic, when they might be better regarded as matching nonsovereign forms of inquiry to the task of interpreting the conditions that flow from the problematization of sovereignty.[23]

Such points are elided by those who argue that all things associated with "postmodernism" entail a complete break with the Enlightenment, modernity, and its virtues. However, if we take a close look at some of Foucault's arguments—which have been influential for many concerned with the politics of identity in international relations—we can show the affinities, if not the similitude, between his thought and the Enlightenment. Indeed, in his reading of Kant's essay "Was ist Aufklarung?" Foucault places himself squarely in the shadow of the Enlightenment.[24] "What is modern philosophy?" he asks. "Perhaps we should respond with an echo," he replies. "Modern philosophy is the philosophy that is attempting to answer the question raised so imprudently two centuries ago: *Was ist Aufklarung?*"[25]

The engagement with Kant is brief, but the incitement to Foucault's thought provided by Kant is extensive. Foucault uses Kant's essay to reemphasize some overlooked Enlightenment themes and resituate himself in relation to them. Specifically, the notion that the Enlightenment is either a specific historical period or a set of codes unique to that period is denied. Instead, a different rendering of the Enlightenment is offered:

> Thinking back on Kant's text, I wonder whether we may not envisage modernity rather as an attitude than as a period of history. And by "attitude," I mean a mode of relating to contemporary reality; a voluntary choice made by certain people; in the end, a way of thinking and feeling; a way, too, of acting and behaving that at one and the same time marks a relation of belonging and presents itself as a task. A bit, no doubt, like what the Greeks called an *ethos*. And consequently, rather than seeking to distinguish the "modern era" from the "premodern" or "postmodern," I think it would be more useful to try to find out how the attitude of modernity, ever since its formation, has found itself struggling with attitudes of "countermodernity."[26]

Modernity, then, is an ethos—a "manner of being" or "practice"[27]—in which attitudes of countermodernity are simultaneously imbricated; an ethos in which the simple oppositions of either/or are confounded by the recognition of the way in which critique and its object are in relations of *agonistic* interdependence rather than contradiction.[28] Via a consideration of Baudelaire, Foucault comes to the conclusion that what is rooted in the Enlightenment is a particular mode of philosophical inquiry, "one that simultaneously problematizes man's relation to the present, man's historical mode of being, and the constitution of the self as an autonomous subject." As such, fidelity to the legacy of the Enlightenment "is not faithfulness to doctrinal elements, but rather the permanent reactivation of an attitude—that is, of a philosophical ethos that could be described as a permanent critique of our historical era."[29]

This ethos inspires both negative and positive features. Negatively, it requires a refusal of what Foucault terms the " 'blackmail' of the Enlightenment," the notion that one has to be either for or against the Enlightenment in analyzing its historical and philosophical features. Positively, the ethos of modernity and the Enlightenment involves what Foucault calls a "limit-attitude." That is, criticism "consists of analyzing and reflecting upon limits." But, again, such criticism cannot be figured simply as a destructive force: "We are not talking about a gesture of rejection. We have to move beyond the outside-inside alternative; we have to be at the frontiers."[30] Such criticism does not produce universal knowledge that is globally applicable, but neither does it lapse into the relative obscurity of particularism, for such contradictory alternatives and the general implications they give rise to are resisted by the force of the philosophical ethos. In this context, the claim that "postmodernism" in international relations is incoherent if it does not escape fully "modernist" assumptions makes little sense, for no one escapes fully modernity when the critical ethos signified by "postmodernism" is appreciated as integral to the Enlightenment project.[31]

Being at the frontiers is the leitmotif of a "critical ontology of ourselves" which "has to be considered not, certainly, as a theory, a doctrine, nor even as a permanent body of knowledge that is accumulating; it has to be conceived as an attitude, an ethos, a philosophical life in which the critique of what we are is at one and the same time the historical analysis of the limits that are imposed on us and an experiment with the possibility of going beyond them."[32] This ethos of criticism is thus far from being simply a negative and destructive enterprise. It is, as Foucault argues in the quote that begins chapter 8 and provides the epigraph for this book, "a matter of flushing out that thought and trying to change it: to show that things are not as self-evident as one believed, to see what is accepted as self-evident will no longer be accepted as such. Practicing criticism is a matter of making facile gestures difficult."[33] Most significantly, this means that the central (but all-too-often forgotten) feature of the Enlightenment is being practiced better by the "postmodern" critics than by the self-proclaimed rationalist defenders of the faith.

Border Crossings

Where once the above objections to the impoverished understanding of "postmodernism" in international relations would have been made in a defensive mode, now they are put forward with an air of resigned exasperation. Where once we were all caught in the headlights of the large North American car of international relations theory, now the continental sportster of critical theories has long since left behind the border guards and toll collectors of the mainstream — who can be observed in the rearview mirror waving their arms wildly still demanding papers and the price of admission — as the occupants go on their way in search of another political problem to explore.[34] Time has moved on for most people, and with it has come a raft of exciting new research in international relations that is indebted, implicitly as well as explicitly, to the Enlightenment ethos articulated by Foucault.

Few things are more problematic and troublesome than the naming of intellectual trends. This has to be constantly borne in mind, because the research being considered here does not constitute a neatly demarcated "school" of thought, it does not often if ever embrace the label of "postmodernism," and many scholars who might be associated with it could easily be identified in other terms. But when considered as the whole it is not, multiple answers abound to the challenge that those who have gained inspiration from the critical themes of continental philosophy should embark on their own research agendas.[35] Of note is work that deals with familiar issues in estranging ways, including research on the performative nature of state identity (particularly its gendered character) in the context of U.S. intervention; studies of the centrality of representation in North-South relations and immigration policies; a deconstructive account of famine and humanitarian crises; interpretive readings of diplomacy and European security; the radical rethinking of international order and the challenge of the refugee; critical analyses of international law and African sovereignties; a recasting of ecopolitics; the rearticulation of the refugee regime and sovereignty; a problematization of the UN and peacekeeping; a semiotic reading of militarism in Hawai'i; and arguments concerning practices of contemporary warfare, strategic identities, and security landscapes in NATO, among many others.[36]

For all the differences, nuances and subtleties, this work incorporates many of the key achievements of "poststructuralism" (meaning the interpretive analytic of "postmodernism"), especially the rethinking of questions of agency, power, and representation in modern political life.[37] It also shares much in common with important and parallel developments in other fields, such as geography.[38] But the burgeoning focus on identity politics and the politics of identity in international relations has not been restricted to those whose debts are most obviously to continental political thought.[39] Important in this regard has been the growth in feminist scholarship, both in terms of the deployment of arguments from writers nominally outside the field (such as the work of Judith Butler, Joan Cocks, and Kathy Ferguson, among others, which is central to *Writing Security*), and the substantive contributions of those nominally inside.[40] Equally important is the growth in postcolonial scholarship, a hybrid category concerned with hybridity, particularly the racialized character of taken-for-granted concepts such as the "nation," "East/West," and "North/South." Drawing on the thought of Homi Bhabha, Franz Fanon, Albert Memmi, Chandra Mohanty, V. Y. Mudimbe, Edward Said, and many others concerned with the Other, this intellectual site offers intersections with the rich veins in anthropology, cultural studies, and literary theory.[41]

Border Raids

At the same time as the interdisciplinary theorizations of the politics of identity have proliferated, the attacks on so-called postmodernism have intensified and more conventional international relations' scholars have begun to appropriate concerns that were previously confined to the critical domains. Indeed, more mainstream writers are now proudly announcing a newfound interest in issues of intersubjective meaning, signified by the focus on "culture," "ideas," "norms," "epistemic communities" and the like.[42] This development might have been the basis for an engagement with critical scholars, but given the assumptions on which it is based, it is unlikely to be so. Instead it has become the basis for an attempt at the further marginalization of their ideas, as the politicized categories of culture and identity are reductively operationalized for the hegemonic interests of North American international relations. Some reflections on the idea of "security culture" will help illustrate what is at stake.

The post–cold war period has seen a new development: concomitant with the focus on culture as a security threat has been the newfound analytic concern with ideational phenomena. Although the latter is often portrayed as a necessary response to the former, they are better understood as being co-dependent practices. This is because each depends on what Appadurai has called the "substantialization of culture," the regarding of "culture" as "some kind of object, thing, or substance, whether physical or metaphysical."[43] Once social practices are signified as culture and rendered as a substance, they are intelligible as variables. These variables can then be operationalized as causal factors that contribute to the way threats are perceived, in response to which security apparatuses are deployed. In this sense, "security culture" highlights the place certain nonmaterial factors occupy in the landscape of international enmity.

This line of argumentation is clearest in *The Culture of National Security*. Within the myopic parochialism of North American international relations' intellectual parameters — where the clash between realism and rationalism, in the form of the neo(realist)/neo(liberal) "debate," governs the field — this collection marks a substantial departure. Its contributors have "rummag[ed] in the 'graveyard' of sociological studies" for an approach that can expand the possible determinants of national security policy. Starting from the proposition that "security interests are defined by actors who respond to cultural factors," the various scholars are attempting to draw in considerations their mainstream interlocutors have previously regarded as epiphenomenal to the structures of international politics.[44]

However, although "culture" constitutes their core category, its undertheorized status in the argument means that the collection's contributors demonstrate all too well that the substantialist perspec-

tive is the default argument. Considered briefly to be one of a num
ber of "summary labels for social factors," "culture" is figured as no
more than that which is not material, the ideas and beliefs that make
up the domestic domain, which can be isolated as variables possessing
at least some causal autonomy.[45] In consequence, "identity" is rendered in essentialist ways as a variable that can be inserted into already existing theoretical commitments.[46]

Variously described as a constructivist argument, the approach of
The Culture of National Security is that "construction" operates in a hierarchy of levels—a familiar metaphor in international relations—affect-
ing either the behavior, properties, or existence of actors. In delineating
the ambit of the argument's concern, it is suggested that "theories
that call attention to lower-order construction effects may or may not
stress higher ones. In this book we focus on the first and, especially,
the second effects, usually taking the existence of states as given."[47]

Despite the claim that "the cultural-institutional context" of national security policy helps "to constitute the very actors whose conduct they seek to regulate"—something that would make the existence of pregiven states difficult—the lack of conceptual depth in
The Culture of National Security constricts any such radical impulses.[48]
This lack of depth, moreover, is proudly acknowledged. "Identity" is
seen as little more than "a useful label" the deployment of which, it
is insisted, should not be read "as a signal of commitment to some
exotic (presumably Parisian) social theory."[49] What we are witnessing
in arguments such as this, therefore, is little more than an attempt to
domesticate "discourse" and related notions, so that the substantive
interests of critical scholars can be mapped onto the preexisting strictures of empirical social science, while the larger metatheoretical (and
thus ethico-political) questions of their positions can be avoided.[50] If
this is the case for a project that might be considered relatively progressive (progressive, that is, given its position relative to even more
conventional perspectives in international relations), then the normalization of the politics of identity is all the more prevalent in the
field as a whole.[51]

Resisting this move requires a comprehensive commitment to the
historicization and politicization of identity politics in all its dimensions. In the first instance, this involves understanding that constructivist arguments tend to operate in one of two predominant ways.[52] In
the first, there is a conception of the volitional agent reigning supreme.
In the context of international relations, this could produce an argument in which policy makers or other agents of the state are regarded
as being engaged in a sort of conscious and deliberate construction

of reality. Such a position might assume, at least indirectly, that policy makers are located outside of the domain of constitution, and have both control and intention over variables such as culture and identity. In the second, language becomes an omnipotent force so deterministic that "it" acts as the governing subject such that all accounts of human agency are expunged. This could produce an argument that emphasized linguistic features and paid insufficient attention to the materiality of discourse.[53]

One of the most significant and negative consequences of constructivism so conceived would be that it could invite a misreading in terms of constructivism-as-philosophical-idealism (so that if policy makers thought differently the world would automatically be different). Such a concern is far from being misplaced. *Writing Security* does not embody a constructivist argument; it is, instead, concerned with the performative constitution of identity. Notwithstanding that, even an admittedly sympathetic critic has claimed (in an argument I would surprisingly not contest) that "the evisceration of political economy" in *Writing Security* means that problems of foreign policy "are rendered as questions of adjusting our thinking."[54] Less sympathetic criticisms of so-called postmodernism (such as the already cited articles of Mearsheimer, Wallace, and Waltz) have not been hesitant to play, in the discipline's time-honored fashion, the idealism card as the first step toward dismissal.[55] If this can be directed at an argument that explicitly distances itself from constructivism, then the risks are all the greater for those who adopt the term.

The other negative consequence of constructivism so conceived is the way in which the assumption of intentional agency (whether of individuals or states) can impoverish even the notion of things being socially constructed. This is prevalent in the mainstream appropriations of critical concerns, and elements of this tendency are clearest in the work of Alexander Wendt. Although Wendt's earliest scholarship argued strongly for the appreciation of the mutually constituted and co-determined nature of agents and structures in international relations,[56] he has nonetheless diminished the place of constitutive relations by concluding that the appropriate research agenda for international relations is a state-centric one.[57] Indeed, Wendt's self-professed modernist constructivism — which he has since dubbed "an 'essentialist' or 'weak' constructivism" — reendorses state-centric realism, with its implication of volitional agents, while marginalizing a more radical understanding of identity.[58]

The often explicit social-scientific preferences exhibited in the Wendt argument, most evident in the concern for international relations theorists to structure their work in terms of a "research agenda" that could offer "causal" and "empirical" answers, effectively strip a politicized concept of its politics.[59] Similarly, for all the effort to go beyond the bounds of the "rationalist problematique" that binds neorealists and neoliberals together,[60] Wendt exhibits an overwhelming but underrecognized commitment to many of the general tenets of that disposition. Wendt wants to maintain that "philosophies of science are not theories of international relations" (hence we should avoid spending too much time on "questions of ontology"),[61] but there seems little escape from the fact that consciously or not, international relations theorists are philosophers of knowledge. The central issue is whether we want to take the constitution and nature of agency seriously—which would by definition require considerable attention to the question of ontology—or whether we are happy in the final instance to merely posit the importance of certain agents. To do the latter involves gliding over another point well made by Judith Butler:

> Agency belongs to a way of thinking about persons as instrumental actors who confront an external political field. But if we agree that politics and power exist already at the level at which the subject and its agency are articulated and made possible, then agency can be *presumed* only at the cost of refusing to inquire into its construction . . . In a sense, the epistemological model that offers us a pregiven subject or agent is one that refuses to acknowledge *that agency is always and only a political prerogative*.[62]

Although Wendt might initially agree that "politics and power exist already at the level at which the subject and its agency are articulated and made possible" (hence his focus on identity- and interest-formation among states), a powerful rationalist pull in his argument curtails the logical consequence of pushing the constitutive nature of political agency to its limits. This commitment can be observed at two key points: when the anthropomorphism of the individual-state analogy is defended by Wendt,[63] and when it is argued that the body is the "material substrate of agency" that remains for the individual once the constitutive properties of the self are stripped away.[64] The latter point is particularly telling, on two counts. First, one of the major contributions of recent political theorizing, particularly feminist scholarship, has been to put in question the assumption of pregiven, material bodies as the unproblematic ground for identity and politics.[65] To overlook such arguments in favor of a (seemingly commonsense) resolution of this complex issue forecloses the potential of Wendt's argument to come to terms with the complexities and contingencies of politics. The second count of interest is that the first suggests Wendt retreats in the end to the (supposedly) secure foundations of the body politic because of his moral commitment to an "epistemic realism" whereby the world comprises objects independent of ideas or beliefs about them.

It is this epistemic realism that constitutes the epistemic conceit that drives much of the mainstream's appropriation of culture, identity, and the like. Figuring the world in terms of an idealist/materialist dichotomy is what enables recidivist realists to insist on the priority of the material, and more progressive wings of the orthodoxy to talk of supplementing the material with the ideational. In this context, the latter is but a different formulation of the same basic assumptions shared with the former. Neither appreciate the problematization of the idealist/materialist dichotomy that results from poststructuralist concerns with performativity.

In contrast, thinking in terms of performativity enables different ways of regarding culture and, as a result, the meaning of "security culture." The line of argumentation represented by *Writing Security* posits "culture" as a relational site for the politics of identity, rather than a substantive phenomenon in its own right. As Appadurai suggests, emphasizing "the dimensionality of culture rather than its substantiality" — the way in which culture "attends to situated and embodied difference" rather than pregiven substance — means we can view culture in a manner radically different from it being simply a variable or context.[66] Instead of diminishing the politicized aspects of culture in those terms, we can see culture as signifying part of the conditions of intelligibility that establish the conditions of possibility for social being. The issue of "security culture" becomes, therefore, not a question of the social context that provides inputs that color the decision-making process, but the way in which culturalist arguments themselves secure the identity of subjects in whose name they speak.[67]

Such formulations are far removed from a concern with the desire to structure political accounts in terms amenable to falsification and testing.[68] Their distance is a result, not only of varying intellectual commitments, but of a fundamentally different view of their intellectual purpose. Broadly speaking, poststructuralists and their allies see their works as interpretive interventions that have political effects, whereas the mainstream (in both its orthodox and relatively progressive guises) perceives itself as engaged in the objective pursuit of cumulative knowledge central to a distinct social science, even as it sometimes acknowledges the difficulties therein.[69] As we shall see in the conclusion, this differing sense of purpose has important ramifications for the prospect of future engagements.

Friendly Fire

Those engagements are not restricted to a simple Manichaean clash between "the mainstream" and "the critics." Just as the above discussion of *The Culture of National Security* illustrated tensions within the social scientific community of international relations, those engaged in the political criticism of world politics exhibit heterogeneous commitments and perspectives.

At least as argued in *Writing Security*, the identity assumptions of poststructuralism constitute a problematization of sovereign accounts of politics common to the mainstream by shifting *from* a concern with the a priori assumptions of agency and pregiven subjects *to* the problematic of subjectivity and its political constitution. In making this move, however, arguments of this kind have been subject to fraternal criticism. Reading this questioning of agency as the death and abandonment of the subject, Iver Neumann has distinguished sharply between "hard-line poststructuralists" and constructivists, and argued that the metatheoretical commitments of the poststructuralists could be disenabling for political interventions.[70]

One of the dilemmas associated with these recent developments in international relations' theorizing is the often contradictory valences indicated by the term "constructivism." While it has been adopted by elements of the mainstream in their appropriative arguments, it has also been deployed by critical scholars sometimes intellectually allied with poststructuralism.[71] Work in this vein has been informed by different philosophical and sociological literatures, and includes a large body of research on security and European identity, an account of Western action in Bosnia, an exegesis of international society, the reconceptualization of "the national interest," especially in the context of United States foreign policy vis-à-vis Cuba, a discursive analysis of United States foreign policy decision making in Vietnam, an exhumation of Slovenian national identity, a reading of NATO enlargement, and a rethinking of the meaning of violence.[72] Three collective enterprises — the many and varied writings of "critical security studies," the edited volumes produced by the SSRC projects on the social construction of sovereignty, and the culture and production of insecurity — are important manifestations of this strand of "constructivism."[73]

To draw distinctions between poststructuralists and critical constructivists goes against an increasingly common tendency whereby the latter term often subsumes the former two (and thus manifests its own politics of naming).[74] It is also a distinction which in the first instance is difficult to make and contentious to suggest, not least because much critical work combines in a productive way the different positions. Individual scholars can easily occupy multiple positions.[75] Nonetheless, the purpose of highlighting the distinction drawn by others is to make an important theoretical point, with particular political consequences, which can sometimes remain submerged. This is because, despite some exchanges, the entailments of the theorization of identity in even critically inclined constructivist arguments are sometimes less fully explicated than would be useful.[76] An engagement with these entailments would enable the issues at stake in Neumann's argument to be better appreciated.

While Neumann is evidently empathetic with the case for the ontological impossibility of a secure and self-enclosed self, he believes poststructuralists dwell on this at the expense of a concern with the epistemology of identity. It is a position akin to the common argument that poststructuralism privileges "deconstruction" over "reconstruction," with the former term meaning negative criticism and the latter signifying positive politics.[77]

The argument of Neumann and others replicates what Foucault called the "blackmail of the Enlightenment." Instead of opting for either/or renderings of the theoretical and political choices we face, i.e., problematizing subjectivity equates with the end of agency and the death of the subject, a more sustained critique of "the limits that are imposed on us and an experiment with the possibility of going beyond them" has to be achieved. This necessarily involves the refusal to bracket off either ontological or epistemological issues (assuming we wish to persist with those categories), for new political enactments both depend on and themselves perform the problematization of subjectivity. This is one of the contrasting commitments that seems to mark an important distinction between poststructuralists and critical constructivists. The former appreciates that the deconstruction of identity both widens the domain of the political to include the ways in which identity is constituted, and contains within it a necessarily affirmative moment through which existing identity formations are denaturalized and alternative articulations of identity and the political are made possible. The latter can appear hesitant to pursue this radical logic to its ultimate conclusions, preferring instead to secure some dimensions of identity as a way of anchoring analysis.

Insofar as critically inclined constructivists posit a limit to the limit-attitude, they replicate elements associated with the more mainstream appropriations from which they want to be distanced. For example, some of the formulations in an argument concerned with a critical account of the construction of national interests manifest a similar intellectual purpose (theory-construction), and can be read as exhibiting similar commitments (purposive agents confronting an external political field) to those of at least the progressive element of the mainstream. Arguing that constructivism is an approach that can provide a theory to account for the constitution of state interests and action, Weldes's article suggests the basic principle of constructivism is "that people act towards objects, including other actors, on the basis of the meanings that the objects have for them." This quote from Wendt—whom Weldes nonetheless goes on to engage critically—suggests a starting point shared with contributors to *The Culture of National Security* that might, given its other entailments and their effects, bring with it more problems than are bargained for. In the context of foreign policy decision makers, the group who it is said does the constructing, this opening assumption is parlayed into the following form: "Drawing on a wide array of already available cultural and linguistic resources, state officials create representations which serve, first, to populate the world with a variety of objects, including both the self (i.e., the state in question) and others."[78]

The distance between these propositions and the starting premise for *The Culture of National Security* (that "security interests are defined by actors who respond to cultural factors") does not appear all that great. The distance from notions of performativity is quite marked, however. In terms of the latter, "there is no power, construed as a subject, that acts, but only...a reiterated acting that *is* power in its persistence and instability. This is less an 'act,' singular and deliberate [such as creation or definition by state officials], than a nexus of power and discourse that repeats and mimes the discursive gestures of power."[79] Of course, none of us fully expunges all traces of the assumptions about agents and the political field problematized by performativity in our arguments, and examples could be isolated in the previous chapters of this book to illustrate that claim. But without a larger context that simultaneously problematizes the seemingly extradiscursive location of policy makers—something well in evidence in *Writing Security*—those traces are accentuated. And in being so accentuated, critical constructivist arguments can be more easily drawn into the realm of judgment where the protocols of "empirical social science" rule, to the detriment of a politicized account of important practices.

The purpose in suggesting that there are substantive issues implied by the distinction others have made between poststructuralist and critical constructivist accounts of identity is manifestly not an attempt to divide and diminish the combined effects of these various critical theories for international relations. To the contrary, the capacity to make distinctions between different presuppositions and their entailments within a broadly understood critical domain of inquiry speaks volumes for both the quantity and quality of research now available in this sector of the field. Instead, the purpose of noting this distinction is to enable a better response to the mainstream appropriations. An attentiveness to the depoliticization of identity studies under way in the field suggests that approaches that do not pursue fully the problematization of subjectivity could contribute, perhaps unwittingly, to this trend.

Mission Statements

This review illustrates the sometimes subtle but always important conceptual distinctions between poststructuralists and others. Illustrating those differences is essential if the disciplinary politics of theorizing identity is to be appreciated. The coincidence of intensified ad hominem assaults on critical scholars, and the appropriation and normalization of their substantive concerns, cannot be overlooked. In the end, two things stand out. First, appropriations of the themes of identity politics by realist and rationalist scholars that are not attuned to the entailments that go with them is likely to satisfy no one. Poststructuralists will rightly decry the depoliticizing and ahistoricizing consequences of the move, while hard-core realists will bemoan what they see as the lack of rigor in even this limited move.[80]

Second, and most important, although a dialogue between poststructuralists and others (in which the legitimacy of the former would be accepted, and some understanding of their work exhibited) is both necessary and would be welcome, in the end it is likely to reveal that the conflicts that materialize themselves in terms of disciplinary approaches are in actuality clashes between fundamentally disparate ethico-political positions. This is evident even in the empathetic critiques of those who share much in common with poststructuralists, where doubts about the move beyond the dichotomy of idealism/materialism, the alleged denial of agency in critical writings, and the perceived problems for politics of these positions are enunciated.[81]

Each of these charges can either be supported or refuted, but only by assuming certain ontological conditions that cannot themselves be validated by anything other than reasoned argumentation.

For example, there is little "evidence," at least in the narrow social-scientific sense, which can unquestionably validate the key assumption of this book—that identity is an inescapable dimension of being, rather than an epiphenomenal property, for both individual and collective subjects. There is plenty of evidence in documentary archives or contemporary political discourse to suggest that "identity" is a site in which political struggles are enacted, and such evidence has been explored at length as a way of justifying the larger claim. But this situation does not mean that a converse position—such as the view that material interests are determinant—necessarily holds, because that starting point would be equally immune to the sort of evidence being demanded for this argument.[82]

The situation is even clearer when it comes to the contestation between poststructuralist writers and the more mainstream scholars of international relations. This is because each group, loosely defined though they are, understands its purpose with regard to intellectual inquiry in radically different ways. Each group, if you like, follows a different mission statement. These contrasting purposes have been signified in the argument above in terms of the contrast between an ethos of political criticism and the rigors of social science, or (as in the Introduction to this book) the differences between a logic of interpretation and a logic of explanation.[83] As a result, the disciplinary ambitions of each group are markedly different; poststructuralists engaged in pursuing the ethos of political criticism are not much troubled by where their research leaves them in relation to the site of international relations, whereas those operating in terms of social scientific procedures are constantly concerned about positioning their argument in such a way as to maximize their disciplinary audience and impact. Where critically inclined constructivists fall in this matrix of issues, which is surely not a series of either/or options, is not wholly clear, a conundrum that might go some way toward indicating the source of the uncertainty about how far to pursue the limit-attitude that is evident in some examples of this scholarship.[84]

These contrasting purposes can also be understood in terms of what Connolly has referred to as "the ontopolitical assumptions"—those judgments about the nature of realities and our capacities to understand them—which necessarily mark competing social and political theories.[85] These ontopolitical assumptions are key, because the agonism demonstrated by competing conceptual accounts of international relations and world politics goes beyond methodological or epistemological disagreements; the agonism is testament to the strongly held assumptions about the nature of our world and our place in it which direct us toward some modes of representation and not others.[86] Although those assumptions must always be revealed, constantly scrutinized, and often reformulated, they are not amenable to "proof" except in terms readable through their own ethico-political assumptions.

This perhaps helps explain why critical scholars of world politics are increasingly and overtly concerned with ethical questions that are inherent to their work. Yet the political consequences of these arguments—such as the way in which the ethos might play out in the specific sites of United States Foreign Policy, for example—has attracted to date little enthusiasm.[87] Not because the proposals are unappealing per se, but because they allegedly do not disclose new options that mark them off completely from those that could be advocated by competing perspectives. In such criticisms lies an important misunderstanding that is worth clarifying by way of conclusion. Even when an argument of this kind shifts to the register of policy, its contribution is not to simply advocate one fixed position. This is not because it is incapable of endorsing or suggesting particular decisions in specific circumstances that should be pursued. Rather, an argument of this kind embodies an ethos that considers critique to be a form of intervention, carrying with it particular assumptions into an already established political formation in order to pry open the space for alternatives. This ethos is therefore primarily concerned with the temporal process of critique and the positions it makes possible. Whether deconstructive, genealogical, or of some other kind, an argument like this is always looking to the limits and how they can be contested, disturbed, or negotiated. Its contribution is to recognize the way such limits establish both the possibility and the insufficiency of particular policy resolutions, to appreciate that despite such deficiencies decisions must be taken only to be simultaneously criticized and taken again, and to enact the Enlightenment attitude by a persistent and relentless questioning in specific contexts of the identity performances, and their inescapable indebtness to difference, through which politics occurs. All of this is necessarily part of an ethico-political position far removed from the disciplinary ambitions of social science, for it maintains that only by pursuing the agonism between closure and disturbance, naturalization and denaturalization, can a democratic ethos be lived.

Notes

A Note about the Revised Edition

1. "Foreign Policy and Identity: Japanese Other/American Self," in *The Global Economy as Political Space: A Critical Reader in International Political Economy*, edited by Naeem Inayatullah, Stephen J. Rosow, and Mark Rupert, Boulder, 1994.

Introduction

1. Equating in an unreflective manner the "United States" with "America" is often considered (with good reason) an ethnocentric move. Nonetheless, throughout this study I use both phrases to represent the object of consideration. For reasons that will be more fully argued in chapters 5 and 6, the retention of a certain undecidability to the naming of (the United States of) America is important to the argument being made here.

2. François Ewald, "Insurance and Risk," in *The Foucault Effect: Studies in Governmental Rationality*, edited by Graham Burchell, Colin Gordon, and Peter Miller, Hemel Hempstead, England, 1991, p. 199.

3. Mary Douglas and Aaron Wildavsky, *Risk and Culture: An Essay on the Selection of Technological and Environmental Dangers*, Berkeley, 1982.

4. U.S. Department of Health and Human Services, *Vital Statistics of the United States 1987: Volume II, Mortality Part A*, Hyattsville, Maryland, 1990, table 1–6. Other diseases, such as diseases of the heart and malignant neoplasms, were the major causes of death.

5. Frank Donner, *Protectors of Privilege: Red Squads and Police Repression in Urban America*, Berkeley, 1990, p. 367. Excluding the Lockerbie disaster, in the thirty years since the beginning of the 1960s, there have been eighty-five explosions aboard civilian aircraft attributed to "terrorism" resulting in 2,143 deaths. Billie H. Vincent, "Aviation Security and Terrorism," *Terrorism* 13, 1990, p. 398. Although not a complete accounting of all deaths resulting from "terrorism," this figure demonstrates — in comparison to the millions who have died in that time from civil war, preventable diseases, or starvation — that the concern surrounding "terrorism" does not correspond with its occurrence.

6. "The threat is posed not merely by actions the other might take to injure or defeat the true identity but by the very visibility of its mode of *being* as other." William

229

E. Connolly, *Identity/Difference: Democratic Negotiations of Political Paradox*, Ithaca, 1991, p. 66.

7. I refer to the policies of the now curtailed McCarran–Walter Act, which excluded from the United States, on ideological grounds, writers like the Nobel Prize winner Gabriel García Márquez.

8. George Bush, "In Defense of Saudi Arabia (Speech of August 8, 1990)," in *The Gulf War Reader: History, Documents, Opinions*, edited by Micah L. Sifry and Christopher Cerf, New York, 1991, p. 197.

9. See Hayden White, *The Content of the Form: Narrative Discourse and Historical Representation*, Baltimore, 1987, especially chapter 1.

10. For a discussion of these entailments, see David Campbell, "Recent Changes in Social Theory: Questions for International Relations," in *New Directions in International Relations? Australian Perspectives*, edited by Richard A. Higgott, Canberra, 1988; Yosef Lapid, "The Third Debate: On the Prospects of International Theory in a Post-Positivist Era," *International Studies Quarterly* 33, 1989, pp. 235–54; and Jim George, "International Relations and the Search for Thinking Space: Another View of the Third Debate," *International Studies Quarterly* 33, 1989, pp. 269–79.

11. See "Speaking the Language of Exile: Dissidence in International Studies," edited by Richard K. Ashley and R. B. J. Walker, *International Studies Quarterly* 34, 1990, pp. 259–416.

12. The charge of "relativism" has become a mantra-like repudiation employed by realists and others seeking to delegitimize an argument such as this. The logic behind this criticism is that any position concerning itself with the constructed nature of reality has to assume (implicitly or explicitly) that all positions are relative to a specific framework, paradigm, or culture, such that we can make no judgments about right and wrong, good or bad. Furthermore, it is often maintained that such an assumption is contradictory, because the relativist is said to resort to a universal: i.e., that all things are relative. For two reasons, I think such a charge is mistaken and misleading. First, the meaning of relativism is usually ascribed by the objectivist critic, but in a way that refuses to question the terms of the debate. Specifically, the charge of relativism rests on the dubious assumption that there is indeed some overarching, universal framework to which one is relative. For all the efforts of philosophers and others over the centuries, I am not aware of any agreement on the existence or nature of such an Archimedean point. Indeed, those factors that are sometimes cited as "universal" — such as tradition or culture—invoke the very intersubjective qualities that the so-called relativist is concerned with. Second, the characteristics subsumed under the term *relativism* by realist critics usually bear the hallmarks of subjectivism rather than relativism. The concern for the lack of standards and truths is usually said to derive from the alleged moral solipsism that results from so-called relativism: the idea that the abandonment of universals leads to an ethical anarchy in which anything goes. But the so-called relativist is concerned with the social and intersubjective nature of paradigms, practices, and standards, and thus rejects the idea that these are the property of individuals. My thinking on these issues has been most influenced by Richard Bernstein, *Beyond Objectivism and Relativism: Science, Hermeneutics, and Praxis*, Oxford, 1983.

13. See Jim George and David Campbell, "Patterns of Dissent and the Celebration of Difference: Critical Social Theory and International Relations," *International Studies Quarterly* 34, 1990, pp. 269–93.

14. Michel Foucault, *Discipline and Punish: The Birth of the Prison*, translated by Alan Sheridan, New York, 1979, p. 31.

15. See Hubert L. Dreyfus and Paul Rabinow, *Michel Foucault: Beyond Structuralism and Hermeneutics*, Brighton, 1983, pp. 118–20.

16. For a good account of these formulations, see Judith Butler, "Contingent Foundations: Feminism and the Question of 'Postmodernism,' " in *Feminists Theorize the Political*, edited by Judith Butler and Joan W. Scott, New York, 1992.

17. Richard Rorty, "Introduction: Pragmatism and Philosophy," in *Consequences of Pragmatism (Essays 1972–1980)*, Brighton, 1982, p. xix.

18. This is different from the claim that there are "alternative conceptual frameworks" through which we can know the world, for such a position eventually collapses into a Kantian understanding, whereby "the world" is a thing-in-itself thoroughly independent of our knowledge. See Rorty, "The World Well Lost," in *Consequences of Pragmatism*.

19. Michel Foucault, "The Order of Discourse," in *Language and Politics*, edited by Michael Shapiro, Oxford, 1984, p. 127.

20. Ernesto Laclau and Chantal Mouffe, *Hegemony and Socialist Strategy: Towards a Radical Democratic Politics*, translated by Winston Moore and Paul Cammack, London, 1985, p. 108.

21. Ibid., p. 110. White has expressed a similar sentiment: "Tropic is the shadow from which all realistic discourse tries to flee. This flight, however, is futile; for tropics is the process by which all discourse constitutes the objects which it pretends only to describe realistically and to analyze objectively." Hayden White, *Tropics of Discourse: Essays in Cultural Criticism*, Baltimore, 1978, p. 2.

22. Michel Foucault, *Power/Knowledge: Selected Writings and Other Interviews 1972–1977*, edited by Colin Gordon, New York, 1980, pp. 100–102.

23. For a general discussion on this theme, see Connolly, *Identity/Difference*.

24. Judith Butler, *Gender Trouble: Feminism and the Subversion of Identity*, New York, 1990, p. 133.

25. Ibid., pp. 136, 140–41, 145 respectively. Emphasis in the original.

26. See Joan Cocks, *The Oppositional Imagination: Feminism, Critique and Political Theory*, New York, 1989. Cocks uses the capital letter for Masculine to signify its status as the norm of the regime.

27. Ibid., p. 61.

28. Foucault, "Two Lectures," in *Power/Knowledge*, especially pp. 106–7.

29. The groups and phenomena objectified as dangers vary with the domain or identity that is being secured. In terms of the sexed body, sexual danger—sometimes in the form of male violence, psychological anxieties, or cultural transgressions—has obviously been the concern. On this issue, see Carole S. Vance, "Pleasure and Danger: Toward a Politics of Sexuality," in *Pleasure and Danger: Exploring Female Sexuality*, edited by Carole S. Vance, Boston, 1984; Ellen Carol DuBois and Linda Gordon, "Seeking Ecstasy on the Battlefield: Danger and Pleasure in Nineteenth-Century Feminist Sexual Thought," in *Pleasure and Danger*; and Judith Walkowitz, "Male Vice and Female Virtue: Feminism and the Politics of Prostitution in Nineteenth-Century Britain," in *Powers of Desire: The Politics of Sexuality*, edited by Ann Snitow, Christine Stansell, and Sharon Thompson, New York, 1983. Alternatively, in European society, the working class has often been targeted as another mode of being, sometimes by association with criminals and the insane. See Colin Gordon, "Governmental Rationality: An Introduction," in *The Foucault Effect*, pp. 38–39; Louis Chevalier, *Laboring Classes and Dangerous Classes*, translated by Frank Jellinek, New York, 1973; and Foucault, "The Dangerous Individual," in *Michel Foucault: Politics, Philosophy, Culture: Interviews and Other Writings 1977–1984*, edited by Lawrence D. Kritzman, New York, 1988.

30. Given the way the state itself has often been considered a sexed body, the centrality of gender norms to the moral space of state identity can be further highlighted. Since the beginning of the nineteenth century, male and female stereotypes have been used to visually represent the nation. See George L. Mosse, *Nationalism and Sexuality: Respectability and Abnormal Sexuality in Modern Europe*, New York, 1985.

31. Benedict Anderson, *Imagined Communities: Reflections on the Origin and Spread of Nationalism*, revised edition, New York, 1991.

32. Charles Tilly, *Coercion, Capital, and European States, A.D. 990–1990*, New York, 1990.

33. In his account of the importance of speed and temporality to politics, Paul Virilio observed, somewhat grandiosely, that "stasis is death really seems to be the general law of the World." Virilio, *Speed and Politics*, translated by Mark Polizzotti, New York, 1986, p. 67.

34. "In a social configuration whose precarious equilibrium is threatened by an ill-considered initiative, security can henceforth be likened to the absence of movement." Virilio, *Speed and Politics*, p. 125.

1. Provocations of Our Time

1. The most striking, though far from the only, example of such an analysis is Francis Fukuyama, "The End of History?" *The National Interest*, summer 1989, pp. 3–18.

2. Fred Halliday, "The Ends of Cold War," *New Left Review* 180, 1990, pp. 5–23.

3. William G. Hyland, *The Cold War Is Over*, New York, 1990.

4. See the debates in *The New Detente: Rethinking East-West Relations*, edited by Mary Kaldor, Gerard Holden, and Richard Falk, London, 1989. For an account of continuities in the "Third World" during this juncture, see Rajni Kothari, "The New Detente: Some Reflections from the South," *Alternatives* 14, 1989, pp. 289–99.

5. Halliday, "Ends of Cold War," p. 7.

6. William G. Hyland, "America's New Course," *Foreign Affairs* 69, 1990, pp. 1–2. For similar statements, see Charles William Maynes, "America without Cold War," *Foreign Policy* 78, 1990, pp. 3–25; and John Lewis Gaddis, "Towards the Post–Cold War World," *Foreign Affairs* 70, 1991, pp. 102–16. The disappearance of danger has led many to ruminate on the challenges of securing the peace. See, for example, *The Cold War and After: Prospects for Peace*, edited by Sean M. Lynn-Jones, Cambridge, Massachusetts, 1991.

7. Hedley Bull, "The Theory of International Relations, 1919–1969," in *The Aberystwyth Papers: International Politics 1919–1969*, edited by Brian Porter, London, 1972.

8. Michael Shapiro, *The Politics of Representation: Writing Practices in Biography, Photography, and Policy Analysis*, Madison, 1987, p. 93.

9. William E. Connolly, *Identity/Difference: Democratic Negotiations of Political Paradox*, Ithaca, 1991, pp. 215–16.

10. See ibid., chapters 1 and 7.

11. See, respectively, Edward Soja, *Postmodern Geographies: The Reassertion of Space in Critical Social Theory*, London, 1989, p. 217; the cover story in *Time*, April 9, 1990; and Colin McCord and Harold P. Freeman, "Excess Mortality in Harlem," *The New England Journal of Medicine* 332, January 18, 1990, pp. 173–77.

12. This term is indebted to Derrida and Lefort. On "erasure" see Jacques Derrida, *Of Grammatology*, translated by G. Spivak, Baltimore, 1976. For the idea of "the markers of certainty," see Claude Lefort, *Democracy and Political Theory*, translated by D. Macey, Minneapolis, 1988.

13. The idea of the "rarefaction of political discourse" was first suggested to me by Richard Ashley.

14. See Jacques Derrida, *Positions*, translated by Alan Bass, Chicago, 1981, pp. 41–44. For suggestive commentaries on this theme, see Rodolphe Gasché, *The Tain of the Mirror: Derrida and the Philosophy of Reflection*, Cambridge, Massachusetts, 1986; and Christopher Norris, *Derrida*, London, 1987.

15. Derrida, quoted in Gasché, *The Tain of the Mirror*, p. 241.

16. For reviews of this extensive literature, see Charles S. Maier, "After the Cold War: Introduction to the 1991 Edition," in *The Cold War in Europe: Era of a Divided Continent*, edited by Maier, New York, 1991; Mary Kaldor, *The Imaginary War: Understanding the East-West Conflict*, Oxford, 1990, chapter 3; and Deborah Welch Larson, *Origins of Containment: A Psychological Explanation*, Princeton, 1985, pp. 4–18.

17. E.g., Arthur Schlesinger Jr., "The Origins of the Cold War," *Foreign Affairs*, 46, 1967, pp. 22–52; Daniel Yergin, *Shattered Peace: The Origins of the Cold War*, revised edition, New York, 1990; Louis J. Halle, *The Cold War as History*, revised edition, New York, 1991. For a review, see Geir Lundestad, "Moralism, Presentism, Exceptionalism, Provincialism, and Other Extravagances in American Writings on the Early Cold War Years," *Diplomatic History* 13, 1989, pp. 527–45.

18. E.g., William Appelman Williams, *The Tragedy of American Diplomacy*, revised edition, New York, 1962; Lloyd Gardner, *Architects of Illusion: Men and Ideas in American Foreign Policy*, Chicago, 1970; Joyce and Gabriel Kolko, *The Limits of Power: The World and United States Foreign Policy*, New York, 1972. Critical reviews of this literature include Robert W. Tucker, *The Radical Left and American Foreign Policy*, Baltimore, 1971; and J. L. Richardson, "Cold War Revisionism: A Critique," *World Politics* 24, 1972, pp. 579–612. For a review that takes issue with some of the revisionist theses, but that is sensitive to the differences among these historians, see Warren F. Kimball, "The Cold War Warmed Over," *American Historical Review* 79, 1974, pp. 1119–36. Labelled "neorevisionist" by Maier for its application of world-systems theory to United States foreign policy, is Thomas J. McCormick, *America's Half Century: United States Foreign Policy in the Cold War*, Baltimore, 1989. There were also works of right-wing revisionism, which charged that U.S. officials toward the end of World War II were too soft on the Soviet Union. See Larson, *Origins of Containment*, pp. 5–6.

19. Kaldor, *The Imaginary War*, p. 37. For an overview, see John Lewis Gaddis, "The Emerging Postrevisionist Synthesis on the Origins of the Cold War," *Diplomatic History* 7, 1983, pp. 171–90. Gaddis's own work is probably the best example of postrevisionism: see his *The Long Peace: Inquiries into the History of the Cold War*, New York, 1987. Postrevisionism has not given the prominence to economic issues some would like, prompting what has been termed a corporatist literature. For an exchange concerning this literature, see John Lewis Gaddis, "The Corporatist Synthesis: A Skeptical View," *Diplomatic History* 10, 1986, pp. 357–62; and Michael J. Hogan, "Corporatism: A Positive Appraisal," *Diplomatic History* 10, 1986, pp. 363–72. Some have seen in this relatively mild debate the prospects for another synthesis, although a number of European historians downplay the corporatist emphasis on the pivotal role of the United States in postwar European economic development. See Lawrence S. Kaplan, "The Cold War and European Revisionism," *Diplomatic History* II, 1987, pp. 143–56.

20. See Edward Thompson et al., *Exterminism and Cold War*, London, 1982; Kaldor, "After the Cold War," *New Left Review* 180, 1990, pp. 25–37; Michael Cox, "From the Truman Doctrine to the Second Superpower Detente: The Rise and Fall of the Cold War," *Journal of Peace Research* 27, 1990, pp. 25–41; Noam Chomsky, *Deterring Democracy*, New York, 1991. For an exchange on this literature, see Halliday, "The Ends of

Cold War"; and Edward Thompson, "Comment: The Ends of Cold War," *New Left Review* 182, 1990, pp. 139–50.

21. See, for example, Hyland, *The Cold War Is Over; The Cold War and After,* ed. Lynn-Jones; Joseph S. Nye, Jr., *Bound to Lead: The Changing Nature of American Power,* New York, 1990; *Sea-Changes: American Foreign Policy in a World Transformed,* edited by Nicholas X. Rizopoulos, New York, 1990; Robert J. Art, "A Defensible Defense: America's Grand Strategy after the Cold War," *International Security* 15, 1991, pp. 5–53.

22. Halle, *Cold War as History,* p. xvi; Yergin, *Shattered Peace,* pp. 7, 9–10.

23. See, for example, Chomsky, *Deterring Democracy,* pp. 19–20.

24. Thompson, "Comment," p. 146.

25. "But the Cold War passed, long ago, into a self-generating condition of Cold War-ism (exterminism), in which the originating drives, reactions, and intentions are still at play, but within a general inertial condition." Thompson, "Notes on Exterminism, the Last Stage of Civilization," in Thompson, et al., *Exterminism and Cold War,* p. 21. "It is ideology, even more than military-industrial pressures, which is the driving-motor of the Cold War...It is as if...ideology has broken free from the existential socio-economic matrix within which it was nurtured and is no longer subject to any control of rational self-interest." Thompson, "Comment," pp. 141–42.

26. Halle, *Cold War as History,* p. 12. Halle's unabashed realism is evident from this statement: "But the historical circumstances, themselves, had an ineluctable quality that left the Russians little choice but to move as they did. Moving as they did, they compelled the United States and its allies to move in response. And so the Cold War was joined." Ibid., p. xvii. His reflections on historiography are published in *Cold War as History* as appendix 1, "A Multitude of Cold Wars."

27. See Jim George, "The Study of International Relations and the Positivist/Empiricist Theory of Knowledge: Implications for the Australian Discipline," in *New Directions in International Relations? Australian Perspectives,* edited by Richard A. Higgott, Canberra, 1988. Quote is on p. 88.

28. See Hans J. Morgenthau, *Politics among Nations: The Struggle for Power and Peace,* 5th ed., revised, New York, 1978, chapter 1.

29. George, "The Study of International Relations," pp. 90–91. See also Mervyn Frost, *Towards a Normative Theory of International Relations,* Cambridge, 1986. For a discussion of the ultimate positivism of the *verstehen* tradition, see David Campbell, "Recent Changes in Social Theory: Questions for International Relations," in *New Directions in International Relations?* ed. Higgott, especially pp. 25–27.

30. "The essential strategic relationship of antagonism between the United States and the Soviet Union constitutes a realm of necessity for U.S. policymakers." Colin S. Gray, *The Geopolitics of Superpower,* Lexington, 1988, p. 3. See also Stanley Hoffmann, *Primacy or World Order: American Foreign Policy Since the Cold War,* New York, 1978. This theme is critically addressed in Charles Nathenson, "The Social Construction of the Soviet Threat: A study in the Politics of Representation," *Alternatives* 13, 1988, pp. 443–83.

31. Richard Rorty, "Thugs and Theorists: A reply to Bernstein," *Political Theory* 15, 1987, p. 578, note 25.

32. Richard Bernstein, "One Step Forward, Two Steps Backward: Richard Rorty on Liberal Democracy and Philosophy," *Political Theory* 15, 1987, p. 551.

33. Walter LaFeber, *America, Russia, and the Cold War 1945–1984,* 5th ed., New York, 1985, chapter 4.

34. NSC-68, "United States Objectives and Programs for National Security, April 14, 1950," in *Containment: Documents on American Policy and Strategy, 1945–1950,* edited by Thomas H. Etzold and John Lewis Gaddis, New York, 1978, p. 385.

35. Ibid., pp. 385, 386, 387.

36. Ibid., pp. 390, 401.

37. Draft study prepared by the Policy Planning Staff, Annex VIII, NSC 68/1, "The Strategy of Freedom," November 10, 1950, in *Foreign Relations of the United States 1950, Volume I: National Security Affairs; Foreign Economic Policy*, Washington, D.C., 1977, p. 406.

38. NSC-68, p. 403.

39. PPS 1, "Policy with Respect to American Aid to Western Europe," May 3, 1947, in *Containment*, ed. Etzold and Gaddis, pp. 102–3.

40. PPS 4, "Certain Aspects of the European Recovery Program from the United States Standpoint (Preliminary Report)," July 23, 1947, in *Containment*, ed. Etzold and Gaddis, pp. 108–9.

41. "Moscow Embassy Telegram 511: 'The Long Telegram,'" in *Containment*, ed. Etzold and Gaddis, pp. 50–63. For an excellent account of the orientalist reasoning of both the "long telegram" and the later "Mr. X" article, see Anders Stephanson, *Kennan and the Art of Foreign Policy*, Cambridge, Massachusetts, 1989, pp. 13–15, 45–53, 73–79. For an analysis of the "long telegram's" figurations of the USSR as a potential rapist and red flood, see Gearóid Ó Tuathail and John Agnew, "Geopolitics and Discourse: Practical Geopolitical Reasoning in American Foreign Policy," *Political Geography* 11, 1992, 190–204. Although a parallel assessment by the senior British diplomat in Moscow shared Kennan's orientalist disposition, Kennan's telegram was significantly more rhetorical in its characterization of the Soviet Union. Interestingly, a Soviet diplomatic cable of the same era — aside from a couple of ritualistic references to "the imperialistic tendencies of American monopolistic capital" — offers a very dry and matter-of-fact analysis of U.S. leadership and policy. See *Origins of the Cold War: The Novikov, Kennan, and Roberts "Long Telegrams" of 1946*, edited by Kenneth M. Jensen, Washington, D.C., 1991.

42. Quoted in John Lewis Gaddis, *Strategies of Containment: A Critical Appraisal of Postwar American National Security Policy*, New York, 1982, p. 40.

43. Quoted in Thomas G. Paterson, *Meeting the Communist Threat: From Truman to Reagan*, New York, 1988, p. 120.

44. Quoted in Gaddis, *Strategies of Containment*, p. 30.

45. NSC-20/4, "U.S. objectives with Respect to the USSR to Counter Soviet Threats to U.S. Security," in *Containment*, ed. Etzold and Gaddis, p. 208.

46. Quoted in Gaddis, *Strategies of Containment*, p. 359.

47. "Memorandum by the Counsellor (Kennan) to the Secretary of State," January 6, 1950, in *FRUS 1950, Volume 1*, p. 128.

48. For example, "The Ambassador in the Soviet Union (Kirk) to the Secretary of State," August 11, 1950, in *FRUS 1950, Volume 1*, p. 367.

49. Matthew Evangelista, "Stalin's Postwar Army Reappraised," *International Security* 7, 1982–83, pp. 110–38. Evangelista also notes that the Soviets rapidly demobilized their postwar military, assigned many of the remaining soldiers to civil reconstruction work, and maintained perhaps half of their divisions at substantially less than full strength. As a result, the popular conception of the Soviet military threat was "illusory." Ibid., p. 137.

50. "Moscow Embassy Telegram #511," in *Containment*, ed. Etzold and Gaddis, p. 63.

51. Quoted in Melvyn P. Leffler, "The American Conception of National Security and the Beginnings of the Cold War, 1945–48," *American Historical Review* 89, 1984, p. 364.

52. "Draft Memorandum by the Counsellor (Kennan) to the Secretary of State," February 17, 1950, in *FRUS 1950, Volume 1*, p. 164.

53. NSC-17, "The Internal-Security of the United States," June 28, 1948, Records Group 273, National Archives of the United States, p. 6.

54. Ibid., pp. 9, 20, 6–7.

55. The one-page revision submitted to the NSC staff read as follows: "1. One purpose underlies every national security policy: to maintain the fundamental values and institutions of the United States. 2. To protect and preserve these fundamental values and institutions of the United States, we set the following objectives: *a.* To maintain a sound, strong United States economy, capable of enabling us to reach our general objectives in *b, c,* and *d; b.* To block further expansion of Soviet power, even at the grave risk of general war; *c.* To reduce Soviet power and influence to a point which no longer constitutes a threat to our security, without unduly risking general war; *d.* To establish an international system based on freedom and justice as contemplated in the United Nations Charter; *e.* To assure internal security against subversion, sabotage and espionage; *f.* To avoid, except as stated in *b* above, general war." NSC Planning Board, "Outline of Revised Basic National Security Policy: General Objectives," RG 273, National Archive.

56. James S. Lay, "Memorandum for the NSC Planning Board," May 7, 1953, RG 273, National Archive.

57. "Suggestions of the Office of Defense Mobilization for Changes in the Planning Board 'Outline of Revised Basic National Security Policy.' Dated April 29, 1953," May 8, 1953, RG 273, National Archive.

58. "Defense Department Changes," May 8, 1953, RG 273, National Archive.

59. NSC 153/1, "Restatement of Basic National Security Policy," June 10, 1953, RG 273, National Archive.

60. NSC 162/2, "Review of Basic National Security Policy," October 19, 1953, RG 273, National Archive.

61. NSC 5501, "Basic National Security Policy," January 6, 1955, RG 273, National Archive.

62. NSC 5602/1, "Basic National Security Policy," March 15, 1956, RG 273, National Archive.

63. NSC 5707/8, "Basic National Security Policy," June 3, 1957, RG 273, National Archive.

64. NSC 5810/1, "Basic National Security Policy," May 5, 1958, RG 273, National Archive.

65. NSC 5906/1, "Basic National Security Policy," August 5, 1959, RG 273, National Archive.

66. Quoted in Paterson, *Meeting the Communist Threat,* p. 199.

67. Address by Secretary Rusk, "The Role of the United States in World Affairs," *Department of State Bulletin* 56, 1967, pp. 770–71.

68. Quoted in Geir Lundestad, "Uniqueness and Pendulum Swings in U.S. Foreign Policy," *International Affairs* 62, 1986, p. 405.

69. Center for the Study of Foreign Affairs (CFSA), *Thinking about World Change,* Washington, D.C., 1990, chapter 1, especially pp. 16–19. Quote is on p. 17. The report was authored by Michael Vlahos, who, as director of the CSFA in the State Department, conducted a series of fifty conferences and seminars involving three hundred academics and policy makers between September 1988 and May 1989 to consider the issue of long-term change. This report is a "synthesis of a year's debate, of questions and of quest." Ibid., p. 8. Although the report offers the disclaimer that its views do

not necessarily reflect those of the State Department, the program members it identifies by name include many well-known figures in the revolving door environment of Washington.

70. On the debates over the extent and nature of the Soviet nuclear threat, see Fred M. Kaplan, *Dubious Specter: A Skeptical Look at the Soviet Nuclear Threat*, Washington DC, 1980; Lawrence Freedman, *U.S. Intelligence and the Soviet Strategic Threat*, 2nd ed., Princeton, 1986; and John Prados, *The Soviet Estimate: U.S. Intelligence Analysis and Soviet Strategic Forces*, Princeton, 1986. In the general debate about Soviet military power, assessments of Soviet defense spending have been important. On their contestable status, see the series of articles by Franklyn D. Holzman: "Are the Soviets Really Outspending the U.S. on Defense?" *International Security* 4, 1980, pp. 86–104; "Soviet Defense Spending: Assessing the Numbers Game," *International Security* 6, 1982, pp. 78–101; and "Politics and Guesswork: CIA and DIA Estimates of Soviet Military Spending," *International Security* 14, 1989, pp. 101–31. Estimations of Soviet military manpower levels have also been crucial (and debatable). See Evangelista, "Stalin's Postwar Army Reconsidered"; and Raymond L. Garthoff, "Estimating Soviet Military Force Levels: Some Light from the Past," *International Security* 14, 1990, pp. 93–116.

71. Sacvan Bercovitch, *The American Jeremiad*, Madison, 1978.

72. Ibid., p. 23. On the literary tradition of European jeremiads and the culture of anxiety in which they operated, see Jean Delumeau, *Sin and Fear: The Emergence of a Western Guilt Culture Thirteenth–Eighteenth Centuries*, translated by Eric Nicholson, New York, 1990.

73. On the two Committees on the Present Danger, see Samuel F. Wells, Jr., "Sounding the Tocsin: NSC-68 and the Soviet Threat," *International Security* 4, 1979, pp. 141–51; Jerry W. Sanders, *Peddlers of Crisis: The Committee on the Present Danger and the Politics of Containment*, Boston, 1983; and Simon Dalby, *Creating the Second Cold War: The Discourse of Politics*, New York, 1990. Examples of the jeremiad-like qualities of the writings of the second Committee on the Present Danger can be found in *Alerting America: The Papers of the Committee on the Present Danger*, edited by Charles Tyroler, Washington DC, 1984. A related and influential analysis — discussed in chapter 6 — is Norman Podhoretz, *The Present Danger: Do We Have the Will to Reverse the Decline of American Power?* New York, 1980.

74. Quoted in Michael T. Klare and Peter Kornbluh, "The New Interventionism: Low-Intensity Warfare in the 1980s and Beyond," in *Low-Intensity Warfare: Counterinsurgency, Proinsurgency, and Antiterrorism in the Eighties*, ed. Michael T. Klare and Peter Kornbluh, New York, 1988, p. 4.

75. CSFA, *Thinking about World Change*, pp. 53–56.

76. President Bush declared after the ceasefire had been put in place: "By God, we've kicked the Vietnam syndrome once and for all." In one of the many subsequent victory celebrations, he stated: "America rediscovered itself during Desert Storm." "A Different Bush Conforms to Nation's Mood," *New York Times*, March 2, 1991, p. 1; and "Glittering TV Show Dulls Democrats' View of '92," *New York Times*, April 5, 1991, p. B6. A more complete analysis of the representation of the Gulf War can be found in my *Politics without Principle: Sovereignty, Ethics and the Narratives of the Gulf War*, Boulder, 1993.

77. On the origins of the term *cold war*, see Halliday, "The Ends of Cold War," p. 7, though this is not the conclusion he draws. For an analysis of cold war discourse that aims to demonstrate its orientalist affinities with (and replacement of) earlier colonialist discourse, see William Peitz, "The 'Post-Colonialism' of Cold War Discourse," *Social Text* 19–20, 1988, pp. 55–75.

2. Rethinking Foreign Policy

1. Toward the end of 1990, the U.S. Congress passed new immigration legislation, but the exclusions mandated in that legislation—which continue to include the Communist Party even after the changes in the Soviet Union and Eastern Europe—have not changed the INS questions of old. See United States, House, *Immigration Act of 1990: Conference Report, 101st Congress,* 2d session, Report 101–955, Washington, D.C., 1990.

2. On the first use of *international,* see James Der Derian, "The Boundaries of Knowledge and Power in International Relations," in *International/Intertextual Relations: Postmodern Readings of World Politics,* edited by James Der Derian and Michael J. Shapiro, Lexington, 1989, p. 3; and Hidemi Suganami, "A Note on the Origin of the Word *International," British Journal of International Studies* 4, 1978, pp. 226–32.

3. For the original formulation of the levels of analysis issue, see J. David Singer, "Levels of Analysis: The International System and the Nation-State," in *Politics and the International System,* edited by Robert L. Pfaltzgraff, 2nd ed., Philadelphia, 1972.

4. For overviews of the field, see James N. Rosenau, *The Scientific Study of Foreign Policy,* New York, 1968; and Patrick J. McGowan and Howard B. Shapiro, *The Comparative Study of Foreign Policy: A Survey,* Beverly Hills, 1973.

5. James Rosenau, "Introduction: New Directions and Recurrent Questions in the Comparative Study of Foreign Policy," in *New Directions in the Study of Foreign Policy,* edited by Charles F. Hermann, Charles W. Kegley Jr., and James N. Rosenau, Boston, 1987, pp. 5–6.

6. Steve Smith, "Foreign Policy Analysis," in *International Relations: British and American Perspectives,* edited by Steve Smith, Oxford, 1985, pp. 46–47; James A. Caporaso, Charles F. Hermann, Charles W. Kegley Jr., James N. Rosenau, Dina A. Zinnes, "The Comparative Study of Foreign Policy: Perspectives on the Future," *International Studies Notes* 13, 1987, p. 32; and Rosenau, "Introduction," p. 4.

7. Rosenau, "Introduction," p. 1.

8. Charles F. Hermann and Gregory Peacock, "The Evolution and Future of Theoretical Research in the Comparative Study of Foreign Policy," in *New Directions in the Study of Foreign Policy,* edited by Hermann, Kegley, and Rosenau, pp. 16–18.

9. See William Bloom, *Personal Identity, National Identity, and International Relations,* Cambridge, 1990, p. x.

10. Steve Smith, "Describing and Explaining Foreign Policy Behavior," *Polity* 17, 1985, pp. 598–99.

11. Rosenau, "Introduction," pp. 1–2. See also Caporaso et al., pp. 32–33.

12. Steve Smith, "CFP: A Theoretical Critique," *International Studies Notes* 13, 1987, p. 48. Some of these issues are noted by Caporaso et al. (see pp. 33, 37–40), though they are not diverted from their attempts to maintain the basic assumptions of CFP.

13. See Richard Ashley, "Foreign Policy as Political Performance," *International Studies Notes* 13, 1987, pp. 51–54.

14. Richard K. Ashley, "Untying the Sovereign State: A Double Reading of the Anarchy Problematique," *Millennium: Journal of International Studies* 17, 1988, p. 253.

15. One of the most influential foreign policy textbooks in international relations begins with a quote from Dean Rusk, cited in part in chapter 1, that nicely illustrates the presumption of a settled identity: "It is quite true that the central themes of American foreign policy are more or less constant. They derive from the kind of people that we are . . . and from the shape of the world situation." Charles W. Kegley Jr. and Eugene R. Wittkopf, *American Foreign Policy: Pattern and Process,* 4th ed., New York, 1991, p. 3.

16. It is important to note that this argument is self-consciously operating only within the terms of a western discourse about western states. The major texts of the discipline of international relations have focused almost exclusively on western history and concerns, and in seeking to problematize the boundaries and entailments of that discourse, I am operating within the confines of its ethnocentricity. It is reasonable to suggest, however, that insofar as this critique is compelling, it opens up a space for refiguring the study of world politics in terms that would not exclude the greater proportion of humanity. To problematize the traditional western narrative on the rise of the state is also to problematize its foundational status for our understanding of international relations. As a consequence, this argument would enable important texts — such as Eric Wolf's *Europe and the People without History*, Berkeley, 1982 — to be brought into the discipline's mainstream.

17. F. H. Hinsley, *Sovereignty*, 2nd ed., Cambridge, 1986, p. 219.

18. Ibid., p. 15.

19. John H. Herz, *International Politics in the Atomic Age*, New York, 1959, p. 43.

20. Hinsley, *Sovereignty*, p. 15.

21. Herz, *International Politics*, p. 44

22. Miller offers a characteristic formulation: "Like all such historical benchmarks, Westphalia is in some respects more a convenient reference point than the source of a fully formed new normative system. Some elements that characterize the modern world, separating us from the Middle Ages, were well established long before 1648; others did not emerge until many years after. Still, the Peace of Westphalia created at least the foundations of a new European system...out of the ruins of the political structures and the idealized rationale for them that had existed more or less unchanged in Europe for the preceding thousand years." Lynn H. Miller, *Global Order: Values and Power in International Politics*, Boulder, 1990, p. 20. For similar representations of the Westphalian moment, see Kenneth N. Waltz, *Theory of International Politics*, New York, 1979, p. 131; and Robert Gilpin, *War and Change in World Politics*, Cambridge, 1981, pp. 29, 36.

23. Herz, *International Politics*, pp. 47–48. Herz was making this argument in order to demonstrate that the advent of nuclear weapons had fundamentally altered the nexus between territoriality and security. He thus wished to maintain that the classical period was at an end. Although this proposition did not alter his edifying account of the rise of the territorial state, Herz was later to retract it. See Herz, "The Territorial State Revisited," *Polity* 1, 1968, pp. 12–34.

24. For discussion of these themes in the literature of contemporary international relations, see R. B. J. Walker, "Realism, Change, and International Political Theory," *International Studies Quarterly* 31, 1987, pp. 65–86; and Walker, "History and Structure in the Theory of International Relations," *Millennium: Journal of International Studies* 18, 1989, pp. 163–83.

25. See, for example, Anthony Giddens, *The Nation-State and Violence: Volume Two of a Contemporary Critique of Historical Materialism*, Berkeley, 1985; Michael Mann, *The Sources of Social Power: Volume 1, A History of Power from the Beginning to A.D. 1760*, Cambridge, 1986; Michael Mann, *States, War, and Capitalism: Studies in Political Sociology*, Oxford, 1988; Reinhart Koselleck, *Critique and Crisis: Enlightenment and the Pathogenesis of Modern Society*, Cambridge, Massachusetts, 1988; John A. Hall, ed., *States in History*, Oxford, 1989; and Charles Tilly, *Coercion, Capital and European States, A.D. 990–1990*, New York, 1990. For a review of some of this literature, see Anthony Jervis, "Societies, States and Geopolitics: Challenges from Historical Sociology," *Review of International Studies* 15, 1989, pp. 281–93.

26. Michael Mann, *The Sources of Social Power: Volume 1, A History of Power from the Beginning to A.D. 1760*, Cambridge, 1986.

27. William E. Connolly, *Political Theory and Modernity*, Oxford, 1988, p. 2.

28. Koselleck, *Critique and Crisis*, pp. 18–19, 17.

29. See Marc Bloch, *Feudal Society*, trans. by L. A. Manyon, Chicago, 1961; and R. W. Southern, *Western Society and the Church in the Middle Ages*, Harmondsworth, England, 1970.

30. The metaphor of "mapping" has an important historical development as its referent, for it was at this juncture that cartographical representations of space came to be applied to whole countries. The first representation of a complete national territory was Christopher Saxon's collection of county maps (published in 1579), which provided a visual and conceptual guide to the kingdom of England and Wales. See Richard Helgerson, "The Land Speaks: Cartography, Chorography, and Subversion in Renaissance England," *Representations* 16, 1986, pp. 51–85.

31. The argument here is intended only to be suggestive of the relationship between the church, the state, and the problematic of identity: it is not intended to be a comprehensive account of the social forces and political practices implicated in the emergence of state forms. For example, this section has skipped lightly over the important issue of the emergence of "policy" and "police" in the seventeenth century as governmental technologies constitutive of the domain of the state, though I pursue this issue a little further in chapter 8. For an account of these "police" regulations in a specific context, see Marc Raeff, *The Well-Ordered Police State: Social and Institutional Change through Law in the Germanies and Russia, 1600–1800*, New Haven, 1983, especially pp. 4–5, 43–56.

32. Koselleck, *Critique and Crisis*, pp. 48–50.

33. Mann, *The Sources of Social Power*, p. 436.

34. Hans Blumenberg, *The Legitimacy of the Modern Age*, translated by Robert M. Wallace, Cambridge, Massachusetts, 1983. The argument to which Blumenberg was offering a critique was being developed by Karl Lowith, *Meaning in History*, Chicago, 1949.

35. Blumenberg argues that "self-assertion" is neither biological nor economic survival, but an "existential program, according to which man posits his existence in a historical situation and indicates to himself how he is going to deal with the reality surrounding him and what use he will make of the possibilities that are open to him." Blumenberg, *Legitimacy of the Modern Age*, p. 138.

36. Ibid., p. 173.

37. Ibid., pp. 214–15.

38. See Carl Schmitt, *Political Theology: Four Chapters on the Concept of Sovereignty*, Cambridge, Massachusetts, 1985.

39. Blumenberg, *The Legitimacy of the Modern Age*, p. xxiv. See the argument in part 1, chapter 8.

40. Ibid., p. xxiv.

41. Geoffrey Hawthorn, *Enlightenment and Despair: A History of Social Theory*, 2nd ed., Cambridge, 1987, chapter 1.

42. Connolly, *Political Theory and Modernity*, p. 11.

43. The concept of a "discourse of danger" comes originally from G. M. Dillon, "The Mediation of the Mediation: Arms Control and a Critical Genealogy of the Canons of the National-Security-Discourse," paper presented to the International Studies Association Annual Conference, London, April 1989.

44. This discussion is drawn from Jean Delumeau, *Sin and Fear: The Emergence of a Western Guilt Culture Thirteenth–Eighteenth Centuries*, translated by Eric Nicholson, New York, 1990.

45. Ibid., p. 112.
46. Ibid., p. 36.
47. Ibid.
48. Ibid., p. 42.
49. Ibid., pp. 96–97.
50. "The definition of difference is a requirement built into the logic of identity, and the construction of otherness is a temptation that readily insinuates itself into that logic." William E. Connolly, *Identity/Difference: Democratic Negotiations of Political Paradox*, Ithaca, 1991, p. 9.
51. Connolly, *Political Theory and Modernity*, p. 13.

3. Foreign Policy and Identity

1. On the importance of a "Hobbesian tradition," see Donald W. Hanson, "Thomas Hobbes's 'Highway to Peace,'" *International Organization* 38, 1984, pp. 329–31; Michael Joseph Smith, *Realist Thought from Weber to Kissinger*, Baton Rouge, 1986, pp. 12–15; and Robert W. Cox, "Social Forces, States and World Orders: Beyond International Relations Theory," in *Neorealism and Its Critics*, edited by Robert O. Keohane, New York, 1986, pp. 211–12. For an example of how this unproblematic understanding informs analysis, see Jack Snyder, "Averting Anarchy in the New Europe," *International Security* 14, 1990, pp. 5–41.
2. Robert Gilpin, "The Richness of the Tradition of Political Realism," in *Neorealism and Its Critics*, ed. Keohane, p. 304.
3. Reinhart Koselleck, *Critique and Crisis: Enlightenment and the Pathogenesis of Modern Society*, Cambridge, Massachusetts, 1988, p. 24.
4. Bull's own view of the relationship between Hobbes's state of nature and the understanding of international relations differs from that he ascribes to the dominant realist tradition. Bull prefers Locke's understanding of the state of nature because it allows him to talk of an anarchical *society* as the defining condition of international relations—a form of social life that, no matter how rudimentary, involves some notion of community that distinguishes it from pure anarchy, although it is still characterized by formal anarchy (meaning the absence of a central and all-powerful source of authority). See Hedley Bull, *The Anarchical Society: A Study of Order in World Politics*, London, 1977, especially pp. 46–51.
5. Hedley Bull, "Hobbes and the International Anarchy," *Social Research* 48, 1981, pp. 717–19.
6. Ibid., p. 720.
7. Thomas Hobbes, *Leviathan*, edited by C. B. Macpherson, Harmondsworth, England, 1968, chapter 13, pp. 187–88.
8. Bull, "Hobbes and the International Anarchy," pp. 720–21.
9. Hobbes, *Leviathan*, chapter 13, p. 187.
10. Ibid., p. 188.
11. Bull, "Hobbes and the International Anarchy," pp. 727, 733; Smith, *Realist Thought*, pp. 13–14.
12. R. B. J. Walker, "History and Structure in International Relations Theory," *Millennium: Journal of International Studies*, 18, 1989, p. 173; Bull, *The Anarchical Society*, pp. 49–50.
13. Koselleck, *Critique and Crisis*, pp. 43–44.
14. Murray Forsyth, "Thomas Hobbes and the External Relations of States," *British Journal of International Studies* 5, 1979, p. 208. See also Hanson, "Thomas Hobbes's 'Highway to Peace,'" p. 351.

15. Koselleck, *Critique and Crisis*, pp. 39–40.

16. Ibid., p. 24.

17. Hobbes, *Leviathan*, chapter 13, p. 187. Emphasis added.

18. David Johnston, *The Rhetoric of "Leviathan": Thomas Hobbes and the Politics of Cultural Transformation*, Princeton, 1986, p. 189.

19. Such as the possibility that Hobbes allows for a robust individuality within the parameters of a minimal order; see Richard E. Flathman, "Absolutism, Individuality, and Politics: Hobbes and a Little Beyond," *History of European Ideas* 10, 1989, pp. 547–68.

20. Hobbes, *Leviathan*, "Introduction," p. 81.

21. Forsyth, "Thomas Hobbes and the External Relations of States," pp. 196–97.

22. Hobbes, *Leviathan*, chapter 17, p. 227.

23. Ibid., p. 168. See Johnston, *The Rhetoric of "Leviathan,"* pp. 98–101 for a discussion of this fear in contrast to the fear of death. Johnston argues later (pp. 111–12) that the irrational fear of things invisible is contrasted by Hobbes to the rational fear of death in such a way that the former is considered a threat to the ordered polity, while the latter is what secures the ordered polity. Johnston concludes that it is thus not possible to argue that the real power of sovereigns comes from their supplementing the fear of death with a fear of things invisible. The argument being made here accepts that one does not supplement the other, but would equally disagree with the notion that one replaces the other. In contrast, using Blumenberg's metaphor of the recovery of positions, it might be more accurate to refuse a complete distinction between the two fears and instead see the fear of death reoccupying the position established by the fear of things invisible. However, because the latter is never fully removed from society, we should employ the notion of a "discourse of danger" to account for the way the fear of death is more complex and nuanced.

24. Johnston, *The Rhetoric of "Leviathan,"* p. 206.

25. William E. Connolly, *Political Theory and Modernity*, Oxford, 1988, p. 29.

26. Hobbes, *Leviathan*, chapter 11, pp. 160–61.

27. Ibid., chapter 13, p. 186.

28. Ibid., chapter 15, p. 209.

29. Ibid., chapter 12, p. 173.

30. Quoted in Johnston, *The Rhetoric of "Leviathan,"* p. 90.

31. Quoted in ibid., p. 123.

32. See, for example, Hobbes, *Leviathan*, chapter 15, pp. 212, 216. For a discussion on the relationship of otherness to the normal individual in Hobbes, see Connolly, *Political Theory and Modernity*, pp. 26–30.

33. *Leviathan*, chapter 29, pp. 363, 364, 371–73, 375.

34. Ibid., p. 369.

35. Johnston, *The Rhetoric of Leviathan*, pp. 104, 131–32.

36. Forsyth, "Thomas Hobbes and the External Relations of States," pp. 196–97.

37. Koselleck, *Critique and Crisis*, p. 41.

38. William E. Connolly, *Identity/Difference: Democratic Negotiations of Political Paradox*, Ithaca, 1991, p. 207.

39. See Michael J. Shapiro, *The Politics of Representation: Writing Practices in Biography, Photography and Policy Analysis*, Madison, pp. 100–111.

40. Richard K. Ashley, "Foreign Policy as Political Performance," *International Studies Notes* 13, 1987, p. 51.

41. For examples of the traditional arguments, see *The Domestic Sources of Foreign Polity*, edited by James N. Rosenau, New York, 1967; and Peter A. Gourevitch, "The Second Image Reversed: The International Sources of Domestic Politics," *International Organization* 32, 1978, pp. 881–912.

42. Richard K. Ashley, "Living on Border Lines: Man, Poststructuralism, and War," in *International/Intertextual Relations: Postmodern Readings of World Politics*, edited by James Der Derian and Michael J. Shapiro, Lexington, 1989, p. 303.

43. Ibid., p. 304.

44. Ashley makes note of this: see "Living on Border Lines," p. 314n. The historical processes via which the state has had differing consequences for gender — processes associated with the development of political economy and the social contract — are the subject of an extensive literature. See, for example, Joan W. Scott and Louise A. Tilly, *Women, Work and Family*, New York, 1978; Varda Burstyn, "Masculine Dominance and the State," in *The Socialist Register*, edited by Ralph Miliband and John Saville, London, 1983; Maria Mies, *Patriarchy and Accumulation on a World Scale: Women and the International Division of Labor*, London, 1986; and Carole Pateman, *The Sexual Contract*, Stanford, 1988.

45. Quoted in Richard K. Ashley, "Imposing International Purpose: Notes on a Problematic of Governance," in *Global Changes and Theoretical Challenges: Approaches to World Politics for the 1990s*, edited by Ernst-Otto Czempiel and James N. Rosenau, Lexington, 1989, p. 255.

46. See the essays in *The Concept of Socialism*, edited by Bhikhu Parekh, New York, 1975.

47. The vast array of ways in which even the social relations of production central to capitalism can be organized has been discussed in Robert W. Cox, *Production, Power, and World Order: Social Forces in the Making of History*, New York, 1987. An account of the role of aesthetic works in the constitution of bourgeois subjectivity is provided by Peter De Bolla, *The Discourse of the Sublime: Readings in History, Aesthetics and the Subject*, New York, 1989.

48. Richard K. Ashley, "Untying the Sovereign State: A Double Reading of the Anarchy Problematique," *Millennium: Journal of International Studies* 17, 1988, p. 257.

49. David Campbell, *The Social Basis of Australian and New Zealand Security Policy*, Canberra, 1989.

50. Ashley, "Untying the Sovereign State," p. 257.

51. See David Campbell, "Security and Identity in United States Foreign Policy: A Reading of the Carter Administration," Ph.D. diss., Australian National University, 1989.

52. For a discussion of the concept of a problematization, see "Polemics, Politics, and Problematizations: An Interview with Michel Foucault," in *The Foucault Reader*, edited by Paul Rabinow, New York, 1984; and Michel Foucault, *The Use of Pleasure: The History of Sexuality, Volume Two*, translated by Robert Hurley, New York, 1985.

53. Ashley, "Untying the Sovereign State," p. 257.

54. Ashley, "Living on Border Lines," pp. 264–66.

55. Michel Foucault, *The Order of Things: An Archaeology of the Human Sciences*, New York, 1971, p. 312. See the discussion in Paul Rabinow, *French Modern: Norms and Forms of the Social Environment*, Cambridge, Massachusetts, 1989, pp. 7–10, 18–24.

56. See Michel Foucault, "Governmentality," in *The Foucault Effect: Studies in Governmental Rationality*, edited by Graham Burchell, Colin Gordon and Peter Miller, Hemel Hempstead, England, 1991.

57. Rabinow, *French Modern*, pp. 10–11; and Michael J. Shapiro, "Representing World Politics: The Sport/War Intertext," in *International/Intertextual Relations*, edited by Der Derian and Shapiro, p. 75. Interestingly, the very concepts of "normal" and "normalized," although obviously having long histories themselves, became formalized in the period between 1759 and 1834. See Rabinow, *French Modern*, p. 10.

58. For accounts that illustrate the ways in which these hierarchies have sequestered gendered understandings, see Wendy Brown, *Manhood and Politics: A Feminist Reading in*

Political Theory, Totowa, New Jersey, 1988; Elaine Showalter, *The Female Malady: Women, Madness, and English Culture 1830–1980,* New York, 1985; Carolyn Merchant, *The Death of Nature: Women, Ecology and the Scientific Revolution,* New York, 1980; and Genevieve Lloyd, "Selfhood, War and Masculinity," in *Feminist Challenges: Social and Political Theory,* edited by Carole Pateman and Elizabeth Gross, Boston, 1986. For a review of the impact of gender on international relations, see Anne Sisson Runyan and V. Spike Peterson, "The Radical Future of Realism: Feminist Subversions of IR Theory," *Alternatives* 16, 1991, pp. 67–106.

59. Quoted in Brown, *Manhood and Politics,* p. 95n.

60. See Koselleck, *Critique and Crisis,* pp. 31–36.

61. See Forsyth, "Thomas Hobbes and the External Relations of States," p. 207.

62. Kathleen B. Jones, "The Trouble with Authority," *differences: A Journal of Feminist Cultural Studies* 3, 1991, pp. 104–27. See also Carole Pateman, " 'God hath ordained to man a helper': Hobbes, Patriarchy and Conjugal Right," *British Journal of Political Science* 19, 1989, pp. 445–63. Cf., Christine Di Stefano, "Masculinity as Ideology in Political Theory: Hobbesian Man Considered," *Women's Studies International Forum* 6, 1983, pp. 633–44.

63. Carl von Clausewitz, *On War,* edited and translated by Michael Howard and Peter Paret, Princeton, 1984, pp. 179–80.

64. For example, the British Foreign Office can be dated from the 1780s. Beginning with only a few officials, it had a staff of only thirty by 1853, and this was to increase by only an additional ten in the subsequent fifty years. For a historical survey of these institutional developments, see *The Times Survey of Foreign Ministries of the World,* edited by Zara Steiner, London, 1982.

65. For discussions of these see, respectively, Benedict Anderson, *Imagined Communities: Reflections on the Origin and Spread of Nationalism,* revised edition, New York, 1991; Stephen Kern, *The Culture of Time and Space, 1880–1918,* Cambridge, Massachusetts, 1983; and *The Invention of Tradition,* edited by Eric Hobsbawm and Terence Ranger, Cambridge, 1983. This literature suggests that nationhood did not precede statehood, thereby removing a common prop for the argument that the nation-state is the unproblematic rendering of a well-established and prior identity associated with "the people." See Immanuel Wallerstein, "The Construction of Peoplehood: Racism, Nationalism, Ethnicity," *Sociological Forum* 2, 1987, especially pp. 383–85.

66. James Der Derian, *On Diplomacy: A Genealogy of Western Estrangement,* Oxford, 1987.

67. Ibid., p. 76.

68. Ibid., p. 199.

69. For the idea that weather reports are an example of a modern discourse of "danger" that naturalizes social order, see Andrew Ross, "The Work of Nature in the Age of Electronic Emission," *Social Text* 18, 1987–88, pp. 116–28.

70. See Michael J. Shapiro, "The Politics of Fear: Don DeLillo's Postmodern Burrow," *Strategies* 1, 1988, pp. 120–41.

71. Ibid., p. 119.

72. Gloria Anzaldúa, *Borderlands/La Frontera: The New Mestiza,* San Francisco, 1987, p. 3.

73. "A horizon is not a geographical or topological concept, but an historic and cultural metaphor." Gustavo Esteva, "Regenerating People's Space," in *Towards a Just World Peace: Perspectives from Social Movements,* edited by Saul H. Mendlovitz and R. B. J. Walker, London, 1987, p. 278.

74. Anne Norton, *Reflections on Political Identity,* Baltimore, 1988, pp. 45–46. For a good example of how a national self was objectified through a representation of dif-

ference, which in turn was in actuality predicated on the assumption of likeness, see Dominguez's discussions of Israeli representations of the Lebanese during the Israeli invasion of 1982. Virginia Dominguez, *People as Subject, People as Object: Selfhood and Peoplehood in Contemporary Israel*, Madison, 1989, pp. 178–87.

4. Foreign Policy and Difference

1. For a discussion of the axiological dimension to strategies of otherness, see Tzvetan Todorov, *The Conquest of America: The Question of the Other*, New York, 1984, p. 185.

2. Richard K. Ashley, "Living on Border Lines: Man, Poststructuralism, and War," in *International/Intertextual Relations: Postmodern Readings of World Politics*, edited by James Der Derian and Michael J. Shapiro, Lexington, 1989, pp. 264–66.

3. Quoted in David George Hale, *The Body Politic: A Political Metaphor in Renaissance English Literature*, The Hague, 1971, p. 11.

4. See "De Corpore Politico, or the Elements of Law," in *The English Works of Thomas Hobbes*, Vol. 4, edited by William Molesworth, London, 1839.

5. Quoted in Michel Foucault, *Madness and Civilization: A History of Insanity in the Age of Reason*, trans. by Richard Howard, New York, 1973, p. 202.

6. Quoted in Walter Laquer, *The Age of Terrorism*, Boston, 1987, p. 66.

7. For studies in which a similar understanding of the body is central, see George Armstrong Kelly, *Mortal Politics in Eighteenth-Century France*, Waterloo, 1986, especially chapter 2; Dorinda Outram, *The Body and the French Revolution: Sex, Class and Political Structure*, New Haven, 1989; and Debra B. Bergoffen, "The Body Politic: Democratic Metaphors, Totalitarian Practices, Erotic Rebellions," *Philosophy and Social Criticism* 16, 1990, pp. 109–16.

8. Quoted in Jacques Le Goff, "Head or Heart? The Political Use of Body Metaphors in the Middle Ages," in *Fragments for a History of the Human Body*, edited by Michel Feher, with Ramona Naddaff, and Nadia Tazi, New York, 1989, p. 17.

9. Hale, *The Body Politic*, p. 35. For an example, see Edward Forset, *The Bodies Natural and Politique* (London 1606), Amsterdam, 1973.

10. Hale, *The Body Politic*, pp. 28–29; Le Goff, "Head or Heart?" p. 14.

11. Ernst H. Kantorowicz, *The King's Two Bodies: A Study in Medieval Political Theology*, Princeton, 1957, p. 196.

12. Ibid., p. 197.

13. Ibid., pp. 193–94.

14. Ibid., pp. 15–16, 18–19.

15. Ibid., pp. 201–2.

16. Quoted in ibid., p. 206.

17. Ibid., pp. 203–9.

18. Ibid., p. 210.

19. Quoted in ibid., p. 213.

20. Quoted in ibid., p. 216.

21. Ibid., p. 223.

22. See Wendy Brown, *Manhood and Politics: A Feminist Reading in Political Theory*, Totowa, New Jersey, pp. 109–10.

23. Catherine Gallagher, "The Body Versus the Social Body in the Works of Thomas Malthus and Henry Mayhew," *Representations* 14, 1986, pp. 83–106.

24. Donna Haraway, "The Biopolitics of Postmodern Bodies: Determinations of Self in Immune System Discourse," *differences: A Journal of Feminist Cultural Criticism* 1, 1989, p. 14.

25. Ibid., p. 24.

26. Ibid., pp. 30, 15.

27. See ibid., pp. 30–32. For an extensive analysis of representation in nuclear strategic discourse, see Carol Cohn, "Sex and Death in the Rational World of Defense Intellectuals," *Signs: A Journal of Women in Culture and Society* 12, 1987, pp. 687–718.

28. Bryan S. Turner, *The Body and Society: Explorations in Social Theory*, Oxford, 1984, p. 114.

29. Mary Douglas, *Purity and Danger: An Analysis of the Concepts of Pollution and Taboo*, London, 1984, p. 122.

30. Ibid., p. 160.

31. See Jean Delumeau, *Sin and Fear: The Emergence of a Western Guilt Culture Thirteen–Eighteenth Centuries*, translated by Eric Nicholson, New York, 1990, conclusion.

32. Quoted in Georges Canguilhem, *On the Normal and the Pathological*, translated by Carolyn R. Fawcett, Dordrecht, Holland, 1978, p. 107.

33. Quoted in ibid., p. 67.

34. Douglas, *Purity and Danger*, p. 2.

35. Michel Foucault, *The Birth of the Clinic: An Archeology of Medical Perception*, translated by A. M. Sheridan Smith, New York, 1975, pp. 31–35.

36. Ibid., p. 35.

37. See Canguilhem, *On the Normal and the Pathological*, part 2.

38. Ibid., part 3, chapter 2.

39. Ibid., p. 105.

40. Ibid., p. 137.

41. See *Degeneration: The Dark Side of Progress*, edited by J. Edward Chamberlin and Sander L. Gilman, New York, 1985; and Sander L. Gilman, *Disease and Representation: Images of Illness from Madness to AIDS*, Ithaca, 1988.

42. See Delumeau, *Sin and Fear*.

43. *Degeneration*, ed. Chamberlin and Gilman, p. xiv.

44. Robert A. Nye, *Crime, Madness, and Politics in Modern France: The Medical Concept of National Decline*, Princeton, 1984.

45. David Kunzle, "The Art of Pulling Teeth in the Seventeenth and Nineteenth Centuries: From Public Martyrdom to Private Nightmare and Political Struggle?" in *Fragments for a History of the Human Body*, ed. Feher et al., p. 60.

46. Nye, *Crime, Madness, and Politics in Modern France*, chapter 6. Somewhat surprisingly, Nye does not comment on the orientalist nature of this designation.

47. Ibid., p. 204.

48. Quoted in ibid., p. 331.

49. Ibid., p. 337.

50. See Judith Walkowitz, *Prostitution and Victorian Society: Women, Class and the State*, Cambridge, 1980.

51. This is how Foucault understood the emergence of "prison fevers" in the middle of the eighteenth century. See Foucault, *Madness and Civilization*, p. 202.

52. This impetus is different from Susan Sontag's desire to expunge all metaphoric thinking from representations of disease, although it finds much of value in her reading of the effects of metaphoric medical discourse. See Susan Sontag, *Illness as Metaphor and AIDS and Its Metaphors*, New York, 1990.

53. See Glenn Hook, "The Nuclearization of Language: Nuclear Allergy as Political Metaphor," *The Journal of Peace Research* 21, 1984, pp. 259–75.

54. Haraway, "The Biopolitics of Postmodern Bodies"; and Emily Martin, "The End of the Body," Distinguished Lecture presented to the American Ethnological Society Annual Meeting, Atlanta, 1990.

55. Sontag, *Illness as Metaphor*, pp. 61, 64–65.

56. Ibid., pp. 82, 83.

57. As Haraway notes, "Science remains an important genre of western exploration and travel literature." Haraway, "The Biopolitics of Postmodern Bodies," p. 5.

58. "U.S. May Still Strike Back, Reagan Hints," *Washington Post*, June 29, 1985, p. A19.

59. Sontag, *Illness as Metaphor*, p. 126.

60. Foucault, *Madness and Civilization*, pp. 6, 7.

61. Ibid., p. 3.

62. Sontag, *Illness as Metaphor*, pp. 135–36.

63. Gilman, *Disease and Representation*, p. 2.

64. Sander L. Gilman, *Difference and Pathology: Stereotypes on Sexuality, Race, and Madness*, Ithaca, 1985.

65. Recognizing the statistical absurdity of the incidence of pathologies among these groups does not depend on the knowledge of hindsight. When the U.S. census results were released in 1841, they purported to show that the total of "insane and feeble-minded" persons in the country totaled 17,000, of whom 3,000 were black. For this to have been plausible, it would had to have been the case that free blacks had an incidence of mental illness eleven times higher than slaves, and six times higher than whites. The excessive claims of these statistics were demonstrated at the time by people who showed that in Worcester, Massachusetts, where the total black population was 151, all but 18 of these people were insane paupers. One does not have to be a conspiracy theorist to see that these statistics provided "scientific" evidence for anti-abolitionist forces. The features of blackness, madness, and a class position came together to support the continuation of slavery as a means of securing the integrity of American society. Ibid., pp. 137–38.

66. Hayden White, *Tropics of Discourse: Essays in Cultural Criticism*, Baltimore, 1978, p. 91.

67. See Gilman, *Disease and Representation*, chapter 15; Paula Treichler, "AIDS, Homophobia, and Biomedical Discourse: An Epidemic of Signification," *Cultural Studies* 1, 1987, pp. 263–305; and Treichler, "AIDS, Africa, and Cultural Theory," *Transition* 51, 1991, pp. 86–103.

68. "Health Dept. Loses in AIDS Rule Dispute," *New York Times*, May 28, 1991, p. A18. The statement was made by Dr. Jonathan Mann, head of the World Health Organization's global program on AIDS between 1986 and 1990.

69. Borrowing from E. P. Thompson's polemic against Althusserian structuralism, Richard Ashley used the idea of an "orrery" — that is, a planetarium, or model of the solar system — to describe the "self-enclosed, self-affirming joining" of various commitments with neorealist discourse. See Richard K. Ashley, "The Poverty of Neorealism," *International Organization* 38, 1984, pp. 226, 228. My use of the term is designed to illustrate the way in which the meaning of something only becomes clear through its location in a chain of difference with something else, a process that involves understanding by association rather than understanding by observation and naturalistic description.

70. These terms are from Foucault, *Madness and Civilization*, pp. 58, 205.

71. "U.S. May Still Strike Back, Reagan Hints."

72. Quoted in Jon Stratton, *Writing Sites: A Genealogy of the Postmodern World*, Hemel Hempstead, England, 1990, p. 82.

73. For discussions of some of these tropes, see Stephen J. Rosow, "The Forms of Internationalization: Representation of Western Culture on a Global Scale," *Alternatives* 15, 1990, pp. 287–301; Hayden White, "The Forms of Wildness: Archeology of an Idea," in *Tropics of Discourse; Anatomy of Racism*, edited by David Theo Goldberg, Min-

neapolis, 1990; Marianna Torgovnick, *Gone Primitive: Savage Intellects, Modern Lives*, Chicago, 1990.

74. Etienne Balibar, "Paradoxes of Universality," in *Anatomy of Racism*, ed. Goldberg, p. 285.

5. Imagining America

1. Michael Walzer, "What Does It Mean to Be an 'American'?" *Social Research* 57, 1990, pp. 591–614. Quote is from p. 602.

2. Michael Kammen, *People of Paradox: An Inquiry Concerning the Origins of American Civilization*, New York, 1980, p. 4.

3. Peter Mason, *Deconstructing America: Representations of the Other*, London, 1990, p. 7; and Jean Delumeau, *Sin and Fear: The Emergence of a Western Guilt Culture Thirteenth–Eighteenth Centuries*, translated by Eric Nicholson, New York, 1990, p. 126.

4. Tzvetan Todorov, *The Conquest of America: The Question of the Other*, translated by Richard Howard, New York, 1984.

5. Ibid., p. 5.

6. Ibid., p. 17. This epistemology was equally to be found in the works of those who differed from Columbus. See Anthony Pagden, "*Ius et factum*: Text and Experience in the Writings of Bartolomé de Las Casas," *Representations* 33, 1991, pp. 147–62.

7. Edmundo O'Gorman, *The Invention of America*, Bloomington, 1961.

8. Ibid., p. 78.

9. This discussion is drawn from O'Gorman, *The Invention of America*, part 2.

10. Quoted in Todorov, *The Conquest of America*, p. 14.

11. O'Gorman, *The Invention of America*, pp. 60–61.

12. Quoted in Todorov, *The Conquest of America*, p. 21.

13. Ibid., p. 30.

14. O'Gorman, *The Invention of America*, pp. 89–90; and Todorov, *The Conquest of America*, p. 22.

15. This discussion is drawn from O'Gorman, *The Invention of America*, pp. 94–124.

16. Mason, *Deconstructing America*, p. 18.

17. See the facsimile reproduction in *The Cosmographiae Introductio of Martin Waldseemüller*, edited by Charles George Herbermann, New York, 1907. The 1507 map was the only one of Waldseemüller's to bear the inscription *America*: he withdrew it from later versions after he became convinced that Vespucci was not the discoverer of the New World. Moreover, it was not until Gerhard Mercator's world map of 1538 that the continent was divided into North and South America. Ibid., pp. 29–30.

18. Louis Montrose, "The Work of Gender in the Discourse of Discovery," *Representations* 33, 1991, pp. 1–41. As with the many feminine names given to newly encountered lands—such as Florida, Guiana, and Virginia (the last so-called because of the belief that Queen Elizabeth was a virgin)—they "might be seen to invite the thrust of European masculinity." Mason, *Deconstructing America*, p. 26. Indeed, the discourses of sexuality, exploration, and colonization came to be intertwined, and "America" came to function as a sexual trope. John Donne, in his "Elegie: To His Mistris Going to Bed," writes: "License my roaving hands, and let them go, / Behind, before, above, between, below. / O my America! my new-found-land." Quoted in Jon Stratton, *Writing Sites: A Genealogy of the Postmodern World*, Hemel Hempstead, England, 1990, p. 150. For a discussion of how the rendering of newly discovered lands as feminine continued into the nineteenth century, see Mary Louise Pratt, "Scratches on the Face of

the Country; or, What Mr. Barrow Saw in the Land of the Bushmen," in *"Race," Writing and Difference*, edited by Henry Louis Gates Jr., Chicago, 1986.

19. O'Gorman, *The Invention of America*, p. 129.

20. Ibid., p. 130.

21. See William E. Connolly, "Identity and Difference in Global Politics," in *International/Intertextual Relations: Postmodern Readings in World Politics*, edited by James Der Derian and Michael J. Shapiro, Lexington, 1989, p. 325; and Paul Gordon Lauren, *Power and Prejudice: The Politics and Diplomacy of Racial Discrimination*, Boulder, 1988, p. 10.

22. Mason, *Deconstructing America*, p. 34.

23. Quoted in Todorov, *The Conquest of America*, p. 34.

24. Cabeza de Vaca, *Adventures in the Unknown Interior of America*, translated by Cyclone Covey, Albuquerque, 1983, p. 25.

25. Ibid., p. 42.

26. Todorov, *The Conquest of America*, p. 36.

27. Bartolomé de Las Casas, *In Defense of the Indians*, translated, edited, and annotated by Stafford Poole, De Kalb, Illinois, 1974, p. 21.

28. Quoted in Todorov, *The Conquest of America*, p. 42.

29. See Lee Eldridge Huddleston, *Origins of the American Indians: European Concepts, 1492–1792*, Austin, 1967, pp. 14–15.

30. "The Requirement, 1512," in *History of Latin American Civilization: Sources and Interpretations*, Volume 1, *The Colonial Experience*, edited by Lewis Hanke, Boston, 1967, pp. 123–24.

31. Ibid., p. 125.

32. Cabeza de Vaca, *Adventures*, p. 57.

33. Quoted in Todorov, *The Conquest of America*, pp. 49–50.

34. Cabeza de Vaca, *Adventures*, p. 55.

35. Todorov, *The Conquest of America*, pp. 46–47.

36. Cabeza de Vaca, *Adventures*, p. 123.

37. Todorov, *The Conquest of America*, p. 175.

38. See "The New Laws, 1542," in *History of Latin American Civilization*, ed. Hanke, pp. 144–49.

39. Quoted in ibid., p. 156.

40. Quoted in ibid., pp. 150–51.

41. Huddleston, *Origins of the American Indians*, pp. 24–25.

42. This background is drawn from Las Casas, *In Defense of the Indians*, pp. 1–9.

43. Quoted in ibid., pp. 163–64.

44. See Huddleston, *Origins of the American Indians*, pp. 10–11.

45. Michael T. Ryan, "Assimilating New Worlds in the Sixteenth and Seventeenth Centuries," *Comparative Studies in Society and History* 23, 1981, pp. 519–38. For an account of how the confrontation with black Africa occurred in the terms described below, and equally failed to unsettle Eurocentric frames of reference, see Katherine George, "The Civilized West Looks at Primitive Africa 1400–1800: A Study in Ethnocentrism," *Isis* 49, 1958 pp. 62–72. For a discussion of how these traditional interpretive frames were applied to all non-Westerners and then fixed and disseminated in European culture through popular travelogues, see Richard G. Cole, "Sixteenth-Century Travel Books as a Source of European Attitudes toward Non-White and Non-Western Culture," *Proceedings of the American Philosophical Society* 116, 1972, pp. 59–67.

46. Mason, *Deconstructing America*, chapter 2. For example, a group of aristocrats who engaged in nocturnal crimes on the early eighteenth-century streets of Lon-

don were referred to as "Mohocks" ("Mohawks"). A similar derivation was that of the "apaches" of nineteenth-century France, as noted in chapter 4.

47. Ryan, "Assimilating New Worlds," p. 525.

48. W. R. Jones, "The Image of the Barbarian in Medieval Europe," *Comparative Studies in Society and History* 13, 1971, p. 378.

49. Nancy Stepan, *The Idea of Race in Science: Great Britain, 1800–1960,* Hamden, Connecticut, 1982, p. xi.

50. See Todorov, *The Conquest of America,* p. 161. Todorov contrasts the master/slave dichotomy of Aristotle with the Christian/non-Christian dualism of Las Casas.

51. For a discussion of these different orientations toward otherness in terms of Columbus's attitude toward the Indians, from which this understanding is derived, see ibid., p. 42.

52. For Derrida's reflections on the inherent ethnocentrism of writing and presence, see Jacques Derrida, *Of Grammatology,* translated by G. Spivak, Baltimore, 1976, especially pp. 101–40.

53. Ibid., p. 43.

54. Ibid., p. 171.

55. "Royal Ordinances on 'Pacification,' 1573," in *History of Latin American Civilization,* ed. Hanke, p. 151.

56. Ibid., p. 150.

57. Ibid., p. 190.

58. Romila Thapar, "The Image of the Barbarian in Early India," *Comparative Studies in Society and History,* 13, 1971, pp. 408–36.

59. Stanley Diamond, "Introduction: The Uses of the Primitive," in *Primitive Views of the World,* edited by Stanley Diamond, New York, 1964.

60. Mason, *Deconstructing America,* chapter 7.

61. Diamond, "Introduction: The Uses of the Primitive," p. vi.

62. See Nicholas P. Canny, *The Elizabethan Conquest of Ireland: A Pattern Established,* New York, 1976.

63. Mason, *Deconstructing America,* pp. 62–63.

64. Quoted in Nicholas P. Canny, "The Ideology of English Colonization: From Ireland to America," *William and Mary Quarterly* 30, 1973, p. 581.

65. Ibid., p. 582.

66. Ibid., pp. 583–86.

67. Quoted in ibid., p. 585.

68. Quoted in ibid., p. 584.

69. Quoted in ibid., p. 588.

70. Quoted in David George Hale, *The Body Politic: A Political Metaphor in Renaissance English Literature,* The Hague, 1971, p. 11.

71. Quoted in Sacvan Bercovitch, *The American Jeremiad,* Madison, 1978, p. 39.

72. Ibid., pp. 41–42.

73. See Sacvan Bercovitch, *The Puritan Origins of the American Self,* New Haven, 1975, especially chapter 5.

74. Michael Zuckerman, "The Fabrication of Identity in Early America," *William and Mary Quarterly* 34, 1977, p. 204.

75. For accounts of this case and its importance for emerging American identity, see Richard Drinnon, *Facing West: The Metaphysics of Indian Hating and Empire Building,* New York, 1990, chapters 1 to 3; Richard Slotkin, *Regeneration through Violence: The Mythology of the American Frontier, 1600–1860,* Middletown, Connecticut, 1973, pp. 58–69; and Michael Zuckerman, "Pilgrims in the Wilderness: Community, Modernity, and the Maypole at Merry Mount," *New England Quarterly* 50, 1977, pp. 255–77.

76. Quoted in Drinnon, *Facing West*, p. 19.

77. See Ben Barker-Benfield, "Anne Hutchinson and the Puritan Attitude toward Women," *Feminist Studies* 1, 1972, pp. 65–96; and *The Antinomian Controversy, 1636–1638: A Documentary History*, edited by David D. Hall, Middletown, Connecticut, 1968.

78. Quoted in Kammen, *People of Paradox*, p. 34.

79. "Description of Virginia and Proceedings of the Colonie," in *Narratives of Early Virginia, 1606–1625*, edited by Lyon G. Tyler, New York, 1907, pp. 108–9.

80. James Axtell, *The Europeans and the Indians: Essays in the Ethnohistory of Colonial North America*, New York, 1981, pp. 43–46.

81. See James Axtell, *The Invasion Within: The Contest of Cultures in Colonial North America*, New York, 1985.

82. See Gary B. Nash, "Red, White, and Black: The Origins of Racism in Colonial America," in *The Great Fear: Race in the Mind of America*, edited by Gary B. Nash and Richard Weiss, New York, 1970.

83. "A Relation of Maryland," in *Narratives of Early Maryland, 1633–1684*, edited by Clayton Colman Hall, New York, 1910, pp. 85–86.

84. This discussion is drawn from Drinnon, *Facing West*, chapter 4.

85. Michael Zuckerman, "Identity in British America: Unease in Eden," in *Colonial Identity in the Atlantic World, 1500–1800*, edited by Nicholas Canny and Anthony Pagden, Princeton, 1987, p. 145; D. W. Meinig, *The Shaping of America: A Geographical Perspective on 560 Years of History*, Volume 1, *Atlantic America, 1492–1800*, New Haven, 1986, pp. 144–45.

86. Meinig, *The Shaping of America*, p. 72.

87. Quoted in Zuckerman, "Identity in British America," p. 146.

88. Winthrop Jordan, "American Chiaroscuro: The Status and Definition of Mulattoes in the British Colonies," *William and Mary Quarterly* 19, 1962, p. 200.

89. Kammen, *People of Paradox*, p. 202.

90. Meinig, *The Shaping of America*, p. 213; Axtell, *Europeans and Indians*, pp. 290–92.

91. Howard Zinn, *A People's History of the United States*, New York, 1980, pp. 24, 43.

92. Zuckerman, "Identity in British America," p. 135.

93. Ibid., p. 135. This tendency was manifested in other colonies established by Europeans. For example, around the Cape colony in seventeenth-century South Africa, Europeans (Dutch settlers) constructed a hedge of bitter almonds to keep the indigenous people at bay. See Alistair Sparks, *The Mind of South Africa*, New York, 1990, p. xv.

94. Ibid., p. 116.

95. See Gary B. Nash, *Race, Class and Politics: Essays on American Colonial and Revolutionary Society*, Urbana, 1986, chapter 2. For accounts of the Indian wars, see *Narratives of the Indian Wars, 1675–1699*, edited by Charles H. Lincoln, New York, 1913.

96. Slotkin, *Regeneration through Violence*, p. 117; Paul Boyer and Stephen Nissenbaum, *Salem Possessed: The Social Origins of Witchcraft*, Cambridge, Massachusetts, 1974, p. 6.

97. Brian Levack, *The Witch-Hunt in Early Modern Europe*, London, 1987, pp. 12–13.

98. Nachman Ben-Yehuda, *Deviance and Moral Boundaries: Witchcraft, the Occult, Science Fiction, Deviant Sciences and Scientists*, Chicago, 1985, p. 38.

99. John Demos, *Entertaining Satan: Witchcraft and the Culture of Early New England*, New York, 1982, p. 13.

100. See Boyer and Nissenbaum, *Salem Possessed*, pp. 11–12, chapter 8.

101. Slotkin, *Regeneration through Violence*, pp. 128–45.

102. Cotton Mather wrote of the Quakers: "If the Indians have chosen to prey upon the frontiers, and outskirts, of the province, the Quakers have chosen the very

same frontiers, and outskirts, for their more spiritual assaults; and finding little success elsewhere, they have been laboring incessantly... to enchant and poison the souls of poor people, in the very places, where the bodies and estates of the people have presently after been devoured by the savages." Quoted in ibid., p. 130.

103. Quoted in Winthrop D. Jordan, *White over Black: American Attitudes Toward the Negro, 1550–1812*, New York, 1977, p. 34.

104. Meinig, *The Shaping of America*, p. 228.

105. Jordan, *White over Black*, pp. 108–9.

106. Ibid., p. 95.

107. Quoted in Lauren, *Power and Prejudice*, p. 22.

108. For a discussion of Jefferson's views, see Jordan, *White over Black*, chapter 12.

109. Stepan, *The Idea of Race in Science*, pp. 1–2. "Race" appeared as a trope long before the nineteenth century, however. It is first evident in thirteenth-century Spanish, Portuguese, and French texts, but does not become more common until the sixteenth century. In French, it primarily referred to belonging to or descending from a family of "noble stock," and thus implied quality. In Spanish, it referred to "defect" or "guilt," and was applied to Jews or Moors who could overcome their race (as defect) by conversion and baptism. Verena Stolcke, "Conquered Women," *NACLA Report on the Americas* 24, 1991, pp. 24–25.

110. Jordan, *White over Black*, pp. 234–39.

111. Meinig, *The Shaping of America*, p. 228.

112. Jordan, *White over Black*, pp. 102–3.

113. Ibid., pp. 116–18.

114. Quoted in Drinnon, *Facing West*, p. 33.

115. Quoted in ibid., p. 55.

116. Quoted in Jordan, *White over Black*, p. 254.

117. Quoted in Meinig, *The Shaping of America*, pp. 288–89.

118. Quoted in Kammen, *People of Paradox*, pp. 63–64.

119. Quoted in Jordan, *White over Black*, p. 94.

120. Meinig, *The Shaping of America*, p. 181.

121. See Leonard W. Levy, *Legacy of Repression: Freedom of Speech and the Press in Early American History*, Cambridge, Massachusetts, 1960.

122. A general discussion of the social transformations in this period is provided by Kenneth A. Lockridge, "Social Change and the Meaning of the American Revolution," *Journal of Social History* 6, 1973, pp. 403–39. For a discussion of the economic disparities, see Nash, *Race, Class and Politics*, chapter 7. For an analysis of the contradictory tendencies of colonial life, see Kammen, *People of Paradox*, chapter 6. For texts of the Great Awakening, see *The Great Awakening: Documents on the Revival of Religion, 1740–1745*, edited by Richard L. Bushmen, New York, 1970.

123. Jack P. Greene, "Search for Identity: An Interpretation of the Meaning of Selected Patterns of Social Response in Eighteenth-century America," *Journal of Social History* 3, 1970, pp. 189–220.

124. Albert J. Harkness, "Americanism and Jenkins' Ear," *Mississippi Valley Historical Review* 37, 1950, p. 89.

125. For the growth in use of the term in the 1760s, see Richard L. Merritt, *Symbols of American Community, 1735–1775*, New Haven, 1966.

126. Meinig, *The Shaping of America*, p. 306.

127. For an analysis of this period, see Gordon Wood, *The Creation of the American Republic, 1776–1789*, Chapel Hill, 1969.

128. For the impact of texts such as the Constitution upon American identity, see Michael Warner, "Textuality and Legitimacy in the Printed Constitution," *Proceedings*

of the American Antiquarian Society 97, 1987, pp. 59–84; *Beyond Confederation: Origins of the Constitution and American National Identity*, edited by Richard Beeman, Stephen Botein, and Edward C. Carter II, Chapel Hill, 1987; and Sheldon S. Wolin, *The Presence of the Past: Essays in the State and the Constitution*, Baltimore, 1989.

129. Carl N. Degler, *Out of Our Past: The Forces That Shaped Modern America*, 3rd ed., New York, 1984, p. 79. Like the French Revolution, the American Revolution was not a "thing" until it had subsequently entered the collective imagination through print. See Benedict Anderson, *Imagined Communities: Reflections on the Origin and Spread of Nationalism*, revised edition, New York, 1991, p. 80; and Michael Warner, *The Letters of the Republic: Publication and the Public Sphere in Eighteenth-Century America*, Cambridge, Massachusetts, 1990.

130. Degler, *Out of Our Past*, pp. 108–11.

131. See Zinn, *People's History of the United States*, p. 68.

132. Geoffrey Hawthorn, *Enlightenment and Despair: A History of Social Theory*, 2nd ed., Cambridge, 1987, p. 192.

133. On classical republicanism, see J. G. A. Pocock, *The Machiavellian Moment: Florentine Political Thought and the Atlantic Republican Tradition*, Princeton, 1975; Bruce James Smith, *Politics and Remembrance: Republican Themes in Machiavelli, Burke, and Tocqueville*, Princeton, 1985; and *The Rising Glory of America 1760–1820*, revised edition, edited by Gordon S. Wood, Boston, 1990.

134. Michael Lienesch, *New Order of the Ages: Time, the Constitution, and the Making of Modern American Political Thought*, Princeton, 1988, p. 43.

135. Hawthorn, *Enlightenment and Despair*, p. 194.

136. John W. Blassingame, "American Nationalism and Other Loyalties in the Southern Colonies, 1763–1775," *Journal of Southern History* 34, 1968, p. 54. See also Cushing Strout, *The American Image of the Old World*, New York, 1963.

137. Zuckerman, "Identity in British America," p. 154.

138. Axtell, *The European and the Indian*, p. 315; and Slotkin, *Regeneration through Violence*, chapter 7.

139. Zinn, *People's History of the United States*, p. 72.

140. Donald H. Stewart, *The Opposition Press of the Federalist Period*, Albany, 1969, pp. 143–44.

141. Quoted in Drinnon, *Facing West*, p. 97.

142. Ibid., p. 99.

143. For an analysis, see Harold H. Hyman, *To Try Men's Souls: Loyalty Tests in American History*, Berkeley, 1959.

144. Levy, *Jefferson and Civil Liberties*, p. 30.

145. Ibid., p. 31.

146. Meinig, *The Shaping of America*, p. 369.

147. Zinn, *People's History of the United States*, p. 92.

148. For discussions of the rise of the American party system, see Noble E. Cunningham, Jr., *The Jeffersonian Republicans: The Formation of Party Organization, 1789–1801*, Chapel Hill, 1957; and Roy F. Nichols, *The Invention of the American Political Parties*, New York, 1967.

149. See Richard Hofstader, *The Idea of a Party System: The Rise of Legitimate Opposition in the United States, 1780–1840*, Berkeley, 1969.

150. John Adams, second president of the United States, declared as much when he wrote: "Republics are always divided in opinion, concerning forms of government, and plans and details of administration. There divisions are generally harmless, often salutary, and seldom very hurtful, except when foreign nations interfere, and by their arts and agents excite and ferment them into parties and factions. Such interference

must be resisted and exterminated, or it will end in America...in our total destruction as a republican government and independence power." *The Works of John Adams,* Volume 9, Boston, 1854, pp. 186–87. Federalist representative Robert Goodloe Harper concurred when he told the Fifth Congress of 1796: "Popular governments, unless quite contemptible...cannot be subverted without the aid of internal division. This division is only effected by means of foreign influence, which supports, and is supported by, domestic faction; therefore, everything that tends, however remotely, to facilitate the alliance between these two deadly foes, is most carefully to be guarded against." Quoted in Richard Buel, *Securing the Revolution: Ideology in American Politics, 1789–1815,* Ithaca, 1972, pp. 194–95.

151. Hofstader, *The Idea of Party,* p. 90.

152. Quoted in Hofstader, *The Idea of Party,* p. 95.

153. For details of the diplomacy of the period, see James A. Hutson, *John Adams and the Diplomacy of the American Revolution,* Lexington, 1980; Jonathan R. Dull, *A Diplomatic History of the American Revolution,* New Haven, 1985; and Robert W. Tucker and David C. Hendrickson, *Empire of Liberty: The Statecraft of Thomas Jefferson,* New York, 1990.

154. Quoted in Tucker and Hendrickson, *Empire of Liberty,* p. 67.

155. Isser Woloch, *Jacobin Legacy: The Democratic Movement under the Directory,* Princeton, 1970, chapter 1.

156. See Eugene Perry Link, *Democratic-Republican Societies, 1790–1800,* New York, 1973.

157. Ibid., p. 190.

158. Ibid., p. 175.

159. *The Works of John Adams,* Vol. 9, p. 192.

160. Orville J. Victor, *History of American Conspiracies,* [1863], *Mass Violence in America,* Volume 1, edited by Robert M. Fogelson and Richard E. Rubinstein, New York, 1969, p. 235.

161. Buel, *Securing the Revolution,* pp. 128–29; and Thomas P. Slaughter, *The Whiskey Rebellion: Frontier Epilogue to the American Revolution,* New York, 1986.

162. Quoted in James Morton Smith, *Freedom's Fetters: The Alien and Sedition Laws and American Civil Liberties,* Ithaca, 1956, p. 24.

163. For details of the mission to France, see William Stinchcombe, *The XYZ Affair,* Westport, Connecticut, 1980.

164. Quoted in Alexander De Conde, *The Quasi-War,* New York, 1966. For another general analysis of the period, see Marshall Smelser, "The Jacobin Phrenzy: The Menace of Monarchy, Plutocracy, and Anglophilia, 1789–1798," *Review of Politics* 21, 1959, pp. 239–58.

165. De Conde, *The Quasi-War,* p. 84.

166. Quoted in Smith, *Freedom's Fetters,* pp. 178–79.

167. Quoted in De Conde, *The Quasi-War,* p. 88. For a description of the Illuminati, a sect of liberal enlightenment thinkers who emerged in the eighteenth-century struggles of the Bavarian counter-enlightenment and then merged with Freemasonry, see Vernon Stauffer, *New England and the Bavarian Illuminati,* New York, 1918.

168. Quoted in Smith, *Freedom's Fetters,* p. 184.

169. De Conde, *The Quasi-War,* p. 78.

170. For the case of Franklin's grandson, see Smith, *Freedom's Fetters,* chapter 10.

171. Ibid., p. 56.

172. See Smith, *Freedom's Fetters.*

173. Hofstader, *The Idea of a Party System,* p. 108.

174. Quoted in Stauffer, *New England and the Bavarian Illuminati*, p. 227.

175. Smith, *Freedom's Fetters*, p. 56.

176. Quoted in Victor, *History of American Conspiracies*, p. 235.

177. *The Works of John Adams*, Vol. 9, p. 193.

178. Pocock, *The Machiavellian Moment*; B. Honig, "Declarations of Independence: Arendt and Derrida on the Problem of Founding a Republic," *American Political Science Review* 85, 1991, pp. 97–113; and Anne Norton, *Reflections on Political Identity*, Baltimore, 1988, chapter 3.

179. Honig, "Declarations of Independence," p. 105. See also Norton, *Reflections on Political Identity*, chapter 5.

180. A number of writers have remarked on this. For example: "In Europe stages of development succeeded each other in time; in America they were juxtaposed in space." Michael Paul Rogin, *Fathers and Children: Andrew Jackson and the Subjugation of the American Indian*, New York, 1975, p. 13. And: "The movement of American history has been spatial rather than dialectic." Pocock, *The Machiavellian Moment*, p. 543.

181. Bercovitch, *American Jeremiad*, pp. 154–55.

182. Jean Baudrillard, *America*, New York, 1989, p. 118. Baudrillard's often pilloried observations echo many of Alexis de Tocqueville's interpretations, particularly in the way that each uses barren landscapes (deserts and wilderness) as representations of the ignorance of nature, culture, and history they observe in America. See Marco Diani, "The Desert of Democracy, from Tocqueville to Baudrillard," paper presented to the Department of Sociology, University of Lancaster, February 1991.

183. Leonard Levy, *Jefferson and Civil Liberties: The Dark Side*, Cambridge, Massachusetts, 1963, p. x.

184. Drinnon, *Facing West*, p. 99.

6. Writing Security

1. For the claim that it is, see Sacvan Bercovitch, *The American Jeremiad*, Madison, 1978, p. 176: "Only in the United States has nationalism carried with it the Christian meaning of the sacred. Only America, of all national designations, has assumed the combined force of eschatology and chauvinism ... Of all symbols of identity, only America has united nationality and universality, civic and spiritual selfhood, secular and redemptive history, the country's past and paradise to be, in a single synthetic ideal."

2. J. G. A. Pocock, *The Machiavellian Moment: Florentine Political Thought and the Atlantic Republican Tradition*, Princeton, 1975, pp. 512, 513. As Pocock argued, one can speak of an "apocalyptic Machiavellianism." Indeed, "the republic—a concept derived from Renaissance humanism—was the true heir of the covenant and the dread of corruption the true heir of the jeremiad." Ibid., p. 545.

3. For accounts of these struggles, see Michael Paul Rogin, *Fathers and Children: Andrew Jackson and the Subjugation of the American Indian*, New York, 1975; Robert M. Utley, *The Indian Frontier of the American West 1846–90*, Albuquerque, 1984; Donald R. Hickey, *The War of 1812: A Forgotten Conflict*, Urbana, 1989; Reginald C. Stuart, *United States Expansionism in British North America, 1775–1871*, Chapel Hill, 1988; and David M. Pletcher, *The Diplomacy of Annexation: Texas, Oregon, and the Mexican War*, Columbia, Missouri, 1973.

4. The documents in *Manifest Destiny*, edited by Norman A. Graebner, Indianapolis, 1968, unequivocally demonstrate how the practices of foreign policy identified in earlier periods performed at this juncture. For discussions of this theme, see A.

K. Weinberg, *Manifest Destiny: A Study of Nationalist Expansionism in American History*, Baltimore, 1935; Frederick Merk, *Manifest Destiny and Mission in American History*, New York, 1963; and Ernest Lee Tuveson, *Redeemer Nation: The Idea of America's Millennial Role*, Chicago, 1968.

5. Thomas R. Hietala, *Manifest Design: Anxious Aggrandizement in Late Jacksonian America*, Ithaca, 1985, p. 264.

6. For accounts of these events, see David Healy, *U.S. Expansionism: The Imperialist Urge in the 1890s*, Madison, 1970; Philip S. Foner, *The Spanish-Cuban-American War and the Birth of American Imperialism, 1895–1902*, New York, 1972; David F. Trask, *The War with Spain in 1898*, New York, 1981; and Michael Hunt, *Ideology and U.S. Foreign Policy*, New Haven, 1987.

7. See Richard Drinnon, *Facing West: The Metaphysics of Indian Hating and Empire Building*, New York, 1990, p. 269.

8. Quoted in V. G. Kiernan, *America, The New Imperialism: From White Settlement to World Hegemony*, London, 1980, p. 115.

9. On the place of these assumptions in foreign aid policies, see Robert Packenham, *Liberal America and the Third World: Political Development Ideas in Foreign Aid and Social Science*, Princeton, 1973. For exhortations about America's democratic purpose, see Gregory Fossedal, *The Democratic Imperative: Exporting the American Revolution*, New York, 1989; and Joshua Muravchik, *Exporting Democracy*, Washington, D.C., 1991.

10. See Alan Trachtenberg, *The Incorporation of America: Culture and Society in the Gilded Age*, New York, 1982.

11. See Nell Irvin Painter, *Standing at Armageddon: The United States, 1877–1919*, New York, 1987; and John Higham, *Strangers in the Land: Patterns of American Nativism, 1860–1925*, 2nd ed., New Brunswick, New Jersey, 1988.

12. Drinnon, *Facing West*, p. 261.

13. Quoted in Walter LaFeber, *The American Age: United States Foreign Policy at Home and Abroad Since 1750*, New York, 1989, p. 152.

14. Quoted in Drinnon, *Facing West*, p. 262.

15. LaFeber, *The American Age*, p. 206.

16. Drinnon, *Facing West*, pp. 266–67.

17. Ernesto Laclau and Chantal Mouffe, *Hegemony and Socialist Strategy: Towards a Radical Democratic Politics*, translated by Winston Moore and Paul Cammack, London, 1985, p. 108.

18. Anders Stephanson, *Kennan and the Art of Foreign Policy*, Cambridge, Massachusetts, 1989, p. 206.

19. Christopher Thorne, *Border Crossings: Studies in International History*, Oxford, 1988, p. 302.

20. David Kolb, *The Critique of Pure Modernity: Hegel, Heidegger and After*, Chicago, 1986, p. 267.

21. Richard Rorty, "Thugs and Theorists: A Reply to Bernstein," *Political Theory* 15, 1987, p. 567.

22. For the multiplicity of possible social orders, see Robert W. Cox, *Production, Power and World Order: Social Forces in the Making of History*, New York, 1987, chapters 2–4. The significance of this is that the disciplining of this myriad of interpretations so as to sustain a particular political identity requires a powerful means of transferring the differences within to the differences between.

23. Quoted in Stephen J. Whitfield, *The Culture of the Cold War*, Baltimore, 1991, p. 5.

24. For a discussion of the function of anticommunism in conservative critiques on the New Deal, see James T. Patterson, *Congressional Conservatism and the New Deal: The Growth of the Conservative Coalition in Congress, 1933–1939*, Lexington, 1967.

25. William Chafe, *The Unfinished Journey: America Since World War II*, New York, 1986, pp. 26–27.

26. Chafe, *The Unfinished Journey*, pp. 93–94.

27. Ibid., pp. 107–8.

28. Ibid., p. 109.

29. Quoted in Whitfield, *The Culture of the Cold War*, p. 24.

30. M. J. Heale, *American Anticommunism: Combating the Enemy Within 1830–1970*, Baltimore, 1990, chapter 3.

31. Quoted in Harold M. Hyman, *To Try Men's Souls: Loyalty Tests in American History*, Berkeley, 1960, p. 316.

32. See Arno Mayer, *Politics and Diplomacy of Peacemaking: Containment and Counterrevolution at Versailles, 1918–1919*, New York, 1967.

33. Hyman, *To Try Men's Souls*, p. 317.

34. Quoted in Heale, *American Anticommunism*, p. 63.

35. Quoted in ibid., p. 107.

36. Quoted in Murray B. Levin, *Political Hysteria in America: The Democratic Capacity for Repression*, New York, 1971, p. 12.

37. Quoted in ibid., pp. 25–26.

38. Quoted in ibid., p. 18.

39. Quoted in ibid., pp. 16–17.

40. The American reaction to the Paris Commune was so vitriolic that the despotism of the Bonapartes was deemed preferable. The *New York Herald* declared that they "were the proper doctors for those virulently revolutionary disorders of Paris." See Samuel Bernstein, "The Impact of the Paris Commune in the United States," in *Revolution and Reaction: The Paris Commune*, edited by John Hicks and Robert Tucker, Amherst, 1973, p. 61. On Chicago's Haymarket bombing, see Paul Avrich, *The Haymarket Tragedy*, Princeton, 1984.

41. Richard Slotkin, *The Fatal Environment: The Myth of the Frontier in the Age of Industrialization, 1800–1890*, Middletown, Connecticut, 1986, chapters 15 and 19. Quotes are on p. 311 and p. 483, respectively.

42. The image of Indians on the frontier was taken one step further when a news reporter for NBC commented in February 1991 that the Soviets had "gone off the reservation" with their efforts to broker a diplomatic solution to the Persian Gulf war.

43. Slotkin, *The Fatal Environment*, pp. 18–19. On the centrality of frontier imagery to the United States space program, see Dale Carter, *The Final Frontier: The Rise and Fall of the American Rocket State*, London, 1988.

44. Slotkin, *The Fatal Environment*, pp. 32–33. See my "Foreign Policy and Identity: Japanese Other / American Self," in *The Global Economy as Political Space: A Critical Reader in International Political Economy*, edited by Naeem Inayatullah, Stephen J. Rosow, and Mark Rupert, Boulder, 1994.

45. See William Appelman Williams, "The Frontier Thesis and American Foreign Policy," *Pacific Historical Review* 24, 1955, pp. 379–95. On the gendering of the frontier as feminine, see Annette Kolodny, *The Lay of the Land: Metaphor as Experience and History in American Life and Letters*, Chapel Hill, 1975. The gendering of newly discovered lands, akin to the frontier experience, is noted in chapter 5.

46. Slotkin, *The Fatal Environment*, p. 531.

47. Any number of groups have been the object of this reasoning. As a war correspondent on the northwest frontier in colonial India, Churchill wrote "But in a land of fanatics common sense does not exist." Accordingly, because it was useless and even dangerous to attempt rational dialogue, he argued that the Afghan "must be crushed." Likewise, Theodore Roosevelt maintained that excessive violence was de rigueur in the Philippines because "the barbarian will yield only to force." Kennan argued the same for Soviet society in the "long telegram," while assessments of the Japanese economic threat have argued that verbal threats are not sufficient. Equally, Henry Kissinger was of the view "that the only thing Asians respect[ed was] brutal power." See, respectively, David B. Edwards, "Mad Mullahs and Englishmen: Discourse in the Colonial Encounter," *Comparative Studies in Society and History* 31, 1989, p. 655; LaFeber, *The American Age*, p. 212; Richard Leaver, "Restructuring in the Global Economy: From Pax Americana to Pax Nipponica?" *Alternatives* 14, 1989, p. 433; and Christopher Thorne, *American Political Culture and the Asian Frontier, 1943–1973*, London, 1986, p. 362.

48. For the importance of violence to the self, see Richard Slotkin, *Regeneration through Violence: The Mythology of the American Frontier, 1600–1860*, Middletown, Connecticut, 1973.

49. Quoted in Michael Kammen, *People of Paradox*, New York, 1980, p. 34.

50. Rogin, *Fathers and Children*, pp. 116–17.

51. Quoted in Kiernan, *America*, p. 28.

52. Quoted in Slotkin, *The Fatal Environment*, p. 318.

53. Quoted in Kiernan, *America*, p. 79.

54. Howard Zinn, *A People's History of the United States*, New York, 1980, pp. 218, 235.

55. Quoted in Whitfield, *The Culture of the Cold War*, p. 73.

56. Congress established the Fish Committee in 1930 to investigate communism, and the McCormack-Dickstein Committee in 1934 to consider a wider range of subversive groups. See Heale, *American Anticommunism*, pp. 102–3, 112.

57. Ibid., pp. 117–18.

58. Quoted in Geir Lundestad, "Uniqueness and Pendulum Swings in U.S. Foreign Policy," *International Affairs* 62, 1986, p. 410.

59. Heale, *American Anticommunism*, p. 123.

60. Quoted in Levin, *Political Hysteria*, p. 24. Original emphasis.

61. Quoted in Whitfield, *The Culture of the Cold War*, p. 81. On Niebuhr, see Richard W. Fox, *Reinhold Niebuhr: A Biography*, New York, 1985.

62. Whitfield, *The Culture of the Cold War*, p. 89.

63. Quoted in ibid., pp. 130, 21, 23, 31.

64. Robert Justin Goldstein, *Political Repression in Modern America: From 1870 to the Present*, Cambridge, Massachusetts, 1978, pp. 351–52.

65. Quoted in Whitfield, *The Culture of the Cold War*, p. 56.

66. Executive Order 9835, "Prescribing Procedures for the Administration of an Employee Loyalty Program in the Executive Branch of the Government," *Code of Federal Regulations Title 3 — The President 1943–1948 Compilation*, Washington, D.C., 1957, pp. 627, 630.

67. Executive Order 10450, "Security Requirements for Government Employment," *Code of Federal Regulations Title 3 — The President 1949–1953 Compilation*, Washington, D.C., 1958, p. 936.

68. Colin Gordon, "Governmental Rationality: An Introduction," in *The Foucault Effect: Studies in Governmental Rationality*, edited by Graham Burchell, Colin Gordon and Peter Miller, Hemel Hempstead, England, 1991, pp. 35–36.

69. E.O. 10450, p. 938. The Eisenhower executive order on security remains in force today as the basis for all security investigations. See Guenter Lewy, *The Federal Loyalty-Security Program: The Need for Reform*, Washington, D.C., 1983. There have been some changes in practice, however. Membership in the Communist Party is no longer a disqualification for employment in the government, and since 1977, the Office of Personnel Management (formerly the Civil Service Commission) no longer asks applicants questions about Communist Party membership, or membership in any group advocating violent overthrow. Furthermore, since 1968 no person has been denied or dismissed from government employment on loyalty grounds or as a security risk (excluding those charged with espionage).

70. Goldstein, *Political Repression*, pp. 374–75; and Frank Donner, *The Age of Surveillance: The Aims and Methods of America's Political Intelligence System*, New York, 1980, p. 27.

71. Foucault's conception of security includes a trait by which the rationality of the procedure "prescribes not by absolute binary demarcation between the permitted and the forbidden, but by the specification of an optimal mean within a tolerable bandwidth of variation." Gordon, "Governmental Rationality," p. 20.

72. *Case Studies in Personnel Security*, edited by Adam Yarmolinsky, Washington, D.C., 1955, pp. 1, 14, 21, 32, 55, 109, 115, 153, 177, 244, 291, 296.

73. Ibid., pp. 12, 18, 89, 91, 206, 210, 211.

74. Andrew Ross, "Containing Culture in the Cold War," *Cultural Studies* 1, 1987, p. 331.

75. Stephanson, *Kennan and the Art of Foreign Policy*, p. 301n.

76. Daniel Yergin, *Shattered Peace: The Origins of the Cold War*, revised ed., New York, 1990, p. 171.

77. National Security Action Memorandum No. 182, "U.S. Overseas Internal Defense Policy," August 24, 1962, Record Group 273, National Archives of the United States, pp. 11, 19–20.

78. Elaine Tyler May, *Homeward Bound: American Families in the Cold War Era*, New York, 1988, pp. 93, 95. In 1953 the State Department released 425 employees because of allegations of homosexuality. On some occasions, loyalty and security investigators asked the question "Have you any reason to doubt his masculinity?" of friends and colleagues. Ralph S. Brown, *Loyalty and Security: Employment Tests in the United States*, New Haven, 1958, p. 258.

79. Heale, *American Anticommunism*, p. 82.

80. Quoted in Whitfield, *The Culture of the Cold War*, p. 19.

81. Quoted in ibid., pp. 43–45.

82. May, *Homeward Bound*, pp. 69, 110–11.

83. See Warren Susman, with the assistance of Edward Griffin, "Did Success Spoil the United States? Dual Representations in Postwar America," in *Recasting America: Culture and Politics in the Age of the Cold War*, edited by Larry May, Chicago, 1989.

84. Indeed, Elaine May has argued that this enframing of identity was an effect of cold war practices. But no matter how distinctive the nuclear family was to the postwar period — and the use of the term *nuclear* suggests that it probably was — the use of sexual norms to maintain a patriarchal, family-centered society was not unique to this period. White domination through slavery in the southern United States was made possible by the construction of a black sexual threat to white women. Not only did this define a racial relationship, in reversing the actual direction of interracial sexual exploitation (it was white men who exploited black women), it reinforced a patriarchal relationship amongst whites. See Michael Paul Rogin, *"Ronald Reagan," the Movie and Other Episodes in Political Demonology*, Berkeley, 1987, pp. 51–52.

85. The racist logic behind this decision was made obvious by Governor Culbert L. Olson of California, when he told (unbelievably) a group of Japanese-American editors in February 1942: "You know, when I look out at a group of Americans of German or Italian descent, I can tell whether they're loyal or not. I can tell how they think and even perhaps what they are thinking. But it is impossible for me to do this with the inscrutable Orientals, and particularly the Japanese." Quoted in Richard S. Drinnon, *Keeper of Concentration Camps: Dillon S. Myer and American Racism*, Berkeley, 1987, pp. 31–32.

86. William W. Keller, *The Liberals and J. Edgar Hoover*, Princeton, 1989, chapter 2; and Richard Longaker, "Emergency Detention: The Generation Gap, 1950–1971," *Western Political Quarterly* 27, 1974, pp. 395–408. On the Internal Security Act, see William R. Tanner and Robert Griffith, "Legislative Politics and 'McCarthyism': the Internal Security Act of 1950," in *The Specter: Original Essays on the Cold War and the Origins of McCarthyism*, edited by Robert Griffith and Athan Theoharis, New York, 1974.

87. Keller, *The Liberals and J. Edgar Hoover*, p. 61.

88. Ibid., pp. 61–62, 163. For the grounds that constituted danger, see Brown, *Loyalty and Security*, chapter 11: "Security by Exclusion: Identifying Risky People."

89. Ibid., p. 157. Because most FBI files were kept in regional offices, this underestimates their total database. In 1972, they opened 65,000 new files. And because each file contained more than one name, more than this number of people were under surveillance.

90. Mark Thomas Connelly, *The Response to Prostitution in the Progressive Era*, Chapel Hill, 1980, pp. 139–46; and Ruth Rosen, *The Lost Sisterhood: Prostitution in America, 1900–1918*, Baltimore, 1982, pp. 34–35. For an analysis of the prewar moral climate that the CTCA so effectively institutionalized, see David Pivar, *Purity Crusade: Sexual Morality and Social Control, 1868–1900*, Westport, Connecticut 1973.

91. "These events [McCarthyism, etc.] were not aberrations outside the nation's history, but the result of a mix of elements essential to the culture and always present, not aberrations, but exaggerations of the commonplace, not the actions and reactions of psychotics or paranoids, but those of so-called normal men." Levin, *Political Hysteria*, p. 3. "There is a tendency to view the application of internal security measures in a liberal polity as aberrant episodes in an otherwise open and democratic process... But these events also suggest a broader pattern in which the liberal state attempts to deal with the tensions and limits implicit in liberalism itself." Keller, *The Liberals and J. Edgar Hoover*, p. 3.

92. See Executive Orders 11605 and 11785, in *Code of Federal Regulations Title 3 — The President 1971–1975 Compilation*, Washington DC, 1976, pp. 580, 874.

93. Longaker, "Emergency Detention," p. 400.

94. Michael Cox, "From Detente to the 'New Cold War': The Crisis of the Cold War System," *Millennium: Journal of International Studies* 13, 1984, p. 266; Robert W. Cox, "The Crisis of World Order and the Problem of International Organization in the 1980s," *International Journal* 35, 1980, p. 370.

95. Paul Kennedy, *The Rise and Fall of the Great Powers: Economic Change and Military Conflict from 1500 to 2000*, New York, 1987, pp. 395–413.

96. For discussions of the domestic disorder in this period, see Thomas Powers, *The War at Home: Vietnam and the American People, 1964–1968*, Boston, 1984; and Kim McQuaid, *The Anxious Years: America in the Era of Vietnam and Watergate*, New York, 1989.

97. Godfrey Hodgson, "Disorder Within, Disorder Without," in *Estrangement: America and the World*, edited by Sanford J. Ungar, New York, 1985.

98. Alan Wolfe, *America's Impasse: The Rise and Fall of the Politics of Growth*, New York, 1981, p. 6. A good example of the anti-Great Society perspective of neoconservatism is David Stockman, "The Social Pork Barrel," *The Public Interest* 39, 1975, pp. 3–30.

99. David Edgar, "The Free or the Good," in *The Ideology of the New Right*, edited by Ruth Levitas, Cambridge, 1986, pp. 63–69.

100. Quoted in ibid., p. 76.

101. Robert Nisbet, *The Twilight of Authority*, New York, 1975. See Peter Steinfels, *The Neoconservatives: The Men Who Are Changing America's Politics*, New York, 1979, especially chapter 3.

102. Sheldon Wolin, "The New Conservatives," *New York Review of Books*, February 5, 1976, p. 8.

103. Samuel P. Huntington, "The Democratic Distemper," *The Public Interest* 41, 1975, pp. 9–38. This article is an edited version of his contribution to the Trilateral Commission's report on "the governability of the democracies." See Michel Crozier, Samuel P. Huntington and Joji Watanuki, *The Crisis of Democracy*, New York, 1975.

104. Huntington, "The Democratic Distemper," p. 37.

105. Daniel Bell, "The End of American Exceptionalism," *The Public Interest* 41, 1975, p. 197.

106. Ibid., p. 211.

107. Norman Podhoretz, *The Present Danger: Do We Have the Will to Reverse the Decline of American Power?*, New York, 1980, p. 79.

108. Ibid., p. 76.

109. Ibid., pp. 38–39. Podhoretz listed Laos, Ethiopia, Mozambique, and Cambodia as among those nations.

110. Ibid., p. 22.

111. Steinfels, *The Neoconservatives*, p. 60.

112. Ibid., pp. 68–69.

113. Ibid., p. 69.

114. Miriam David, "Moral and Maternal: The Family in the New Right," in *The Ideology of the New Right*, ed. Levitas.

115. Quoted in ibid., p. 156.

116. Zillah Eisenstein, "The Sexual Politics of the New Right: Understanding the 'Crisis of Liberalism' for the 1980s," *Signs* 7, 1982, pp. 567–75. In the influential economic text *Wealth and Poverty* (Ronald Reagan distributed copies to his cabinet in 1981), George Gilder argued that the family also contains male sexuality in a way that aids the economy. Marriage, for Gilder, creates a sense of responsibility that forces men to channel their sexual energies toward the economy: "A married man . . . is spurred by the claims of family to channel his otherwise disruptive male aggressions into his performance as a provider for wife and children." According to Gilder, it is "familial anarchy," not capitalism or its malpractice, that causes poverty. Quoted in Eisenstein, "The Sexual Politics of the New Right," p. 576.

117. Donner, *The Age of Surveillance*, p. 453. For an interesting catalog of how these issues were recycled through the 1960s, see the covers of *Life, Time, Newsweek*, and other magazines reproduced in Michael Ryan and Douglas Kellner, *Camera Politica: The Politics and Ideology of Contemporary Film*, Bloomington, 1988.

118. Andre Kaspai, "Le Cancer Americain," *Histoire* 42, 1982, pp. 6–18. Cf. Michael T. Klare, *Beyond the "Vietnam Syndrome:" U.S. Interventionism in the 1980s*, Washington DC, 1981.

119. Fred Halliday, *The Making of the Second Cold War*, 2nd ed., London, 1986.

120. See Donner, *The Age of Surveillance,* pp. 452–463.

121. Ibid., p. 457. In an effort to beef up the quantitative dimensions of danger, the State Department compiles statistics on the number and type of targets among U.S. interests with overseas operations. In 1989, they found 182 incidents, but many of them can be considered as something other than "terrorism." Included, for example, was the holdup of a Coca-Cola truck in the Philippines, vandalism against a Unisys office in Denmark, and industrial relations protests by Korean workers against the American Chamber of Commerce in Seoul. See "Special Report: Business Targets," *Terrorism* 13, 1990, pp. 455–69.

122. Frank Donner, *Protectors of Privilege: Red Squads and Police Repression in Urban America,* Berkeley, 1990, p. 367. For a quite extraordinary argument in favor of understanding adherence to the views of "the left" as an indicator of "terrorism," see Herbet A. Kampf, "Terrorism, the Left Wing, and the Intellectuals," *Terrorism* 13, 1990, pp. 23–51.

123. "Newly Released Documents Provide Rare Look at How FBI Monitors Students and Professors," *Chronicle of Higher Education,* February 10, 1988, p. A1, 13. For a detailed analysis of the FBI's COINTELPRO dealings, see Ward Churchill and Jim Vander Wall, *The COINTELPRO Papers: Documents from the FBI's Secret Wars against Dissent in the United States,* Boston, 1990.

124. Donner, *The Age of Surveillance,* p. 462.

125. Miriam Davidson, "Militarizing the Mexican Border," *The Nation,* April 1, 1991, p. 408.

126. David Cole, "Secret Tribunal," *The Nation,* May 6, 1991, p. 581; "Crime Bill Would Establish Alien Deportation Tribunal," *New York Times,* June 1, 1991, p. 6; David Cole, "Don't Let White House Order Secret Trials of Political Cases" [letter], *New York Times,* June 2, 1991, p. E18; "U.S. Drops Plan for Alien Tribunals," *New York Times,* June 21, 1991, p. A14.

7. Rewriting Security

1. For a discussion of this formulation, see Richard K. Ashley, "Untying the Sovereign State: A Double Reading of the Anarchy Problematique," *Millennium: Journal of International Studies* 17, 1988, pp. 252–59.

2. One example among many is Antonin Kratochvil and Marlise Simons, "Eastern Europe: The polluted lands," *New York Times Magazine,* April 29, 1990.

3. Some American politicians have recognized this and, as a consequence, sought to delegitimize this potential by reinvoking a cold war discourse. Conservative Republican Congressman Newt Gingrich has stated that "35 percent of the environmental movement is just stupid; their solutions are essentially socialism." Quoted in David Corn, "Beltway Bandits," *The Nation,* June 4, 1990, p. 768.

4. For a consideration of the representational practices immanent in the policy discourses of crime and foreign policy, see Michael J. Shapiro, *The Politics of Representation: Writing Practices in Biography, Photography, and Policy Analysis,* Madison, 1988, especially pp. 42–47, 111–23.

5. "Address to the Nation on the National Drug Control Strategy," September 5, 1989, *Public Papers of the Presidents of the United States: George Bush 1989 Book II,* Washington DC, 1990, p. 1304.

6. The White House, *National Drug Control Strategy,* Washington, D.C., 1991, p. 1.

7. Ibid. Note the way "Nation" is capitalized. A common practice in some U.S. government reports, it symbolically distinguishes the United States from other nations, and endows America with a quasi-transcendental air.

8. See Peter Andreas and Coletta Youngers, "U.S. Drug Policy and the Andean Cocaine Industry," *World Policy Journal* 6, 1989, pp. 529–62; Waltrud Q. Morales, "The War on Drugs: A New U.S. National Security Doctrine," *Third World Quarterly* 11, 1989, pp. 147–69; and Jonathan Marshall, *Drug Wars: Corruption, Counterinsurgency, and Covert Operations in the Third World*, Forestville, California, 1991, p. 62.

9. Marshall, *Drug Wars*, p. 29; Edward Jay Epstein, *Agency of Fear: Opiates and Political Power in America*, revised edition, New York, 1990. Nixon went to great lengths to target Turkey as the source of heroin, and increased the enforcement budget from $43 million in fiscal year 1970 to $292 million in fiscal year 1974. Interestingly, although Nixon's penchant was clearly the law and order dimension of the issue, funding for treatment was greater than enforcement, increasing from $59 million to $462 million in the same period. This means that the current concentration on enforcement over treatment—signified by the fact that since 1980 the drug budget has appropriated three-quarters of its money for the agencies of law and order—is something for which both Reagan and Bush have exceeded Nixon. See David F. Musto, *The American Disease: Origins of Narcotic Control*, expanded edition, New York, 1987, pp. 254–63.

10. See Musto, *The American Disease*. International efforts have continued unabated to the present day. In 1989 a group of seven nonpermanent members of the United Nations' Security Council—led by Algeria and Brazil—rebutted an attempt by Britain, the United States and the Soviet Union to have the council declare drug trafficking "a threat to international peace and security." The opposition wanted the General Assembly to handle the issue, and a special session of the assembly was held in February 1990 to address the issue. See "Security Council Bars Drug Fight," *New York Times*, October 11, 1989, p. A12; *Resolution and Decision Adopted by the General Assembly at Its Seventeenth Special Session 20–23 February 1990*, United Nations GA/8005, New York, April 3, 1990. Although this session recognized drugs as a "scourge," a source of violence, and a major health problem, it resisted making them a security issue per se.

11. Cited in Craig Reinerman and Henry G. Levine, "Crack in Context: Politics and Media in the Making of a Drug Scare," *Contemporary Drug Problems* 16, 1989, pp. 537, 541–42. In so doing, the media was only continuing a long tradition of sensationalizing reports of crime. One study found that the print media highlights violent and sensational crime, does not report crime in a manner representative of official data, exaggerates fears of victimization, and is generally supportive of police views. See H. L. Marsh, "Newspaper Crime Coverage in the U.S. 1893–1988," *Criminal Justice Abstracts* 21, 1989, pp. 506–14.

12. "Drugs: The Enemy Within," *Time*, September 15, 1986.

13. From 1981, funding grew from $1.7 billion to a proposed $11.7 billion in 1992. It increased 82 percent—from $4.2 billion—after Bush took office. See *National Drug Control Strategy*, p. 133. The Clinton administration consolidated this increase, with $12.2 billion spent in FY 1994 and $16 billion requested for FY 1998. Office of National Drug Control Strategy, *National Drug Control Strategy*, Washington, D.C., February 1995, p. 113; and ONDCP *News Briefs*, March-April 1997.

14. James A. Inciardi, "Beyond Cocaine: Basuco, Crack, and Other Coca Products," *Contemporary Drug Problems* 14, 1987, p. 482. Emphasis in original. The DEA's special report of August 22, 1986 was largely ignored by the media. Once "the war on drugs" was underway, it was also largely ignored by the DEA.

15. *National Drug Control Strategy*, pp. 5, 8–9.

16. Reinarman and Levine, "Crack in Context," pp. 546, 551. The figure was 750,000 for heroin and 300,000 for cocaine. NIDA's category of frequent use refers to use in the previous week, thereby generating a higher figure.

17. Quoted in Epstein, *Agency of Fear,* p. 183. The conclusion applied to both licit and illicit drugs at a time when administration statistics showed that there were nine million alcoholics but only 100,000 heroin addicts.

18. See Inciardi, "Beyond Cocaine."

19. George F. Will, "Drugs Are Already Déclassé," *Washington Post,* September 6, 1989, p. A23. Interestingly, Will began this column — which ran the day after Bush's address to the nation — with the premise that "martial metaphors miss the point" because only moral leadership will prevail.

20. The breakdown of the status of drug consumers is as follows: 60 percent hold full- or part-time jobs, 12 percent are students, 5 percent are homemakers, 10 percent are unemployed, and 5 percent are "other." *National Drug Control Strategy,* p. 70.

21. "Study: White Students More Likely to Use Drugs," *Washington Post,* February 25, 1991, p. A4. This survey has been criticized for excluding those who dropped out of school and refusing to ask about crack. The project director was quoted as saying, however: "We recognize that this tells us only a portion of the story, but it's a portion of the story that has been overlooked a great deal. The majority of nonwhite youth do complete high school and, among these individuals, rates for both illicit and licit drugs are generally lower than average."

22. "Crack, Bane of Inner City, Is Now Gripping Suburbs," *New York Times,* October 1, 1989, p. A1.

23. Reinarman and Levine, "Crack in Context," pp. 544–45.

24. Norman Zinberg, "Mandatory Testing for Drug Use and AIDS," in *Toward a National Policy on Drug and AIDS Testing,* edited by Mathea Falco and Warren I. Cikins, Washington, D.C., 1989, p. 66; Alexander Cockburn, "Getting Opium to the Masses: The Political Economy of Addiction," *The Nation,* October 30, 1989, p. 482.

25. U.S. Department of Health and Human Services, *Vital Statistics of the United States 1987,* Washington, D.C. 1988, table 5–4. Heroin, methadone, and other opiates were listed as causing 595 deaths; marijuana, cannabis derivatives, LSD, amphetamines, and caffeine (all in one category), were listed as resulting in 165 deaths. These figures accord with the estimate of the National Council on Alcoholism, which reported 3,562 deaths in 1985 from all illegal drugs. Ethan A. Nadelmann, "The Case for Legalization," *The Public Interest* 92, 1988, p. 24.

26. Reinarman and Levine, "Crack in Context," pp. 544–45; Cockburn, "Getting Opium to the Masses," p. 482.

27. In addition to the *National Drug Control Strategy,* see United States Senate, Committee on the Judiciary, Majority Staff Report, *Fighting Crime in America: An Agenda for the 1990s,* 100th Congress, 1st session, March 12, 1991. This report, which demonstrates how the Democrats are willing partners in the hype of "the war on drugs," begins with the statement: "The epidemic of violent crime has swept the entire nation." Three reasons are asserted: drugs, deadly military-style assault weapons owned by drug gangs, and demographic trends (that show an increase in the teenage population, which increases the number of people in the cohort supposedly prone to criminal activity).

28. *Fighting Crime in America,* pp. 5–7.

29. E. J. Misham, "Narcotics: The Problem and the Solution," *Political Quarterly* 61, 1990, p. 460.

30. Paul J. Goldstein, "The Drugs/Violence Nexus: A Tripartite Conceptual Framework," *Journal of Drug Issues* 15, 1985, pp. 493–506. Some contend that this understanding of the nexus is too static and limited, ignoring the overarching issues of political

economy. See Ansley Hamid, "The Political Economy of Crack-related Violence," *Contemporary Drug Problems* 17, 1990, pp. 31–78.

31. William F. Wieczork, John W. Welte, and Ernest L. Abel, "Alcohol, Drugs, and Murder: A Study of Convicted Homicide Defenders," *Journal of Criminal Justice Studies* 18, 1990, pp. 217–27. Of those one-half, 39 percent were under the influence of alcohol alone, while 13 percent had consumed both alcohol and drugs. The study also made the interesting finding that black offenders had the least involvement with substance abuse prior to the homicide. These figures are not surprising when one considers that a considerable amount of medical evidence suggests that heroin and other opiates actually decrease violent responses on behalf of users. As the 1973 National Commission on Marijuana and Drug Abuse concluded: "Assaultive offenses are significantly less likely to be committed by... opiate users." Quoted in Epstein, *Agency of Fear*, p. 30.

32. Paul J. Goldstein, Henry H. Brownstein, Patrick S. Ryan, and Patricia A. Bellucci, "Crack and Homicide in New York City, 1988: A Conceptually Based Event Analysis," *Contemporary Drug Problems* 16, 1989, p. 663.

33. This figure has nonetheless increased. From 1976 through 1983, the proportion of homicides attributable to narcotic situations remained relatively stable at 1.7 percent to 2.0 percent. In 1985 the figure climbed to 2.9 percent, then 3.9 percent (1986), 4.9 percent (1987), and 5.6 percent (1988). In absolute numbers, this means that some 1,400 of the nearly 20,000 murders in 1989 were drug-related. See FBI, *Crime in the United States 1980*, Washington, D.C., 1981; *Crime in the United States 1985*, Washington, D.C., 1986; and *Crime in the United States 1989*, Washington, D.C., 1990. "Narcotic drug laws" were listed as the murder circumstances for 6.2 percent of all homicides in 1991, declining to 5 percent in 1995. The absolute numbers for this period reflected a fall from 1,353 to 1,010 murders. *Crime in the United States for 1995*, table 2.14, p. 30. Available at http://www.fbi.gov/publish.htm.

34. Goldstein et al., "Crack and Homicide in New York City," p. 682. Of course, the identification of a homicide as drug-related is an interpretive act subject to ambiguity and error. There is a strong possibility of overreporting in this category: there are bureaucratic pressures to highlight the prevalence of drugs (high-intensity drug-trafficking areas like New York receive additional funds), and the general climate might produce a tendency for ambiguity to be resolved by the ascription of drugs as the context. As an instance of the latter, consider the case in which three college age youths beat to death a gay man in New York City. Because the victim was a consumer of cocaine, the police first listed the incident as a drug-related homicide. But after protests, it was reclassified as an antigay hate crime. See "Guilty Plea in Slaying of Gay Man," *New York Times*, August 6, 1991, p. B1.

35. "The crack distribution scene is undoubtedly violent. However, the crack phenomenon does not appear to have greatly influenced the overall homicide rate in New York City... In both nature and number, crack related homicides largely appear to be replacing other sorts of homicides rather than just adding to the existing homicide rate." Goldstein et al., "Crack and Homicide in New York City," p. 683.

36. The Justice Department's Bureau of Justice Statistics conducts a National Crime Victimization Survey of people at least twelve years old in 50,000 households across the country to ascertain how many have been victims of all categories of crime, except murder. Begun in 1975, it then reported that just over 32 percent of households were affected; by 1990 that was down to just under 24 percent. One of the breakdowns in the survey further cast doubt on a watertight drugs/crime nexus: the West was the region with the highest rate of crime in all categories, yet it contains only one of the five

government-designated high-intensity drug-trafficking areas. In contrast, the Northeast, which includes New York, was the region with the lowest rate of crime in all categories. Two other points problematize the representation of crime as emanating from the inner cities and "infecting" the predominantly white suburbs: (1) When the survey began, both blacks and whites experienced the same rate of crime; by 1990, that equality had been altered, with nearly 28 percent of black households compared to 23 percent of white households experiencing some form of crime. (2) The poor suffered the highest rate of violent crime and, except for robberies, the higher the income of a household the less frequent the experience of crime. See "A 15-year Decline in Crime Found in Survey of Homes," *New York Times,* August 9, 1991, p. A12.

37. Jerry Fagan and Ko-Lin Chin, "Initiation into Crack: A Tale of Two Epidemics," *Contemporary Drug Problems* 16, 1989, pp. 596–97.

38. The FBI's Uniform Crime Reports show that just over two-thirds of all drug arrests in 1989 were for possession alone. The remaining one-third were for sale/manufacture. Of the possession arrests, 23 percent were for marijuana and just under 35 percent for heroin and cocaine. The bulk of law enforcement in "the war on drugs" is thus being targeted against the most personal and minor of offenses. See *Crime in the United States 1990,* p. 171.

39. For one study among many supporting these conclusions, see Charles E. Faupel and Carl B. Klockars, "Drugs-Crime Connections: Elaborations from the Life Histories of Hard-core Heroin Addicts," *Social Problems* 34, 1987, pp. 54–68. The most egregious attempt to link drugs and crime through the idea that consumers resort to illegal activity to finance their habits has to have been the completely unsubstantiated claims of New York Governor Nelson Rockefeller in the 1960s and President Nixon in the 1970s. Rockefeller declared that "addicts" had to steal $1 billion worth of goods in New York, when the total amount of reported theft in that state never exceeded $100 million. Nixon's drugs–crime statistics were equally fabricated and inflated. His administration produced an estimate of $18 billion in theft allegedly caused by addicts, a figure that was *twenty-five times* greater than the total sum of all property stolen and unrecovered in the entire United States throughout 1971. See Epstein, *Agency of Fear,* chapters 2, 22.

40. Bennett's statements, for example, came in a written response to Milton Friedman's call for the decriminalization of drugs, a proposal Friedman had first floated in 1972 during Nixon's war on drugs. See "A Response to Milton Friedman," *Wall Street Journal,* September 19, 1989, p. A30. Bennett was particularly vehement in rebutting such arguments, claiming that they were the product of failed liberal intellectuals (a claim that must have offended Friedman!). See "Bennett Rebuts Legalization Ideas," *Washington Post,* December 12, 1989, p. A10. In this respect, it is worth noting that Bennett was at the time having considerable trouble with the (legal) drug of his choice. Upon becoming the "drug czar," he declared that he was quitting smoking his usual two packs of cigarettes a day, but nine months later he was unable to kick the habit and was consuming Nicorette gum, each stick of which contains half as much nicotine as a cigarette. See "Drug Czar Still Hooked on Nicotine," *Washington Post,* December 7, 1989, p. A25. When questioned about his continuing addiction and how he reconciled it with this public vehemence to drug use and legalization, Bennett returned to the drugs-crime nexus he had rebutted in replying to Friedman; the difference, he replied, was that "I didn't do any drive-by shootings." See "Bennett Rebuts Legalization Ideas."

41. Craig Reinarman, "The Social Construction of an Alcohol Problem: The Case of Mothers Against Drunk Driving and Social Control in the 1980s," *Theory and Society* 17, 1988, p. 91.

42. Quoted ibid., p. 111. Gusfield is not denying that drunk driving is a problem or that the fatalities it produces are a tragedy. Rather, his concern is with the dynamics behind the singling out of the drunk driver as a special category of traffic offender, a category that attracts more opprobrium than, say, those who speed or those who drive unsafe cars. Moreover, Reinarman, Gusfield, and other analysts are interested in the heightened attention given to drink driving and the rise of activist groups like Mothers Against Drunk Driving at a time when both the consumption of alcohol and the incidence of alcohol-related problems is declining. See Howard F. Stein, "In What Systems Do Alcohol/Chemical Addictions Make Sense? Clinical Ideologies and Practices as Cultural Metaphors," *Social Science and Medicine* 30, 1990, p. 991. These concerns have direct relevance for the current "war on drugs." On their relationship to cocaine, see Craig Reinarman, Dan Waldorf, and Sheigla Murphy, "Scapegoating and Social Control in the Construction of a Public Problem: Empirical and Critical Findings on Cocaine and Work," *Research in Law, Deviance, and Social Control* 9, 1987, pp. 37–62.

43. Quoted in Jefferson Morely, "Contradictions of Cocaine Capitalism," *The Nation*, October 2, 1989, p. 346.

44. Lee P. Brown, "The Illegal Use of Drugs," *Vital Speeches of the Day* 54, 1988, p. 727. Original emphasis.

45. See M. J. Heale, *American Anticommunism: Combating the Enemy Within 1830–1970*, Baltimore, 1990, pp. 54, 70, 74.

46. Brown, "The Illegal Use of Drugs," p. 728. He also declared that "the surgeon general of the United States should declare the drug problem an epidemic and engage a total commitment from the medical profession to address this social cancer."

47. Musto, *The American Disease*, pp. 5–6, 218–19, 244–45, 17, 83, 220.

48. Mathea Falco, "Introduction," in *Toward a National Policy on Drug and AIDS Testing*, ed. Falco and Cikins, p. 17.

49. Douglas Crimp, "AIDS: Cultural Analysis/Cultural Activism," in *AIDS: Cultural Analysis, Cultural Activism*, edited by Douglas Crimp, Cambridge, Massachusetts, 1988, p. 8. A year before being appointed by Reagan, Servas was editor of the *Saturday Evening Post* and claimed both to have worked at National Institutes of Health (NIH) and to have discovered a cure for AIDS—both of which the NIH denied.

50. Ibid., pp. 8, 134. The myth of black difference has been carried on by advocates of "the war on drugs," like Los Angeles police chief Daryl Gates. In 1982, when asked to explain how so many black suspects died from police choke holds, he responded: "We may be finding that, in some blacks, when [the choke hold] is applied, the veins or arteries do not open up as fast as they do in normal people." Joe Domanick, "Field Marshall Daryl Gates," *Mother Jones* 16, 1991, p. 39.

51. Martin Walker, "Sentencing System Blights Land of the Free," *Guardian Weekly*, June 30, 1991, p. 10. While "the war on drugs" has been the single biggest factor in the increased number of people entering prison (now running at 1,500 people per day), the United States has long had a more repressive criminal justice system than the rest of the world. The consequence is that America's rate of incarceration for all sectors of the population is by a considerable margin the world's highest at 426 people per 100,000 population. This is almost twice the rate in the former Soviet Union (268), and much greater than Britain (97) or South Africa (33). Many advocates of a tough crime approach argue that increasingly harsh sentencing will act as a deterrent, but the fact that the United States already has the most severe sentencing guidelines in the world suggests that this is unlikely. For example, one in four inmates is serving a sentence of fifteen years or more, and one-half are in for seven years or more. In the Soviet Union, only 10 percent serve ten or more years, most serve for less than five years, and the

majority of prisoners spend two-thirds of their sentence on parole. These statistics among others suggest that the United States is a disciplinary society in which the prison system plays an integral role in constituting the bounds of subjectivity. For this argument, see Thomas L. Dumm, *Democracy and Punishment: Disciplinary Origins of the United States*, Madison, 1987.

52. Morris J. Blachman and Kenneth E. Sharpe, "The War on Drugs: American Democracy under Assault," *World Policy Journal* 7, 1989–90, p. 141.

53. "Airport Anti-Drug Nets Snare Many People Fitting 'Profiles,'" *New York Times*, March 20, 1990, p. A1. In many cases, the "brief" stop has amounted to hours of harassment. In the case of Linda Jones, a *Detroit News* reporter stopped twice at the Detroit airport after returning from trips, the officers making the stops offered the following reasons: On the first occasion it was because she was "foreign and appeared nervous." On the second occasion, when pressed, the agent stated, "I'm from the old school. I see a person like you, I wonder to myself: Where's her husband? Where's her boyfriend?" Ms. Jones is black (albeit an American citizen), wears her hair in braids, and was once carrying a Caribbean scarf.

54. Blachman and Sharpe, "The War on Drugs," pp. 139–40; *National Drug Control Strategy*, pp. 115–20.

55. Duncan A. Simpson, "Does a 'Drug-Free Federal Workplace' Also Mean a 'Fourth Amendment Free Workplace?" *Labor Law Journal* 40, 1989, pp. 547–66; and Falco, "Introduction," p. 16.

56. Nat Hentoff, "Just Say No to the USIA," *Washington Post*, June 17, 1989, p. A19.

57. *National Drug Control Strategy*, pp. 72–73.

58. U.S. Bureau of the Census, *Statistical Abstract of the United States 1990*, 110th edition, Washington DC, 1990, table 874. This means that one in three businesses employing 500–999 workers and 45 percent of businesses employing over 1,000 workers have drug-testing programs.

59. Falco, "Introduction," p. 12.

60. Russell Luculano, "Private Sector Concerns," in *Toward a National Policy on Drug and AIDS Testing*, ed. Falco and Cikins, p. 54.

61. *Maintaining a Drug-Free Environment: The Hopkins Commitment*, Baltimore, 1990, pp. 8–10.

62. David Wagner, "The New Temperance Movement and Social Control at the Workplace," *Contemporary Drug Problems* 14, 1987, pp. 539–56.

63. Epstein, *Agency of Fear*, chapter 2.

64. "Bennett Mulls Drug-Abuser Boot Camps," *Washington Post*, May 8, 1989, p. A1.

65. *National Drug Control Strategy*, p. 37.

66. Interestingly, a State Department report makes a similar observation. In a section on "America in the 1990s," it states: "Cigarettes, alcohol, and drugs have become the tragic props of a national morality play. Just as the old teetotalers sought through booze banning to confront their fears of a 'mongrelized' America, so the new temperance movements try to exorcize their sense of national loss through personal healing." Center for the Study of Foreign Affairs, *Thinking about World Change*, Washington, D.C., 1990, p. 54.

67. Quoted in Peter Dale Scott and Jonathan Marshall, *Cocaine Politics: Drugs, Armies, and the CIA in Central America*, Berkeley, 1991, p. 2.

68. Charles B. Rangel, "Yes We Can Do Something for Colombia," *Washington Post*, August 24, 1989, p. A23.

69. Quoted in John Lewis Gaddis, *Strategies of Containment: A Critical Appraisal of Postwar American National Security Policy*, New York, 1982, p. 203.

70. United States Senate, Subcommittee on Terrorism, Narcotics and International Operations, *Drugs, Law Enforcement and Foreign Policy*, 100th Congress, 2d session, S. PRT. 100–165, Washington, D.C., 1989, p. 1.

71. Ibid., p. 11. The quote is from General Gorman's testimony, cited approvingly in the executive summary.

72. See *National Drug Control Strategy*, p. 25; Michael Massing, "In the Cocaine War... The Jungle Is Winning," *New York Times Magazine*, March 4, 1990. The *National Drug Control Strategy* has a variety of figurative modes, however. It begins, for example, with a clear expression of a medical and economic representation of the problem by noting that Bush's first NDCS "described drug use as 'a broad epidemiological phenomenon, progressing in individuals and passing through sectors of the population at different rates, in different degrees, with different effects.'" It also described drug use as "the result of a market, in which the variable 'supply' of drug sellers and variable 'demand' of drug buyers meet in a combustible mix." Ibid., pp. 1–2.

73. For a discussion of this aspect of United States Foreign Policy, see D. Michael Shafer, *Deadly Paradigms: The Failure of U.S. Counterinsurgency Policy*, Princeton, 1988.

74. Scott and Marshall, *Cocaine Politics*, p. 23; Andreas and Younger, "U.S. Drug Policy"; Marshall, *Drug Wars*, chapter 2. For the Reagan-Bush interpretation, see Elliot Abrams, "Drug Wars: The New Alliance against Terrorists and Traffickers," *Department of State Bulletin*, 86, 1986, pp. 89–92.

75. For a refutation of the connection, see Edmundo Morales, *Cocaine: White Gold Rush in Peru*, Tucson, 1989, pp. 133–45.

76. Quoted in Scott and Marshall, *Cocaine Politics*, p. 24.

77. Of course, the invasion of Panama in December 1989 had the drug war as one of its pretexts. More particularly, Operation Blast Force in Bolivia in 1986 saw 170 U.S. military personnel directly involved in combat with DEA agents and Bolivian forces against suspected cocaine laboratories over a four-month period. Operation Snow Cap, which began in Peru in 1988, involved one hundred U.S. civilians and fifty Green Berets, alongside DEA agents, helping Peruvian forces in helicopter strikes against alleged laboratories. See Michael Klare, "Fighting Drugs with the Military," *The Nation*, January 1, 1990, pp. 8–12. Much of the support for these initiatives comes from the State Department's Bureau of International Narcotics Matters, which runs (with the assistance of the Pentagon) an air force of fifty-three planes in South America using pilots who have Vietnam or CIA experience. See Andreas and Younger, "U.S. Drug Policy," p. 554; and "Management Woes Hobble U.S. Air Fleet in Drug War," *New York Times*, June 13, 1991, p. A1.

78. George Bush, "Remarks to Members of the National Association of Attorneys General," March 13, 1989, *Public Papers of the President*, pp. 335–37; Bush, "Remarks to Drug Enforcement Administration Officers in New York City," *Public Papers of the President*, March 9, 1989, pp. 309–12.

79. The Nixon administration also employed the Pentagon in its war on drugs, though to a more limited extent than current policy. When seeking to arouse domestic opinion on the issue and target Turkey's poppy supply in 1971, the Defense Department gave a presentation on "the relationship of... dissent and drugs" to media executives, and sent SR71 spy planes to photograph growing areas in all source countries. Epstein, *Agency of Fear*, p. 149.

80. Peter Reuter, "Can the Borders Be Sealed?" *The Public Interest* 92, 1988, pp. 51–65; Miriam Davidson, "Militarizing the Mexican Border," *The Nation*, April 1, 1991, pp. 406–9; "New Radar Fence Is Erected," *Washington Post*, April 25, 1990, p. A4; Blachman and Sharpe, "The War on Drugs," p. 149; Jack Anderson and Dale Van Atta, "High-Tech War on Drugs Floundering," *Washington Post*, August 28, 1989, p. D8.

81. United States Foreign Policy has at one time or another facilitated if not allowed the trafficking of heroin in Afghanistan, Pakistan, and Southeast Asia, and the smuggling of cocaine in Central America. For example, the Afghan mujahadeen were by 1985 not only receiving hundreds of millions of dollars in U.S. military aid, they were known to be the source of two-thirds of America's heroin supply. The Kerry report, after all, substantiated charges that the covert operation to aid the contras in the Reagan administration enabled the entry of cocaine into the United States, some of the funds from which found their way back to the Nicaraguan insurgents. For the other cases, see Alfred McCoy, *The Politics of Heroin in Southeast Asia*, New York, 1972; and Marshall, *Drug Wars*, chapter 4.

82. Quoted in Epstein, *Agency of Fear*, p. 34.

83. Ibid., p. 81.

84. Quoted in Marshall, *Drug Wars*, p. 31. Marshall notes that there was evidence that Bulgaria and Laos were involved; but then, at least indirectly, so was the United States. Once freed of national office, Schultz came to advocate the legalization of drugs. "Schultz on Drug Legalization," *Wall Street Journal*, October 27, 1989, p. A16.

8. The Politics of Theorizing Identity

1. In Michel Foucault, *Politics, Philosophy, Culture: Interviews and Other Writings 1977–1984*, edited by Lawrence D. Kritzman, translated by Alan Sheridan and others, New York, 1988, pp. 154–55.

2. See Yale H. Ferguson and Richard W. Mansbach, *The Elusive Quest: Theory and International Politics*, Columbia, 1988; and Yale H. Ferguson, *The State, Conceptual Chaos, and the Future of International Relations Theory*, Boulder, 1989.

3. See Kenneth Waltz, "Reflections on Theory of International Politics: A Response to My Critics," in *Neorealism and Its Critics*, edited by Robert O. Keohane, New York, 1986; K. J. Holsti, "Mirror, Mirror on the Wall, Which Are the Fairest Theories of Them All?," *International Studies Quarterly* 33, 1989, pp. 255–61.

4. Fred Halliday has offered a relatively mild statement along these lines: "IR has also been affected by the spread of discourse theory and varieties of postmodernism, but not, I have to say, with very fruitful results." Fred Halliday, "International Relations: Is There a New Agenda?" *Millennium: Journal of International Studies* 35, 1991, p. 67. A more strident, and more common, formulation has been offered by Stephen Walt: "In short, security studies must steer between the Scylla of political opportunism and the Charybdis of academic irrelevance. What does this mean in practice? Among other things, it means that security studies should remain wary of contemporary tangents that have seduced other areas of international studies, most notably the 'postmodern' approach to international affairs ... Contrary to their proponents' claims, postmodern approaches have yet to demonstrate much value for comprehending world politics; to date, these works are mostly criticism and not much theory ... In particular, issues of war and peace are too important for the field to be diverted into a prolix and self-indulgent discourse that is divorced from the real world." Stephen Walt, "The Renaissance of Security Studies," *International Studies Quarterly* 35, 1991, p. 223.

5. See, in particular, Richard K. Ashley and R. B. J. Walker, "Reading Dissidence/Writing the Discipline: Crisis and the Question of Sovereignty in International Studies," *International Studies Quarterly* 24, 1990, pp. 367–416.

6. A good example of this tendency is Robert Keohane's essay on the perils of postmodernism for a feminist contribution to international relations, in which he confidently asserts a range of conclusions about postmodernism without citing a single

postmodern theorist. Moreover, those assertions depend on a systematic misreading of many postmodern attitudes, such that what we are left with is a "strategy of condemnation by refraction." William E. Connolly, *Identity/Difference: Democratic Negotiations of Political Paradox*, Ithaca, 1991, pp. 51–54. See Robert O. Keohane, "International Relations Theory: Contributions of a Feminist Standpoint," *Millennium: Journal of International Studies* 18, 1989, pp. 245–53.

7. Derrida, for example, has never used the term *poststructuralism*, and has always insisted that deconstruction was no more than an interpretive strategy and never a school of thought. Jacques Derrida, "But beyond ... (open letter to Anne McClintock and Rob Nixon)," *Critical Inquiry* 13, 1986, p. 167. Equally, Foucault — who never used either term to describe his work and once joked "What are we calling postmodernity? I'm not up to date" — stated that "I do not understand what kind of problem is common to the people we call postmodern or poststructuralist." Michel Foucault, "Critical Theory/Intellectual History," in *Politics, Philosophy, Culture*, ed. Kritzman, pp. 33, 34. Indeed, there was something of a major intellectual conflict (later resolved at a personal level) between Derrida and Foucault during which, ironically, Foucault expressed concerns about deconstruction akin to those today employed by critics against "postmodern" as a whole. See Edward Said, "Michel Foucault, 1926–1984," in *After Foucault: Humanistic Knowledge, Postmodern Challenges*, edited by Jonathan Arac, New Brunswick NJ, 198h, p. 7. Judith Butler has elaborated in an interesting fashion some of the dimensions of this issue:

"On this side of the Atlantic [the United States] and in recent discourse the terms 'postmodernism' or 'poststructuralism' settle the differences among those positions in a single stroke, providing a substantive, a noun ... It may come as a surprise to some purveyors of the continental scene to learn that Lacanian psychoanalysis in France positions itself officially against poststructuralism, that Kristeva denounces postmodernism, that Foucaultians rarely relate to Derrideans, that Cixous and Irigaray are fundamentally opposed ... Lyotard champions the term, but he cannot be made into the example of what all the rest of the purported postmodernists are doing. Lyotard's work is, for instance, seriously at odds with that of Derrida, who does not affirm the notion of "the postmodern," and with others for whom Lyotard is made to stand ... Is the effort to colonize and domesticate these theories under the sign of the same, to group them synthetically and masterfully under a single rubric, a simple refusal to grant the specificity of these positions, an excuse not to read, and not to read closely?" Judith Butler, "Contingent Foundations: Feminism and the Question of 'Postmodernism,'" in *Feminists Theorize the Political*, edited by Judith Butler and Joan W. Scott, New York, 1992.

8. In addition to the remarks concerning this issue in the Introduction, the ambit of these concepts has been well articulated in Thaïs Morgan, "Is There an Intertext in This Text? Literary and Interdisciplinary Approaches to Intertextuality,' *American Journal of Semiotics* 3, 1985, pp. 1–40; David Carroll, *Paraesthetics: Foucault/Lyotard/Derrida*, New York, 1987; and Derrida, "But beyond." As Derrida has noted, "we say 'writing' for all that gives rise to an inscription in general, whether it is literal or not and even if what it distributes in space or time is alien to the order of the voice: cinema photography, choreography, of course, but also pictorial, musical, sculptural 'writing.' One might also speak of athletic writing, and with even greater certainty of military or political writing in view of the techniques that govern those domains today." Jacques Derrida, *Of Grammatology*, translated by G. Spivak, Baltimore, 1976, p. 9.

9. The charge of political quietism has two aspects: (1) the claim that "postmodernism's" alleged abandonment of ethical standards has licensed a free-for-all poli-

tics; and (2) the claim that there is no affirmative politics open to those who find value in "postmodernism's" attitude. In response to these lines of thought, both Derrida and Foucault (their differences notwithstanding) have acted and argued for an affirmative politics in a variety of guises. Derrida, who was once arrested in Czechoslovakia for giving seminars to dissident intellectuals that offended the authorities, stated in an interview: "Deconstruction, I have insisted, is not neutral. It intervenes." Derrida, "But beyond," p. 168; and Derrida, *Positions*, translated by Alan Bass, Chicago, 1981, p. 93. For an overview of Derrida's writings in relation to this issue, see Richard Bernstein, "Serious Play: The Ethical-Political Horizon of Jacques Derrida," *The Journal of Speculative Philosophy* 1, 1987, pp. 93–117. Foucault has been described by Kritzman as "the leading French intellectual of his time to identify with various socio-political causes" (including prison reform, the socially marginalized, conscripted soldiers, Eastern European dissidents, and Solidarity, among others). Larry Kritzman, "Foucault and the Politics of Experience," in *Politics, Philosophy, Culture*, ed. Kritzman, pp. xviii-xix. Foucault has articulated his understanding of political action in a number of interviews, especially those in *Politics, Philosophy, Culture*, ed. Kritzman. For a compelling interpretation of Foucault's political commitment, see Tom Keenan, "The 'Paradox' of Knowledge and Power: Reading Foucault on a Bias," *Political Theory* 15, 1987, pp. 5–37.

10. Richard J. Bernstein, *Beyond Objectivism and Relativism: Science, Hermeneutics and Praxis*, Oxford, 1983, p. 18.

11. For a review of the contributions of these scholars, see Jim George and David Campbell, "Patterns of Dissent and the Celebration of Difference: Critical Social Theory and International Relations," *International Studies Quarterly* 34, 1990, pp. 269–93.

12. Connolly, *Identity/Difference*, p. x.

13. See the various papers in "Beyond the Blocs," *Current Research on Peace and Violence III*, edited by Pertti Joenniemi, Tampere, Finland, 1990–91.

14. Examples of this concern are easy to identify among Western strategists. See Jack Snyder, "Averting Anarchy in the New Europe," *International Security* 14, 1990, pp. 5–41; and John J. Mearsheimer, "Back to the Future: Instability in Europe after the Cold War," *International Security* 15, 1991, pp. 5–56.

15. "Study of War Changes as East Does," *New York Times*, January 16, 1990, p. A20.

16. "U.S. Needs More Help in Gulf, Cheney tells NATO," *New York Times*, December 8, 1990, p. 7.

17. "Rifts Imperil Europe's No-Border Plan," *New York Times*, April 16, 1990.

18. France has a number of policies that are animated by a chauvinism similar to that evidenced in the United States. For example, the Mirguet amendment to article thirty-eight of the 1958 French constitution (promulgated on July 18, 1960) "declared the necessity to fight against all threats to public hygiene and specifically names tuberculosis, cancer, alcoholism, prostitution and homosexuality as objects of attack." Cited in Michel Foucault, "Sexual Morality and the Law," in *Politics, Philosophy, Culture*, ed. Kritzman, p. 272n. Likewise, the French government proclaimed new and exclusionary immigration rules in 1991. See "Immigrants—The Real Issue," *Guardian Weekly*, June 30, 1991, p. 13; and "France Unveils Strict New Rules on Immigration," *New York Times*, July 11, 1991, p. A5.

19. Paul Virilio, *Popular Defense and Ecological Struggles*, translated by M. Polizzotti, New York, 1990, p. 64.

20. G. M. Dillon, "The Alliance of Security and Subjectivity," in *Current Research on Peace and Violence III*, ed. Joenniemi, pp. 101–24.

21. Ibid., p. 114.

22. Colin Gordon, "The Soul of the Citizen: Max Weber and Michel Foucault on Rationality and Government," in *Max Weber, Rationality and Modernity*, edited by Sam Whimster and Scott Lash, London, 1987. This direction of Foucault's later work has been elaborated in *The Foucault Effect: Studies in Governmental Rationality*, edited by Graham Burchell, Colin Gordon, and Peter Miller, Hemel Hempstead, England, 1991.

23. Gordon, "The Soul of the Citizen," p. 297. For a fuller discussion of pastoral power, see Michel Foucault, "Politics and Reason," in *Politics, Philosophy, Cutlure*, ed. Kritzman.

24. Michel Foucault, "Afterword: The Subject and Power," in *Michel Foucault: Beyond Structuralism and Hermeneutics*, edited by Hubert L. Dreyfus and Paul Rabinow, Brighton, 1982, pp. 214–15.

25. *Michel Foucault, The History of Sexuality, Volume 1: An Introduction*, translated by Robert Hurley, New York, 1980, pp. 139–40.

26. Foucault, "Politics and reason."

27. Ibid., p.80.

28. Ibid., p. 79.

29. Foucault, *The History of Sexuality, Volume 1*, p. 137.

30. Colin Gordon, "Governmental Rationality," in *The Foucault Effect*, ed. Burchell, Gordon, Miller, p. 27.

31. Ibid., p. 20.

32. Foucault, *History of Sexuality, Volume 1*, p. 25.

33. On occasions, the performative nature of security discourse is explicitly revealed, as in French President Giscard d'Estaing's 1976 speech to the Military Academy: "Alongside the supreme means of ensuring our security," he declared, "we need the presence of security. In other words, we need to have a social body organized around this need for security." Quoted in Paul Virilio, *Speed and Politics*, translated by Mark Polizzotti, New York, 1986, p. 122.

34. Quoted in Gordon, "The Soul of the Citizen," p. 304.

35. For a discussion of this tendency, see Daniel Deudney, "The Case against Linking Environmental Degradation and National Security," *Millennium: Journal of International Studies* 19, pp. 461–76.

36. See Michel Foucault, "The Two Lectures," in *Power/Knowledge: Selected Interviews and Other Writings 1972–1977*, edited by Colin Gordon, New York, 1980.

37. See Michel Foucault, "The Ethic of Care for the Self as a Practice of Freedom," in *The Final Foucault*, edited by James Bernauer and David Rasmussen, Cambridge, Massachusetts, 1985.

38. Foucault, "Afterword," pp. 221–22.

39. Gordon, "Governmental Rationality," p. 5.

40. Charles Tilly, *Coercion, Capital and European States A.D. 990–1990*, New York, 1990, p. 102.

41. See Alberto Melucci, *Nomads of the Present: Social Movements and Individual Needs in Contemporary Society*, edited by John Keane and Paul Mier, Philadelphia, 1989. The activism surrounding AIDS is an excellent example of how the interpretation of a danger can both rearticulate identities in response to the disciplinary strategies of the state and extend the domain of "the political" into that arena previously considered cultural. See *AIDS: Cultural Analysis, Cultural Activism*, edited by Douglas Crimp, Cambridge, Massachusetts, 1988.

42. Judith Butler, *Gender Trouble: Feminism and the Subversion of Identity*, New York, 1990, p. 148.

Epilogue

1. "Killed by Son of Mafia Thug," and "A Son to be Proud of, Says Acidman," *Daily Mail,* 18 October 1996.

2. The identity politics of immigration in Britain have been well examined in Roxanne Lynne Doty, "Immigration and National Identity: Constructing the Nation," *Review of International Studies* 32, 1996, pp. 235–55; and Kathryn A. Manzo, *Creating Boundaries: The Politics of Race and Nation,* Boulder, 1996, especially chapter 4.

3. For an account of the media's part in this debate during the 1997 election campaign, see "Sowing the Seeds of Rebellion," *The Guardian,* 18 April 1997.

4. "Goodbye, Xenophobia," *The Observer,* 4 May 1997.

5. This thought prompts a clarification. In chapter 5 of this book I called America "the imagined community par excellence," though in chapter 6 this was qualified to an extent with the observation that, while "America is not exceptional in combining nationalism, eschatology, and chauvinism... America is an intensification of this structural quality" whereby the *aporia* in identity has to be overcome. Although this has been singled out by John Ruggie in his account of identity and United States foreign policy, I think Iver Neumann is correct to observe that "it makes little sense to insist that the United States would be more imagined than other collectives." Although I would maintain that the absence for the United States of the "mystical foundations of authority" (to use Derrida's phrase) available to other collectives in their efforts to secure identity and identify security intensifies the representational crisis, this does not make one "more imagined" and the other "more real" for, as Balibar observes, only imagined communities are real. See John Ruggie, "Past as Prologue? Interests, Identity, and American Foreign Policy," *International Security* 21, 1997, p. 110; Iver Neumann, "Self and Other in International Relations," *European Journal of International Relations* 2, 1996, p. 158; Jacques Derrida, "Force of Law: the 'mystical foundation of authority,'" in *Deconstruction and the Possibility of Justice,* edited by Drucilla Cornell, Michael Rosenfeld, and David Gray Carlson, New York, 1992; and Etienne Balibar, "The Nation Form," in Etienne Balibar and Immanuel Wallerstein, *Race, Nation, Class: Ambiguous Identities,* London, 1991.

6. On these issues, see, respectively, William E. Connolly, "Drugs, the Nation and Free-Lancing: Decoding the Moral Universe of William Bennett," *Theory and Event* 1, 1997 [as of 1997, available at http://muse.jhu.edu/journals/theory_&_event/]; Michael J. Shapiro, "Value Eruptions and Modalities: White Male Rage in the '80s and '90s," *Cultural Values* 1, 1997, pp. 58–80; Christopher Hitchens, "Look over your Shoulder," *London Review of Books,* 25 May 1995; Jodi Dean, "The Familiarity of Strangeness: Aliens, Citizens, and Abduction," *Theory and Event* 1, 1997; Roxanne Lynne Doty, "The Double-Writing of Statecraft: Exploring State Responses to Illegal Immigration," *Alternatives* 21, 1996, pp. 171–89, and Michael J. Shapiro, "Narrating the Nation, Unwelcoming the Stranger: Anti-Immigration Policy in Contemporary 'America,'" *Alternatives* 22, 1997, pp. 1–34. Much recent scholarship, most obvious in the "New Americanists" series edited for Duke University Press by Donald E. Peace, has addressed similar concerns. See, for example, *National Identities and Post-Americanist Narratives,* edited by Donald E. Peace, Durham, 1994; and Priscilla Wald, *Constituting Americans: Cultural Anxiety and Narrative Form,* Durham, 1995.

7. See, for example, "Pentagon Imagines New Enemies to Fight in Post–Cold War Era," *New York Times,* 17 February 1992; Judith Miller, "The Challenge of Radical Islam," *Foreign Affairs* 72, 1993, pp. 43–56; Samuel P. Huntington, "The Clash of Civilizations?" *Foreign Affairs* 72, 1993, pp. 22–49; and "Asteroid Defense: 'Risk Is Real,' Plan-

ners Say," *New York Times*, 7 April 1992. Similar concerns are analyzed in Bradley Klein, *Strategic Studies and World Order*, Cambridge, 1994.

8. I have considered these in, respectively, "Identity, Sovereignty, Responsibility: Reflections on Post-Cold War Moral Cartography," in *The Return of Culture and Identity in International Relations Theory*, edited by Yosef Lapid and Friedrich Kratochwil, Boulder, 1995; *Politics without Principle: Sovereignty, Ethics and the Narratives of the Gulf War*, Boulder, 1993; and *National Deconstruction: Violence, Identity, and Justice in Bosnia*, Minneapolis, 1998. An example from Bosnia indicates the persistence of particular figurations. During that war an American diplomat referred to Bosnian Serb territory as "Indian country" — while U.S. units in IFOR named their bases and areas using frontier references (e.g., Fort Apache) — thereby invoking a frame of reference common to U.S. military expeditions at home and abroad since the nineteenth century. The comment is attributed to Robert Frasure by Robert Holbrooke in the latter's article, "The Road to Sarajevo," *The New Yorker*, October 21–28, 1996.

9. One empathetic reviewer of this book remarked that "Campbell's thesis in this regard [about post–Cold War discourses of danger replicating those of the cold war] is being proved even as we speak," while another marginally more skeptical reviewer argued that this was "debatable." For the former, see Sankaran Krishna, "The Importance of Being Ironic: A Postcolonial View on Critical International Relations Theory," *Alternatives* 18, 1993, pp. 391, 411n. The latter remark comes from Gearóid Ó Tuathail, "Dissident IR and the Identity Politics Narrative: A Sympathetically Skeptical Perspective," *Political Geography* 15, 1996, p. 652n.

10. The latest attacks can be found, respectively, in William Wallace, "Truth and Power, Monks and Technocrats: Theory and Practice in International Relations," *Review of International Studies* 22, 1996, p. 311; Stephen Krasner, "The Accomplishments of International Political Economy," in *International Theory: Positivism and Beyond*, edited by Steve Smith, Ken Booth, and Maryisa Zalewski, Cambridge, 1996, pp. 124–25; Fred Halliday, "The Future of International Relations: Fears and Hopes," in *International Theory*, ed. Smith, Booth, and Zalewski, pp. 320, 327n; and Øyvind Østerud, "Antinomies of Postmodernism in International Studies," *Journal of Peace Research*, 33, 1996, pp. 385–90.

11. Justin Rosenberg, "The International Imagination: IR Theory and 'Classic Social Analysis,'" *Millennium: Journal of International Studies* 23, 1994, pp. 85–86. My full response can be found in "Political Excess and the Limits of Imagination," *Millennium: Journal of International Studies* 23, 1994, pp. 365–375, alongside responses from others.

12. Ibid., p. 101.

13. For the first presentation of these views, see Robert O. Keohane, "International Institutions: Two Approaches," *International Studies Quarterly* 32, 1988, pp. 379–96. Despite many criticisms of Keohane on this point — see, for example, a number of the contributions to the special issue of *International Studies Quarterly* 34, 1990 — Keohane later restated his earlier arguments without any attempt to respond to his critics. See Judith Goldstein and Robert O. Keohane, "Ideas and Foreign Policy: An Analytic Framework," in *Ideas and Foreign Policy: Beliefs, Institutions, and Political Change*, ed. Judith Goldstein and Robert O. Keohane, Ithaca, 1993. Keohane's methodological dicta have been legislated for the entire social sciences in the collaboration that produced Gray King, Robert O. Keohane, and Sidney Verba, *Designing Social Inquiry: Scientific Interference in Qualitative Research*, Princeton, 1994. For a good discussion of the assumptions behind this, see Roland Bleiker, "Forget IR Theory," *Alternatives* 22, 1997, pp. 64–65.

14. John Gerard Ruggie, "Territoriality and Beyond: Problematizing Modernity in International Relations," *International Organization* 47, 1993, pp. 139–74. I consider Ruggie's argument in more detail in *National Deconstruction,* chapter 1.

15. The quote comes from William Connolly and is discussed in note 6 of chapter 8.

16. John J. Mearsheimer, "The False Promise of International Institutions," *International Security* 19, 1994/95, especially pp. 36–47. The reading of "postmodernism" as a form of philosophical idealism — presumably because of a simplistic understanding of the centrality of language and discourse — is not uncommon. See Wallace, "Truth and power," p. 311; and Kenneth Waltz, "Reflections on Theory of International Politics: A Response to My Critics," in *Neorealism and Its Critics,* edited by Robert O. Keohane, New York, 1986.

17. See John A. Vasquez, "The Problems and Pitfalls of Postmodern Theorizing," in *International Relations Theory Today,* edited by Ken Booth and Steve Smith, Oxford, 1995. Some good reviews of "postmodernism" do exist. See, especially, Richard Devetak, "Postmodernism," in Scott Burchill and Andrew Linklater et al., *Theories of International Relations,* London, 1996.

18. Hayden White, "Historical Text as Literary Artifact," in his *Tropics of Discourse: Essays in Cultural Criticism,* Baltimore, p. 91.

19. Judith Butler, "Contingent Foundations: Feminism and the Question of 'Postmodernism,'" in *Feminists Theorize the Political,* edited by Judith Butler and Joan W. Scott, New York, 1992, p. 4.

20. Foucault's points are discussed below. As for Derrida, see Rodolphe Gasché, *Inventions of Difference: On Jacques Derrida,* Cambridge, Massachusetts, 1994, p. 124. Interestingly, Lyotard, who is usually taken to be the progenitor of "postmodernism" with the publication of the *Postmodern Condition* in 1979, has since expressed reservations about his use of the term *postmodern,* shying away from its periodization, and instead arguing that "postmodernity" is a moment within modernity. For this argument, see Jean-François Lyotard, "Re-writing modernity," *Substance* 54, 1987, pp. 3–9.

21. Fredric Jameson, *Postmodernism: or, the Cultural Logic of Late Capitalism,* Durham, 1991, p. ix.

22. Ibid., p. xii.

23. The distinction between the interpretive analytic and the cultural problematic is sometimes made in terms of, respectively, poststructuralism versus postmodernism. See Butler, "Contingent foundations," p. 6; and R. B. J. Walker, *Inside/Outside: International Relations as Political Theory,* Cambridge, 1993, pp.187–88. In chapter 8 I averred from identifying my arguments in terms of either "poststructuralism" or "postmodernism." But under the constant disciplinary pressure of having to name one's position, I would now hesitantly accept the former while persisting — because of the argument being made here — with my distance from the latter.

24. For a critical analysis of Foucault's consideration of Kant, see Geoffrey Galt Harpham, "So . . . What *Is* Enlightenment? An Inquisition into Modernity," *Critical Inquiry* 20, 1994, pp. 524–56.

25. Michel Foucault, "What Is Enlightenment?" in *The Foucault Reader,* edited by Paul Rabinow, New York, 1984, p. 32.

26. Ibid., p. 39.

27. Michel Foucault, "Politics and Ethics: An Interview," in *The Foucault Reader,* p. 377.

28. The notion of "agonism," a Foucauldian neologism discussed in chapter 8, helps overcome the more stilted notion of contradiction. Michel Foucault, "Afterword: The

Subject and Power," in Hubert L. Dreyfus and Paul Rabinow, *Michel Foucault: Beyond Structuralism and Hermeneutics*, Brighton, 1982, p. 222.

29. Foucault, "What Is Enlightenment?" p. 42.

30. Ibid., p. 45.

31. This claim is nonetheless evident in at least two accounts of international relations theory (the first of which is markedly more sophisticated than the second): Chris Brown, " 'Turtles All the Way Down': Anti-Foundationalism, Critical Theory and International Relations," *Millennium: Journal of International Studies* 23, 1994, p. 227; and Roger D. Spegele, "Richard Ashley's Discourse for International Relations," *Millennium: Journal of International Studies* 21, 1992, pp. 147–82.

32. Ibid., p. 50.

33. Michel Foucault, "Practicing Criticism," in *Politics, Philosophy, Culture*, ed. Kritzman, New York, 1988, pp. 154–55. In *National Deconstruction* I have expanded on the above and articulated an "ethos of political criticism" by which to understand the approach to inquiry I adopt.

34. I owe the first metaphor to James Der Derian, "The (S)pace of International Relations: Simulation, Surveillance, and Speed," *International Studies Quarterly* 34, 1990, p. 296.

35. This challenge was first issued by Thomas Biersteker in "Critical Reflections on Post-Positivism in International Relations," *International Studies Quarterly* 33, 1989, p. 266. Although it has in effect been answered from day one—see the contributions to the special issue of *International Studies Quarterly* 34, 1990, for some of the political accounts—it is now indisputably dealt with. Of course, the Keohanes of this world would disagree, but that is because their demands for scholars to have a research agenda is not a neutral invitation that can be answered by undertaking, as the work cited here does, one's own research agenda. Keohane's demand for fidelity to a research agenda is a demand that work which depends on fundamentally distinct metatheoretical assumptions abandon those precepts in favor of a research agenda the strictures of which Keohane wishes to legislate.

36. Cynthia Weber, *Simulating Sovereignty: Intervention, the State and Symbolic Exchange*, Cambridge, 1994; "Something's Missing: Male Hysteria and the U.S. Intervention into Panama," *Genders* 19, 1994, pp. 171–97; "Dissimulating Intervention: A Reading of the U.S.-led Intervention into Haiti," *Alternatives* 20, 1995, pp. 265–77; and *Faking It: U.S. Hegemony in a Post-Phallic Era*, Minneapolis, 1999. Roxanne Lynne Doty, "Foreign Policy as Social Construction: A Post-Positivist Analysis of U.S. Counterinsurgency Policy in the Philippines," *International Studies Quarterly* 37, 1993, pp. 297–320; *Imperial Encounters: The Politics of Representation in North-South Relations*, Minneapolis, 1996, "The Double-Writing of Statecraft," and "Immigration and National Identity." Jenny Edkins, "Legality with a Vengeance: Famines and Humanitarian Relief in 'Complex Emergencies,'" *Millennium: Journal of International Studies* 25, 1996, pp. 547–75. Costas M. Constantinou, "NATO's Caps: European Security and the Future of the North Atlantic Alliance," *Alternatives* 20, 1995, pp. 147–64, and *On the Way to Diplomacy*, Minneapolis, 1996. Michael Dillon, "Sovereignty and Governmentality: From the Problematics of the 'New World Order' to the Ethical Problematic of the World Order," *Alternatives* 20, 1995, pp. 323–68; *Politics of Security: Towards a Political Philosophy of Continental Thought*, London, 1996; "The Sovereign and the Stranger," in *Sovereignty and Subjectivity*, edited by Jenny Edkins, Nalini Persram, and Veronique Pin-Fat, Boulder, forthcoming 1997; and "The Scandal of the Refugee: Some Reflections on the 'Inter' of International Relations and Continental Thought," in *Moral Spaces: Rethinking Ethics and World Politics*, edited by David Campbell and Michael J.

Shapiro, forthcoming. Siba N'Zatioula Grovogui, *Sovereigns, Quasi-Sovereigns, and Africans: Race and Self-Determination in International Law*, Minneapolis, 1996. Thomas C. Kuehls, *Beyond Sovereign Territory: The Space of Ecopolitics*, Minneapolis, 1996. Nevzat Soguk, *States and Strangers: Refugees and Displacements of Statecraft*, Minneapolis, 1998. François Debrix, *Re-envisioning Peacekeeping: Simulation, the UN, and the Mobilization of Ideology*, Minneapolis, 1999. Kathy Ferguson and Phyllis Turnbull, *Oh, Say, Can You See? The Semiotics of the Military in Hawai'i*, Minneapolis, 1998. Klein, *Strategic Studies and World Order*, and "Politics by Design: Surveying the Landscapes of the New Security Debates," paper presented to the British International Studies Association Annual Meeting, Durham, 16–18 December 1996. Chris Hables Gray, *Postmodern War*, London, 1997. James Der Derian, *Virtual Security*, forthcoming. Michael J. Shapiro, *Violent Cartographies*, Minneapolis, 1997. Finally, *Challenging Boundaries: Global Flows, Territorial Identities*, edited by Michael J. Shapiro and Hayward R. Alker, Minneapolis, 1996, collected the work of twenty-one authors who explore the dynamics of identity politics in disparate global domains.

37. Richard Ashley, "The Achievements of Poststructuralism," in *International Theory*, ed. Smith, Booth, and Zalewski, especially pp. 245–46.

38. See Klaus-John Dodds, "Geopolitics and Foreign Policy: Recent Developments in Anglo-American Political Geography and International Relations," *Progress in Human Geography* 18, 1994, pp. 186–208; Gearóid Ó Tuathail, *Critical Geopolitics: The Politics of Writing Global Space*, Minneapolis, 1996; "Special Issue: Critical Geopolitics," edited by Simon Dalby and Gearóid Ó Tuathail, *Political Geography* 15, 1996; and the literature reviewed in Gearóid Ó Tuathail, "Political Geography III: Dealing with Deterritorialization," *Progress in Human Geography* 20, 1997, forthcoming.

39. For an array of perspectives working within the rubric of identity, see *The Return of Culture and Identity in International Relations Theory*, edited by Yosef Lapid and Friedrich Kratochwil, Boulder, 1995; and *Identities in International Relations*, edited by Jill Krause and Neil Renwick, London, 1996. The best overview is Neumann, "Self and Other in International Relations."

40. For examples of feminist international relations, see Cynthia Enloe, *The Morning After: Sexual Politics in the Post–Cold War Era*, New York, 1993; *Feminism/Postmodernism/Development*, edited by Marianne Marchand and Jane Parpart, London, 1995; *Gendered States: Feminist Revisions of International Relations Theory*, edited by V. Spike Peterson, Boulder, 1992; Jan Jindy Pettman, *Worlding Women: A Feminist International Politics*, London, 1996; Christine Sylvester, *Feminist Theory and International Relations in a Postmodern Era*, Cambridge, 1994; J. Ann Tickner, *Gender in International Relations: Feminist Perspectives on Security*, New York, 1992; Sandra Whitworth, *Feminism and International Relations: Towards a Political Economy of Gender in Interstate and Non-Governmental Organizations*, London, 1994; Marysia Zalewski, *The Man Question in International Relations*, forthcoming. Good overviews of this literature can be found in Marianne Marchand, "Reconceptualising 'Gender and Development' in an Era of 'Globalisation,'" *Millennium: Journal of International Studies* 25, 1996, pp. 577–603; Christine Sylvester, "The Contributions of Feminist Theory to International Relations," in *International Theory*, ed. Smith, Booth, and Zalewski; and J. Ann Tickner, "Identity in International Relations Theory: Feminist Perspectives," in *The Return of Culture and Identity in IR Theory*, ed. Lapid and Kratochwil. A sense of the contestations between different theorizations of identity in feminist scholarship can be gained from Cynthia Weber, "Good Girls, Little Girls and Bad Girls: Male Paranoia in Robert Keohane's Critique of Feminist International Relations," *Millennium: Journal of International Studies* 23, 1994, pp.

337–49; Marysia Zalewski, "The Women/'Women' Question in International Relations," *Millennium: Journal of International Studies* 23, 1994, pp. 407–23.

41. For an overview specific to international relations, see Phillip Darby and A. J. Paolini, "Bridging International Relations and Postcolonialism," *Alternatives* 19, 1994, pp. 371–97; and *At the Edge of International Relations: Postcolonialism, Gender and Dependency*, edited by Phillip Darby, London, 1997. Within international relations—if in the wake of these developments this sense of enclosure in a disciplinary site continues to make any sense—the work, among others, of Roxanne Doty, Siba Grovogui, Sankaran Krishna, Kate Manzo, Nevzat Soguk, and Christine Sylvester can be regarded in these terms. This emphasizes the fluid and transgressive nature of thought, because writings organized under the sign of a single author can be considered in multiple ways.

42. See, in particular, *Ideas and Foreign Policy*, ed. Goldstein and Keohane. In *When Knowledge Is Power: Three Models of Change in International Relations*, Berkeley, 1990, Ernst Haas combines an indebtedness to a Foucauldian theme with a cursory dismissal of the relevance of Foucault.

43. Arjun Appadurai, *Modernity at Large: The Cultural Dimensions of Globalization*, Minneapolis, 1996, p. 12.

44. Peter J. Katzenstein, "Introduction: Alternative Perspectives on National Security," in *The Culture of National Security: Norms and Identity in World Politics*, edited by Peter J. Katzenstein, Ithaca, 1996, pp. 1–4.

45. Ronald L. Jepperson, Alexander Wendt, and Peter J. Katzenstein, "Norms, Identity, and Culture in National Security," p. 33; Elizabeth Kier, "Culture and French Military Doctrine before World War II," pp. 187, 203; Alastair Ian Johnston, "Cultural Realism and Strategy in Maoist China," p. 217; Robert G. Herman, "Identity, Norms, and National Security: The Soviet Foreign Policy Revolution and the End of the Cold War," p. 283; and Thomas U. Berger, "Norms, Identity, and National Security in Germany and Japan," pp. 318, 325, all in *The Culture of National Security*, ed. Katzenstein.

46. Jepperson, Wendt, and Katzenstein, "Norms, Identity, and Culture in National Security," p. 59. Identity is said to come in two basic forms, one of which is "those that are intrinsic to an actor (at least relative to a given social structure)." As an instance of this, the argument claims that "being democratic, for example, is an intrinsic feature of the U.S. state relative to the structure of the international system." It is not difficult to appreciate that a position that regards certain identities as "intrinsic," and includes among the intrinsic qualities highly contestable concepts such as "democracy," is reductionist in its representation of politics.

47. Ibid., p. 41.

48. Katzenstein, "Introduction," p. 22.

49. Jepperson, Wendt, and Katzenstein, "Norms, Identity, and Culture in National Security," p. 34. It is fair to note that the authors do acknowledge the existence of poststructuralist scholarship (p. 46), but that acknowledgment involves neither a recognition of the conflicting conception of identity it involves, nor an engagement that works through those differences.

50. The politics of this position are evident in Peter J. Katzenstein, "Introduction: Alternative Perspectives on National Security," in *The Culture of National Security*, ed. Katzenstein, where the research agenda demands of Keohane are endorsed. A cautious appreciation of the difficulties of meshing social-scientific and interpretive dimensions can be found in Ruggie, "The Past as Prologue?" pp.124–25.

51. For an analysis of this larger literature, see Mark Laffey and Jutta Weldes, "Beyond Belief: Ideas and Symbolic Technologies in the Study of International Relations," *European Journal of International Relations* 3, 1997, pp. 193–237.

52. Judith Butler, *Bodies That Matter: On the Discursive Limits of "Sex."* New York, 1993, pp. 4–12. This point is developed further in *National Deconstruction*, chapter 2.

53. For example, studies that style themselves solely as "discourse analysis," often found in journals such as *Discourse and Society.*

54. Ó Tuathail, "Dissident IR and the Identity Politics Narrative," p. 652. My contestation of this reading would center on the way it depends on the very dichotomous structure of ideal/material problematized by notions of discourse and performativity.

55. Testament to this tendency is evident from the lengths Ruggie has to go in order to prevent such a reading of his account of interests and identity in United States foreign policy. See Ruggie, "Past as Prologue?" pp. 117–20.

56. See Alexander Wendt, "The Agent-Structure Problem in International Relations Theory," *International Organization* 41, 1987, pp. 335–70. For a poststructuralist critique, see Richard K. Ashley, "Living on Borderlines: Man, Poststructuralism, and War," in *International/Intertextual Relations: Postmodern Readings of World Politics*, ed. James Der Derian and Michael J. Shapiro, Lexington, 1989, pp. 276–77.

57. Alexander Wendt, "Anarchy Is What States Make of It: The Social Construction of Power Politics," *International Organization* 46, 1992, p. 424.

58. Alexander Wendt, "Identity and Structural Change in International Politics," in *The Return of Culture and Identity in IR Theory*, ed. Lapid and Kratochwil, p. 50. One of the substantive moves in this article is to transpose the supposedly "national" frame of previous arguments to the larger domain of collective identity in international relations. While I agree with those who have observed that the argument of *Writing Security* and *Politics without Principle* could be specified to a greater extent when it comes to considering the potential differences between, say, "American" and "Western" formations, I would contest the view that this book offers only an argument about national identity that is unrelated to collective international identity. That is because the central theme of *Writing Security* concerns the way in which the domains of inside/outside and domestic/foreign are performatively constituted. As such, the "national" is brought into being in a relationship with the "collective," which arises at the same time; neither precedes the other, as the objections might be read as suggesting. For one such objection, see Jennifer Milliken, "Intervention and Identity: Remaking the West in Korea," in *Cultures of Insecurity: States, Communities and the Production of Danger*, edited by Jutta Weldes, Mark Laffey, Hugh Gusterson, and Raymond Duvall, forthcoming.

59. Wendt, "Anarchy Is What States Make of It," pp. 425–26.

60. Ibid., pp. 391–392.

61. Ibid., p. 425.

62. Butler, "Contingent Foundations," p. 13.

63. Wendt, "Anarchy Is What States Make of It," p. 397n.

64. Ibid., p. 402.

65. See, in particular, Butler, *Bodies That Matter.*

66. Appadurai, *Modernity at Large*, pp. 12–13. Beginning a conversation between anthropology and international relations on the subject of culture in the context of security is one of the achievements of *Cultures of Insecurity*, ed. Weldes et al.

67. For arguments along this line, see Michael J. Shapiro, "Strategic Discourse/Discursive Strategy: The Representation of 'Security Policy' in the Video Age," in

Reading the Postmodern Polity: Political Theory as Textual Practice, Minneapolis, 1992; and Klein, *Strategic Studies and World Order*.

68. For a clear illustration of the differing analytic commitments that inform these contrasting approaches, compare the "methodological" formulations in Johnston, "Cultural Realism and Strategy in Maoist China," in *The Culture of National Security*, ed. Katzenstein, pp. 221–28, with Shapiro, "Strategic Discourse/Discursive Strategy," pp. 108–10.

69. For an interesting reflection on some of the epistemological limits to the orthodox commitments, see John Gerard Ruggie, "Peace in Our Time? Causality, Social Facts and Narrative Knowing," *American Society of International Law Proceedings*, 89th meeting, 1995, pp. 93–100.

70. Neumann, "Self and Other after the Death of the Sovereign Subject." This is the conclusion to his *Uses of the Other: European Identity and World Politics*, Minneapolis, 1998, a version of which was presented at the International Studies Association Annual Conference in Toronto, March 1997, where the quoted remark was made.

71. Self-designation as constructivist by critically inclined scholars is especially clear in Barry Buzan and Ole Wæver, "Slippery? Contradictory? Sociologically Untenable? The Copenhagen School Replies," *Review of International Studies* 23, 1997, p. 241; Jutta Weldes, "Constructing National Interests," *European Journal of International Relations* 2, 1996, pp. 279–80; and Laffey and Weldes, "Beyond Belief," p. 195. The many meanings of the term are evident in one of Alexander Wendt's usages, where it is simultaneously applied to all critical theorists *and* to a very select group within the mainstream. Wendt, "Constructing International Politics," *International Security* 20, 1995, pp. 71–72. To avoid being implicated in this understanding, those cited here often distinguish themselves as "critical constructivists," "social constructivists," or "critical social constructivists."

72. See, for example, Ole Wæver et al., *Identity, Migration, and the New Security Agenda in Europe*, London, 1993; Wæver, "Securitization and Desecuritization," in *On Security*, edited by Ronnie Lipschutz, New York, 1995; "European Security Identities," *Journal of Common Market Studies*, 34, 1996, pp. 103–33; and Barry Buzan, Ole Wæver, and Jaap de Wilde, *Security: A New Framework for Analysis*, Boulder, 1997. Erik Ringmar, *Identity, Interest and Action: A Cultural Explanation of Sweden's Intervention in the Thirty Years' War*, Cambridge, 1996. K. M. Fierke, "Multiple Identities, Interfacing Games: The Social Construction of Western Action in Bosnia," *European Journal of International Relations*, 2, 1996, pp. 467–97. Timothy Dunne, "The Social Construction of International Society," *European Journal of International Relations* 1, 1995, pp. 367–89. Jutta Weldes, "Constructing National Interests," *European Journal of International Relations* 2, 1996, pp. 275–318; Weldes and Diana Saco, "Making State Action Possible: The United States and the Discursive Construction of 'the Cuban problem,' 1960–1994," *Millennium: Journal of International Studies* 25, 1996, pp. 361–95; and Weldes, *Constructing National Interests: The U.S. and the Cuban Missile Crisis*, Minneapolis, forthcoming. Jennifer Milliken and David Sylvan, "Soft Bodies, Hard Targets, and Chic Theories: U.S. Bombing Policy in Indochina," *Millennium: Journal of International Studies* 25, 1996, pp. 321–59. Lene Hansen, "Slovenian Identity: State Building on the Balkan Border," *Alternatives* 21, 1996, pp. 473–96. David Mutimer, "Making Enemies: NATO Enlargement and the Russian 'Other,'" paper prepared for the International Studies Association Annual Conference, Toronto, March 1997. Vivienne Jabri, *Discourses on Violence: Conflict Analysis Reconsidered*, Manchester, 1996.

73. *Critical Security Studies*, edited by Keith Krause and Michael C. Williams, Minneapolis, 1997; *State Sovereignty as Social Construct*, edited by Thomas J. Biersteker

and Cynthia Weber, Cambridge, 1996; and *Cultures of Insecurity,* ed. Weldes et al. It should be stressed that although different renditions of "constructivism" are deployed by the editors of these collections to characterize the common ground, they incorporate contributions from across the entire disciplinary perspective.

In place of "constructivism," Jabri's *Discourses on Violence* prefers "structurationist," a term once used but now seemingly abandoned by Wendt.

74. Laffey and Weldes, "Beyond Belief," p. 223n; Michael C. Williams and Keith Krause, "Preface: Toward Critical Security Studies," in *Critical Security Studies,* ed. Krause and Williams, p. xxi.

75. Any number of scholars could be cited in this regard, but see in particular Iver B. Neumann, "Russia as Central Europe's Constituting Other," *East European Politics and Societies* 7, 1993, pp. 349–69; *Russia and the Idea of Europe: A Study in Identity and International Relations,* London, 1995; and *Uses of the Other.*

76. For a theoretically poor critique of constructivism, see Bill McSweeny, "Identity and Security: Buzan and the Copenhagen School," *Review of International Studies* 22, 1996, pp. 313–26. A response can be found in Buzan and Wæver, "Slippery? Contradictory? Sociologically Untenable? The Copenhagen School Replies."

77. The de/reconstruction distinction is obvious in Brown " 'Turtles All the Way down,' " pp. 217–18. It is echoed in Williams and Krause, "Preface," in *Critical Security Studies,* ed. Krause and Williams, pp. xiii–xv. Contesting this framing of the issue, theorizing the violence of difference and representation, and demonstrating how the inherent ethicality of poststructuralist thought is a precondition for political interventions are major goals of my *National Deconstruction.*

78. See Weldes, "Constructing National Interests," p. 279, 281. It should be emphasized that this is neither the sum of Weldes' position nor necessarily the desire of her argument.

79. Butler, *Bodies That Matter,* p. 225.

80. These criticisms were leveled at Peter Katzenstein by James Der Derian and Stephen Krasner, respectively, at a conference on international norms held in Jerusalem in June 1997.

81. I have in mind here Krishna, "The Importance of Being Ironic," and Ó Tuathail, "Dissident IR and the Identity Politics Narrative." These have been effectively engaged in a debate of commendable tone by, respectively, James Der Derian, "The Pen, the Sword, and the Smart Bomb: Criticism in the Age of Video," *Alternatives* 19, 1994, pp. 133–40; and Simon Dalby, "Writing Critical Geopolitics: Campbell, Ó Tuathail, Reynolds and Dissident Skepticism," *Political Geography* 15, 1996, pp. 655–60. Ó Tuathail has responded in "The Patterned Mess of History and the Writing of Critical Geopolitics: A Reply to Dalby," *Political Geography* 15, 1996, pp. 661–65. Another lengthy review worth noting for its constructive criticism is Regina U. Gramer, "On Poststructuralism, Revisionism, and Cold Wars," *Journal of Diplomatic History* 19, 1995, pp. 515–24. All of the above have numerous points that could be engaged in a detailed and finely grained response, but rather than seek to resolve each point I prefer to leave the debate open.

82. I am responding here to some of the points raised in Steve Herbert, "Review Essay," *Political Geography* 15, 1996, p. 644. For an interesting argument about identity and political analysis, see Richard Handler, "Is 'Identity' a Useful Cross-Cultural Concept?" in *Commemorations: The Politics of National Identity,* ed. J. R. Gillis, Princeton, 1994.

83. In these terms, I have argued that to understand world politics, some in international relations might better regard themselves as exploring the "philosophical an-

thropology of everyday life on a global scale." Campbell, "Political Prosaics, Transversal Politics, and the Anarchical World," in *Challenging Boundaries,* ed. Shapiro and Alker, p. 24. The contrast with the disciplinary ambitions of an argument like Rosenberg's is noted in my "Political Excess and the Limits of Imagination," especially p. 371.

84. In a draft for the *Cultures of Insecurity* collection, George Marcus concluded that "the volume itself, as noted, positions itself within the discipline, wanting to be heard, through its 'constructionist' identity tolerated by the mainstream, rather than be considered 'beyond the pale' like the more radical poststructuralist scholars to which it is nonetheless very sympathetic intellectually. Still, what remains is a certain ambiguity about whether the project that this volume represents wants to remain a recognized reserve with the discipline for its own self-identified constituency, dedicated to critical commentary and alternative analyses in relation to mainstreams, or whether it wants to have a transformative effect through some sort of complex responses from and with the mainstream of security studies in IR." George Marcus, "Forward," mimeo, xvii.

85. William E. Connolly, "The Irony of Interpretation," in *The Politics of Irony: Essays in Self-Betrayal,* ed. Daniel W. Conway and John E. Seery, New York, 1992. I consider this argument in more detail in *National Deconstruction,* especially chapter 2.

86. Essays that suggestively illuminate related points include Bleiker, "Forget IR Theory," and Paul Saurette, " 'I mistrust all systematizers and avoid them': Nietzsche, Arendt and the Crisis of the Will to Order in International Relations Theory," *Millennium: Journal of International Studies* 25, 1996, pp. 1–28.

87. See Neumann, "Self and Other in International Relations," p. 160; Jean Manas, "Beyond Right and Wrong? Thoughts Engendered by a PostModernist Critique of the Gulf War," *Harvard Journal of International Law* 36, 1995, pp. 245–58; and Chris Brown, "Review Article: Theories of International Justice," *British Journal of Political Science* 27, 1997, p. 295. These remarks were all directed at the political options for United States Foreign Policy discussed in chapter 8, and were expanded in the final chapter of *Politics without Principle.* They could not take account of the way in which this challenge has been taken up with respect to Bosnia in *National Deconstruction.*

Index

David Campbell is professor of international politics at the University of Newcastle. He has also taught at Keele University and The Johns Hopkins University. Campbell is the author of, among other works, *Politics without Principle: Sovereignty, Ethics, and the Narratives of the Gulf War* and *National Deconstruction: Violence, Identity, and Justice in Bosnia* (Minnesota, 1998).